PERSEPHONE

A Study of Two Worlds

PERSEPHONE

by

D. STREATFEILD

The Julian Press, Inc.

NEW YORK

First published 1959
by The Julian Press, Inc.,
80 East 11th Street,
New York 3, N.Y.

© D. Streatfeild 1959

Printed in Great Britain
by Butler & Tanner Ltd.
Frome and London

Contents

Introduction

IT is often helpful to know how a book came to be written: it is therefore worth explaining that the present study is connected with a work of fiction, to the writing of which I devoted my leisure over a period of years, and which I subsequently abandoned. Several years later, reading Hadley Chase's *No Orchids for Miss Blandish*, I came upon an episode which corresponded with a passage in my own story in a manner so extraordinarily close that it was impossible to pass the resemblance over as a coincidence.

The episode concerned was briefly as follows. In *No Orchids* Miss Blandish has been kidnapped by gangsters but is rescued by a rival gangster who takes her to his flat, intending to return her to her father, from whom he hopes for a reward. She, however, unaccountably objects to being restored to him: she hits her rescuer over the head with a chair, tears the telephone cable from its connection, locks the door and throws the key out of the window. She insists on the inevitability of recapture by Slim Grisson, her kidnapper and ravisher, and he duly arrives, knifes his rival and asserts his connubial rights on the spot.

In my own story the hero, returning to his rooms, finds a girl, to whom he had started to make love, waiting for him outside the door. He had earlier discovered that this girl was the mistress of his superior, a man in an influential official position who also holds him in his power in another connection, and had for that reason decided to have no more to do with her. She, however, has fallen in love with him and is determined to keep him: she therefore insinuates herself into the flat and refuses to leave. When he threatens to have her removed by the police and goes to the telephone there is a scuffle which ends in her tearing the telephone cable from its connection, and the couple end in one another's arms.

At first sight the parallelism may seem slight enough, being confined to the striking but trivial elements of the struggle and the tearing of the telephone cable from the wall, but in addition to these there were certain resemblances—again superficial, but none the less striking—between my hero and Slim Grisson: the former, for instance, also, although in quite another connection, kills with a knife, and although he is seen in a completely different light and, in my story, plays an entirely different role, he possessed certain personal idiosyncrasies which were reminiscent of Slim. These were enough to make a profound impression on me: I received the impression that in Hadley Chase's rendering of the scene I was recognizing something that I had seen before: it was rather as though I had witnessed an isolated scene from a play in an unknown language, had attempted afterwards to reconstruct the plot of the story of which this scene formed a part, and was now reading another attempted reconstruction by somebody in a like position. I felt, in short, a strong conviction that Hadley Chase and I had, as it were, witnessed the same vision, or dreamed the same dream, and had each attempted to give an account of it as he understood it, each being under the necessity of adapting it to some extent to the requirements of his story.

This reaction was, of course, a purely subjective matter: I am not attempting to found any hypothesis on it, but relate it simply because it was in fact the starting-point of this study, and because it introduces the main thesis which I shall attempt to establish on the basis of other, more objective evidence. The force of the impact which this experience made on me can, perhaps, only be fully appreciated by somebody who has attempted to write fiction. He will know how the writer, turning his eyes inwards, conjures up characters and situations, believing that he has 'created' them; how he wrestles with these products of the free fantasy, explaining and rationalizing them, fitting them into the overall plan of the story, and, as he does so, finding out more about them, or, as he believes, 'inventing' characteristics, backgrounds, thoughts and purposes for them. He is intimately aware of how each episode arose, of how it was

2

shaped and fitted into the plot, of the considerations which led to the choice of each detail, and of the way in which vague and nebulous forms were progressively clarified, filled in and built up into the finished product. The whole process seems such a private and personal matter that the discovery that the experience has been shared, that the details which he believed that he had evolved and worked out for himself must, in fact, have been objectively present, though unrecognized, from the start (for they had already been seen by somebody else) comes as a profound shock. For although it seems obvious to us that if two people watch the same play at the theatre they will see and hear the same things, we believe that what goes on 'inside our heads' is strictly private; this privacy of thought, indeed, is one of our most prized possessions, and it is always with something of a shock, generally accompanied by slight feelings of resentment, that we discover that somebody else has 'read our thoughts'. Yet here I was confronted by convincing evidence that what I had discovered 'inside my head' had been equally accessible to somebody else.

The experience led me to embark on an analysis of *No Orchids* from a symbolical viewpoint, and in the process I perceived that the parallelism between the episodes related above was by no means so superficial as it appeared at first sight. The rule for this kind of analysis is to ignore the explanations and rationalizations provided by the writer, and to concentrate on what actually happened, and on the outcome; one must regard the characters in the drama as independent, autonomous persons, with their own motives (evidence confirming that this is in fact the case will be adduced in due course); one must assume that the writer may not have fully understood these motives, or may have distorted or misrepresented them to some extent in obedience to the requirements of his plot, and must attempt to reconstruct them from the actions related. If we proceed on these lines it becomes apparent that the two episodes reveal the following common basic elements: (*a*) the girl is where she ought not to be, i.e. she belongs to a principle of authority from whose control she has been removed or has escaped; (*b*) this has occurred in connection with her love for a man who is at odds with, and is fundamentally hostile to, the principle of authority; (*c*) she is alone with a man in a closed room; (d) when an attempt is made to establish communication with the principle of authority, which would break up the love-affair, she frustrates it; (e) the forbidden union of the lovers is consummated. In my story the girl goes to her lover of her own free will, whereas Miss Blandish is represented as being taken by force against her will, but her behaviour on this occasion reveals clearly enough that her real motive was no different, namely the consummation of her love for the rebel against authority.

That, then, was the true basis of the inner-world drama which Hadley Chase and I had both witnessed, and which we each attempted to interpret according to our respective and very different viewpoints. The perspicacious reader may already discern some of its implications, as well as some parallels with greater and better-known versions of the theme; an attempt will be made to elucidate some of them in the following chapters. For the moment we must postpone any attempt at interpretation, taking this opportunity merely to state the basic thesis which it will be our purpose to establish in the course of this study.

This is that there exists an inner world, which lies 'outside' our personal minds, and in which they are contained in exactly the same way as our bodies are contained in the outer world revealed by the senses. The inner world is no less 'objective' than the outer: i.e. in certain respects it is the same for all observers, although their particular view of it, and their individual interpretations of what they perceive in it, must necessarily vary to some extent, exactly as the particular views and interpretations made by individuals of certain aspects of the outer world vary.

A host of objections will inevitably spring up in the mind of the average reader in face of this pronouncement, reminiscent as it is of the woolly theories of many spiritualists, occultists and the like. I can only ask him to approach my attempt to establish it with an open mind, for it is not a regurgitation of hazy subjective emotions, but a serious attempt to suggest a system of reference which may help us to understand some of the problems of our times. It is also written in full awareness of the importance of the problems of the outer world, from which we derive our daily bread: one of my principal themes, indeed, is the necessity of strict discrimination between these two worlds; but this is only possible if we have some understanding of the nature of the inner. The basic patterns on which the two are constituted, and the laws which govern them, are fundamentally different: failure to recognize this fact, and to take sufficient account of the laws of the inner world, often leads to misunderstandings and false valuations which have a disastrous effect on our outer-world life.

I shall attempt to show that the inner world is *real*: no more, but also no less real than the outer. Inner-world factors, acting according to their own laws and not to those of the outer world, affect our minds, and our minds determine our actions: that, perhaps, is obvious, but the belief is commonly held today that our minds are no more than mirrors of the outer world, and possess no inherent, independent and autonomous contents of their own. Hence we believe that all we need do in order to make the best of life is to concentrate on the laws of the outer world: once they are fully understood, we believe, we cannot go wrong, because we shall be able to adapt ourselves perfectly to our environment. We overlook the fact that we have an inner as well as an outer environment, and that we must adapt ourselves to the former no less than to the latter. When factors deriving from our inner environment force themselves on our attention we are impatient with them and attempt to explain them away in outer-world terms, or we brush them aside as mere atavisms, vestigial remnants of our less enlightened past which can be relied upon to melt away and disappear in due course when subjected to the healthy air of outer-world understanding. We either insist that the inner world is not real, and is therefore unworthy of attention, or else we attempt to treat it as a subordinate department of the outer. This is a very dangerous tendency, for to ignore and neglect the unalterable patterns of the mind is no less disastrous than to ignore and neglect outer-world facts; inner-world factors, exactly like those of the outer world, will assert themselves whether we recognize and accept them or not, and if we refuse to recognize and accept them the consequences will be no less serious than those which ensue from ignoring or misunderstanding the forces of the outer world.

For my obvious dependence on the system of Jung, and for

my constant references to and quotations from his works, I make no apology. For many years I have found his ideas not only an unfailing source of inspiration and help in personal life, but also the key which makes all human behaviour intelligible. This is undoubtedly due to an individual orientation which the reader may not share, and I shall presently explain my personal position in this matter. If the reader cannot accept this basic approach to life—for which I do not claim any absolute or exclusive validity—there is nothing to be done: even if he allows himself to be convinced by the arguments, the system will remain something alien which he cannot assimilate to his conception of the meaning of life, and he will not benefit from it. I believe, however, that there are many people in the world today who might benefit greatly from a better understanding of Jung's system if they were not initially prejudiced against it.

A not uncommon viewpoint on this matter is one which I recently saw explicitly stated, namely that Freud was the 'scientist' of the modern psychological movement, whereas Jung's principal contribution to it was the restoration of the irrational element of 'soul' to modern thinking. The danger in this sweeping generalization is that today the mere word 'science' enjoys such enormous prestige that people are apt to regard it as tantamount to truth. If they do make any reservation in this respect it is generally only to the effect that science is not concerned with 'values': in order to form a basis for our judgments on what is good, beautiful and the like we must, they admit, look elsewhere, but where understanding is concerned, and above all in practical matters, science is regarded as infallible. Psychology is regarded nowadays as a branch of practical medicine, and medicine is a science: hence the belief that Freud's system is essentially 'scientific', whereas Jung's is primarily concerned with 'the irrational', denotes a strong bias against the latter. Jung's system, it implies, is all very well as an academic curiosity: he has interesting things to say about the symbolism of myths, the meaning of alchemy and the like, but when it comes to practical matters we must turn to Freud. It is even a common affectation among people of a scientific turn of mind to say that they do not understand what Jung is talking about; in a later chapter we shall find a scientist complacently asserting that he cannot begin to understand what philosophers are talking about, and then advancing his own views on philosophical questions, revealing in the process considerable ignorance and very inadequate reflection. The epitome of this attitude is embodied in the dictum of some writer, quoted by Maud Bodkin,[1] to the effect that 'the Zurich school' only offers 'a fresh bunch of superstitions': this gentleman has at least the candour to say openly what the others politely infer.

But the essence of what we loosely call 'science' is a discipline or general method, which demands that hypotheses be set up on the basis of observation of the outer world, and then established by 'experiments' which can be repeated at any time. The scientific experiment is a contrived demonstration, whereby it can be established whether the hypothesis is true or false, and every stage of the procedure, as well as the materials used, must be capable of exact control and definition by the experimenter. It is at once obvious that this discipline can only be applied to the field of psychology in a very limited sphere, for the mind cannot be segregated from its environment in a test-tube and subjected to influences which can be exactly controlled and defined by the psychologist: Freudians, in fact, can no more devise a set experiment to demonstrate the existence and properties of the Oedipus complex than Jungians can do the same for the collective unconscious. In this sense, then—and, as every scientist will admit, it is the essential sense of the concept of 'science' as generally understood—there are no grounds for maintaining that the system of Freud is any more 'scientific' than that of Jung.

Nevertheless the prejudice against Jung's system is prevalent. I shall attempt to elucidate the reasons for this in the following chapters, and in the meanwhile ask the reader to approach the problem with an open mind, for it may well be that any reluctance or aversion which he may feel towards accepting some of the features of Jung's system are based on an unadmitted prejudice. He must, above all, resist the temptation of rejecting ideas out of hand because they are of an unfamiliar type, disguising this fear of the unfamiliar from himself under the cover of some such evasion as that 'he does not understand':

[1] Maud Bodkin: *Archetypal Patterns in Poetry.*

7

he will find it quite possible to understand if he is prepared to make the necessary effort, and only then will he be in a position to reach a sound and balanced judgment on the question of whether he agrees or not.

But although it is not possible to apply the scientific method to psychology in the precise form in which it is applied in the more familiar fields of chemistry, physics and biology, if we adopt a somewhat wider definition of the word science we can justifiably claim that it is possible to approach the study of psychology in a scientific spirit. If we define a science as a coherent and consistent system of understanding in a particular field of experience, then psychology, the study of the mind or soul, can perfectly well qualify as a science. In order that it may so qualify, however, we must evolve an acceptable terminology in which to define the subject-matter of our enquiries, and it is in this that our greatest difficulty lies, for the systematic study of the inner world is still at an elementary stage.

The basis and framework of any science consists of the terms which are used in it, for each of which a precise definition has been worked out, so that it is always clear to exactly what any statement refers. The working out, the development, the differentiation and the precision of these terms actually constitute the science: scientific advance consists mainly of the introduction of fresh terms, with the concomitant definitions which clarify and fix the concepts to which they apply. This is a slow and continuous process: no science is born like Athene, fully armed.

Thus today the term 'electricity' means virtually nothing to the physicist, because in the context of his subject it might mean almost anything. He will want to know if the term is to be understood as referring to a current or a static charge, a distortion in space represented by a mathematical formula, a free electron or any of a hundred phenomena associated with these things, for each of which he has evolved a clearly circumscribed scientific term. Two hundred years ago the word still meant something: it was the mysterious power which caused scraps of paper to adhere to a piece of amber which had been rubbed, and was believed to be a specific property of amber. By modern standards such a definition is useless; yet its invention was the first step in the development of the whole body of modern theory connected with the subject. One must start somewhere.

In the study of the contents and structure of the inner world, therefore, the investigator, still groping in darkness, is compelled to identify such phenomena as he can and to give them a name by which they can be provisionally fixed and recognized. There can be no doubt whatever that later investigators will find many of these terms inaccurate, unsatisfactory or even misleading, and will introduce a richer, more highly developed terminology to take their place. Nevertheless they will offer posterity a point of departure, even if it be only something to depart from. Even the theories of phlogiston or of the corpuscular nature of light had their value in the clarification to which their refutation gave rise, for, as Socrates demonstrated, the *reductio ad absurdum* of a false hypothesis is an important step towards the establishment of a true one.

In this embryo science, therefore, we must be content, for the time being, to accept much inaccuracy and uncertainty. In the absence of an accurate terminology and of closely defined standards with which to compare individual phenomena it must inevitably happen that we are sometimes uncertain exactly what we are talking about. When we believe that we have isolated an image or entity of the mind we suddenly find it mysteriously changing its attributes, merging into another image or disappearing altogether. The difficulty may be that we are in reality concerned with two separate entities or tendencies, merged in a combination in which we are unable to discriminate between them, in much the same way as the physical scientists of last century were unable to distinguish between the various isotopic forms of the same element; or it may be that the entity with which we are concerned, being a living process, does in fact change its form as it develops, as the caterpillar changes into the butterfly; or again its aspect may depend entirely on the viewpoint from which we are considering it. All these matters must be taken into account, and for the time being we simply have not collected enough material, or devoted enough consideration to the subject, to allow us to advance very far.

Any attempt at over-precise definition, therefore, is liable to defeat its own ends. The images of the mind are like fishes,

INTRODUCTION

slippery things: until we have devised efficient instruments of thought with which to lay hold of them and retain them in the light while we undertake a detailed examination of their anatomy and behaviour they are apt to slide back into the dark waters of the unconscious before we have got very far; and after such an experience they are apt to become shy and hide themselves in the depths. It is better, for the time being, to coax them to the surface and to make what observations we can without disturbing them.

The alternative to this tentative and admittedly provisional approach to the subject is to attempt to reduce everything, in the Freudian manner, to concrete, outer-world terms, under the impression that we then know exactly what we are talking about. When, for instance, we discern a mental image of the male sex which is associated with authority we name it the 'Father-image' and seek to prove that it must be derived from the relationship of the infant to its concrete, personal father—a matter which everybody can easily grasp without going to the trouble of mastering unfamiliar concepts and developing a new mode of thought. This is what Jung describes as the 'reductive' tendency of the Freudian system, because it seeks to reduce mental phenomena to the status of mere reflections of physical facts and concrete situations. It is retrogressive and leads nowhere.

I believe that one of the most important causes of the prejudice against Jung's teaching is that it demands the acceptance of the existence or reality of entities of an unfamiliar nature, such as the collective unconscious and the Archetypes. The meaning of the terms existence and reality is a difficult question, and in order to understand and accept the implications of Jung's system, and of the inner world generally, it is necessary to have devoted some thought to it. It is a subject to which, not unnaturally, people do not normally devote much attention: they use the terms in a rough-and-ready colloquial manner which is adequate for all ordinary purposes, and in consequence, when it is suggested that inner-world entities such as the collective unconscious exist and are real, they imagine that they are being asked to believe that these things are of the same nature as tables and chairs, corporeal human beings, and similar objects to which they are accustomed to accord the properties of reality and existence. In the circumstances it is

10

understandable that they should object. But if the meanings of the terms reality and existence are analysed it will be found that they can be legitimately applied to inner-world entities without doing violence to that well-tried system of outer-world interpretation which is provided by modern science. It is only a question of making a serious attempt to understand what the new terminology means: the Inquisition was alarmed and angered by Galileo's ideas about gravity because they did not understand what he was talking about, but Galileo himself would almost certainly have been unreceptive to the conception of the curvature of space, and for the same reason. The problem of the nature of reality and existence, in its relationship to the theory of two worlds, will be examined in the second part of this volume.

My hostility to the system of Freud will already have been noted, and it will become progressively more apparent. It is fairly generally known that Jung and Freud parted company owing to an insuperable divergency of views, and some little animosity, both between them and their followers, inevitably resulted from the breach. In order to forestall any misunderstanding it will be advisable for me to state at the outset that I have no part in any feud which may exist between the rival schools: I am not 'a Jungian', in the sense that I have no connection with the Zurich school, or, indeed, with any psychologists. My views on psychology are derived solely from private reading and from the study of the human material with which I have been brought into contact in the course of a life devoted to various pursuits completely unconnected with psychology. Like many people of my generation I 'discovered' the psychology of the unconscious from the works of Freud at the end of my schooldays, when they were beginning to become widely known among the lay public. I at once became an enthusiastic adherent of the system (although purely as an intellectual diversion), but after a few years my interest died because, as I realized even then, it led nowhere so far as I was concerned. Soon afterwards, however, my interest in the modern psychological movement was revived by reading Herbert Silberer's *Probleme der Mystik und ihrer Symbolik*,[1] which opened up a new

---

[1] English transl., *Problems of Mysticism and its Symbolism.*

world of thought for me. This work had appeared in 1914, when only the first of Jung's major works—*Wandlungen und Symbole der Libido*[1]—had yet been published; at that time Jung himself had not yet broken away completely from Freud's ideas, and Silberer still accepts them without question. Nevertheless his approach differs radically from Freud's, in that his thinking is not 'reductive': he does not attempt to explain away all symbolism by reducing it to the status of a distorted representation of outer-world fact, but, on the contrary, he follows it into the world of mind and seeks to discover the nature of that world and the laws which govern its contents, in contrast to those of the outer world. He accepts the inner world as a reality.

At the time, of course, I did not fully understand all this, but I can still remember the impression which I received then (some twenty-five years ago) that here at last was a psychologist who worked 'upwards' and not 'downwards'. Today I should use the terms 'inwards' and 'outwards'.

Later again I began to read Jung's works, but was not immediately captivated by all his theories. His basic approach seemed to me intrinsically right in the same way as Silberer's did, but to begin with I rejected a number of his conclusions, which I either could not accommodate to my system of thought at the time, or else could not find substantiated in my own observation of life. It has only been in the course of some twenty years of completely independent thought and observation that I have become convinced that this system (with the addition of a few extensions of my own) does provide an intelligible and acceptable explanation of life as I understand it. I still disagree with it in a few minor points, to which I have alluded in various places in this study, but in the main I have come to accept this system on the basis of my own observation, and, it may be added, of some bitter experiences. I regard it as a guide to real life, not as an intellectual diversion. And lastly, deeply though I revere Dr. Jung (whom I have never met), and great though my gratitude to him is, I am not his disciple, but an independent investigator who has found his theories more helpful than any others.

This preference on my part is easily explained on the basis

[1] English transl., *The Psychology of the Unconscious*.

of Jung's system itself: Freud's thinking is extraverted, whereas Jung's and Silberer's is introverted, and my own tendency is markedly in the latter direction. It is of the essence of Jung's theory of extraversion and introversion that these two attitudes of mind, with the whole system of values and principles to which they give rise, are fundamentally opposed, but that they are nevertheless complementary, and that neither is intrinsically better, truer or in any way superior to the other. In the first instance, therefore, it might seem that there is not necessarily anything to choose between these two opposing psychological systems: they might represent two views of the same truth as seen from opposite viewpoints, in which case the only balanced and comprehensive view of the subject would be the one which takes account of both. The extravert's meat is the introvert's poison, and *vice versa*: extravert thinkers, therefore, might be expected to derive most benefit from following Freud's system, while those whose thought is introverted should cleave to Jung's—and they should 'agree to disagree'.

This conclusion, however, is open to two objections: in the first place Jung, by formulating this polarity, may claim to have established a system which transcends it; and in fact, although his tendency remains introverted, and although he reached his impartial standpoint by following an introverted line of thought, he does almost invariably succeed in maintaining his impartiality by having a due regard for the extravert viewpoint: it is only very occasionally that introvert prejudices slip past his guard. In this respect, therefore, his system does seem more catholic and comprehensive than Freud's, and while I know from personal experience that the introverted thinker can learn to understand a great deal about that profoundest enigma for him, the extravert viewpoint, from a study of the works of Jung, I am convinced that the extraverted thinker will derive no clue concerning the nature of introverted thought from those of Freud.

In the second place the very nature of the subject demands an introverted rather than an extraverted approach. The concretizing, particularizing tendency of extraverted thinking is eminently well suited to the study of, e.g., botany or zoology (Charles Darwin was a typical extravert thinker), but it is out of place in the investigation of the mind, for the latter, although it contains the concrete and the particular, is abstract and tends towards the universal in its structure and nature.

Hence it seems to me that while nobody can deny the importance of Freud's pioneering work in the study of the psychology of the unconscious, and while a certain number of his basic conclusions remain unchallenged, yet the later developments, and even some of the basic tenets of his system are at best one-sided and incomplete, and at worst misleading and retrogressive in the context of the study of the mind. His conception of instinct, in particular, seems to me entirely fallacious, as I shall attempt to demonstrate, and on that conception a large part of his system rests. Jung's system, on the other hand, seems to me to embrace all that is of fundamental value in Freud's, while at the same time going beyond it in its own sphere and, in addition, making contributions to thought, the import of which far transcends the limited sphere of medical psychology. I must make it quite clear, however, that I speak without any practical knowledge of psychotherapy: I am convinced, from personal experience, that Jung's system can be of the greatest assistance to the layman who applies it perseveringly to the treatment of his own psychological difficulties, but I am not in a position to make any pronouncements on the respective merits of the two systems as applied by practitioners to the cure of more serious mental derangements. But this last is surely only a secondary aspect of a psychological system, the ideal function of which is to enable the layman to understand the nature of mind, and thereby to escape the necessity of psychiatric treatment.

There are one or two other matters, in connection with which the approach adopted in this study runs counter to prevalent forms of thought, and for which it is therefore better to prepare the reader in advance. The first, which may arouse opposition in the minds of those who are unaccustomed to the assumption of an unconscious element in the motivation of almost all human behaviour, will arise from the apparently arbitrary manner in which thoughts, feelings and motivations unknown to the authors are inferred from the contents of their works. The complete and positive acceptance of this viewpoint is perhaps only possible to those who have studied human behaviour in its light over a number of years, and, in particular, have convinced themselves of its applicability to their own minds. Such unconscious contents, like all other material which is not immediately comprehensible to the conscious mind, are revealed in the first place by the intuitive function in a manner which, by its very nature, is not susceptible of rational explanation. The material thus intuitively produced, however, can subsequently be worked over, analysed and rearranged by the processes of rational thought until it can be shown to be either compatible or incompatible with a logically coherent system or world-picture which embraces other material as well. If it proves compatible, if it 'fits in' with what we have already established as incontrovertible, the new idea may be accepted as scientifically valid.

The history of the development of the natural sciences abounds in examples of this process: the discoverer 'gets an idea' in the form of a flash of insight, and then proceeds to establish its factual validity by means of patient experimentation and analysis. This process can be applied to the symbolical material contained in a poem in precisely the same way as to the structure of a complex molecule as revealed by its chemical and physical properties. The only difference lies in the manner in which the material is analysed and the nature of the standards by comparison with which its properties and correlations are defined.

Several centuries of intensive investigation and speculation have been required in order to establish the methods and standards of the physical sciences in their present form; in comparison with them the sciences of the mind are still in their infancy, and their methods and standards crude, uncertain and unfamiliar. It is for this reason that it is often harder to accept conclusions derived from purely symbolical or mental material than those deduced from the behaviour of physical bodies in accordance with the familiar and established methods of the natural sciences. But it is only necessary to mention the name of Galileo in order to realize that this was not always so.

If, therefore, the conclusions intuitively reached from the study of the symbolical content of poems and works of fiction can be shown to be capable of arrangement in a logically coherent system which is not incompatible with other known facts, we are bound to accept them as no less 'true' than the

deductions of physicists in regard to the electron, or of econo-
mists in regard to monetary trends. And if these conclusions
indicate that a great deal of human behaviour is motivated by
mental factors of which we are not conscious, we must accept
that fact also. It is mortifying, but it is true. *A fortiori* we may
conclude that when a creative artist gives his fantasy free rein
he will inevitably bring to expression things which are not
present in his conscious mind—of the existence of which, in fact,
he is completely unaware. Consciously he may be concerned
only with the technique of his art and with some rational theme
which he wishes to communicate, but the apparently fortuitous
choice of characters and situations, of words and images, may
reveal a whole world of the mind which has little or no connection with the content of the writer's consciousness. The reader
will be able to judge for himself whether such conclusions are
justifiable.

Another point concerns the approach to religious themes.
Today it is perhaps hardly necessary to apologize for 'free
thinking' in such matters; in face of the predominantly materialistic outlook of the times the need is rather to explain an
attitude which accepts any kind of divine principle as a reality.
Since this question leads straight to one of the main themes of
the study it will be well to clarify it at the outset. We shall be
concerned with the contrast between two worlds: the inner
world which lies beyond and around the conscious mind and the
outer world of which the body and other individuals form part.
This distinction, which is no more and no less absolute than
any other conceptual dichotomy, has been adumbrated by Jung
in his differentiation between the introverted and extraverted
functioning of the mind;[1] in a much later work[2] he also makes
the distinction between factual and what he calls 'psychological'
truth. If, he says in illustration of his thesis, it had long been
universally held that the river Rhine flowed back in a circle
to its own source, then the idea must be held to be psychologically true quite irrespective of its factual erroneousness, for such
a notion could not be widely accepted over a long period unless
it corresponded with, and gave expression to, some universal

[1] In *Wandlungen u. Symbole der Libido*; English transl., *The Psychology of
the Unconscious.*
[2] *Antwort auf Hiob.*

content or structure of the mind. If it lacked the attribute of psychological truth it would long ago have been forgotten like any other improbable traveller's tale. The notion, in fact, represents an inner or psychological truth: the error arises only in referring it to the outer-world, factual phenomenon known as the river Rhine. There must exist, in order to account for the existence of the legend, an abstract 'type' or mental image of a river which returns to its source, and this may be held to exist objectively if it is found to occur independently in a number of human minds at different times and places. The fact that no concrete material river has ever been known to conform to such a picture by no means invalidates the objective existence of the image; on the contrary it tends to substantiate it, for we must ask ourselves how it then comes about that so many people have for so long shown a disposition to believe anything so incompatible with the characteristics of the outer world which they know.

The same consideration applies to religious legends: they are necessarily true in the psychological or inner-world sense by virtue of the fact that they have at some time exerted a fascination over the minds of men and have, incidentally, thereby changed the course of history; like an international treaty, a business contract or an act of parliament they produce consequences which affect our lives although they exist only 'on paper', or in other words in our minds: therefore we can deny them neither truth nor reality. The question of their historical or factual truth is quite another matter, and, from the inner-world point of view, completely immaterial. We cannot, as Jung points out, prove that the events described in the Gospels (or, for that matter, in the Edda, the Koran or the Vedantas) did not occur as historical facts: all that we can say is that it is highly improbable. But even if the negative proof were available it would not alter the psychological truth of the stories. So far as Christianity is concerned we must learn to distinguish between the inner image of the Christ and the historical character (or possibly characters) called Jeshu or something similar, who once caused a disturbance in Palestine. Whoever the latter may have been, and whatever he, or they, may have done, the image of the Redeemer exists, and has always existed, as a living force in the human mind (and, incidentally, no 'vegetation myth' is required to account for it, or can account for it.) The Virgin Birth, the Crucifixion and the Resurrection are all psychological truths which have found symbolical expression again and again throughout history, and which are still being revealed in the creative works of the present day. This viewpoint, which will be elaborated in the course of the study, is surely not incompatible with a proper reverence for those ideas which many people still hold sacred.

The idea that a story which is factually true has greater significance or importance than one which is 'invented' is, moreover, a sign of inferior thinking. There exists an abundance of cheap magazines, produced for the poorly educated, which find it worth implying by their titles that the stories contained in them are 'true', and superficial thinkers constantly reiterate the proverb that truth is stranger than fiction. There is here a glimmering of understanding of the contrasting natures of the two worlds, for the word 'strange' evidently implies incredible, striking or significant. What the proverb is really saying is that the outer world ('truth') is normally less coherent, striking and significant, and that it contains less meaning than the inner world ('fiction'); but that occasionally outer-world events do occur whose dramatic or significant quality is so marked that it transcends the limits of outer-world plausibility which writers of fiction normally impose on themselves. We do in fact normally judge the interest and significance of outer-world events, as distinct from their practical implications, very largely by the standards of the inner world. Practical considerations apart, therefore, it is the form of the inner world in which we are really interested: it is the event which has dramatic quality, which is moving, striking, inspiring, shocking (for negative values may be no less arresting and significant than positive ones) which we single out, remember and rejoice in telling to one another. 'Truth', in the sense of the record of factual events, acquires interest (practical considerations apart) in proportion to its similarity to 'fiction'. The factual truth or untruth of a religious legend concerning events which are said to have occurred centuries ago can obviously have no practical repercussions at the present day: the wine-bill for the marriage feast at Cana has been paid long since and Lazarus is dead, whether for the first or second time is immaterial now. The only importance of the Gospel stories today lies in their inner-world value—in the psychological truths (not merely the ethical principles) which they reveal—and that, of course, is very great. If, when we come to analyse and identify the elements of which their message is composed, we find that the same elements are embodied in other stories, and sometimes in a far less edifying form, that is nothing for anybody either to be distressed or to crow about: the stories remain, and neither their value nor their beauty is in any way lessened by such considerations. The inner-world truths which they embody are realities of the mind, capable of influencing us and our actions, and are therefore no less 'real' or 'true' than that which we can touch or see. If their significance is universal it is hardly to be expected that their content should be unique: among the countless millions of human beings who have concerned themselves with human problems which are basically the same throughout the ages, a number must inevitably have discovered the same spiritual or inner-world realities, and have brought them to expression according to their idiom and their capacity. If some of these revelations are inferior, or even objectionable, that does not detract from the value of the others. Anybody is free to maintain that the Gospel stories are superior to any other versions of the same theme and I should not join issue with him; the identity of this theme with that of other stories, on the other hand, however inferior the latter may be in their aesthetic or ethical form, is a fact which cannot be denied and which it is an intellectual duty to insist upon.

Another point to which it is as well that the reader's attention should be drawn in advance is a purely formal one. Contrary to the usual practice I have given a brief synopsis of all the works to which I have devoted detailed consideration. In my experience nothing is more annoying or discouraging than the assumption, so commonly met with in works of this nature, that the reader must be familiar with all the more important works of literature, or the blithe observation that the work in question is 'easily available for reference'. No author, if he is not writing purely for specialists or professional scholars, has the right to expect his readers either to have all the classics fresh in their memories or else to devote days to the study of works which are often lengthy and diffuse, simply in order that they may be able to follow his argument. I am, of course, painfully aware of the fact that such synopses can only be grotesque travesties which are liable to give a completely distorted impression of what may be a great original, but it seems to me that this defect, regrettable though it is, must be accepted as the price of intelligibility. I can only hope that my readers will be moved to consult the originals of any of these works with which they are not familiar, and that my dissection of them will not prevent their finding the same pleasure and inspiration in them that I have found.

I have adopted the same principle with regard to the works of Jung. His system represents advances in thought in spheres far wider than that of medical psychology, and it is not always easy of assimilation. His various theories, moreover, are scattered among a considerable number of works, some of which are not easy reading, and those who do not read German will find that the quality of the earlier translations into English leaves very much to be desired.[1] I have therefore acted on the assumption that it would not be safe to presume any great familiarity with his system in the average reader, for few people in these days have the time or enjoy the tranquillity necessary to master such a considerable body of work. Accordingly I have done my best to provide summaries of the main heads of his system piecemeal as they arise. By presenting them thus separately in the context of the examples to which they apply I hope that I have made what might otherwise be an indigestible body of condensed theory somewhat more readable. Those to whom Jung's system is already familiar will be able to skip these interpolations: for others I hope that they will provide an elementary introduction which may inspire a study of the originals.

This volume is part of a larger whole, which I hope to publish under the general title *A Study of Two Worlds*. I have attempted to make it self-contained, but at the same time to embody in it an adumbration of the scope of the whole study.

[1] The translation of the new complete edition of Jung's works in English, now in course of publication, is, on the other hand, admirable.

PART I

MISS BLANDISH IN THE UNDERWORLD

I Persephone

No Orchids for Miss Blandish was one of the most successful books of its decade. Not only were several million copies of the book itself sold but a film was made of the story, and Miss Blandish's name became literally a 'household word' which could be used on the stage, or even in B.B.C. programmes, in the assurance that it would be familiar to the widest circles of the public. Miss Blandish, in fact, became one of the great legendary figures which inhabit the communal mind; she belongs almost to the company of Sherlock Holmes, Tarzan, Alice and Peter Pan.

It is clear that a phenomenon of this magnitude can be attributed to one cause only: the figure in question must correspond to something which is universally present in the minds of contemporary people: it must constitute something which they want to talk about, which fits into their views and feelings about life; which helps them to express themselves and thus to come to terms with the problems of existence. Miss Blandish is a typical mythological figure, a portrayal, that is to say, of a symbolical destiny expressed in terms of human life. Images of this nature are universal in humanity and are to be found in the myths and legends of all peoples at all times: there is no essential difference at all between the story of Miss Blandish's descent into the underworld and that of Persephone, evolved over two thousand years ago and still familiar to us.

Such a conclusion is not immediately acceptable. Persephone seems so remote, and we learnt about her at school, which puts her story into a moralizing, instructional category that seems infinitely far removed from the unedifying tale of Miss Blandish. And we have tidied away the old myth by 'explaining' it:

Persephone, we say, 'represents' the vegetation which disappears in the winter and returns in the spring, and with that superficial rationalization we believe that we have accounted for her. We shall return later to this question of explaining away myths: at present it will suffice to point out that this particular explanation is completely inadequate. Demeter, the mother, 'represents' vegetation, and she remains forlorn above the earth: why was it necessary to invent the additional figure of a virgin daughter? And what has the latter's rape to do with the vegetation theme—where does Pluto come into it? The Greeks were quite aware of the parallel between Persephone's periodical disappearance and return and the cycle of vegetation, but many of them saw far more in the story than that, for it constituted the basic theme of the mysteries of Eleusis, which were perhaps the most important of all manifestations of the mystical element in classical religion. It is evident that for the ancient world the Persephone myth must have played a part similar to that which the story of the Crucifixion and Resurrection has played in the Christian world: it expressed in symbolical form certain basic spiritual facts with which every human being is concerned. For the wide popularity and the profound and beneficent spiritual effects of the mysteries on those who participated in them are attested by a number of reputable contemporary authorities; they were available to all who spoke Greek and bore no blood-guilt, and the resultant diversity of personalities among the participants, from the simplest to the most cultured and intellectual, would hardly all have been so moved and inspired by a superficial allegory of such an obvious nature as that of the vegetation-cycle.

The disreputable story of *No Orchids* would seem at first sight to stand in cross contrast to such sacred themes. It is characterized by a daring treatment of sex and violence, and any comparison between such sadistic lewdness and the themes of classical legend, even though they no longer form part of our religious beliefs, is repugnant to our finer feelings. But so is the story of Persephone a tale of sex and violence: not only the daughter, but the mother also is raped.[1] The atmosphere of anxious propriety of the schoolroom, and of the schoolbooks from which we learn the story, is apt to obliterate this fact.

[1] By Poseidon. See Jung and Kerenyi: *Einführung i. d. Wesen d. Mythologie.*

There is no reason why spiritual truths should not be expressed in terms of sex and violence: it may not be desirable, but the fact remains that it often happens. The people who evolved the myth of Persephone and the secret revelations of the Eleusinian mysteries were not compiling moralizing tales for school-children any more than Hadley Chase was when he wrote *No Orchids*: they, and he, had become dimly and introspectively aware of a tragic symbolical destiny which demanded expression, and each of them set about bringing it to expression in the contemporary idiom. It is our task as investigators to look behind the idiom, to think away the gangsters and millionaires and night-clubs of *No Orchids* just as we think away the personified divine principles of the ancient myth, in an effort to discover what the stories really mean. All that matters is what happened, not what the respective authors suggest to account for why it happened.

Until we have examined the material of *No Orchids* in greater detail we cannot go further into its possible parallels with the Persephone legend; I have introduced the matter here at the outset in order to give some indication of the kind of material for which we may be on the lookout. My thesis is that Miss Blandish's enormous popularity can only be accounted for by elements in her story which have some significance apart from the mere superficial handling of it. It would be foolish to deny that much of the popular appeal of the book did lie in the lewd and gruesome episodes in which it abounds. Sex and horrors have always been popular themes, and today the purveying of such matter has become a prosperous industry, yet no figure from the horror fiction, or indeed from any fiction, of her decade found anything like the same universal acceptance as Miss Blandish. *No Orchids* remains a classic, still to be found on the shelves of respectable libraries, and although its popularity has now faded it can confidently be predicted that in due course it will revive. Thus although it is true to say that if the story had been written in a less sensational form it would not have reached quite such a wide public, it is no less true that if it had contained no more than sensationalism it would never have been remembered.

As G. F. Orwell said in an article devoted to it, *No Orchids* is a brilliant piece of writing; yet the wide public among whom it has found acceptance are not unduly critical in such matters: they are concerned with the substance rather than the style, and subsequent works by the same author, in which seductions and horrors are no less brilliantly described, have made little impression. The significance of *No Orchids* lies in the story, and that story exercised its fascination on the intellectual critic and writer Orwell no less than on the great unenlightened public. It must contain something of universal significance.

Before turning to the work itself it is necessary to dispose of one important point, namely the dependence of *No Orchids* on another work: William Faulkner's *Sanctuary*.[1] In the following chapters we shall find numerous examples of such derivations of one work from another. There is no question of plagiarism: it is rather a matter of inspiration. The function of the writer of fiction is to discern the essential and significant elements in human situations and to present them in the form of a coherent and acceptable story: it is immaterial from what source his materials are derived. They may come from actual events in the outer world, from his own unaided fantasy or from the works of other writers: all that matters is his ability to present them in the most telling form. We can speak of plagiarism only when a writer, at a loss for ideas, deliberately sets out to remodel an existing work, which has proved successful, in a disguise in which, he hopes, it will not be recognized. The dividing line between such a servile imitation and the case in which existing literary material has acted as a source of inspiration and a spur to emulation is hard to define, yet in its results it is obvious enough. It is well known, for instance, that a great many of Shakespeare's plots were derived from existing legends and tales, yet no reasonable person would accuse Shakespeare of plagiarism on that account. What happened was evidently that Shakespeare, reading the stories in question, discerned their underlying meaning or pattern, and that he was impelled to produce his own fresh rendering of it. The situation is similar to my own experience related in the introduction to this enquiry: it is a case of two individual minds interpreting the same universal experience, and it can take place even when the

[1] I am indebted to Dr. H. L. R. Edwards for drawing my attention to this point, and also to *No Orchids* itself.

two minds in question have no external knowledge of one another's productions. More commonly, perhaps, one of the interpretations is the immediate consequence of its author's having read the other, but that is immaterial. Shakespeare read a crude medieval legend concerning dynastic conflicts at the court of Denmark and discerned in it the bare bones of a situation which he presented in the complex psychological form of *Hamlet*: that presentation is his own rendering of a universal mental pattern which necessarily existed in a potential state in his mind even before he had read the ancient epic of the troubles at Elsinore, and it is therefore only a matter of secondary importance to discover exactly what item in his reading turned his attention to it.

This matter of the interaction of the personal or particular and the universal parts of the mind is one of the principal themes of this study and will be further elucidated in later chapters; at this point we may introduce the subject by a brief outline of Jung's theory of the Archetypes.

THE ARCHETYPES

When a fresh human life is inaugurated by the impregnation of an ovum the resultant zygote or elementary embryo is a single cell which differs in hardly any external particular from that from which a dog or a horse, or even a sea-urchin will develop. Nevertheless we can say with certainty that if this entity survives for a few months it will have attained a recognizable human form. In the vast majority of cases it will then grow into a man or woman between five and six feet in height, and almost invariably it will possess two eyes, a nose, two hands and so forth. Individual variations between certain limits are normal, and exceptional conditions during childhood and gestation may produce striking abnormalities; nevertheless we can be absolutely confident that this microscopic creature will in no circumstances grow to a height of twenty feet, nor will it develop feathers, or a carapace, or even a digestive system capable of breaking down cellulose as a cow's can. These characteristics do not belong to the human pattern which is already present, in a potential state, even in the single cell of the fertilized ovum.

The adult human being who will eventuate after about twenty years, therefore, may be seen as the product of the interaction of two factors: on the one hand the unvarying and universal pattern of the species, and on the other the particular factors affecting the individual being. The latter are partly endogenous, arising from the particular combination of genes in the original zygote, and partly extragenous, deriving from the particular conditions to which the individual organism has been subjected during its development; the endogenous elements are on the borderline and may be included among either the universal, racial components or the individual ones, according to how closely we circumscribe the hereditary factor, but the elements arising from influences which take effect after conception are clearly a part of the individual existence as distinct from the general pattern of the race or stock. The colour of the eyes, for instance, may be solely determined by the parental stock, but the effects of disease or abnormal nutrition during gestation or childhood are purely individual.

The typical characteristics of the species, however, are not confined to physical forms: they embrace typical mental tendencies or behaviour-patterns as well. Tortoises are not only equipped with a carapace but with the impulse to draw head and limbs into its protection when alarmed; nightingales sing, spiders spin webs, and human beings pick things up with their hands and investigate them. We can, therefore, be confident that the human embryo will develop not only a recognizable human form but that, gross abnormalities apart, it will come into possession of a complete and stereotyped set of human behaviour tendencies as well: not only the body, but the mind also, has a typical, unvarying, universal generic substructure. This is the universal mind in which we all participate just as we participate in the basic anatomical structure of our species.

We shall be concerned later with the specific manner in which this universal human mind acts through the mechanism of the instinctive reactions and the intermediate levels of the unconscious mind; it will be sufficient for the moment to draw attention to its contrast with the individual element in the mind. In humanity the potentiality of individual variation in the mental sphere infinitely exceeds what is possible in the physical: it is in this respect that we have so far differentiated

28

ourselves from the rest of the animal creation as to justify the conception of an entirely separate plane of human existence. It is the faculty of adding to our generic mental heritage by means of learning from individual experience which we have brought to such an extraordinary pitch that each human individual has come to regard himself as a closed, self-contained, personal mind, entirely cut off from his generic mental roots. In our concentration on the particular we have lost sight of the universal.

Nevertheless the development of each individual mind remains confined within the pattern of generic potentialities exactly as that of the body does. The possibilities of individual variation within the universal pattern are infinitely greater in the mental than in the physical sphere: in the swimming-bath there is little difference between one man and another: one has blue eyes and the other brown; one is taller by perhaps a fifth of his total stature than the other; but they go home and one sits down to write a treatise on mathematics and the other to mend shoes, one resumes the responsibilities of empire and the other returns to picking pockets. Yet the philosopher and the statesman can no more evade or transcend the typical patterns of the human mind than the cobbler and the pickpocket can: their minds, like their bodies, are formed in the same generic mould and have been built up on the same generic foundations by the action of the same generic impulses. The only differences between them lie in the particular manner in which their individual mental experiences and peculiarities have interacted and combined within this framework to produce that complex of mental habits, skills, standards of value and guiding ideas which we call the personality.

The difference between one human personality and another may be truly immense and fraught with immense consequences: nevertheless it cannot transcend the limits of the essentially human. Similarly, in the physical sphere, two men may have utilized their identical basic human endowment differently, in that one has learnt to swim while the other has not; this constitutes an individual difference in capacity which in certain circumstances may be of vital importance in that one will survive where the other drowns. But the very importance of this difference lies precisely in the fact that both are subject to the same basic and unalterable limitation, namely that they cannot survive under water. One of them has taken account of this universal human limitation and has adapted the universal human potentialities to it in learning to keep his head above water when out of his depth; the other, having failed in this, must pay the penalty. But if the swimmer, failing to understand the nature of the problem, had attempted to overcome the generic human inability to live under water simply by keeping his head under water for as long as he could, with the intention of eventually training himself to remain there indefinitely, he would never have learnt to swim and would have drowned as surely as the other who had never concerned himself with the problem. He would have failed to understand, and thus to circumvent, the inherent limitations of his human constitution.

In the sphere of the mind it is exactly the same. The highest individual attainments of which we are capable are achieved by adapting human potentialities to human limitations, and the inability to understand, or the failure to accept the latter must lead to disaster. In the course of this study we shall find numerous examples of this tragic fact.

The mind has learnt to recognize the limitations of the body, but it is harder for it to appreciate its own. Possibilities which transcend or differ from the factors by which the conscious mind is moulded, or on which it has been built up, simply do not exist for it, for it possesses no means of apprehending them. Since, therefore, there is nothing with which it can compare its own nature it cannot recognize that nature in its entirety. Perceiving some of the things which it can do, it is apt to assume that it is potentially capable of doing anything, and is for ever embarking on enterprises which ignore the limitations of which it is not aware. The majority of human disasters, as we shall see, can be attributed to this tendency; yet, on the other hand, the same tendency is the mainspring of human achievement, for it is precisely by the initiative which impels us to attempt what has never before been attempted that we have grown great. It is, therefore, vitally necessary that we should learn to form as clear a picture as possible of the nature of our innate impulses and insurmountable limitations no less than of our potentialities.

If the mind were not equipped with some mechanism which warned it to desist when it was attempting the mentally impossible the human race could not have survived. This mechanism acts by presenting to the conscious mind images in the form of visions, inner voices, dreams, emotions or simply 'ideas' which in some way run counter to or contrast with the conscious attitude. They derive from a primitive level of the mind which disposes only of an archaic, symbolical language which differs from that of the highly developed, educated conscious mind and is not immediately comprehensible to the latter. If the conscious mind fails to understand these messages it may persist in some enterprise or attitude which ignores the inherent limitations of the mind in the same way as an attempt to live under water ignores those of the body; in such a case mental sickness will result. The conscious mind, on the other hand, may learn to accept these warnings and to interpret them correctly, in which case the error of its ways will be revealed to it and it will be in a position to amend them.

Modern psychology seeks to teach the conscious mind to interpret these messages. Freud recognized their symbolical nature but related them exclusively to outer-world situations: they represent, in his system, merely disguised wish-fulfilments which the conscious mind refuses to entertain in their 'true' form because of their unacceptability by conventional moral standards, or for other similar reasons. Jung, on the other hand, sees in them something far more fundamental: they are expressions, or intimations, of the basic structure of the mind itself: not merely allegorical representations of concrete situations. Such allegorical representations, he admits, do occur when the unconscious mind is simply rectifying some oversight or ill-considered judgment of the conscious mind: he quotes the example of a patient whose mental capacity he had underrated, and whose figure thereupon appeared to him in a dream standing above him on a high tower. Interpreting this dream as the resurgence, from his unconscious mind, of impressions of the superior qualities of the patient to which he had paid insufficient conscious attention, and which had therefore been repressed by the attitude suitable to a mentally inferior person which he had adopted towards her, he informed her frankly of his mistake and amended his attitude: naturally, as he says, with the best results.

But behind and beyond such more or less trivial intimations

of minor errors which anybody, if he takes the trouble, can identify in his day-to-day dreams and fantasies, Jung discerned a body of more generalized or abstract symbols of far wider import. As might be expected such figures occurred with peculiar persistence in the dreams, fantasies and delusions of the mentally sick, but they corresponded in an inexplicable way with the figures of myth and legend, from the most ancient fables to contemporary poetry and fiction. Dissatisfied with Freud's contention that these parallels, some of which he had himself discerned, simply indicated the prevalence in all individual minds at all times of repressed concrete wishes (mostly of an incestuous nature) Jung advanced the hypothesis that they should rather be regarded as revelations by the mind of its own generic structure. This structure, being the mould in which the individual conscious mind is formed, the foundation on which it has been built up, and the impulses by which it was built and which are active in it, is normally inaccessible to consciousness. For so long as the conscious mind confines itself to its legitimate activities, indeed, there is no need for it to have any knowledge of its own background; it is only when its natural spirit of enterprise entices it into undertakings which do violence to the inherent limitations of the mind as a whole that it stands in need of restraint. When this happens the offended part, or structure, of the universal mind calls attention to itself in exactly the same way as, for instance, the digestive system, normally unconscious, calls attention to itself if we persist in eating unsuitable food.

The mind, like the body, must be regarded as a whole, all of whose parts and functions interact and depend on one another; like the body, moreover, it has certain specific modes of reaction to specific stimuli or provocations; just as the body reacts with a raising of the temperature, a lowering of the blood-pressure, inflammations, discharges and the like, so does the mind react with certain definite emotional states, impulses, obsessions and so forth. These mental reactions may be identified and described exactly like physical symptoms and, for convenience, may be treated as separate entities just as a fever or an inflammation may be so treated. Roughly speaking it may be said that these specific modes of reaction of the universal mental disposition or structure of humanity are the manifestations of what Jung has called the Archetypes. They may be recognized in their universal occurrence just as specific physical symptoms may be recognized, and valid conclusions may be drawn from their presence; nevertheless it must be remembered that they are modes of reaction of the unitary mind of which they are parts, and not strictly circumscribed entities existing in their own right. Similarly the wise doctor will always bear in mind that it is not the fever which he has to cure but the patient's whole organism, which is producing the fever as a reaction to some unsatisfactory condition. I say the patient's organism and not the patient himself advisedly, for in mental sickness it is the universal part of the mind affected by the patient's faulty conscious attitude which has to be considered, not merely his individual personality: in a sense the patient himself is the disease.

An important characteristic of the Archetypes is that they habitually present themselves to the conscious mind in the form of images which tend to behave in a certain way. These images are often visual, although they may take other forms as well, and consist of human figures, animals, objects and scenes, and in situations in which some or all of these occur in relation to one another. Typical examples are a wise old man, a woman of supernatural beauty and power, a sword which breaks and must be mended, the birth of a divine child, imprisonment, the menace of an armed man appearing from the darkness, the sun at its rising, setting and zenith. These may be described as typical Archetypal figures or images: they are not, of course, the Archetypes themselves, any more than the body of a man or his activities are the man himself, but they are living realities, no less than the body and actions of the man are realities: they possess power and exert their influence on the mind no less than the man's body and actions exert their influence on the outer world.

I have described the Archetypes as warning signals and modes of reaction similar to the symptoms of physical sickness, but they must not be regarded as exclusively pathological phenomena. The mind, like the body, has its requirements when in normal health and will draw attention to them when they are in need of satisfaction; like the body it demands alternations of exercise and rest, nourishment from external sources and evacuation of its own waste products, a routine complying with its inherent rhythms as a rule, varied by occasional stimulating irregularities. In addition to these parallels with physical existence it has its own typical modes of activity and quiescence, evolution, involution, dichotomy, reunification and self-renewal. All of these are represented by Archetypal images and situations: the processes themselves, or the hypothetical 'structures' of the mind by and through which they take place, may be regarded as the actual essence of the Archetypes, although with the proviso that we cannot, in the last resort, define what anything mental 'is'. *A fortiori*, to brush the question aside with the claim that mental phenomena 'are' no more than disguised representations of concrete, outer-world situations is merely puerile, for the situations of the outer world possess the character of situations solely by virtue of the attitude of the mind.

The mind, like the body, maintains its individual existence by virtue of a complex system of equilibria between counter-balancing forces: in the last resort such a particular pattern of equilibrium between non-individualized elements is the nearest notion we can form of the essence of living individuality. If this equilibrium is endangered the survival of the individuality is threatened, and the activity of the ultimate Centre of the individual is always directed to restoring it. The means which it brings into action for this purpose are the Archetypal modes which are revealed to consciousness in the form of the Archetypal images. When they are thus revealed it may be assumed that they are active: they are living forces tending purposefully in a given direction governed by the inherent laws of their natures, which in turn are part of the inherent structure of the Psyche or universal mind of man. The appearance of Archetypal images in consciousness, therefore, although not necessarily an indication of a pathological or morbid condition of the mind, does indicate that equilibrium is endangered and that measures are being taken to restore it: they are themselves the expression of healthy reaction to the disturbing influences. These disturbing influences, moreover, must themselves be the consequences of the activity of one of the Archetypal modes, since the mind is not capable of functioning in any other manner: the disturbance indicates that one or other of the modes has temporarily achieved an undue preponderance and requires to be checked by countervailing tendencies.

The equilibrium of the mind, like that of the body in walking, is in a permanent condition of flux and transition, for only thus is progress possible. A state of permanent, static equilibrium would imply stagnation, and life demands change. A rich and vivid experience of Archetypal images, therefore, may be a concomitant of intense mental advance: it is characteristic of the spiritually creative no less than of the mentally sick. As a corollary we may conclude that the creative process, being associated with a precarious mental equilibrium, is a dangerous one, and of this we shall find ample confirmation.

Bearing these points in mind we may return to our two stories.

THE STORIES

William Faulkner's *Sanctuary* was published in 1931, eight years earlier than *No Orchids*, and, unlike as the two works are in many respects, the parallels between them are striking. Faulkner, of course, is a writer of far greater literary pretensions —and higher status—than Chase: he is, indeed, the holder of a Nobel Prize. *Sanctuary*, among other things, is a sociological study of the Deep South in the 'twenties, but this aspect of the work, together with its psychological subtleties, is not our concern here: I mention them merely in order to avoid giving the impression that the two works are comparable from the literary point of view, which they are not. We are concerned here only with a common element in Archetypal symbolism, such as is to be found equally in such remote material as the Persephone myth: this element, on which *No Orchids* is based, constitutes only one thread in the complex plot of *Sanctuary*. But in addition to the parallels in this theme, and in the portrayal of the characters, attention should be drawn to another characteristic in which the two works correspond: that is in the predominant grey misery of the feeling-tone, the insistence on the cruel and the sordid, the atmosphere of bleak hopelessness and exhaustion which pervades both books. This atmosphere is in itself an Archetypal image and represents an integral part of the story.

35

The relevant elements from *Sanctuary* are as follows. A college girl, the daughter of an old-school Southern Gentleman, sets off on a drunken spree with a pseudo-Southern-Gentleman who cannot hold his liquor; they are stranded at a remote house where an illicit whisky still is run by a gangster named Pop-Eye (for these are the days of Prohibition). This Pop-Eye is a killer; he is also a degenerate with such a peculiar nervous constitution that he cannot touch alcohol and is completely and irremediably impotent. His lusts, however, are aroused by the girl, whom he abducts, after taking her virginity by a revolting device.[1] He then keeps her confined in a brothel in a neighbouring town, satisfying his desires by watching her copulating with another man, whom he procures for the purpose and subsequently kills. There is an elaborate sketch of the brothel-keeper, a large and imposing lady who compensates for her sordid occupation by an extreme genteelness in her private life. Under this treatment the girl is completely demoralized, degenerating into an addict of alcohol and sex; she is eventually rescued, and, Pop-Eye not being available, is persuaded by her terrible father to accuse an innocent man of her rape. This man is lynched by the angry mob, and Pop-Eye is subsequently hanged, quite somewhere else, for a murder that he does not happen to have committed. This unedifying story closes with the girl and her father in Paris, under the leaden sky of a grey afternoon that will evidently continue for ever.

The parallelism of *No Orchids* is immediately evident. It opens with a conspiracy by a gang of small-time crooks to steal the fabulous diamonds worn by Miss Blandish, the only daughter of the local millionaire. At the hold-up, however, they have the misfortune to kill her play-boy escort, and since Miss Blandish was a witness to the crime whom they dare not release they decide to abduct her and hold her for ransom. On their way to their hide-out, a remote house in the country, they have the misfortune to be seen by a member of the Grisson gang, big shots who cannot bear to see such a profitable proposition as

---

[1] By the use of the core of a corn-cob. An interesting parallel is provided by the ancient Greek custom of performing the deflowering (regarded as dangerous to the male partner) by means of an ithyphallic image of Leukippos, a girl who had been transformed into a boy. See *Paulys Real-Encycl. d. Class. Altertumswiss.*, art. 'Leukippos.'

Miss Blandish left in the hands of small fry. They therefore pursue the original captors to the hide-out, where they murder them all three, and remove Miss Blandish to their town house.

Slim Grisson, the leader of the gang, is introduced as a pervert whose only pleasure lies in killing and torturing. Hitherto he had taken no interest in women, but he now falls irretrievably in love with Miss Blandish. The real head of the gang, however, is Slim's mother, Ma Grisson, a terrible old woman who has organized her son's successes, relieving him of the responsibility for everything except the actual murdering. The only other noteworthy member of the gang is a handsome philanderer named Eddie, who is portrayed with considerable sympathy.

After the ransom money has been collected Miss Blandish's continued existence is nothing but a source of danger, and Ma would like to 'rub her out'; Slim, however, refuses to allow it: he keeps her 'as a plaything', and even gives her back her diamonds, which thereupon disappear from the story. Ma, in her maternal fondness, persuades Miss Blandish, with the aid of drugs and beatings with a rubber hose, to submit herself to Slim's bestial lusts, and in these circumstances she is held in captivity for several months. Her father, John Blandish, the millionaire, dissatisfied with the failure of the police to rescue her, hires a private detective named Fenner who succeeds in tracking her down.

The Grisson mob have by this time installed themselves in a fortified place, equipped with steel shutters and defended with great fire-power. An army of police is mobilized and this stronghold is captured after a great battle in which the entire Grisson mob, with the sole exceptions of Eddie and Slim, are eliminated in a glorious hecatomb.

But this victory is unavailing, for when the police penetrate to the inmost recesses of the citadel, where Miss Blandish had been held captive, they find that she and Slim have flown. Their absence is due to the incident described in the Introduction: Rocco, the rival gangster, has removed Miss Blandish, and Slim has gone in search of her; she has unaccountably resisted the attempt to restore her to her father, preferring to wait for Slim; now he has her again, and he carries her off on his last flight.

In the end he is caught and shot down, and Miss Blandish recaptured. But once again she unaccountably refuses to return to her old life. Of Slim she says, 'He's not dead. He's with me now, I know he is. At first I thought I was wrong, but now I know I've got him with me. He wouldn't leave me alone, ever —and he never will.' She then throws herself from a window and thus ends the tale.

But there is a bitter postscript. A rich lady, whose car has been held up in the confusion resulting from Miss Blandish's fall from the window, sends her chauffeur to enquire what has happened. On being told she comments acidly that the victim was no doubt another silly girl who had got herself into trouble over a man.

That, of course, is the true theme of the story, and in it we may discern a significant parallel with the Persephone myth.

PERSEPHONE

Persephone, the virgin daughter of Demeter, was raped, or, more politely, carried off to the underworld by its ruler, Pluto or Hades. So, also, was Miss Blandish, her Pluto going by the name of Slim. Demeter, left forlorn in the upper world, approached Zeus (who in most versions was Persephone's father) with the demand for the return of her daughter; in some versions she imposed her will by refusing to allow any vegetation to grow upon the earth in the meanwhile. Whether willingly or under this compulsion Zeus acceded to her request, ordaining the return of Persephone to the upper world; but then it was found that while in the underworld she had eaten a pomegranate[1] given her by Pluto, and in consequence of this he decreed that she must spend part of each year in the underworld with her husband, returning to her mother in the world above only for the remainder.

Now this eating of the pomegranate, if taken as a rational explanation of Persephone's fate, is obviously nonsensical: in order to find any meaning in the story we must interpret it symbolically. As I have already mentioned the rule for doing this is to look first for the final outcome of the action, ignoring the explanations offered as to how and why it came to pass,

---

[1] In some versions only one seed; in others a part, either one third or the half.

and then to consider the action itself: to try, in fact, to discover what actually happened in the Archetypal drama which the writer or mythographer is interpreting. In this myth the final outcome is that Persephone, the daughter or princess of the upper world, is condemned to divide her existence between the two worlds: each, in fact, has asserted a valid claim on her. The upper world claims her by right of origin, but the claim of the lower world came into existence in the course of the story: it is with the creation and establishment of this claim that the myth is concerned. What, then, actually happened? In the first place the ruler of the lower world became enamoured of the princess of the upper world and carried her off against her will. So far no claim had been established, for Zeus, the supreme authority, at first ruled that Persephone be restored to her mother; then, however, it became apparent that Persephone, during her sojourn in the underworld, had done something, this time of her own free will, which bound her to her ravisher with a bond against which even the authority of Zeus availed nothing. The most that he could do was to obtain her periodical liberation for a limited period.

We have not far to look for an explanation of Persephone's fateful action, for the pomegranate, for obvious reasons connected with its manner of bursting, has always had a sexual connotation;[1] Persephone, then, is quite simply bound irrevocably to the underworld by the loss of her virginity to her lover. We must, however, beware of interpreting this conclusion in outer-world terms: the myth is no simple allegory based on the ancient custom of carrying off the bride, or anything superficial of that kind. The final outcome at once rules out such an interpretation, for the mortal bride belongs henceforth solely to her husband and there should be no question of removing her

[1] Cf *Paulys Real-Encycl. d. Class. Altertumswiss.*, art. 'Persephone': ' . . . the ancient marriage custom in which the bride, on first entering her husband's house, was presented with a pomegranate as a love- and fertility-charm.' And, with regard to the binding force contained in the eating of the pomegranate: 'The fact that Kore (i.e. the basic type of Persephone) is bound for ever to the realm of shadows by her eating of the pomegranate . . . is an old fairy-tale theme which occurs already in Egypt. The person who has partaken of food and drink in the world beyond is eternally bound to the underworld and can never again return permanently to the world of the living.'

from him, even for a limited period: we must seek the meaning elsewhere.

Turning now to Persephone's own attitude in the matter we find that her incarceration in the underworld is traditionally regarded as being distasteful to her: she is commonly pictured as longing to return to her mother, and their reunion is seen as an ecstatic fulfilment of hope deferred. But this might perhaps be a polite convention: we have, in fact, the opinion of four contemporary interpreters of this drama who all, quite un-equivocally, assert the contrary view. In the first place we have the two stories under discussion, in both of which the ravished heroine is by no means anxious to return to the world of polite virginity: Faulkner shows her as merely converted to the vicious ways of the underworld, but Chase, sensing the underlying symbolism and bringing it out more clearly, leaves us in no doubt that it is to the person of her lover that Miss Blandish cleaves. This love, it is true, is represented in the most unattractive colours and Miss Blandish is ostensibly its passive and unwilling victim; nevertheless she violently resists Rocco's attempt to deliver her from her supposed tormentor, and in the end, when her lover is taken from her, she follows him to the depths to which he has returned. Further evidence of her love will be discussed later.

The next witness is Thornton Wilder, whose evidence is embodied in a playlet entitled *Persephone and the Devil*. The subject is a puppet-show which goes wrong: the action is intended to represent the Persephone myth, but no puppet for Pluto being available his part is taken by a conventional medieval devil. The operators are careless and inattentive, and in consequence Persephone twice throws herself into the arms of the devil instead of fleeing from him, in the second case preferring him to her mother, who has come to reclaim her. It is interesting to note that here the classical Pluto, who has come to be seen as a kingly and not unacceptable figure, is revealed in his true light. In antiquity he was held in such horror that his name was never mentioned.

Lastly we find the same theme in a book by a woman: Mary Mitchell's *Warning to Wantons*. This is the amusing story of a super-civilized and flirtatious French girl who is abducted by a jealous rival and deposited in the bed of a young peasant in a fantastically remote Balkan village. Hitherto she had lived for all the refinements of civilized luxury, and life in the village is inconceivably primitive and squalid; nevertheless, although she, too, is rescued, she prefers to return to her rustic lover.

Confirmation of this conjecture from classical sources is also not wanting, for both Virgil and Lucan show Persephone as unwilling to return to the upper world. The latter, indeed, represents her as having conceived such a repugnance and hatred for her mother that the latter in her despair became an addict to opium.[1]

On a superficial view one might be inclined to advance the sordid interpretation that these stories have no more edifying message than that the enjoyment of physical love outweighs, for woman, all other considerations. But that leaves the underworld element out of account, and, most particularly, it is incompatible with the undoubted mystical importance which the Persephone myth, in the form of the Eleusinian Mysteries, enjoyed in the ancient world. The story must have some deeper meaning.

One point which does emerge is the importance which virginity and its sacrifice play in the destiny of woman. Once again the outer-world implications of this matter are not sufficient to account for the creation of myths about it: it is an obvious fact that in most social environments the role and status of an individual woman is completely transformed on the bridal night, and such obvious facts do not give rise to myths. We are not concerned with individual women but with the Archetype of womanhood, a figure existing in the universal mind; until we have found out more about her we must leave the question of who Persephone or Miss Blandish is, why she falls to such an ignoble lover, of what her mission in the underworld consists, and why she belongs to two different worlds.

[1] *Cf Paulys Real-Encycl. d. Class. Altertumswiss.*, art. 'Persephone', in which full references are given.

II   The Barrier

THE picture of two worlds at war is an ever-present theme in *No Orchids*. On the one hand there is the upper world of law and order, of virtue and rectitude, ruled by John Blandish and defended by his minions, the detective Fenner and the police; on the other the underworld of crime, vice and licence, ruled by Ma and her gangsters. These two worlds hate one another with an implacable hatred, and whenever they are brought into contact there is bloodshed. The means of bringing them into contact is Miss Blandish, for each acquires a claim on her and it is about her person that the conflict rages.

This situation, of course, is of the essence of every thriller, the excitement and tension of which is maintained by this picture of the conflict between two opposing factions for the possession of some object of great value. The antagonists are commonly represented nowadays as the police and the criminal gang, or our own secret service and that of another country; in *Treasure Island* it was Squire Livesey's men and the pirates. But the pattern is already to be found in the Book of Job, in which the antagonists appear as God and Satan. That is the fundamental formula: the conflict is between constituted authority and the established order on the one hand and the rebellious powers of the dispossessed on the other.

It is necessary for the reader to be persuaded to take sides, and generally the choice falls on the conventional side of constituted authority; occasionally, on the other hand, it is for the deserving rebel—the Robin Hood type—but that, for the moment, we may ignore. In *No Orchids* we are on the side of authority, for although the powers of law and order and of Blandish rectitude are anything but attractively portrayed their antagonists are seen in an even worse light. And Fenner the detective, ruthless and brutal though he is, resembles the traditional hero more closely than does any other character. The orientation thus revealed is important in the sequel.

THE TREASURE

If we go back to Job we find that the object of value around which the conflict rages is the soul of man; in modern times it has assumed a more concrete form, being seen as an object of pecuniary value such as a jewel, or something of critical importance, such as secret plans; in the fairy-tales and legends we also find the idea of the treasure of gold and jewels, or simply of the kingdom. The latter form is of course irreconcilable with a modern context, for kingdoms today do not pass so easily from hand to hand; one of the last exploitations of this particular image is to be found in the famous nineteenth-century thriller *The Prisoner of Zenda*.

Now G. F. Orwell, in an interesting article devoted to *No Orchids*, interprets the whole story as the struggle for power. It is evident, from his last book, *Nineteen Eighty-Four*, which will be the subject of later consideration, that towards the end of his life he was obsessed with this Nietzschean idea, in the light of which he interprets modern political trends. Nietzsche's ideas also will be the subject of discussion in a later volume, but I may anticipate at this point by saying that the form in which that misguided philosopher presents his doctrine of the universal struggle for power is an over-simplification and a distortion of the truth. 'Power' is a difficult and variable concept which cannot be utilized in a philosophical context without further definition; if this is nevertheless done, as Nietzsche did it, the consequence is that suggestions of coercion and tyranny are apt to be unconsciously embodied in propositions in which they may be completely irrelevant.

Nevertheless Orwell's thesis contains a germ of truth, for the Treasure, the object of contention between the rival forces, does include power, in the sense of the capacity to guide and to act, among its attributes. The forms in which the Treasure is seen substantiate this: the possession of the kingdom represents the ability to utilize its resources, that of the treasure of jewels or gold symbolizes the capacity to influence and act conferred by riches, that of the secret plans the ability to succeed in some venture. All these forms are summed up in the basic image of the 'soul', which in this context means the final ability of the individual to decide and to act. This is the object of contention between the rival powers of God and Satan in the story of Job, for the dramatic tension in the legend hinges on the choice with which the protagonist is faced between the two tendencies which are striving for his allegiance. But in the event Job, and Faust after him, discovers a third possibility: he contrives to retain his freedom of choice for himself, for he refuses either to be intimidated by the demonstrations of Jahweh's might or to be beguiled by the blandishments of Satan as expressed through the mouths of his friends and his wife ('curse God and die'). Thereby he wins a moral victory over both contestants and, in effect, compels Jahweh to improve himself: this theme is brilliantly elaborated in Jung's *Antwort auf Hiob*.

The theme of the contest for the Treasure, therefore, does not simply consist in the straight fight between two opposing forces for the possession of 'power' (much as Marx sees the struggle for the possession of 'the means of production') as it must seem to do for so long as the Treasure is represented as an inanimate object without volition of its own: it consists, on the contrary, of the struggle to obtain the allegiance of a free agent. The Treasure, in the last resort, is the power of free decision potentially possessed by every conscious individuality. But for so long as the individual is subject to unconscious impulses that freedom is only potential, not actual, for we cannot reject a tendency of which we are not aware. While this is the case the individual is not really free: he is truly the passive and helpless object of the rivalry of forces over which he has no control— no more than the jewel or the secret plans which can be stolen, taken by force or sold. The Treasure, the power of free decision, is not in his possession: in the language of psychology he is subject to compulsions because the source of his will is inaccessible to him. It is imprisoned in his unconscious mind.

A psycho-therapist once said of a patient in this condition:

44

'The patient says that she cannot; the nurse says that she will not; the truth is that she cannot will.' The condition is not confined to those under medical care.

This situation constitutes one of the principal themes of this study and its further elaboration must be left until later. The conclusion implicit in it is that each of us must undertake the quest of the Treasure for himself if he is not to remain the helpless puppet of blind forces; to do so it is necessary to adventure into the field of battle of the contending forces of the Opposites and to expose ourselves to all the pains and dangers which that entails.

The nature of the Treasure is not so much to be seen in the element of power which belongs to it as in its supreme value. Value, in the last resort, derives from need—a fact which is expressed in the economic theory of 'marginal values'. The attainment of the Treasure is in many cases the only way of spiritual survival and therefore, for those who have reached this precarious position of the mind—and they are often the most gifted, the creative personalities—it is the most valuable of all things. That supreme value, moreover, is not confined to the individual, for the problems with which he has to deal are those of the universal part of the human mind, or the collective unconscious. If he succeeds in solving them for himself he has contributed towards their collective solution by the whole society of which he forms a part. The manner in which he makes that contribution consists in the production of a creative work or in the setting up of a creative example in the form of his own life and performance.

The realization of the possibility of this way of salvation is pre-eminently revealed in the appearance of the Treasure in human form, for that implies that it is seen as something living, with its own volition and intelligence, capable of taking a hand in its own destiny. This development is presented in striking form in *No Orchids* in the substitution of Miss Blandish herself for her diamonds. I think that there can be little doubt that this author sat down to write his thriller without the slightest idea of how it was going to develop; or, if he had a complete plot in mind, that he soon abandoned it and allowed his characters to follow their own propensities. There are several indications of this, which will be discussed in their place; for

45

the moment I wish merely to draw attention to the effect produced by the appearance of Miss Blandish herself.

I have suggested that Faulkner's *Sanctuary* probably provided the inspiration for *No Orchids*, and some of the more detailed parallels between the two works will be discussed later. The derivation appears in two quite separate spheres: the more important is the symbolical, seen in the basic plot of *No Orchids* and in the rendering of the principal characters, but a second is to be found in the literary manner adopted in its earlier chapters. We may consider the latter first.

Sanctuary is scrupulously realistic in its background: the author's intention, which he has very convincingly carried out, is to present an objective picture of a world which actually existed. How true it is I am unable to say, but the effect is impressive in the same way as, for instance, the earlier part of Flaubert's *Madame Bovary* is impressive: the reader feels that this is no fabulous world inhabited by synthetic or idealized personages but a picture of 'real life', that is to say of ordinary people with ordinary, self-contradictory characters, following their humdrum destinies in a world of limited means, small pleasures and petty aspirations. Madame Bovary herself later runs away with the story, the latter part of which develops into a wild fantasy, impressive in quite a different way; Faulkner, however, with an iron self-discipline which Flaubert lacked, keeps both feet firmly on the ground to the bitter end. Nothing is allowed to happen simply as one might wish it to happen; no character is allowed to outgrow the human limitations allotted to him at the outset; no liberties are taken with the intractable, incoherent, unpoetic nature of the outer world. Fantasy, in fact, is studiously and consistently disguised in the garb of a meticulous and impartial psychological and sociological study.

It is a fair conjecture that the author of *No Orchids* set out to write his own book in the same strain. Gangsters were to be the mean, shoddy creatures which most of them really are: we are told in the opening scene of the 'shabby suits and cracked shoes' which they wear; and they were to frequent the kind of cheap, prosaic places which they really do frequent: the memorable opening scene of the book is set in no luxurious night-club, nor yet in a sinister den of vice, but in Minny's hash-house, an ordinary, shabby little eating-place. Then a true-to-life down-

46

at-heel crook appears and forms the unromantic but plausible plan of holding up Miss Blandish in order to steal the diamonds which she will be wearing for her birthday party.

But, as we shall see later, the symbolical elements, even in this opening scene, are already bursting out of the realistic frame, and the author has to take drastic steps to reduce them to order. Having done so he continues with his project, but his resolve is short-lived: it collapses in the moment when Miss Blandish appears on the scene. She is a vision of purity and beauty, a personification in herself of all that is desirable. The Archetypal image of the Treasure is immediately projected on to her figure, and henceforth she herself is the priceless object around which the conflict rages. The shabby little gangsters are no longer good enough: the brighter the light, the blacker the shadow, and the magic of Miss Blandish calls up from the shadows the sombre powers of the Grisson mob. Out of the night emerges Slim, the killer, with his knife, his polished shoes and his yellow eyes; behind him follows the awful figure of Ma, the Devil's Grandmother, attended by all the minor fallen angels. The tawdry glitter of the diamonds fades before the glory of Miss Blandish and no more is heard of them until Slim casually returns them to his love. It would be impossible to devise an apter way of indicating that she herself has usurped their position as the object of contention.

From the strictly rational point of view there is no purpose in this change from the diamonds to Miss Blandish as the lost treasure which must be regained, nor in the double kidnapping, first by the original gang and then by the Grisson mob. The latter point is adroitly utilized later in providing a false trail for the police, but it is improbable that it was deliberately devised for the purpose. If the author, at the outset, had visualized Miss Blandish's falling into the hands of Slim the obvious sequence would have been to have him see her by chance, fall in love with her beauty and kidnap her for that reason: such a plot would have proved no less effective than the one he eventually devised. But in view of what he actually wrote it is a reasonable conjecture that he set out to write a story somewhat in the realistic vein of *Sanctuary*, but, of course, with an entirely original plot. When Miss Blandish appeared, however, both these resolutions collapsed. In the first place the symbolism of *Sanctuary* forced itself on him and he was compelled to allow Miss Blandish to follow her true inner-world destiny, which was that of Persephone as presented in *Sanctuary*. In the second place the short-lived vein of realism was happily abandoned, for Miss Blandish, like Emma Bovary, ran away with the story, soaring with it to realms of unbridled fantasy. The Grisson mob are no longer possible, and from the conscientious dinginess of Minny's hash-house and Dan's hide-out we are transported into a setting of improbable luxury so vague that the writer has not even troubled to think out who does the house-work. In *Sanctuary* such details are never overlooked.

I have spoken of Miss Blandish's running away with the story: this must not be understood as a figure of speech implying merely that the writer became so preoccupied with this character that he overlooked other matters: it means far more than that. Miss Blandish, or Persephone, is an Archetypal image, and as such she has a will of her own. She not only represents, but is, a definite pattern of the mind with its own attributes and its own mode of behaviour, and she will always insist on following her true nature and her inherent destiny. If attempts are made to thwart her in this she will find means of circumventing them: we shall find examples of this in the further course of this study. This autonomous nature of the Archetypes, revealed by their self-willed behaviour when they appear in fantasy, is a cardinal point in my thesis; it will be amply substantiated by further examples, but for the present I can do no better than quote Jung on the subject.

These entities [he writes in *Antwort auf Hiob*] are the Archetypes of the collective unconscious, which are the cause of complex representations such as mythological themes. Representations of this type are not invented but appear to the inner awareness, for instance in dreams, as ready-made images. They are spontaneous phenomena, which are independent of the will, and it is therefore justifiable to attribute a certain degree of autonomy to them. Therefore they are not only to be regarded as objects, but as subjects with their own laws. It is, of course, possible to describe them, from the viewpoint of consciousness, as objects, and to explain them up to a point, just as it is possible to describe and explain a living person; in this case, of course, their autonomy must be disregarded. But if the latter is taken into consideration they must unavoidably be treated as subjects, that is to say that spontaneity and purposefulness, or a kind of consciousness and freedom of will must be admitted in them. One observes their behaviour and takes account of their pronouncements. This dual viewpoint, which it is necessary to adopt in face of every relatively independent organism, produces, of course, a dual result: on the one hand an account of what I do to the object, on the other of what that object does—and on occasion of what it does to me.

This characteristic autonomous behaviour of the Archetypal figures is attested by many writers of fiction: the following passage, chosen at random, will serve to illustrate the familiar pattern. Pierre Benoit, in *l'Ile Verte*, is describing his feelings when about to start a novel:

. . . I was going to be master of time and space, my own master, master of everything, except of the ghosts which I was about to create. However rigorous the plan to which I proposed to coerce them, I knew well that they would not follow it; that hardly would they have issued from within me than they would escape me; that they would live their own lives, in which I should count for little; that they would compel me to share all their passions—to weep, to suffer and to love with them.

Two points in this passage deserve particular notice: first the reference to the writer's mastery of time and space, for, as we shall see later, this freedom is characteristic of the inner world, in contrast to the outer, which is essentially the pattern of what is bound by them; secondly the assertion that the writer is compelled to share the emotions of his 'creations'. He must do so because they are no mere allegories or artefacts, but living symbols which not only represent, but actually *are* factors working in his mind. To this point we shall return shortly.

THE BARRIER

Up to this point we have considered the theme of the two worlds only in the form revealed in the rival factions which we found contending for the Treasure; this image, however, is a basic element of the story, as it is of many stories, and we may now turn to other forms in which it appears.

A point which strikes the attention of the reader who is alert for symbolical features is the frequency with which the telephone appears in the book. The telephone is, of course, an essential concomitant of modern life, but then so are the radio and the aeroplane, and neither of these plays any part in the story; telephoning, on the other hand, has a peculiar importance. The symbolical significance of telephoning is that it is a communication with somebody who is somewhere else: present but not here. The awareness of such unseen presences has always played a part in fantasies, myths and legends: in old times people would hear voices (there is a special word in Arabic—*hatefeh*—meaning 'the voice of an unseen speaker') or, in a more realistic type of story, the device of the smuggled letter was employed. Instances of this latter device will be met with hereafter. But the invention of the telephone, which so strikingly produces that voice of the unseen speaker, has provided the intuitive faculty, to which its symbolical significance is at once apparent, with a new and far more telling image. Evidence of the use to which intuitive fantasy puts even such modern inventions may be found in the delusions of the insane: the up-to-date paranoiac no longer believes that he is being persecuted with the Evil Eye or by having pins stuck into his waxen effigy: he maintains that his oppressors make use of 'radar waves'. To the unconscious the new magic is no different from the old, for it is concerned only with its symbolical aspect. I may add that my own unconscious consistently makes use of images derived from motoring.

The use of the symbol of the telephone which is made in *No Orchids* is striking. Several of the major characters make their first appearances, so to speak, at the other end of the telephone: we hear their disembodied voices before we meet them in the flesh. These include both John Blandish and Ma Grisson; Anna, whom we shall meet later, has to be rung up no less than three times before she makes up her mind to a definite entrance: then she is first seen in a telephone box. Now when an author wishes to introduce new characters there is nothing to prevent his simply causing them to walk on to the scene, or, if that should prove inconvenient, he may transport us into their presence. The fact that this author so consistently introduces his characters by telephone suggests that he is strongly aware of a Somewhere Else; it expresses his feeling that these figures are always present, in the background, out of sight. They may not

be 'here', present to our consciousness, but they are always
'there', liable to take a hand in the course of events.[1]

Another significant symbolical feature is the appearance in
the early morning of people who have been driving all night.
This occurs in the opening scene, in which the First Gangster,
Bailey, has dropped into Minny's hash-house to get his break-
fast after an all-night drive, and it is repeated on several
occasions later in the story: constantly we find the cars from the
night, dust-stained, with their pale, tired occupants, appearing
in the early morning: when we wake up they are there. Once
again we have the inference of that Somewhere Else, out of
which the motorists make their sudden appearance, and now
we have a clue concerning its nature: it has to do with the dark
world of sleep, of dreams and of the unconscious. In the ancient
myths the sun thus appears in his chariot or boat after his long
night journey through the underworld: it is the image of the
rebirth of consciousness after sleep. It may be worth mentioning
that in the act of awaking I myself frequently dream of arriving
at the end of a journey (generally by sea) whereas when falling
asleep I have visions of departure. The point in the present
context is that one of the contents of that Somewhere Else has
emerged into the light of consciousness, of Here, just as dreams
occurring just before we wake are retained in the conscious
memory.

Lastly we find the Barrier. We meet with it on four distinct
occasions, in three of them under precisely that name: barrier.
In the office of Fenner, the detective, there is 'a strong wooden
barrier', and behind it sits Paula, his secretary—a glamorous
blonde; then at the Paradise Club, the headquarters of the
Grisson gang, there is a steel barrier, vaguely identified with the
cloakroom, and behind it sits Maisey the check-girl—a
glamorous blonde. Again, there is the barrier behind which
sit the professional dancing-partners at another night-club:
Fenner strides past it, exchanging a wisecrack with the girl who
sits there: we are told that she is a blonde, and since she is a
'hostess' at a glamorous night-club we may assume that she is
glamorous too. Finally there is the counter at Minny's hash-
house: this is the first appearance of the Barrier, in the

[1] The same use of the symbol of telephoning is strongly marked in
Kafka's *Trial* which will be considered in a later volume of this series.

important opening scene of the book, and although it is not given precisely that name we can identify it by the presence behind it of the waitress, another glamorous blonde. To her we shall return shortly; for the moment we may concentrate on the Barrier itself. The fourfold repetition of this image of the Barrier and the Blonde is too much for coincidence and we may conclude that it has some important significance.

A barrier is something which separates: it excludes but it also contains, and its essential meaning is that the objects on either side of it are prevented from coming into contact. Here, then, we have another rendering of the all-pervading theme of dichotomy, of the existence of two distinct worlds which may be in communication with one another but are essentially separate. We have already noted one factor which separates them, and that is the conflict between the two factions represented by John Blandish and Ma Grisson, but there may be others. This barrier, however, is always visualized as having a door through which it is possible to pass, even the counter in the hash-house being evidently equipped with the usual flap or gate, for the waitress presently emerges from behind it to serve the customers and clear the tables. The particular part of the Barrier which is brought to our notice, in fact, is the point where there is a gate through it, and it is at this point that we always find the Glamorous Blonde. She is the guardian of the threshold, a function which we shall find confirmed in other works.

In order to form some idea of the nature of the two worlds thus separated we may turn to the memorable opening scene in Minny's hash-house. It is an impressive passage according to any literary standards, and that is probably due to two factors: in the first place it is intensely and vividly visualized, and in the second it is full of symbolical elements. To some of these we have already referred and others will appear in due course. It is the morning of an intensely hot day, and in spite of the early hour the atmosphere is already drained and exhausted. The dinginess of the scene and the shabbiness of the characters who first appear is conveyed with great skill, and the feeling tone is grey and unhappy, for Bailey the gangster is tired after his all-night drive and depressed, since business is not going well. The dingy, crude, unsatisfactory, exhausting aspect of life is presented with harsh insistence.

REALISM

I have already referred to this grey hopelessness of tone which pervades *Sanctuary* and much of *No Orchids* as well, although nowhere more strikingly than in this opening scene, and suggested that it is an integral part of the theme of the two stories. To some extent it is associated with the realist attitude, the essence of which is its insistence that life as it is differs very much from life as it appears in fantasy: it is more complicated, less coherent, more limited and circumscribed by accidentals; it is generally less intensely tragic, but at the same time far less pleasurable. The growth of the Realist movement in the literature of the nineteenth century represents an important differentiation of consciousness which goes hand in hand with the growth of the scientific mentality; nowadays we can no longer slip unconcerned through the barrier which divides fact from fancy as the medieval romancer could: the story-teller must either be a realist or a declared writer of fables, allegories or fantasies. Our awareness of the separate existence of two worlds, an outer world of fact and an inner world of fantasy, has grown far more acute, and we have to face the problem of reconciling the two. The necessity of this reconciliation will be one of our principal themes in this enquiry; it is not to be achieved by the prevalent contemporary tendency to accord the property of reality solely to the outer world, dismissing the inner as 'no more than' ideas, or fancies, or wishful thinking, or escapism, or psychology. This is what Jung describes as the 'nothing but' or 'no more than' (*nichts wie*) attitude, and it is a very dangerous one, for the inner world is intensely real, and if we attempt to deny its reality we shall involve ourselves in troubles no less disastrous than we should if we attempted to deny the reality of 'facts'.

Faulkner, we saw, maintained this realistic attitude consistently throughout his book, but Chase, to whom it was clearly less congenial, abandoned it early. He was, no doubt, inspired to attempt it by *Sanctuary*, or by other works in the same vein, but that was no mere slavish imitation; he must, on the contrary, have been struck and impressed by the atmosphere it creates, or in other words he reacted to its inner message. This fact is substantiated by the element of pessimism and hopelessness which pervades the story, even when the outer form of realism has been abandoned. The enlargement of his free fantasy allows him to indulge in far more uninhibited horrors, and more of a certain cynical light-heartedness, than Faulkner ever permits himself, yet the awareness of the dreary unsatisfactoriness of life in This World always remains in the background.

The final abandonment of the limitations of realism accompanies the appearance of Miss Blandish, yet we may already discern the first impulse towards it in the opening scene: it comes with the waitress, who is described as follows: 'She had worked on herself until, from a distance, she looked as good as any movie star. But when you got near she wasn't so hot. She patted her tight yellow curls and stretched. Bailey thought she was wearing a false front.'

The whole episode, as I have said, is intensely and vividly visualized, and here the visual image is that of a ravishing blonde proffering a well-developed bosom across the counter. But the realist intention will not permit of such a vision of glamour in the dingy surroundings of the hash-house, so the author hastily assures us that her charms are counterfeit. It is a neat evasion but, as we shall see, quite useless, for the Blonde is not so easily dismissed: she will shortly reappear, complete with bosom, and this time no doubts will be cast on its authenticity. The background obviously demands a slattern, ruthlessly depicted, and as such Faulkner would have presented her.

This sudden irruption of an other-world fantasy-figure into the carefully controlled picture of this-world dreariness reveals the nature of the impulsion which led to the writing of the story. It is to be a venture into the world beyond the Barrier, reached through the gate which the Blonde guards, and with which she is identical. As we shall see later it is she who has the power of admitting to her charmed world those who find favour with her. Admission is only to be gained with her consent, and by those who come to her alone; any attempt to storm the Barrier by force can only be successful at the expense of bloodshed, and even if it succeeds it is fruitless. The Blonde is of an amorous disposition: that is the only reason why it is possible to gain admission. But this feminine frailty entails a desire to detain her lovers in dalliance with her at the gate, and

54

if they succumb to her charms they will progress no further into the world she guards. It is therefore necessary, if we wish to penetrate more deeply into the other world, to repel her advances as courteously as possible, as we saw Fenner doing at the night-club, and press on into the recesses beyond. Nevertheless the Blonde remains the embodiment of that whole inaccessible world as we see it from this world: she is the first adventure which we meet on the other side of the Barrier, and the quest of the Treasure which lies beyond is, in the last resort, no more than the quest of the undisclosed part of her nature. This important aspect of her image will concern us at some length in later chapters.

THE OTHER SIDE

The other world is not simply the world of pipe-dreams and escapism, of personal fantasies of self-glorification and impossible delights, indulged in as a compensation for the unsatisfactory nature of life in this world. Such things may, of course, enter into its composition, but it is far more than that. It is hard to indicate its nature to those who have little or no acquaintance with it, but in some respects to enter it is like going to a play. With a little practice the observer is able to watch the happenings which occur there without guiding or influencing them: they go forward autonomously according to their own laws. They are, of course, often fragmentary and do not make sense, and in such a case it is a mistake to attempt to force coherence or sense into them by conscious standards. If the observer is utilizing his fantasy for the purpose of writing a story or a play he will, of course, be compelled to do so, but unless he has developed the faculty of going along with his fantasies and discerning their underlying tendencies sufficiently to avoid distorting their true nature he will get into difficulties. This is because, although he is not composing or 'making' his fantasies he cannot avoid participating in their content, and that content has an emotional component. The fantasies have a purpose, for they are Archetypal processes brought into play by the necessity of restoring equilibrium, to the mind: if that purpose is misunderstood and thwarted by conscious interference the images react exactly as though they were human beings similarly provoked; they become hostile and visit their frustration on the subject in the form of unpleasant emotional attacks. Feelings of anxiety and horror, shame and depression amounting to despair are the consequence. These conditions, if they become habitual, constitute a very real danger to physical no less than to mental health: they are among the risks entailed by frequentation of the inner world, and they constitute the reason why preoccupation with it is commonly stigmatized as unwholesome, dangerous or even sinful. Such an attitude, however, can do nothing but harm, for it is impossible to evade the claims and the problems of the inner life, and any misguided attempt to do so may lead, as we shall see, to really serious consequences involving others besides the immediate victim.

This, then, is the Archetypal world, the inner world of the universal mind or collective unconscious. Those whose conscious minds have come into contact with it—who have partaken of nourishment in the world of shadows—are inescapably bound to face and work out its problems, in their minds and in their lives, to the bitter end; others may safely resign themselves to the guidance of the mores of a sound community. This may sound a hard fate, and in some ways it is one, but the inner world offers great rewards as well as penalties: apart from subjective joys no less than those which the outer world has to offer there is the supreme gift of creativeness, which brings spiritual life and the power of self-renewal from the inner to the outer world.

Gustav Meyrink, whom we shall discuss later, called this world, with its richness of manifold forms, its delights and horrors, the Other Side,[1] a designation of which I shall make use from time to time because of its aptness and power of suggesting the true nature of a source of spiritual life, and sphere of experience, which is in effect the other side of our human nature—the hidden side normally concealed by the obtrusiveness of personal consciousness.

Creative personalities develop a familiarity with the Other Side at an early age, and throughout their lives they are oppressed by a sense of its segregation from This World, and

[1] Derived from the title of Alfred Kubin's fantasy *Die Andere Seite*. This important book, which was a source of inspiration to both Meyrink and Kafka, will concern us in a later volume.

filled with a nostalgic longing to live exclusively in it. But the hard and ineluctable law of the Barrier, and of the existence of two separate worlds which it implies, denies the possibility of amalgamating these two incompatible modes of experience. Each has to be approached and dealt with separately, according to its own nature, and it is not until we have learnt to understand the separate, distinct and often contrasting laws which govern these two natures that we can set about the task of reconciling the two worlds between which we, like Persephone, are compelled to share our lives. When this has been accomplished, and not before, it may be possible to build up a harmonious manner of existence in which its due importance is allotted to each world, and the two are brought together in a kind of mating which produces a perpetual, creative self-renewal. But before we can bring about the union it is necessary first to carry out the separation: we must, in fact, concentrate on the distinctions and the contrasts between the two worlds.

This pattern of development is embodied in the basic principle of mystical alchemy, according to which it is necessary first to separate out the two opposing elements inherent in the mysterious *materia prima* in order then to bring them together in fruitful union.[1] With this supreme symbolical image we shall be concerned throughout this investigation.

The initial concentration on the separateness and incompatibility of the two worlds is apt to produce, in creative personalities, a feeling of disgust and repugnance for This World, which is seen as a true vale of tears in which we are imprisoned for the greater part of our lives. The Other Side is the source of all spiritual life and spiritual values, and the goods of This World appear by contrast transient and cheap, its environment impoverished and lifeless. In a later volume we shall find this contrast superbly expressed by Keats in one of the masterpieces of poetry, and later again by Emily Brontë in her works, her life and her death; in *No Orchids* we have the same theme presented in an unconventional and unexpected form. This disreputable thriller is not, perhaps, a masterpiece of literature, but it is profoundly experienced and fundamentally true.

[1] See Herbert Silberer: *Probleme der Mystik u. ihrer Symbolik*; English transl. by Jelliffe: *Problems of Mysticism and its Symbolism*; and Jung: *Psychologie u. Alchemie*; English transl. No. 12 in Collected Works.

Hadley Chase, then, struck and impressed by the rendering, in *Sanctuary*, of feelings which he shared about the miseries and deprivations of life in This World, set out to give his own rendering of it and produced the opening scene of *No Orchids*. But this awareness of the shortcomings of one world implies a corresponding awareness of the superiorities of the other: setting out to portray the wretchedness of life as it is he necessarily had at the back of his mind a vision of life as it might be—as it ought to be. The same, of course, applied to Faulkner and to Flaubert when they set out to write *Sanctuary* and *Madame Bovary* respectively: Faulkner, with an astonishing continuity of conscious purposefulness, succeeded in restraining and concealing this immanent vision of beauty and delight throughout; Flaubert, less self-disciplined, allowed his shallow *petite bourgeoise* to transform herself into a creature of wild and extravagant passions, whose figure offers occasional glimpses of a vision of unearthly and elemental beauty.

Chase succumbs early to this vision in the person of Miss Blandish, but even she, as we have seen, has a precursor in the form of the hash-house waitress whose charms are so hastily disowned. The reason for this hurried dismissal was that the author was already all too familiar with her (as so many men are) and knew that she represents the first hazard which is met after passing the Barrier. To succumb to dalliance with her precludes the further prosecution of the quest of the Treasure; and that is not all, for, as we shall see, it has its own disastrous consequences as well. This time he is determined not to allow himself to be detained at the threshold, but to penetrate deeply into the mysterious world of the Other Side and to discover what is going on there. Accordingly he dismisses the waitress as unworthy of attention and resolutely pursues the vision of the Treasure, which he still sees as a diamond necklace. But when he brings it to consciousness he discovers that it is not the diamonds which he seeks but their wearer. She is only the Blonde again, but she is more than the waitress, for something has been added to her, and into the nature of that something we have now to enquire. I have already said that the quest of the Treasure is in the last resort nothing else than the quest for the complete nature of the Blonde, and here we find confirmation of the fact.

THE INHABITANTS OF THE OTHER SIDE

The determination to penetrate more deeply than hitherto beyond the Barrier is indicated by two symbolical elements in the opening scene. The first is the early hour: it is the beginning of a new day, of a new enterprise. Bailey has been driving all night, and now he appears in the light of morning, whereupon the plan for securing the diamonds is immediately formed: in other words an unconscious content which has been working its way out of the darkness now appears in the light of consciousness and a fresh resolution is reached. The second point is the heat: it is the Indian *tapas* or creative effort which is thus represented, or the alchemistical stage of cooking, which activates the processes of transmutation. This symbolism of heat is often found in dreams.

Hereupon the Blonde appears, but her charms are dismissed as counterfeit and Bailey accordingly, after a little polite flirtation with her, presses forward with the business in hand and leads us to the diamonds. The enterprise has been successful: a penetration has been effected into the world beyond the Barrier, and the first result is that a number of characters from *Sanctuary*, who had evidently taken up their abode on the Other Side, come tumbling out. Most of them have been so transmuted by their residence in the unconscious that they are unrecognizable at first glance: only one, the father, remains virtually unchanged.

To start with there is the girl who is ravished, Miss Blandish herself. She has changed from the shallow, inherently vicious high school student so subtly portrayed by Faulkner into something strangely colourless, sometimes pathetic, and occasionally raised to a certain sublimity by her sufferings. Although Chase attempts to follow his model, which must have become conscious at some time during the development of the story, by suggesting the demoralization which ought to result from her adventures, he fails to convince even himself. Miss Blandish enjoys so much of his respect that he does not even give her a first name: he refers to her thus formally right to the bitter end. She remains strangely innocent and unspoiled throughout, a suffering, bewildered wraith in the underworld, and she only comes to life twice: once in the strange interlude in which she refuses to be taken from Slim, and again in her tragic end. On both these occasions she shows courage and spirit, quite unlike the mean depravity of her original: she is no character study, but a true heroine: in fact Persephone.

It is the same with Slim. He enters with a blare of brass: Satan incarnate. He immediately carries out two murders, one of them by stabbing a helpless man in the abdomen and staying to watch the lengthy process of his demise. At this point the author spares himself no pains to build up this character into a monstrosity of horror. Then Slim falls in love with Miss Blandish, and that is to be an added horror, for she, of course, could not possibly reciprocate his loathsome passion. But that is the author's mistake, for Slim and Miss Blandish suddenly take matters into their own hands. They insist on their love-affair, and when the author makes tentative efforts to break it up it is Miss Blandish who objects.

Now, by degrees, Slim becomes less loathsome: we see him more in the light of the fighter who 'likes a tough spot' than in that of the sadistic pervert. Then we notice that whereas Miss Blandish habitually lives upstairs Slim is continually climbing stairs: this activity of his is described too often, and with too much circumstance, to be a mere coincidence. Freud, as everybody knows, has laid it down that climbing stairs symbolizes copulation, and that may well be the case—sometimes; but it is obvious that the basic meaning of climbing stairs is that of raising oneself to a higher level, and that is what Slim is attempting to do: striving upwards, out of the underworld to Miss Blandish's level. This exertion takes its toll of him, and as the story progresses we hear more and more often how tired he is. Clearly the author's attitude towards him has changed: he is still ferocious, but since he has defied his terrible mother for Miss Blandish's sake he is no longer contemptible. And when at last his creator has to kill him off he is a little sorry for him: 'The thin white face, upturned, looked pathetically defenceless.' Slim had slipped into the role of hero: nothing but the original impotence and the joy in killing remain of Faulkner's strange, detached, idiosyncratic Pop-Eye. Yet, in parenthesis, it is interesting to note that two of Pop-Eye's idiosyncrasies—his invariable black suits and his incessant cigarette-smoking—are spread over three characters in a sequel to *No Orchids*, *The Flesh of the Orchid*, to which I shall refer later.

The father has changed from a Southern Gentleman into a Yankee Industrialist, but otherwise there is no difference. In both books he stands for unyielding authority and a harsh unbending insistence on what he pleases to regard as his honour; he represents the implacable arbiter of rectitude, who visits the sins of the fathers on the children.

It is in Ma Grisson that the most astounding transmutation is revealed, for it is only in her repellent but awe-inspiring physical appearance that she is identifiable with Faulkner's almost engaging whore-house madame, with her lady-like tea-parties and her sighs for her deceased husband. But Ma is a far less ambiguous figure: she is the root of all evil: it is her remorseless cruelty, her scheming viciousness which provide the mainspring for all the discreditable activities of the underworld.

These characters now begin to act the story which has been staged in the opening chapters. They are living figures, which are truly and literally working out their destinies in the mind of the writer, and in many other minds besides. It is his virtue that he has recorded their doings with intuitive honesty, and has thus foreshadowed a solution to a situation of deadlock which affects our whole civilization. I have already given several instances of their autonomy, of the manner in which they pursue their own courses with scant respect for the intentions of the author. In the first place there was the substitution of Miss Blandish for the diamonds; then there is the gradual assumption by Slim and Miss Blandish of the roles of hero and heroine and Miss Blandish's inexplicable refusal to be rescued. We shall find another example in the story of the transformations of the Glamorous Blonde, which it will be convenient to consider next.

III The Glamorous Blonde

THE REHABILITATION OF THE BLONDE

CHASE's characters, in the strongest contrast to Faulkner's, are no psychological characterizations but the pure unalloyed products of the symbol-creating fantasy. Faulkner is concerned to work out how a given personality would behave in certain circumstances in the outer world; his creative intuition has furnished him with a primal Archetypal pattern to which he remains faithful in its essentials, but that pattern is overlaid by and cunningly woven into a highly developed and complex picture of the outer world which is evidently the product of meticulous and sensitive observation. Chase's fantasy is restrained by no such complexities: he simply calls up his characters and, in Jung's words, 'observes their behaviour and takes account of their pronouncements'. It is therefore all the more instructive, from our present point of view, to observe what happens, as the story progresses, to that figure of the Blonde who made such an unwelcome irruption into the opening scene and had to be dismissed in order that the story might take its course.

The writer holds fast to his resolve to ignore her until he has called up the figure of Miss Blandish and witnessed her abduction, but then he breaks down. The Blonde has been banished into the depths of the unconscious, but now he can no longer resist the temptation of making contact with her, and he does so by telephone. In the opening scene it had suddenly occurred to him that the hash-house must have a waitress, and when he turned his attention to her, there, in a flash, stood the Blonde, alluring and provocative; now it occurs to him that Riley, the

Second Gangster, must have a mistress. She is called Anna, and Riley rings her up from the hide-out to which Miss Blandish has been taken; from the other end of the wire she tells plaintively of her loneliness and weeps for her enforced chastity. In other words, although as the result of her banishment she is not Here she is still very much alive in the Somewhere Else, and she is as amorous as ever. After this Riley is killed by Slim.

After she has been rung up three times the Blonde, in the form of Anna, sneaks in—from a telephone box—and now she is refreshed and decked out with all the glamour of the Other Side. Her hair is 'like burnished gold' and her figure 'has it in the right places': there is, in fact, no longer any suggestion that her front might be false. Nevertheless her underlying identity with the waitress is betrayed by a striking image: each of them is described as moving 'as quickly as a lizard', an analogy which occurs nowhere else in the book.

Such a ravishing figure is almost as impossible in the role of mistress to a small-time and unsuccessful crook as she was in the hash-house, and Faulkner would no doubt have portrayed this second-rate gangster's moll as hard and faded or coarse and brash. But by this time Chase had abandoned all attempt at realism.

Throughout the story we find only three female characters: Miss Blandish, Ma Grisson and the Blonde in her various transformations. Miss Blandish is herself a development of the Blonde and Ma represents a special problem which we must postpone until later. Concentrating our attention for the moment on the Blonde we shall find the author progressively filling out and enriching her figure from the crude, erotic picture of the waitress into that of quite an acceptable human being. The interesting point is that he does not do this, as Faulkner might have done, on the basis of observations of objective women, but clearly in accordance with the requirements of the Blonde herself and, one might say, at her instigation.

To Anna, on her first entry, there clings something of the nocturnal and mysterious aura of the Other Side. After a brief appearance in the light of day, when she emerges from her telephone box and her charms are tantalizingly glimpsed, she disappears again into the night, where she remains for a while as a mysterious invisible presence of sinister import. With her own hand she kills the man whom she suspects of having betrayed her lover to his murderers, and she devises a cunning scheme to saddle Eddie and Slim with her crime.

The two gangsters, however, shoot their way out of their predicament and Eddie, fleeing from the police, takes refuge in a hotel bedroom which is occupied by an anonymous and very glamorous blonde in black pyjamas. She not only conceals him from his pursuers but also invites him to spend the rest of the night with her. Ostensibly we never hear of her again, but it is clear enough who she was and why she did it. She was sorry, and she did not wish to let slip an opportunity; it was only against her will that she had been pressed into the part of ruthless avenger; it did not suit her character, which, at this stage, consists of one attribute only, namely lechery. At the first opportunity she relapses into her natural role. Later on, resuming the personality of Anna, she continues the liaison with Eddie which she had thus initiated under the cloak of anonymity. These episodes lead to nothing, and it is clear that the Blonde's escapades were once again leading the author into difficulties. Her behaviour had become altogether too preposterous, and once more he dismisses her and returns to the theme of Miss Blandish, which, by this time, has assumed the central place in the story.

Persistently, however, the Blonde reappears, although only after a considerable interval, and now there is a distinct change in the author's attitude towards her. She has lost the quality of mystery and elusiveness: he now has a firm grip on her and, in the figure of Anna, he deals with her accordingly. It transpires that she had 'carried a gun' for the late Riley—she still keeps it in her handbag—and that is a significant point to which we shall revert later. Eddie, however, has little difficulty in wresting the gun from her, whereupon she forgets her dead lover and throws in her lot with the victor. After that she becomes a strip-tease dancer and develops several human traits: she is hot-tempered and she also begins to demand from Eddie something more than mere cohabitation. In the end she goes over to the camp of righteousness, seeking to betray the Grisson mob to the police, and is accordingly liquidated.

There are two minor appearances to record: in the first the

Blonde appears in a collective guise as the whole chorus—the Girls. Eddie, visiting a night-club in the morning, finds them rehearsing and indulges in a little friendly slap and tickle. Then she makes a fleeting appearance as a jolly fat girl, on whose prowess in the field of love the author enlarges; but in this guise she nearly causes a fight between Rocco and Slim, which is only prevented by the sudden materialization of the dread figure of Ma herself, armed with a tommy-gun. Both these episodes are important for symbolical reasons, to which we shall return later.

The Blonde has still two major metamorphoses to run through. She is Maisey, the cloakroom girl, a good-natured, generous, harmless creature who, however, true to her original nature, succeeds in getting herself seduced by Rocco. She is first tortured and finally despatched by Slim. And lastly there is Paula, Fenner's secretary. Her figure is as lovely as ever, her hair as blonde, and her eyes even larger. We are perfunctorily assured that 'her brains were not her strong point', but in fact she develops quite considerable wit and charm. She is competent, helpful and disinterested—even chaste, albeit against her will, for Fenner imperturbably repels her continual advances. She is thereby redeemed, and becomes the only female character to survive this story. Here at last we find the Blonde in quite a civilized and presentable guise: she has progressed enormously since her first guilty appearance in the hash-house, so hastily disowned.

The Blonde cannot be lightly explained away as 'a sexual fantasy', for that leaves the whole question of her development unexplained. The progress which we have already traced shows a trend away from simple animal promiscuity towards some intimation of a higher ideal, and the unfolding of something in the nature of a full human personality. If we label her simply 'repressed sex', then there is no reason why she should not remain for ever in the form of that eminently convenient 'wish-fulfilment' the anonymous and uninhibited blonde in the hotel bedroom. But no, she will not: she insists on producing a whole repertory of feminine characteristics, some of them, such as Anna's temper and sentimental demands, directly opposed to the wish-fulfilment, others, such as Paula's competence and devotion, quite irrelevant to it. In the case of Paula, who is the final and culminating metamorphosis, moreover, the wish-fulfilment does not take place at all. And, as we shall see, her crowning venture consists in the assumption of the fate of Miss Blandish herself, with all its mystical and tragic implications.

THE NATURE OF THE BLONDE

(i) *Symbolical Material*

The question of who or what the Blonde is, and of why she behaves as she does, may be approached from two viewpoints, the first based on symbolism and the second on the scientific study of instinct.

A point of departure for the symbolical investigation is to be found in her association with water. A detail which has not yet been mentioned in connection with the crucial opening scene is that the hash-house, surprisingly enough in view of its general shabbiness, has just received a morning wash-down, from which the floor is still wet, and the same detail occurs again when Eddie, on his early visit to the night-club, finds the girls rehearsing: there also the floor is still wet from its morning scrub. Evidently, then, this feature occurs spontaneously to the writer when he thinks of girls in the early hours of the day; taken by itself it might not justify any conclusion, but the image occurs again in a slightly different form in connection with Anna. When she is living with Eddie she quarrels with him, again on waking up in the morning, and he dumps her, pyjamas and all, in the bath and turns on the shower. We see her, angry and soaking, emerging from the tub and dripping pools on the bathroom floor. This image has a dual connotation: in the first place the Blonde is being washed or cleaned, an idea with which we shall be concerned later in connection with the bath which Liza receives on entering Higgins' household in Shaw's *Pygmalion*; for the moment, however, we may concentrate on the more fundamental idea of a female figure emerging from the water, as we saw Anna doing.

This image is Archetypal: the first example which comes to mind is Aphrodite emerging from the sea;[1] then we have the

---

[1] More specifically from the foam which collected around the severed member of Uranus which had been thrown into it (Hesiod). This matter will be considered in its place.

host of mermaids and other aquatic females who emerge from their element in order to seek the love of men in both classical and Germanic myths. The Sirens are a case in point: it will be remembered that it was necessary to press past them, ignoring their seductive singing, in order to avoid disaster. Lorelei provides another version of the same theme. Then, again, the future beloved is frequently met at a well: in addition to Rebecca in the Old Testament we find examples in the Arabian Nights and in Ferdosi's *Shahnameh*, the legendary epic of Persia. In the medieval romances there is the Lady of the Lake, seen by Keats as La Belle Dame sans Merci who enslaves knights, and the fairy Melusine, to whom attention has been drawn by Jung. Melusine married a human knight, but was compelled from time to time to assume a fish's tail and resort to a fountain; she plays an important part in alchemistical symbolism. In contemporary literature we have a striking example in the Leni of Kafka's *Trial*, who has a membrane between two fingers, suggesting the webbed foot of an aquatic bird or frog, while among other examples to be considered later there are Haggard's Stella Fregelius, who emerges from the sea and at last returns to it, the mermaid in Wilde's *The Fisherman and his Soul*, and the Hans Andersen mermaid who is associated with Selena in Sloane's *To Walk by Night*.

There are thus sufficient grounds for associating Chase's Blonde with a symbolical or Archetypal figure who has preoccupied the creative mind from time immemorial; her aqueous origin is one of her essential attributes and it is apt to slip unnoticed into any visualization of her image. These attributes of the Archetypal images are not easy to account for, but it is an incontestable fact that they do occur quite spontaneously and universally; they always have occurred, at any rate since human beings have recorded their inner experiences in the form of myths and the like, and they occur in such widely separated places and civilizations as virtually to rule out any question of communication by outer-world means. We can only conclude that they exist in that medium which Jung has called the collective unconscious and which is to a considerable extent unaffected by the limitations of time and space. The fact that we can offer no plausible explanation of this medium in terms of physics or chemistry, or even of physical biology, does not prove that it cannot exist; neither Jung nor any other responsible investigator makes any claim to know 'what it is': we can only record the forms in which it presents itself to our consciousness and make such deductions as we can on the basis of our records. We must avoid the puerile reaction of dismissing the unfamiliar as 'nothing but' psychology, or mysticism, or symbolism, or we shall fall into the error of those who dismissed the theories of Galileo or Darwin as nothing but diabolically inspired delusions. If it can be shown that a something, which for convenience we may designate the collective unconscious, manifests itself universally and coherently to our conscious minds, then we must admit that it exists, whatever it may be; and if it can be shown that these manifestations are accompanied by ascertainable and definable outer-world effects then we cannot deny its reality. The theory of the collective unconscious is a hypothesis designed to explain observed facts, just as the hypotheses of the conservation of matter and energy, and of their transformation one into the other, are so designed. The hypothesis stands or falls in accordance with its ability to explain the observed facts; if it stands, then the entities which it presupposes must be accepted as 'real': the collective unconscious, in fact, must then be accepted as no more and no less 'real' than the abstract conceptions of matter and energy.

Returning to the Blonde, we have noted that she reveals similarities with a universal figure who is seen rising from water in order to seek the love of men. The sea, or water in general, is one of the principal symbols of the unconscious, and particularly of the collective unconscious. Further, one of the most characteristic versions of this image is that of the mermaid, whose upper half is human, whereas her lower half is that of a fish. We thus have the suggestion that the figure is half human and half animal, half personal and half universal. Another version, of course, is that of the sphinx. She is emerging, and while the upper half of her has attained the light of consciousness the lower is still embedded in the darkness of the unconscious. It is, in fact, concealed, and here we find another important feature of that significant figure of the hash-house waitress standing behind her counter, for the visual image is that of the upper half of a woman whose lower parts are concealed. This image is recognizable in a Venus Anadyomene by

Titian,[1] standing up to her thighs in water, and in Wagner's vision of Erda emerging from the ground as far as her waist; the heroine of a Russian novel, to which I have lost the reference, also makes her first appearance standing naked in a river up to her waist, and I know of another version in an unpublished story by an acquaintance.

With that we may leave the symbolical material for the moment. It has suggested that Chase's Blonde is a manifestation of a universal Archetypal figure whose characteristics may be summarized as follows: she originates in the waters of the collective unconscious and is frequently seen in the act of emerging from them; her upper half is conscious, human and desirable, but her lower half is concealed and partakes of the non-human, in some respects subhuman nature of her origins; and finally, she seeks the love of men. It may be added that in order to attain this object she must obviously emerge completely, and the Germanic myth tells us that her purpose is to attain a 'soul'.

(ii) *The Instinctual Basis*

A great deal of modern thinking is based on the unconsidered acceptance as axiomatic of the maxim *Nihil in intellectu quod non prius in sensu*—there is nothing in the intellect which was not previously in the senses. The implication is that the outer world is the sole source of mental images, that the mind is no more than a blank and formless receptacle into which ready-made materials are admitted from somewhere outside it. Such a notion is of course preposterous and can easily be demolished by logical argument, but in the predominantly extravert-materialist atmosphere of the modern world it is apt to be accepted uncritically by those who are not given to analytical thinking, and these include many who are given to expounding theories, even on psychology. We are not here concerned with the philosophical aspect of the matter, but simply with the observed fact that the mind does possess its own inherent images and that these, far from being derived from the outer world, are

[1] Lord Ellesmere's collection. National Gallery of Scotland. The variant with the waitress behind the counter is exemplified by Manet's *Bar aux Folies Bergère* (Home House Coll.—Tate Gall.).

often projected into the latter and seen where they do not exist in the objective sense.

We may start at once with the pronouncement of a scientist. N. Tinbergen, in his completely factual and scientific work *The Study of Instinct*, writes as follows: 'The strict dependence of an innate reaction on a certain set of sign-stimuli leads to the conclusion that there must be a special neuro-sensory mechanism that releases the reaction and is responsible for its selective receptivity to such a very special set of sign-stimuli', and again: 'How does a young cuckoo recognize and select a mate of its own kind? It had never seen a cuckoo before.'

In other words this scientific investigator finds himself led by his meticulously controlled observations and experiments to the conclusion that the young cuckoo, for instance, is born with a special arrangement of nerve-connections which react to certain characteristics of the cuckoo species and to those of no other. Precisely what these characteristics are cannot be established with certainty until a large number of experiments has been carried out: the significant points may consist of some aspect of the visual appearance, some typical behaviour-pattern, the characteristic call or a combination of all or any of them. For our present purposes the essential point is that there must exist in the mind of the young cukoo an inherent potential image, defined in the form of some complex of sensory impressions, which corresponds to certain characteristics of the image of an objective, outer-world cuckoo. When the latter impinge on the cuckoo's senses they are recognized—not, of course, in the sense of conscious, human recognition, but nevertheless recognized— solely by virtue of the pre-existent image.

This innate image is the mental counterpart of the physical 'neuro-sensory mechanism': if the one exists the other must necessarily exist also, for they are two aspects of the same thing. It is a little hard for the mind moulded by contemporary materialistic ideas to accept the real existence of such an image, independently of the outer-world situation with which it is associated, but here again Tinbergen provides us with proof. If any typical instinctive behaviour-pattern, he tells us, is not activated by its proper outer-world stimulus for an excessive period it will tend to come into action of itself, and the animal will carry out the appropriate reactions to a situation which does not exist in the outer world: such reactions he calls 'vacuum activities'. Captive starlings, for instance, will go through the actions of picking up non-existent insects, and ducks will carry out the performance of taking cover from a bird of prey which is not there. It is to be presumed that when these actions were taking place the corresponding images of the insects and the hawk respectively were in some way present in the birds' minds. Subjective experience is ultimately incommunicable, and we can never tell what is present to any consciousness other than our own; nevertheless, if it were not possible to draw some valid conclusions regarding the contents of other minds life would be impossible. We know from our own experience that we only behave in certain manners when we believe that the appropriate situation exists; we may be mistaken, but the image of the situation in question is present in our minds none the less, and it is that image which has called forth the appropriate reaction. We know from the delusions of the insane, and even from the reactions of the sane in certain circumstances, that mental images may present themselves which have no connection whatever with the objective situation as seen by the detached observer; we know that the image must be present in the mind because the person affected not only reacts in the appropriate way but assures us that the situation in question does exist in fact.

There is, therefore, no objection to assuming that innate mental images such as that which enables the cuckoo to recognize its mate are always present in the mind in a latent state. Normally they are only activated and brought to consciousness by the appearance of the appropriate stimulus emanating from the outer world, but in certain circumstances it is perfectly possible for them to present themselves of their own accord. In other words a cuckoo brought up in captivity and never allowed to see or hear another cuckoo would be inherently capable of 'imagining' one.[1]

[1] I must insist that neither in this passage nor in any other am I crediting animals with anything in the nature of human consciousness. When the cuckoo sees (or hears) its potential mate, or the duck sees a hawk, the sensory experience in question must be perceived as a separate image, distinct from its environment, since it becomes the focus of attention. We cannot imagine a bird's mental processes, but we can deduce from its

We must, however, be very much on our guard against the tendency to project elaborate, highly differentiated and comprehensive contents, such as are typical of the human conscious mind, into the minds of animals, or, for that matter, into the human unconscious, which is of a far simpler, more primitive nature than the conscious mind. The ornithologist's picture of the cuckoo is a very detailed and comprehensive one: he knows the length of its legs, the shape of its beak, its typical colouration and its appearance from every conceivable viewpoint and in every position. He will be able to identify every one of these components of the complete image when seen separately: the plumage, for instance, and perhaps the feet; and observing the flight, or the stance, or the typical actions of another bird he will be able to say which of them resemble those of the cuckoo and which differ from them. It would obviously be wrong to

behaviour that it has mental processes of some kind; when anything becomes the focus of its attention it is therefore justifiable to say that it is present to its mind, or to its consciousness, for consciousness exists at various levels. If a sensory stimulus complying with a certain definite pattern invariably releases a certain reaction, complying also with a certain generalized pattern which is too complex to be regarded as a simple reflex, we cannot escape the conclusion that something of the nature of what we humans experience as an image in the mind is involved in the process. The animal cannot, as we can, separate itself from the experience and see itself experiencing it, but that does not alter the fact that the experience evidently occurs, and that it is concerned with an image, for the animal is not a machine and is capable of learning to adapt its reaction, within certain limits, to a given type of sensory experience. If the characteristic reaction-pattern occurs in the absence of the appropriate sensory stimulus it is fair to assume that it is accompanied by the appearance of the appropriate image in the mind in a form similar to that in which it occurs when the objective stimulus is present. Human beings confirm that such things occur in their minds, and the fact that they can turn the light of ego-consciousness on to the experience does not mean that the experience is in itself a product of ego-consciousness, for it is now a commonplace of psychology that human beings experience many things that are not admitted to ego-consciousness. The animal, therefore, may be assumed to experience mental images in the manner in which a human being experiences those things which are not admitted to his ego-consciousness, or which are 'repressed' and confined to the unconscious part of the mind. If these are subsequently recovered and brought to consciousness they are found to be no less clear and definite than conscious contents, although they lack the associations and differentiations supplied by the higher part of the human mind to those experiences which are admitted to ego-consciousness.

assume that the cuckoo recognizes all these features in its mate; what it does recognize we do not know for certain, but it is certainly something much more restricted. It must be sufficient for it to be able to differentiate between a cuckoo and any other species of bird, but that is all. It does not know a complete cuckoo as we know it, but only certain typical attributes of the species, the images of which almost certainly exist quite separately and independently of one another in its mind.

This point may be illustrated by Lack's[1] experiments with robins. The robin normally attacks all other members of its species which trespass on its territory, with the exception of its mate, but it is on the whole tolerant of other species. Lack determined to discover precisely what it was that released the instinctive attack reaction, and for this purpose made use of various portions of a stuffed robin, which he set up in the territory of wild robins. Here is an excerpt from his results:

Similar experiments were tried with a complete stuffed adult robin in which the red breast and white abdomen were painted over with brown ink. This specimen had previously elicited violent attacks from wild robins, but after its red colouring had been changed to dull brown it was no longer attacked by any. It was particularly remarkable to find that wild robins which would not attack this complete robin with a brown instead of a red breast, yet exhibited typical threat display to a bundle of red breast feathers lacking head, wings, tail, legs and even the body!

Further experiments, inspired by the observation that the robin did sometimes pursue small birds of other species, led him to the following deduction:

Hence I came to the conclusion that the robin's fighting behaviour ought not to be considered as a unity, and that it was really composed of three separate actions, namely flying-in-pursuit, threat display and striking, and that each of these actions had its own signal, flying-in-pursuit being elicited by the sight of a small bird flying away, threat display by the sight of red breast feathers, and striking by an object with the shape of a robin.

The robin's only relations with others of its species consist of ejecting trespassers (or being ejected), mating and feeding its

[1] David Lack: *The Life of the Robin.*

young;[1] as to the feeding it is not discriminating, being prepared to place food in the beak of any bird which emits the
appropriate chirping sound, even if it be of another species. It is
therefore apparent that in the robin's mental world no such
entity as a complete robin exists; it knows only a repertory of
isolated images to which it instinctively reacts and which,
therefore, may be regarded as being present to its consciousness. There are the visual impressions of small birds flying, of
red feathers, and of shapes which (we know but he does not)
resemble his own; then there are the auditory impressions of
song and of birds demanding to be fed. There is no reason
whatever to suppose that there is any connection in the robin's
mind between these various phenomena such as that which, to
our minds, binds them together in the concept 'robin': on the
contrary they presumably represent, to him, a miscellany of
separate things which occur in his world.

The sole exception is provided by the mate, who occupies a
unique position in the world of robins of both sexes. Once they
have accepted one another the pair share a territory from
which they eject all other robins, but very rarely do they exhibit
hostile behaviour towards one another. Mistakes do occasionally occur, but on the whole the robin is able to identify its
mate even at a considerable distance, though by what characteristics it does so has not yet been discovered. The mate,
therefore, is the one and only individual being which the robin
normally knows (although, strangely enough, it may learn to
identify an individual human being). In other words it is only
in this single situation that the tendency of the mind to separate
off a single element from the confused stream of experience and
to endow it with identity is brought into play. This process,
which I have described as individuation, is perhaps the most
important of all those which occur in the human mind: this
matter will be elaborated in a later chapter. In the robin at
least it is found associated with instincts concerned with mating,
and what applies to the robin may conceivably have some
application to other species, including our own. This idea
evidently opens a promising line of enquiry, but this is not the
place to embark on it.

Another series of observations which provide invaluable

[1] This applies to the cock. Some of the hens congregate during the winter.

74

material for the investigation of the mental aspect of instinctual behaviour has been made by Konrad Lorenz.[1] One very striking example is the following: Lorenz was observing the hatching of a duck's egg which had been artificially incubated: when the duckling emerged it showed no reactions until he happened to make a movement, but then it turned towards him and gave the sound which he describes as that of 'greeting' in the species, and thenceforth it attached itself to him as mother. If he moved away it immediately gave distress signals and followed him as far as it could; he was compelled to imitate the typical quacking sounds uttered by the mother duck when leading her brood, and if he failed to do so for any length of time the duckling gave out distress signals to which he was compelled to respond, even in the middle of the night. By the exercise of infinite patience he succeeded by these means in filling the role of mother and rearing it successfully. Repeating the experiment with goslings he found his self-imposed task even harder. The goslings, more discriminating than the duckling, did not accept him on the evidence of movement alone: it was not until he quacked that he became their mother. Furthermore they were not prepared to accept his quacking when it emanated from a point some six feet above their heads: it had to come from the proper height. He was therefore reduced to adopting a squatting position, but when he did so and quacked properly he found that his family followed him around quite happily and allowed him to lead them to their food.

Four points emerge from these investigations. The first is the unreliability and sometimes the unsuitability of an instinctive pattern as soon as it is removed from the environment in which it was developed. The duckling's impulsion to project the mother image on to the first large moving object seen, while perfectly suitable in an environment in which eggs are never incubated by any other agency than the mother who laid them, miscarried when transferred into a world of artificial incubators. The same obviously applies to the instincts of the human species, which are still adapted to savage life. We are apt to project a 'purpose', involving foresight of the ultimate goal, into the workings of nature, but nothing of the kind, of

[1] K. Lorenz: *Er redete mit dem Vieh, den Vögeln und den Fischen*; English transl., *King Solomon's Ring*.

course, exists. Natural selection works simply by trial and error. Many human instincts are completely unsuited to a civilized environment, and a great deal of our time and effort are taken up in circumventing their workings. We cannot alter them: they can only be accepted as an inescapable burden from our primitive past. We should, for instance, find life a great deal easier if we did not suffer from an innate impulse to attack our fellows when we disagree with them, and other examples of such unsuitable reactions will appear in the following chapters.

The second point concerns the great variability of the selectivity of instinctive reactions as regards the object which releases them. The selectivity of the duckling's mother-recognition image was obviously exceedingly low, since an object as dissimilar from the proper one as a human being could be accepted by it; that of the goslings was somewhat higher, since a human being behaving normally would not have satisfied it: the stature, and above all the characteristic sounds demanded are typical of the proper object and would in all but the most exceptional circumstances provide an insurance against miscarriage. Nevertheless, even in the gosling, the selective mechanism did not require that this object should possess, e.g., feathers and a beak, and it is fair to conclude that these features simply do not exist in the mental world of the gosling or duckling.

The duck's mating patterns, on the other hand, present an example of extreme selectivity, for the choice of a mate of the exact sub-species of the subject is safeguarded by the small 'flag' of brightly-coloured feathers, arranged in a geometrical design, which are found on the duck's wing. These flags vary in design from one sub-species to another, and Tinbergen states that individuals of related sub-species, although almost indistinguishable in general appearance from those of the subject's own, are refused as mates unless this tiny detail is of the appropriate pattern; in other words we might say that the emotional importance of this apparently trivial superficial marking must be disproportionately great in the duck's love-life. Reactions of this nature he describes as 'isolating mechanisms'.

At this point it is worth asking why the selectivity of the recognition elements should vary so widely. The answer is that they have developed fortuitously and happen to meet the demands of the natural environment. The lower the selectivity of the recognition element is, the greater is the probability of mistaken projections or miscarriages of the instinct; if, however, the reproduction rate of the species suffices to cover the losses incurred by such miscarriages the position remains stable and no higher selectivity need be developed. If, on the other hand, there arises in the species a strain equipped with a more highly selective recognition image, and if that strain happens for any reason to be better fitted for survival in the environment of the moment, then it will gradually outnumber and finally oust the strains with the lower selectivity, and the image of higher selectivity will become part of the normal equipment of the species. I say 'for any reason' advisedly, for it need not be the higher selectivity itself which possesses the survival value: it may be genetically associated with some characteristic of a totally different nature in which the higher survival value resides: say, for example, a higher resistance to cold, a longer neck or a larger liver. In such a case the higher selectivity of the recognition-image will be, so to speak, carried as excess luggage by the species and will tend to persist, or even to become intensified far beyond the optimum point.

Nature has no foresight, and there is no guarantee that the natural devices for dealing with any particular problem are necessarily the best possible solutions: it can only be asserted that in the given circumstances they are adequate, since otherwise the species in which they are embodied would have died out. In consequence natural species reveal many characteristics which have been developed far beyond the optimum point of usefulness—sometimes to grotesque exaggerations which can be nothing but a handicap in competition, when conditions become unfavourable, with other species not so encumbered. As examples the extravagances in the plumage of many male birds—the peacock's tail is the crowning instance—and the senseless elaboration in the structure of some flowers may be quoted. The incredibly intricate social organization of some insects is another case in point, for what do they gain by it? Other closely related species survive very well without it.

The fossil beds are encumbered with the relics of abortive experiments, in which some particular feature has, so to speak, got out of control and exaggerated itself to impossible proportions, eventually dragging the species with it to extinction.

There have been creatures which developed such enormous and rigid carapaces, or grew to such a monstrous size, that they were scarcely capable of moving; plants which developed foliage of such luxuriance that they were unable to survive the smallest decrease in the water-supply; animals which specialized so excessively in the utilization of some particular food that they became exclusively dependent on it and died out when it was no longer available, and innumerable others, the causes of whose failure we do not know. The great new developments such as the conquest of the dry land and of the air, the regulation of body-temperature, etc., have been achieved by inconspicuous species which had not specialized, or carried any particular tendency to exaggerated lengths, for it was they which possessed the greatest powers of adaptation.[1]

There is, of course, a lesson in this for the human species, which has become phenomenally successful (in that it has spread over the whole globe and greatly outnumbers any other mammal species) through the exaggerated development of the cerebral processes to a degree infinitely beyond what is required for mere survival. It is an open question whether this species may not have specialized too far: perhaps it has passed the point of no return,[2] beyond which no further increments have any positive value. In this case, unless it succeeds in reversing the trend of attaching exaggerated importance to the intellect, it is doomed to extinction, probably through self-destruction.

However this may be, we must beware of the facile assumption that any instinctive pattern is necessarily the best possibility, even in the environment in which it grew up, let alone in an alien one. Civilization represents an environment in many respects alien to that in which the human instincts were developed, and the conscious mind itself constitutes the most important element in that alien environment.

The third point concerns the mechanism of projection. The

[1] See H. G. Wells, Julian Huxley and G. P. Wells: *The Science of Life*.

[2] This term is coming to be currently misused: it does not mean a situation from which retreat is impossible, but derives from the economic theory of diminishing returns, which states that each successive investment of work or capital into a closed system will produce a lower proportional return of produce or profit than the one before, until the point of no return is reached, when the system is producing at its maximum potential capacity and all further investment in it is nugatory.

Archetypal mother-image in the duckling does not only consist of the single distinguishing characteristic of a large moving body: that is only the recognition-element in a much wider complex which includes the relationship which the duckling is impelled to set up with the object recognized. The mother, once recognized and accepted, becomes that-which-must-be-followed; she is the source of reassurance from fear, and the centre of life, separation from which engenders violent feelings of anxiety. This powerful emotional complex was projected on to Lorenz solely because he had inadvertently activated its recognition-element, and if he had not found the means of satisfying the duckling's emotional demands by behaving in the appropriate manner it would have experienced intense mental distress. The application of this situation to human life is obvious.

The fourth point, finally, is that true instinctive behaviour consists of an indiscriminate conglomerate of specific reactions to specific stimuli which have no connection with one another, *at the instinctual level*, in the mind of the subject. The human observer, however, discerning common factors in a number of separate responses, is apt to group them together in classes and to presuppose some underlying scheme, or even purpose, connecting them. Such a scheme or purpose, however, exists solely in his own mind, from which it is projected on to the material. Nothing of the kind exists in nature, or in any mind at the instinctual level. Thus Lack discovered 'that the fighting behaviour of the robin ought not to be considered as a unity, and that it was really composed of three separate actions . . . and that each of these actions had its own signal . . .' It is only in the observer's mind that these three separate responses are subsumed in the abstract concept 'fighting'; in the robin's mind, and in any mind at the instinctual level, they have no connection at all.

Each separate response has been developed separately in the process of natural selection, and they are connected, if they are connected at all, solely through the reactions of the environment. Thus a bird lays eggs and the sight of the eggs, which have now become part of the environment, evokes an impulse to sit on them. As a consequence the eggs hatch, and the sight of the open beaks of the young birds evokes in the mature bird the impulse to place food in them. The human observer groups these two reactions together in the class 'parental instincts' and may even go so far as to speak of 'the reproductive instinct' (in the singular) by which concept he presupposes (whether he knows it or not) an underlying scheme or purpose which co-ordinates all the bird's responses, from the collection of the first twig for the nest, through the selection of a mate and coition, to the feeding of the young. Such a scheme or purpose, however, can only exist in a mind, and there is no mind other than the conscious mind of a human being which is capable of producing it.

In fact the only co-ordination between these various responses is in the outer world, or the bird's environment. The bird does not know that sitting on the eggs will cause them to hatch: it simply happens that they do, just as it may happen that they are stolen by a rat or a crow. The impulse to incubate has grown up concomitantly with the development of eggs which required to be kept warm: in the cuckoo, however, it has disappeared, being replaced by the practice of laying eggs in the nests of other birds; thus although parenthood and the existence of its own young are completely absent from the cuckoo's mind its eggs are hatched just the same.

When the young appear they are helpless and require feeding, and the impulse, which forms part of the equipment of the species, to place food in the characteristically open beaks, has grown up concomitantly with that requirement. The bird simply reacts to these stimuli, which are produced by the environment, although some of them may be indirectly caused by its own behaviour; it will, of course, incubate eggs other than its own—or even china ones—and if stimulated by the characteristic food-call will place food in any open beak that presents itself. More significant still: this response may be evoked by the sight of any orifice of a suitable size. Lorenz quotes the example of a bird which repeatedly tried to push food into the ear of a human being on whose shoulder it was accustomed to sit, and I have read of another bird—I think a robin—which had been trained to take food from between the lips of a lady, and on one occasion responded by pressing a fat grub into them. Lorenz attributes the behaviour of the bird he mentions to affection, but I think it far more probable that both birds simply responded to the sight of the orifice in the manner in which they would respond to that of the open beaks of the young in the nest.

We must, therefore, be perpetually on the alert to avoid falling into the trap of presupposing the existence of complex, co-ordinated, purposeful 'instinctive' trends in the mind where none can exist. There is no harm in grouping together a number of responses, which do in fact normally occur in a regular sequence, under some such appellation as 'the mating pattern', but only provided that we always bear in mind that the grouping is made solely for our convenience and that *no coherent scheme or overall purpose of such a kind exists in any mind at the instinctual level.*

THE INSTINCTS IN MAN

The study of human instincts is made extremely difficult by the presence in the human unconscious of a large class of contents which do not derive directly from them. Some of these, as we shall see, are engendered by reaction to the activities of the conscious mind while others, belonging to the collective unconscious, are accretions from the long millennia of primitive life and the civilizations of the past. These latter, in my view, are probably not strictly speaking innate: they are not, that is to say, transmitted by the biological mechanism of the chromosomes as the true instincts presumably must be; nevertheless they are absorbed by every child from the unconscious mental environment in which it grows up, so uniformly and so invariably that they may be regarded as part of the racial or generic mind. They are integral constituents of the Archetypal patterns, accretions to the instinctual nuclei around which these are built up.

For most purposes it is not necessary to distinguish between these elements. The unconscious mind, or at least any particular Archetype when activated, acts as a whole and may be studied under the form of the comprehensive images and patterns to which it gives rise. In one respect, however, it is useful to make a distinction, and that is in the matter of the susceptibility of the respective elements to deliberate alteration. The 'special neuro-sensory mechanisms' in which the instinctive reactions are based are obviously no more capable of change than those which control the digestive or other involuntary processes of the body. They may be capable of adaptation to a limited degree, but the basic pattern of their functioning is part of our unalterable generic nature. It is, therefore, impossible to change our instinctive reactions; we can inhibit and guide our responses to them when they reach the stage which is subject to voluntary control, but nothing that we can do (with the possible exception of a cerebral operation, if the precise location of the nerve-structures in question were known) can prevent the stimulus from producing the impulse towards the appropriate reaction. Thus if I am subjected to a stimulus which produces the reaction of fear, such as a violent and unexpected noise, nothing can prevent the impulse towards the appropriate reaction, which is to run away and hide, from manifesting itself in my mind. Simple people who are frightened by thunder commonly pull the bedclothes over their heads,[1] but if I am ashamed of such conduct I may inhibit the response by an effort of the will; if I am regularly and repeatedly subjected to this stimulus over a considerable period, moreover, as in the case of a bombardment, or even of living in a noisy street, my unconscious mind may itself take over the inhibition, so that I cease even to be aware of my alarm. Nevertheless a conflict is set up in my mind in either case, and it is an established fact that prolonged subjection to such conditions will take its toll of the nervous constitution.

The elements of the collective unconscious which derive from unconsciously absorbed human traditions, on the other hand, are almost certainly not based in neuro-sensory structures. Having been acquired during life they are presumably capable of being changed or eradicated. This cannot be achieved by a simple effort of the conscious will, but it is probable that prolonged concentration on them, combined with a clear understanding of their nature, may result in depotentializing them.

[1] I have been told of another pretty example of such an unsuitable instinctive response in the behaviour of a man disarming a high-explosive shell: he held it at arm's length. Obviously, if it had exploded, the additional two feet or so by which he was thus removed from it could not possibly have saved him from annihilation; but he was dealing with something dangerous, and instinct demanded that he should keep as far away from it as possible.

As an example the reaction to a uniform may be quoted. The uniform, not in its literal sense but in that of a special type of clothing or adornment associated with privileged position, is and has been for millennia the badge and symbol of authority, for even in primitive tribes the chief and the medicine-man are distinguished by special adornments. As a consequence it is a well-known fact that any person wearing any type of unusual and striking clothing (provided that the impression he makes is not merely ridiculous) or adorned with chains, stars, feathers or even metal buttons or a belt, enjoys more prestige with his fellows than one normally clad. One may recognize the fact and be under the impression that one is immune to the reaction, but it almost certainly occurs none the less. I myself, for instance, having been in the army, still have dreams involving military insignia as symbols of rank and authority, although (or possibly because) my conscious attitude towards such things is deprecatory.

Now the reaction to authority as such is based in true instinct, for it is the pattern of subordination to parents or other adults of the species with which young animals of almost all species are equipped at birth; gregarious species, moreover, almost invariably possess an additional tendency to submit to a herd-leader, and the human species is strongly gregarious. No human being, therefore, can ever rid himself of this tendency to self-subordination: he must of necessity project it on to some object, but the vital question concerns the choice of object which he makes. Conceivably, also, the tendency to look for visible distinguishing marks (or even for aural ones, for obedience can often be obtained by shouting) is also based in instinct, for in some other species, at any rate, the older males who act as leaders are equipped with exaggerated antlers, manes or similar marks of mature virility; they also often bellow or roar. In man the only corresponding natural characteristic is the beard, which does not attain an impressive length until comparatively late in life, and it is a fact that authority figures in dreams and fantasies are very frequently bearded.

The tendency to look for some such visible distinguishing mark in the authority-object is, therefore, possibly also ineradicable; artificial adornments, however, are purely human and cannot therefore have existed for long enough to give rise to the development of a special neuro-sensory mechanism in the infinitely slow process of biological change. Their acceptance as marks of the authority-image, therefore, must be by way of substitute: they are purely mental accretions to the instinct-based authority-image. As such, although they may be very deeply rooted in the unconscious, as my own experience, mentioned above, demonstrates, they must be inherently capable of change. By learning to differentiate between these two elements, the unalterable tendency to self-subordination and the alterable marks by which the authority-image is recognized, it should be possible to discover the most suitable object for the projection of the latter. Something in the nature of a spiritual deity is obviously indicated, but it must be remembered that the objects of projection cannot be arbitrarily chosen by the conscious mind. Projections arise from the unconscious, and any attempt to coerce it in its choice provokes violent opposition. It is the duty of the conscious mind to identify, investigate and criticize the objects chosen by the unconscious in accordance with its own higher standards, and if they prove unsatisfactory it must endeavour, in a concilatory spirit, to detach the projection; it is compelled, however, to wait in patience until the unconscious has found a superior substitute which accords with the latter's own requirements. Nevertheless the mere recognition of the fact that a projection is in operation tends in itself to weaken its force, since the conscious mind is alert to its workings.

We may summarize our general conclusions regarding the instincts as follows.

1. Instincts are innate behaviour-patterns, universal throughout the species, which must be based on definite nerve-structures in the brain. Nerve-structures do not change during individual life; the true instincts may therefore be regarded as ineradicable and unalterable.

2. The physical nerve-structure is associated with a mental 'image', which must therefore also be held to be as universal in the species as the latter's anatomy, and as persistent as the relevant nerve-structure.

3. Such images consist of various components: some are associated with the various senses, of which the visual is on the whole the most important although the others are also involved. These constitute the recognition-element whereby the subject

'recognizes' the stimuli produced by outer-world objects—i.e. he responds to them—although he may never before have experienced them. E.g. the cuckoo recognizes a potential mate although it has never before met with another cuckoo.

4. When this instinctive recognition occurs the subject projects the remaining elements in the image on to the object in question; the result is that whatever this object may actually be in the outer-world sense the subject henceforth sees the characteristics of his own inner-world mental image incorporated in it. E.g. Lorenz's duckling, having projected the 'mother-image' from its own mind on to Lorenz, henceforth regarded him as its mother (in its own sense—not in ours). In the inner-world, psychological sense, in fact, Lorenz actually was its mother and its outer-world mother did not exist.

5. The remaining components which are thus projected are largely emotional and are accompanied by impulses to set up certain relations with the chosen object. Thus Lorenz's duckling was placed in a situation of emotional dependence on him and was impelled to set up the relationship of remaining close to him and demanding reassurances of his presence by the exchange of vocal signals.

6. The selectivity of the recognition-element varies enormously in the same pattern as between different species, and in the same species as between different patterns. E.g. the mother-recognition element was found by Lorenz to be considerably more highly selective in goslings than in the duckling, and among ducks the mate-recognition element is far more highly selective than the mother-recognition element. These variations may well be fortuitous and need not necessarily possess any survival value in themselves. All that we can say of them is that in the natural environment in which they have grown up they represent at least the minimum selectivity necessary to ensure the survival of the species, but they may very well exceed it. In an alien environment they are very likely to be either inadequate or excessive, and civilized humanity lives in an environment completely alien to that in which its instincts were developed.

7. True instinctive behaviour consists of a heterogeneous conglomerate of separate, distinct and independent responses to specific stimuli. Many of these normally occur in a regular and connected sequence simply because each response normally

gives rise to a consequence in the outer world, which incorporates the stimulus producing the next response. Situation A incorporates the stimulus producing response A'; this normally brings about situation B, which incorporates the stimulus releasing response B', this the situation C evoking response C' and so on. It is legitimate to see such sequences as 'patterns' involving the interaction of the mind and the environment, but there is no justification for assuming that response B', and still less C', is inherent, to the mind at the instinctual level, in response A' or in situation A; still less is it permissible to invent such concepts as 'the reproductive instinct' or 'the sexual instinct', etc., which presuppose an overall scheme or purposeful plan in any mind at the instinctual level.

8. The mental images by comparison with which the objects producing the stimuli are recognized normally become conscious only in the form of projections when evoked by sensory perception of an external object. E.g. a man, seeing an attractive girl, becomes conscious of his mate-recognition image in her person: he projects it on to her, which endows her, for him, with the attribute of desirability and sets up an emotional relationship to her image in his mind. This activates an impulse to approach her, and if he meets with the response which normally follows such an approach in the mating pattern of the species the next situation is created, to which he responds by making love to her.

Even in the animal world, however, Tinbergen informs us that 'vacuum activities' occur; i.e. in the prolonged absence of any stimulus emanating from the outer world the response takes place of its own accord, the animals behaving exactly as they would do if stimulated by the appropriate outer-world object. Although the animals are not conscious in the human sense, it is permissible to assume that the recognition-element— the image of the stimulus—is present in their minds on such occasions in much the same form (whatever it may be) in which it is present when evoked by an outer-world object. In human subjects there can be no doubt that this occurs, and although the human being is normally able to distinguish between 'true' and 'imaginary' sensory perceptions, in various abnormal conditions he loses this capacity and experiences hallucinations. In any case the emotional response and the impulse to adopt the appropriate behaviour are activated by the appearance of the image even when it is known to be imaginary, although normally in a weaker degree, and although the subject is able to inhibit any behaviour which might be unsuitable in the circumstances.

The human capacity for reflection and introspection implies the ability to hold a succession of 'imaginary' forms—i.e. such as are not produced by sensory perception of the outer world— before consciousness, and it is easy to see that such a train of thought or imagery will inevitably frequently produce the characteristic forms which stimulate the instinctive responses.

THE MATING PATTERN IN MAN

It is no longer possible completely to disentangle the true instinctive responses from among the various components which make up the human mating pattern. The true instincts of the species must have been formed in the time of our pre-human and earliest human ancestors; there has been no time, in the immensely slow process of biological change, for them to alter appreciably since then. (Taking three generations to the century the entire five thousand years during which civilization has existed only cover one hundred and fifty generations.) Since the conscious mind has taken over the direction of our lives, more-over, the fine adjustment of the true instincts has ceased to have any direct bearing on the survival of individuals and the number of offspring which they successfully rear, both of which have become almost entirely a matter of chance. Natural selec-tion, therefore, has ceased to be a factor of importance in determining the genetic inheritance of the species, and that includes the true instincts. Hence it may be taken as certain that the true instincts of the species have become virtually stabilized since the earliest human times; civilization itself, of course, cannot have made the slightest difference to them, for it is not innate but acquired by each individual after birth, and acquired characteristics cannot be transmitted by biological heredity.

The importance of our instincts, however, has by no means diminished on that account: paradoxically, it has, if anything, increased. For we now find ourselves living in an environment to which our instinctual equipment is completely unsuited, yet our instinctive responses have by no means lost their power. They still represent the source of our most intense experiences and most powerful impulses, but their natural manner of expression has become, in nearly every case, so incompatible with our mode of life that a large proportion of our efforts have perforce to be directed to circumventing them. For instance, as I have already mentioned, our true instinctive response to opposition from another member of our own species is to make a physical attack on him; but opposition in civilized life is often a question of intellectual disagreement which can only be satisfactorily eliminated by dispassionate logical argument. When we attempt this, however, we find our mental processes obscured and distorted by the surging effects of the emotional component of our instinctive response to the opposition which we feel. Most of the complex social regulations and codes which have had to be set up and enforced by every community since primitive times have been attributable to the necessity of preventing people from killing one another and otherwise indulging their natural instinctive responses, and then to dealing with the complex and powerful mental forces engendered by the habitual repression of those responses. There are, unfortunately, no such things as civilized instincts.

The word instinct, of course, is loosely used in a colloquial sense to indicate any mental capacity or impulse which is not founded on rational thinking or straightforward feeling. Thus we talk of somebody having an instinct for making money, for wearing the right clothes, or for picking quarrels. There is no objection to this, provided that it is confined to casual conversation in which everybody knows more or less what is meant and there is no necessity to be pedantically precise. Such a loose colloquialism, however, is inadmissible in scientific or philosophical thought, in which precision is essential, and if by the term instinct we mean those innate and universal responses to specific stimuli which have been described above, then we must confine it strictly to them and find other designations for everything which does not conform to the definition.

If we adhere to this rule we have to admit that we are not in a position to identify with certainty more than a very few of the true instinctive components in the mating pattern of humanity. It is impossible to find any human community, even the most primitive, in which the true instinctive responses have not been overlaid by notions and conventions deriving from conscious thought, and attempts to reconstruct what the mating pattern must have been before this happened must remain the purest surmise. A certain amount may be tentatively conjectured on the basis of a close observation of ourselves, and of analogies from the animal world, but it is very little.

All that we can assume with reasonable certainty is the following.

(a) There must be a recognition element, enabling individuals of either sex to identify a suitable mate, i.e. a member of the same species and opposite sex, and, for the male, a female in the child-bearing age-group.

(b) This identification must release an impulse to approach or to attract acceptable mates.

(c) It is reasonably certain, from observation of our own behaviour and by analogy with the animal world, that the activation of the mate-recognition element is accompanied, particularly in the male, by an attitude of hostility and pugnacity directed towards members of his own sex.

(d) It is reasonably certain, from the same sources, that after the initial approach the couple must have a tendency to go through some ritual of courting before the mating is finally established and accepted.

(e) There must be an impulse to coition, but the question of the stimulus by which it is released is highly uncertain. This matter will be considered later.

Nothing beyond this can be established with any degree of certainty; the question whether humanity is by instinct monogamous or polygamous, for instance, remains obscure. Monogamy, of course, does not necessarily imply a life-long partnership: such indissoluble marriages do occur in the animal world but it is more usual for monogamous species to change their partners from one mating season to another. It would, however, be interesting to know whether our earliest ancestors stayed together until the offspring were at least weaned, or whether they lost all interest in one another as soon as coition had taken place.

As regards coition, the emotional importance of this single

brief episode in the larger pattern is probably mainly a product of conscious thought. In the animal world, rape, for anatomical reasons, being impossible, it is necessarily the female who decides on the moment for coition, a fact which she indicates by giving some signal which acts as a release to the male's response, which then occurs spontaneously. There is no reason to suppose that there is any more connection in the male's mind between his initial approach and this response than there is between the bird's impulse to incubate her eggs and that of subsequently feeding the young which result from it. It may safely be assumed that the animal male approaches the female because he is impelled to approach and no more, and that if the signal is not given by her he is not impelled to do anything further. This, at least, may be observed among dogs, who will follow the trail of a bitch on heat for long distances, and will even wait for a considerable time outside her house until she appears; once she has done so, however, and the impulse to seek and approach has thus been satisfied, the dog, if he receives no encouragement, will only hang around for a surprisingly short time before he loses interest and goes away. Situation B has failed to eventuate and so the sequence comes to an end, for there is nothing in the mind of the dog to carry it any further. He may reappear on the following day, but that is only because the process has begun again at the beginning. I go into these rather unsavoury details because they are important in understanding the Blonde, and because they serve to show the fallaciousness of the popular concept of 'a sexual instinct' in which all responses are grouped around and related to the single act of coition.

It is only man, with his power of voluntary imagination, who sees the single act of coition inherent in every aspect of the relationship between the sexes. It is almost certain that this attitude has no counterpart in his true instinctual nature, in which coition has probably no more and no less importance than it has for the animals. That, of course, does not mean that it is not in fact of far greater importance to him than it is to them, but the reason for the disproportionate importance which it has assumed in his emotional life is to be sought, not in his instinctual nature but in its symbolism, for to man it is the supreme symbol of the fruitful union of the opposites, and as such it brings relief from the tensions engendered by them in his mind.

THE RECOGNITION-ELEMENT

Turning now to the characteristics by which early man must have recognized his mate, we may conclude that the importance which has always and universally been attached to female beauty indicates that they were predominantly visual. This is not quite such a truism as it may sound, for woman's visual interest in man is far less pronounced. Feminine hearts, of course, are undoubtedly susceptible to male good looks, but it is notable that in English the words 'beautiful' and 'pretty' are reserved for women. Women are generally far less preoccupied with the appearance of the male body in general than men are with that of the female; it is not possible to sell even a woman's magazine by portraying a handsome man on the cover,[1] whereas it is well known that almost anything can be sold with the help of the picture of a pretty girl. Men, in fact, are always spontaneously alert for a sight of the typical female form, which can be relied upon to 'catch their eye' even when they are absorbed in other matters. Women, on the other hand, are very susceptible to the charms of the male voice; this latter is a definite sexual characteristic and it is permissible to assume that it was first used as a mating call. The success enjoyed among women by singers, and particularly by crooners, needs no emphasis.

There can be no reasonable doubt that man, like the cuckoo, is equipped from birth with a special neuro-sensory mechanism which enables him to recognize his mate, and that this mechanism reacts predominantly to visual stimuli. In terms of the mind this proposition takes the form that in man's unconscious mind there is always a potential image of woman consisting predominantly of the visible distinguishing marks of her sex.

[1] This may be attributed to the fact that women's reaction to male good looks is far more personal and individual than that of man to the characteristic appearance of sexually desirable womanhood—there is no masculine equivalent of the Blonde; hence no picture of male perfection has the same universal appeal to women as that of female perfection (purely as a picture) has for men. This substantiates the hypothesis that the visual element is absent, or at least weak, in the female's mate-recognition image.

This fact has always been known to those who have access to the collective unconscious, such as the story-tellers, as the following tale indicates. It comes from that invaluable mine of symbolical material *The Thousand Nights and One Night* ('the Arabian Nights') which is a collection of legends and anecdotes compiled, probably in Egypt, not later than the fourteenth century, some of its constituents, however, showing evidence of considerably greater antiquity. The story relates how an embittered father, distressed by what he regarded as the calamitous effects produced by woman in the life of man, determined to bring up his young son in total ignorance of the existence of the opposite sex. In this he was successful until his son reached the age of puberty, but then the lad happened to catch sight of a group of girls. He was immediately captivated and demanded to know to what use these delightful creatures might be put; needless to say that he soon discovered the relationship between the sexes. Like the cuckoo he recognized something which he had never seen before, a performance which would be impossible in the absence of a pre-existent image. The story, of course, is not to be taken as a record of outer-world fact: it proves nothing in the sense in which the scientific investigations which we have been considering prove our hypotheses in the outer-world, factual sense: it is the statement of a psychological or inner-world truth, namely that the recognition-image of the mate exists independently in the mind.

The doctors of the Kaballah have said that the male is not without the female, and as a logical proposition that is of course a truism, since maleness exists solely by virtue of the existence of its counterpart, femaleness, just as the seller, as such, exists solely by virtue of the existence of the purchaser; but this particular proposition represents a living mental pattern. An even more striking statement of the thesis is to be found in the Jewish legend of the demon Lilith, Adam's first wife, who was with him before woman, in the person of Eve, had even been created. This, of course, was why God said, 'It is not good that the man should be alone.'[1]

[1] Gen. ii. 18.

THE PIN-UP GIRL

It was a source of wonder to me to find the tents of soldiers condemned to prolonged celibacy in desert encampments decorated with pictures of luscious nudes: for why stimulate and exacerbate an appetite which cannot be satisfied? Yet the practice was universal. The reason why I missed the point was that in those days I still believed in the existence of 'the sexual instinct': to my mind the idea of coition was inherent in the mate-recognition image, and so it seemed to me, as to St. Anthony of Egypt, that if coition is ruled out it is better to banish the picture of the opposite sex from the mind altogether. Needless to say that I was as wrong as he was, for she is a constituent of the mind and cannot be banished from it.

Once we have eliminated the idea of 'the sexual instinct' the situation becomes clearer. There is no sexual instinct, but a series of separate stimuli and responses which may, if outer-world conditions are favourable, follow one another in the regular sequence of the complete mating pattern. In the state of nature, however, this does not always happen, any more than it does in civilized life: it may be assumed with certainty that the animal normally makes a number of false starts, similar to those of the dog pursuing the bitch described above, before the sexual union is finally consummated. When such a false start is made the pattern is simply broken off and starts again at the beginning, and it may be assumed that the animal does not suffer intense mental distress or violent feelings of frustration on each such occasion: dogs, at any rate, show no signs of it. The reason, of course, is that the dog does not know why he is pursuing the bitch: he is simply impelled to do so, and, when he has found her, that, for the moment, is enough: the instinctive response has been satisfied and no stimulus for the release of any further response has been received. The instinctual nature of the dog, therefore, is completely satisfied, and if the bitch will have no truck with him he goes off cheerfully on other concerns and immediately forgets her. If the stimulus to the next stage, in the form of inviting behaviour from the bitch, is received, an entirely new situation arises: a fresh response has been elicited and must be satisfied, and if the affair were broken off at this stage it presumably would induce emotional distress.

Man's sexual constitution, of course, differs from that of the dog in that more frequent evacuation is physiologically demanded; nevertheless it is a fair conjecture that in the state of nature our earliest human ancestors were not successful in achieving sexual intercourse every time their sexual interest was aroused, any more than other animals are. False starts and the breaking off of the sequence after the initial stage must inevitably have been frequent, for even in animal life it is not always that both partners are prepared for coition at the same moment, and that no disturbing extraneous circumstances intervene. Hence it may be assumed that man's instinctive responses in the matter were adapted to these circumstances, in which they grew up, in that the first, or recognition-and-approach stage in the mating pattern was more frequently—perhaps far more frequently—activated than the later one of invitation-and-coition. It is moreover probable, as I have suggested above, that the female may have demanded an intermediate stage of courtship before proceeding to the final stage, which was certainly dependent on her initiative.

The status of courtship in humanity as a true instinctive pattern cannot be proved, but it seems to me probable that it is one, since it exists in many animal species: in humanity, moreover, it is widespread, if not, perhaps, universal. This in itself proves nothing regarding its instinctual status, but the feminine trait of coyness by which it is characterized does seem to be spontaneous and universal, and it elicits a response in man. As types, men like persuading, and women being persuaded, and these characteristics may be observed in many departments of life other than the purely sexual.

In the light of these considerations it is fair to assume that man's instinctive mating pattern is adapted to circumstances which decree that the initial, mate-recognition element will be activated far more frequently than the later stages: it is natural and normal for his sexual interest to be aroused far more often than sexual intercourse takes place, and no frustration, repression or emotional stress need be occasioned, so far as the instincts are concerned, by the breaking off of the sequence at an early stage.

The simple soldiers thus showed far more insight than St. Anthony: it was women they lacked far more than copulation.

94

They needed women in the first place to look at, then to talk to and flirt with and persuade, and only lastly to go to bed with. Since they could not have the two latter stages they at least found a substitute for the first: the pin-up girls at least satisfied the craving to see and recognize the outer characteristics of femininity, and that is an urge which calls for satisfaction more continually and frequently than the later ones.

The urge to see and recognize a suitable mate is almost permanent in man; even when a man's physiological needs are completely satisfied he will still look up when a pretty girl passes. It does him good merely to see her: her image releases libido from the depths of the unconscious part of the mind and makes it available to the conscious part, thus brightening and enlivening the whole picture of the world. The urge persists even when he has no further physiological needs to satisfy, for it is part of the structure of the mind, based in a 'neuro-sensory mechanism' which exists in its own right, irrespective of the body's requirements. Proust, with his penetrating insight, describes how the ageing *viveur* Swann, his days numbered by an incurable disease and certainly no longer capable of or interested in sexual intercourse, could still be seen gazing deep into the *décolletés* of the ladies as he bowed over their hands.

The image of woman, as we shall see, is for man the dispenser of the Waters of Life.

Thus man is for ever alert for the sight of sexually attractive woman, and the mere spectacle is beneficial to him, whether it leads to anything further or not. Generally it also does him good to flirt mildly with her too, and all this may be completely 'innocent' and unblemished by even the faintest *arrière-pensée*; he may be an exemplary husband and sincerely love his wife, to whom he remains absolutely faithful, but that has nothing whatever to do with his need for wider superficial feminine contacts. The situation is exactly the same with women: all women, whether they know it or not, enjoy being gallantly approached by any man, even when they have not the slightest interest in him. The approach in itself is a compliment to their femininity, and as such it satisfies the first stage of the mating pattern, equivalent to the recognition-and-approach stage in man. It thus does any woman good to be singled out for attention by any man and (provided that his approach is not in any way objectionable or embarrassing, and that she has not got her eye on somebody else) it is a source of pleasure to her and she will generally react accordingly; but this need have no further implications than the masculine flirtatiousness described above.

Both sexes, of course, have physiological needs also, which can only be satisfied after their own manner, but, at the instinctual level, the two requirements are almost entirely separate. In the higher regions of the mind, of course, the situation is entirely different, the question of the identity of the partner in sexual intercourse being of the greatest importance; for to any person of sensibility the intimacies involved are almost unendurable in partnership with anybody to whom he or she is not united by strong positive emotional bonds. At this level human beings are human and lay the preponderant emphasis on the individual personality; at the mate-recognition level, which is purely instinctive, they are merely animals and are interested only in sign-stimuli. If husbands and wives appreciated this distinction better a lot of trouble would be saved. If a man 'looks at other women' or a woman at other men, or if either flirts, that is in itself no reason whatever for assuming that he or she is dissatisfied with the marriage-partner.

Thus at last we come back to the Blonde. She is the essence of the pin-up girl, the mate-recognition image pure and simple, but distorted by the conscious knowledge of the later stages of the mating pattern. She displays all the outward and visible distinguishing marks of 'the optimal mate' (as Tinbergen describes the phenomenon)—the prominent breasts of sexual maturity, the slender waist of youth, etc.—in exaggerated form, but in addition to this she is supremely lecherous. In this lechery she departs from her instinct-based origin, for the mate-recognition image is not in itself the exciter of erotic feelings: if the instinctual pattern is left to itself these do not arise until later, for first the mate must be approached and courted, and it is only when the appropriate feeling relationship has been established between the couple that she will make the responses which, in turn, act as the 'sign-stimulus' releasing the male erotic response. Thus, at the instinctual level, the female at this stage is neither objectively, in herself, nor as an image in the mind of man, an erotically-toned entity: she is a challenge to courtship and no more.

96

Man, however, can no longer follow his instincts without interfering with them. He thinks erotic thoughts *in vacuo*, and when the mate-recognition image appears, either in fact or in fantasy, he projects the resultant lecherous feelings on to her figure: it is his concupiscence which she bears. Jung points this out in connection with that highly erotic epithalamium the Song of Songs: the beloved's nose, neck and breasts are compared to towers, which is evidently a phallic symbolism in which the lover projects the characteristic of his own excitement on to the person of the beloved. It is also the explanation of the pistol which Anna carries in her handbag—a characteristic phallic symbol contained in a characteristic vaginal one. She had been threatening and hostile, but as soon as Eddie wrests the pistol from her she becomes amenable and sets up house with him. The meaning of this little allegory is that the Blonde is not purely feminine: she contains a concealed male element which must be removed from her before she can become a satisfactory mate, and in this connection it is worth noting that the liaison between Eddie and Anna is the only more or less satisfactory love-affair in the whole book, filled though it is with casual cohabitations. It is also worth noting that on his last flight Slim quite gratuitously dresses Miss Blandish up in a suit of Rocco's; this is entirely pointless, as obviously a girl in ill-fitting man's clothes would be more conspicuous than in her own. Later, moreover, he goes to some trouble to restore her external femininity, so that here we have another picture of sexual ambivalence. This concealed male element in the Blonde may lead to fantasies of Lesbianism, a theme which has preoccupied a number of creative artists: notably, in undisguised form, Proust and Rodin, and, in a concealed form, Dickens.

The trouble is that the conscious mind has broken through the proper sequence of the mating pattern, leap-frogging the approach and courtship stages and proceeding direct from the mate-recognition image to the act of coition. This is unavoidable, for once the conscious mind has learnt about coition it cannot be prevented from seeing it as inherent in the mate-recognition image. If, however, the young man or boy in whom this occurs keeps to the rules and leads a normal life, flirting with more or less respectable girls of his own standing, no harm is done, for then he experiences the feminine responses of the courtship stage and his own responses to them, and learns to enjoy the experience. It is, as I have suggested, largely immaterial whether such flirtations lead to anything further or not: both parties benefit by them simply as such, and both learn to understand the feeling background, not only of the opposite sex but also of their own.

If, on the other hand, the boy is shy of girls and avoids them, because, like Slim, 'he is afraid they might laugh at him', he never experiences this essential aspect of sexuality. His shyness is probably largely attributable to feelings of guilt concerning his secret erotic thoughts, and the more he avoids women and broods on sexual themes in solitude the greater grow his feelings of guilt and consequently his shyness; thus a vicious circle is set up and he is in danger of becoming a misogynist. His physiological requirements remain to be satisfied, and with these he may deal either in solitude or by recourse to prostitutes. The result is very much the same in either case: he habitually short-circuits the middle stages of the mating pattern and never discovers those aspects of sexuality which are concerned with the feelings as opposed to the senses. This course of development is convincingly described by James Joyce in *Portrait of the Artist as a Young Man*.

As an alternative to real women (for prostitutes are not real women so far as he is concerned) this introverted and imaginative type concentrates on the Blonde, who is no more than a hollow simulacrum, compounded of the outward distinguishing marks of feminine sexuality and activated solely by masculine lust. She is thus often seen as an automaton or doll—numerous examples of this symbolism will be given in a later volume, when we come to examine this situation in closer detail. The original nebulous, inchoate image, which is the result of bringing the functioning of the relevant neuro-sensory mechanism to consciousness in the absence of an object externally perceived, becomes in course of time developed, enriched and filled out by the introjection[1] of elements derived from external objects, either in the form of living women, or in that of illustrative

---

[1] This word is used in various senses by psychologists. As used in this study it means the converse of projection: in projection attributes of the inner image are imposed on the object; in introjection attributes of outer objects are added to the inner image.

material or descriptions in writing. This occurs up to a point with all inner images: even the duckling, for instance, adds the visual impression received from the object it has accepted as mother to the pre-existent mental pattern of which, as we have seen, it is not originally a part. In other words the duckling, on hatching, although it already possesses a potential 'notion' of what its future mate will look like, has no corresponding ideas about its mother, of whom it requires only that she must move and quack; later it learns to recognize her by sight, whoever or whatever 'she' may be. That already constitutes an introjection, and if the duckling were endowed with the power of voluntary, conscious imagination it might go on to build up an idealized image of motherhood.

The constant application of this process to the image of the Blonde results in building it up into a synthetic compendium of feminine anatomical characteristics developed to a degree of exaggeration rarely to be met with on this earth. Compared with such a figure the erotic attractions of most flesh-and-blood girls make a poor showing, and beside her straightforward masculine lecherousness most of them appear aggravatingly inhibited. This leads to a point of great importance, for such a vision of Aphrodite is nowadays no longer the rare possession of a few imaginative introverts: on the contrary, the contemporary cult of film-stars with sensational bust and waist measurements and uninhibited private lives suggests that the Blonde has become the collective ideal of womanhood in the West. This situation is obviously connected with the teachings of Freud: the concept of 'the sexual instinct', directed solely towards copulation, and the thwarting of which may have such disastrous effects, has by now percolated to the masses and taken effect on the collective mind; the cinema and the abundance of cheap illustrative material in modern life have also obviously a lot to do with it. But the notion of the relationship between the sexes as an artificial superstructure built up solely on the pleasure provided by the orgasm is, as we have seen, totally at variance even with the true instincts, let alone with the higher or specifically human components of the mind. It leads to the habitual leap-frogging of the intermediate stages of the mating pattern and consequently to the immediate juxtaposition of the recognition and erotic elements, which tend to become identified thereby. Thus the contemporary young man no longer sees in a pretty girl a pleasant companion with whom he can enjoy himself in flirtation, and to whom he may make love eventually if they find that they appeal to one another, but an object, not even for proper intercourse, but for 'petting'. He has no use for purity or restraint: on the contrary, he demands that she must be 'sexy': she must, in fact, conform as closely as possible to the image of the Blonde. The girls, with lipstick, brassieres and skin-tight trousers, do their best to comply, and nowadays we find the greatest ladies apeing the allurements of the prostitute.

The social questions involved in all this are outside the scope of this work: I wish merely to indicate that the problem of sexual behaviour represented by the Blonde is a very real one, and that it is becoming increasingly widespread. From the social point of view there are two sides to the question, and the contemporary trend has at least the merit that it is an attempt to abolish the harsh distinction between 'pure' and 'fallen' women, with all that that implied, which disfigured the Victorian era. The question with which we are concerned here is that of the psychological background, for the Blonde, as we shall shortly see, represents far more than mere sexual behaviour.

In the Blonde we are dealing, not with objective woman as she actually is, but with the image of woman in the mind of man. Women, being by nature pliable and desirous to please, will do their best to conform to the ideal set up for them by men, but that is beside the point. Our interest lies in what man wants, or believes that he wants, as it is revealed in the picture of the Blonde; and this is not because of its effect on his sexual behaviour, which is a comparatively minor point, but because of the light it throws on his general mental attitude. In the Blonde he is seen to desire woman's outer similitude inhabited by his own lust—a figure supremely portrayed in Swinburne's Faustine.

There have been all kinds of other ideals of womanhood. At various times and places it has been customary for men to see her as austere and queenly, as ethereal, or as gentle and submissive; man has sometimes been moved to regard woman as a sublime mystery, sometimes as an ideal of purity, and sometimes as the source of his inspiration or of his sins. It goes without saying that all these notions are merely projections and have nothing whatever to do with objective women as they actually exist, for women have always been, as they are today, ordinary, self-contradictory human beings, very like men. What we are concerned with, therefore, is a content of the mind which is seen either in projection, in the form of the pin-up girl and her flesh-and-blood equivalents, or else directly as an inner image—as the Blonde.

This erotically-toned image of the recognition-elements of the mating pattern, representing the outer form of woman but lacking both the courtship element in the mating pattern and all the higher mental aspects of man's relationship to her, is, of course, nothing new. In a later volume we shall find that it was an important component in the make-up of the classical goddesses: the Blonde, in fact, differs very little from Aphrodite —or, paradoxically, from Artemis, who was anything but chaste. Individual men have always known her, but she has not always corresponded with the collective ideal. In the Middle Ages, for instance, although as the Lady Venus she was still well known, the emphasis was placed on a very different aspect of womanhood—that of the Queen of Heaven. The Lady Venus, moreover, in her appearances as the Lady of the Lake, the queen of elfland, Melusine etc., is not only a sorceress but also the repository of supernatural wisdom—an attribute notably lacking in the Blonde, with whom the adjective 'dumb' is pre-eminently associated.

We are interested in discovering why the image of woman in the mind of man has taken on this aspect at the present time. Is it merely the consequence of Freudianism? I think rather the reverse: the theories of Freud are to be regarded as one of the consequences rather than as the cause of the general attitude. To what, then, is the latter to be attributed?

We shall shortly see that this generalized symbolical image of woman which appears spontaneously in the minds of men has been identified by Jung as an Archetypal image which he has named the Anima, and we may anticipate here by using this term for convenience of reference. The answer to our question is best to be found by putting it in another form: what does the Anima want? What does she seek to achieve by presenting herself in this guise? We have just noted that she has other roles at her disposal; why, then, does she prefer at the present time to adopt that of the Blonde?

I am not, of course, naïvely imputing conscious motivation to a disembodied content of the mind, but this method of considering the purpose behind symbolical phenomena as though they were the purposes of the symbol itself is a valuable one which will be constantly used in this study, and the reader must familiarize himself with it. Provided that we accept the proposition that such phenomena have any purpose at all—i.e. that they are produced for a purpose by something, whatever it may be—it is clear that this approach merely represents a convenient abbreviation. We say, for instance, that the purpose of the telephone-bell is to inform us that a call has been put through, but nobody will accuse us on that account of imputing conscious volition to the bell. We know perfectly well that the purpose, in the strict sense, resides not in the mechanism but in the minds of the officials of the telephone service who have had the bell fitted; in the last resort, indeed, it is to be found in our own minds, those of the subscribers, who wish for audible notification of a call. The answer to the question 'why is the bell ringing?' is therefore 'so that I may know that somebody wishes to speak to me'. It is not strictly correct, for it should be 'the bell has been fitted so that I may know when somebody wishes to speak to me, and it is ringing now because a connection with my line has been made at the exchange'; for it may, after all, be a wrong number. But such a form of words is superfluous and cumbersome, the short answer sufficing for people who are familiar with such devices.

Similarly the question 'why is the Anima behaving in this way?' is 'because she wants such and such', and this will suffice for those who are familiar with the theory of the Archetypes. The full answer would be 'the Archetypal symbols have been evolved with the purpose of bringing to the notice of the conscious mind certain mental situations which it has no other means of learning about. The Anima is now appearing to the conscious mind in this form because the condition associated with it obtains.' If it be asked in whose mind the purpose which brought about the evolution of this symbol resided, the answer is that it was in our own, just as it was in our own minds that the purpose which produced the telephone-bell existed. But just as it was not the conscious mind of any particular subscriber which caused the bell, or the telephone service, to be introduced, but the sum total of the requirements of all potential subscribers, most of whom had never consciously considered the question, so are the Archetypes the product of the collective unconscious mind. Humanity as a whole requires certain information regarding what is going on in the unconscious part of its mind, and so it has unconsciously evolved the Archetypal symbols: they have a purpose, although that purpose was never consciously formulated in any individual mind.

This method of treating the Archetypal symbols as living, purposeful entities has also the advantage, as Jung points out, that it helps us to objectivize and visualize the influences which they represent. The speedometer in a car does not only provide factual information: it also helps the novice to visualize such speeds as thirty or sixty miles per hour which, hitherto, have been mere abstractions to him. As a driver he must learn to deal with them as practical realities, and if he approaches the question in the light of the idea that the purpose of the speedometer is to tell him when he is going too fast, then the process is greatly assisted. In the matter of symbolism we are all novices, and the concept of the mental factors represented by, say, the Anima, are far harder for most people to translate into terms of reality than is that of abstract speed. The novice must first convince himself that they exist at all, and it is often easier for him to do so if he treats the symbols in the same light as outer-world realities. These symbols, as we have seen, really do behave in a characteristic, significant and apparently autonomous manner, just as the pointer of the speedometer does, and what we have to discover is what their behaviour means; in doing so it is helpful to ask ourselves 'what they want'.

It is, therefore, perfectly legitimate to ask what the Anima wants when she appears as the Blonde, provided only that we bear in mind the fact that the wanting does not, strictly speaking, reside in her, since she possesses no independent mind, any more than the telephone-bell does. Her desires are the desires of an aspect of the collective, unconscious part of the human mind, in which all individual minds participate.

Her purpose, then, is obviously in the first place to draw

attention to herself, since she makes use of the recognition element in the mating pattern for which man is permanently on the alert, whether he wills it or not. This implies that she (the Anima, not objective woman) is in danger of being neglected or overlooked; when she presented herself as the Queen of Heaven she was in no such case: what she then required was evidently respect and reverence, but today she is prepared to forgo everything else provided only that attention is paid to her.

Men (apart from exceptional individuals) are obviously in no greater danger of forgetting their sexual nature today than they ever were: it is not simply with the purpose of promoting sexual intercourse that the Blonde is making such a parade of her sexuality. It might be contended that in the aftermath of Victorian morality men are still in danger of paying too little respect to the sexual side of life, and the fact that the Blonde is so particularly conspicuous in the Anglo-Saxon countries, in which the repression and humbug of Victorian morality was carried to its greatest extremes, lends colour to this suggestion. In most parts of the Continent a far more broad-minded and realistic attitude towards sexual questions obtained throughout the nineteenth century, and in these places the cult of the Blonde is less developed. That, however, is only the superficial aspect of the matter: the significance of the Blonde goes far deeper.

Carrying the matter to a higher (or perhaps deeper) plane we may seek the answer in that inexplicable tendency of the Blonde's, which we have noticed in *No Orchids*, to develop sentimental and other psychological traits which run counter to the simple 'wish-fulfilment' of sexual intercourse: she is not prepared to remain in the crude and ignoble role of the blonde in black pyjamas: she aspires, evidently, to become something more than a mere appeaser of male concupiscence. Here, on the superficial plane, we may find a statement of the personal problem of those men whose interest in women is solely erotic —those who habitually short-circuit the intermediate, approach-and-courting elements in the mating pattern, in order to proceed direct from recognition to coition. This, as we have seen, is probably contrary to the true instinctual pattern, although that cannot be taken as scientifically proved; however that may be it unquestionably does violence to those elements of the image of womanhood which have been added to the instinctual nucleus in the course of human mental development. These, as I have suggested, form part of the collective unconscious and are unconsciously and involuntarily absorbed by everybody from his mental environment. However cynical he may believe himself to be on the subject of women, no man can really free himself from the influence of the feeling values which have grown up round her figure in the course of centuries: I refer to such matters as the respect and protectiveness due to her, the challenge which she represents, and the respect and confidence which must be won from her in return. These things, together, probably, with the characteristic instinctive responses of courtship, form an integral part of the universal image of the Anima which exists potentially in every man's mind; if his relationship to women is to be satisfactory he must bring them to consciousness and do justice to them.

It is not, however, solely a question of a man's relationship to women, important though that is, but of his whole feeling life. It is noticeable that all the elements mentioned, even including the instinctive responses of courtship, are matters of feeling as contrasted with the intellect or the senses. The inference, therefore, is that the Blonde's purpose when she insists on her temperament and her sentimental demands at the expense of the simple fulfilment of sexual desire, is to raise these aspects of the totality of her nature to the surface: here we find part of the explanation of her appearance in an incomplete form, either with her lower half concealed, as behind the counter, or as a mermaid in which it is not yet humanized. The Blonde, in fact, is an incomplete version of the Archetype of the Anima: a version in which the feeling values have been overlooked and remain concealed in the impersonal unconscious.

Once again, however, this matter is not confined to sexual behaviour, nor even to a man's general relations with women, for the feeling life extends to far wider spheres. The trouble is not simply that his feeling relations with women are inferior and inadequate, but that his whole feeling life is; that is the general cause of which the defective sexual pattern is merely a consequence or special case. This question of the repression of one or other of the mental functions is a wide one with which we cannot deal at this juncture: those who are acquainted with Jung's theory of the mental functions and psychological types will appreciate the point, which will be considered in detail in the next volume of this series. It must suffice for the moment to say that thinking and feeling are opposites, and where the one is cultivated to excess the other is habitually repressed; men tend (although there are plenty of exceptions) to prefer thinking to feeling, and women (although also not without exception) the reverse. To man, therefore, woman, as his opposite and counterpart, tends to symbolize the feeling life in general; since her image also stands for the unconscious mind, and the greater part of his feeling life is often inaccessible in the unconscious, the symbolism has a double application. In the unconscious the feelings degenerate and become inferior and often dangerous, which explains Slim's sadistic tendencies; in order that this condition may be cured it is necessary that the domination of the one-sided, repressive conscious attitude be broken and the feeling life as a whole accepted in consciousness, where it can be brought into contact with civilized values and refined by the higher part of the mind. What this means in terms of life will not be clear to those who are not acquainted with Jung's system, but it is unfortunately impossible to elucidate the matter at this point.

This brings us to part of the explanation of Miss Blandish's mission: she must descend into the underworld of the unconscious in search of her counterpart and lover, who has been denied access to the world above, in order that she may raise him to the light of consciousness. It is not merely the personal problem of those individuals in whom the feeling life is repressed by an intolerant conscious attitude based on the function of thinking, but the problem of the age, for we have raised the intellect to the position of an infallible divinity, and are in serious danger of losing our psychic equilibrium in consequence. That is why it is so vitally important that the Anima should draw attention to herself and beguile man, by any means, however unworthy, to concern himself with her. If only he does so there is at least a chance that she may be able to teach him the error of his ways. As we have already noted she is wise after her manner, although at the moment she is studiously concealing the fact in order to avoid arousing the mistrust of men.

Lastly, moving to a plane still higher, or deeper, we may consider the Blonde's role of guardian of the door which leads through the Barrier. This is a matter concerning which we have not yet collected enough information for a full discussion, but I may anticipate by saying that it is a matter of the Two Worlds, or of man's two natures, the one individual, the other generic. As I have suggested above, in our obsession with personal consciousness we have largely cut ourselves off from our universal roots, which are to be found in the unconscious mind, and this is an even graver danger than our loss of feeling values: some of its more serious implications will be discussed later in this study. The Anima therefore, assuming the ignoble externals of the Blonde, stations herself at the door in order to lure men into the world of the Other Side. If they trust her and understand how to deal with her she will act as their guide in these mysterious regions, and they will be able to return to This World wiser, freer, and possibly in possession of the Treasure of wholeness.

The Anima, who is the Queen of Heaven as well as the hash-house waitress, is, as we shall see shortly, nothing less than man's soul. We have seen her as a mermaid rising from the waters of the unconscious in search of the love of man, in order that she may win a soul: that is only another way of saying that she is man's soul seeking the completeness that only his love can give her.

IV *The Irreconcilables*

THE DICHOTOMY OF THE SPHERE

No Orchids is the record of an expedition beyond the Barrier into the world of the Other Side, and the predominant characteristic of that world is that it is devastated by the bitter conflict of two rival factions. The conflict is not at first conspicuous, for the earlier episodes of the story are concerned mainly with the abduction of Miss Blandish; it is true that that at once leads to a conflict, but at first it is only the enmity between two gangs with which we are concerned. But as the story progresses, and the writer penetrates more deeply into the hinterland of the Other Side, the dichotomy crystallizes out into the opposition of two clearly defined parties, each representing definite principles: they are the upper world of John Blandish and the underworld of Ma Grisson. Once these two characters emerge the conflict assumes larger proportions and eventually envelops the whole scene: it reaches its climax in the pitched battle between the Blandish police army and the Grisson gang in which the latter's stronghold is taken by storm.

The situation, we have seen, has its mythological prototype in the Persephone myth in which the princess of the upper world is also ravished by the ruler of the underworld, and we can now discern another parallel: the story of the rape of Helen and the Trojan War. The plot may therefore be regarded as Archetypal, that is to say as representing a fundamental mental pattern, and we have now to attempt to discover in what this schism of the mind consists.

Attention has already been drawn to the way in which the

theme of dichotomy pervades the book: not only is it manifested in the conflict between the opposing factions for the possession of Miss Blandish, but also in the division between This World and the Other Side; it is, however, important to appreciate that these two cleavages are not identical: the two halves into which each of them divides the totality of the world of the mind are not the same.

This point is of vital importance in the study of the mind, and failure to appreciate it has led to many misconceptions. It can best be illustrated by the analogy of the sphere.

Parmenides envisaged the totality of all things[1] in the form of a sphere, and this image is of great and far-reaching importance. The sphere is the only body which appears the same from every point of view; no point on its surface is inherently distinguishable from any other point; and it is the body which contains the largest volume for a given superficies: regarded as a container it holds the maximum possible content. For these reasons it has always been the symbol of perfection and completion, for however one looks at it it remains the same, no part of it has greater significance or importance than any other (as, for instance, the apex of a cone has) and its content cannot be increased by any change of shape. It is the essence of wholeness.

As a result of these properties it is possible to divide a sphere into halves along an infinite number of planes and the result will always be the same: we obtain two hemispheres similar in every respect to one another and also exactly similar to the hemispheres resulting from bisection along any other plane. This is the position in its purest and most absolute form: it suggests that in whatever way we divide the totality of Being, or as we say nowadays, of experience, we shall obtain basically the same result, that is to say two halves which are fundamentally interchangeable and which are always capable of re-unification into the same perfect whole. We may, for our own purposes, differentiate between the two hemispheres by colouring one of them red and the other blue, but such a distinction is superficial, arbitrary and fundamentally irrelevant:

[1] The 'ent' or essence of Being, which is imperishable, whole, indivisible, continuous, unchangeable, perfect and evenly extended in every direction: therefore a sphere.

ultimately, on the highest plane, where such accidentals are of no account, we are left with two perfect halves, indistinguishable from one another and whose only characteristic is that they are halves of the perfect Whole.

The image is strikingly expressed in the famous passage on the origin of sexual love in Plato's *Symposium*. Aristophanes describes the original human beings as follows:

Secondly, the shape of each human being was wholly in the round, with circular back, circular sides, four hands, four legs, circular neck and one head with two faces looking opposite ways, four ears, double genitals and everything my description implies.[1]

Jove then bisected each being 'as men slice apples for pickling, or cut eggs with a hair', turning the faces and subsequently the genitals to the 'inner' side of the resulting hemispherical beings. The consequence was as follows:

Now, when their natural state had been bisected, each half yearned for and tried to approach the other! Round each other they threw their arms, entwining themselves in their desire to fuse. . . .

As our study progresses we shall find the significance of this symbolism confirmed in one example after another: I may anticipate by saying here that the figure of a single human being, divided vertically, each half revealing the characteristics of one of the sexes, and with two heads, or two faces on one head, is the conventional image of REBIS, the 'double thing' of medieval alchemy.

The basic meaning of this picture is the division of the original perfect Whole into two corresponding halves, the Opposites, resulting in the 'desire for reunion' between the halves, which arises from the actual incompleteness of each in itself, and from the ever-present, potential completeness which consists of the union between the two. The union of the sexes is pre-eminently the symbol of this union between opposites which are at the same time counterparts of one another; their union results, of course, in restoring the original unity in the form of the child.

We are dealing here with a figure of the mind, not with a

[1] Freemasons may recognize something in this description.

mere allegory of the facts of biology. If regarded in the latter light the parable would be merely silly; the appearance of the sphere, in any case, denotes that there is more in it than that. This is only a single particular case of the general principle of dichotomy in which, instead of colouring our two hemispheres red and blue, we have named them male and female. And, incidentally, Plato maintains that there were originally three sexes: double males, double females and androgynes. Heterosexual love is the attraction between the two halves of an androgyne, but the bisection of the other two produces male and female homosexuality. In other words we have here a statement that the two halves are really indistinguishable: that union with the counterpart is in the last resort the subject's union with himself, seen from a different viewpoint. If the subject identifies himself with maleness then he necessarily has a counterpart which appears as female, but it is perfectly possible, as we shall see later, for him to identify himself with femaleness, or with the androgyne, instead.

The trouble about this wholeness, seen as the sphere, as an object of thought, is that its parts are all indistinguishable from one another and its form invariable from whatever point of view we regard it. We can think of it only as an undifferentiated whole, and beyond that point we can make no progress. But in order to live we must see the world as something distinct from ourselves with which we can establish relationships, and here already we have a dichotomy, consisting in the division of totality into the hemispheres of subject and object, or self and not-self. With the implications of this differentiation we shall be concerned later. Again, in order to understand life we must endow objects of our experience with individuality, seeing them as identities over against the remainder, which is everything else, but not the identity in question. Proceeding further, we discover similarities and dissimilarities between the various identities which we have established: one class is living, the other inanimate, one pleasant, the other unpleasant, and so on: here we have further dichotomies into classes or categories, each consisting of a pair of opposites. The functioning of the conscious mind, in fact, consists basically in discrimination, which means the dichotomy of the totality of experience, or Being as it presents itself to us, into pairs of opposites, each of which implies its counterpart. With this theme we shall also be concerned later: it is sufficient for the moment to indicate that conscious life may be symbolized as a continuous series of bisections of the perfect sphere which lies beyond and behind all appearances, and which contains all possibilities in an undifferentiated state within itself.

The result of carrying out this process over a period of years may be visualized in the image of a private reproduction of the absolute, universal sphere, and this is the personal mental world of the individual in question. This replica, however, differs from its universal prototype in that the individual has made it comprehensible to his own perceptions by arbitrarily identifying points on its surface and establishing their relations to one another. The result is something like a terrestrial globe, the uniform surface of which is marked off by lines of longitude and latitude and covered with a complex pattern of identifiable areas. It is now no longer immaterial from what point of view the sphere is regarded, nor along which plane it is bisected: each bisection, although still producing two hemispheres of identical form which retain the property of potential reunion to re-establish the perfect whole, is characterized by the different marked areas which are separated by it.

To take the terrestrial globe as an example, if we bisect it along the Equator we obtain the conventional northern and southern hemispheres, the peninsula of India being contained in the former. If, however, we tilt the plane of bisection through some twenty degrees, so that the point on the line of cleavage nearest the North Pole is on the same longitude as India, the latter area will now be included in the hemisphere containing the South Pole. The two new hemispheres differ very little from the former two and may still reasonably be designated northern and southern, but the slight difference in the plane of bisection has resulted in the transference of an important area from one to the other.

In the mental world such a transference may be exemplified by a man's attitude to, say, his own body. Seen from certain points of view it is part of the hemisphere of self as opposed to that of not-self, but if the viewpoint is only slightly changed it becomes part of the outer world from which the subject, seeing itself as a mind, is separate. Thus an athlete, while training for a race, is treating his body as something external to himself on which he is working very much as he might on a horse which he was preparing for the same purpose. During the actual race, however, his viewpoint changes and he is identified with his body, which becomes part of himself as contrasted with his competitors; he now no longer stands over against it as an object, deciding that this will be beneficial for it and the other harmful, but is identified with it in the effort which mind and body are making in unison. (Sir Winston Churchill brings out this point in a passage in *World Crisis* in which he says that a horseman should train his horse as though it were worth ten thousand pounds and ride it as though it were worth half a crown, an analogy which he applies to the utilization of military and naval forces in war.)

Failure to understand this matter leads to false identifications. Thus, if we divide the sphere of totality into male and female, and again into positive and negative, the resultant hemispheres are very similar but not identical. Failure to appreciate the difference leads to such false assertions as that the masculine 'is' positive and the feminine negative. As an approximation this statement may be serviceable, but it is no more strictly true than would be the assertion that the feminine was beautiful and the masculine ugly, the former dark and the latter bright, or true and false, heavy and light, or any other irrelevant pair of opposites. We have to guard against the tendency to pick out one particular line of bisection and to attempt to understand everything in its terms: philosophers, particularly, are liable to attempt to force the whole of existence into such Procrustean beds.

Each dichotomy is individual and unique and the resultant pair of opposites differs, however slightly, from every other pair. Only the fact of dichotomy itself, and its specific and irreducible implications, are universally valid: these are the production of a pair of opposites which are the counterparts of one another; between them there is tension which itself consists at one and the same time of the opposites of repulsion and attraction, hatred and love; and finally the opposites inherently contain the potentiality of fruitful reunion.

In *No Orchids* the sense of duality which pervades the story represents the principle of dichotomy and the resultant tension in general, but the two forms in which we have so far found it expressed represent two distinct cleavages. That between This World and the Other Side represents the division between two modes of the mind, the personal and the universal (or generic) respectively; that between the factions of John Blandish and Ma Grisson, on the other hand, is the conflict between the principles of constituted authority and the rebellion of the dispossessed. We may now turn for further information on the subject to the persons of the two leaders of the factions, who are the representatives of the principles concerned.

THE CAUSE OF THE CONFLICT

We have already noted that both Blandish and Ma make their first appearances as disembodied voices on the telephone; this reveals that they reside in the further reaches of the Other Side: they are not immediately perceptible, although they are always present in the background. Furthermore, we have seen that once they appear the latent conflict, which has been in the air from the start, flares up and involves everybody—even the empty-headed Blonde is compelled to take sides.

Here again we have the symbolic representation of an important characteristic of the mind. The process of differentiation by bisection of the sphere is essentially a working of the conscious mind. In the collective or universal part of the unconscious mind, the nature of which we shall consider later, the process of discrimination has not yet been applied: its contents, therefore, exist in a state of undifferentiated potentiality in which the opposites have not yet been separated out and the tension between them has not therefore come into existence. It is only when any such content reaches the conscious mind that the latter seeks to make it intelligible by splitting it up into pairs of opposites. Thus there exist in the mind two departments, or areas, or modes of functioning, in one of which everything is, so to speak, unitary, not yet being seen in the light of the polarities self—not-self, subject—object, particular —universal, good—bad, inner—outer, spirit—matter and so forth, whereas in the other everything is so seen and is thereby allotted a place in the personal scheme of ideas and values. This dichotomy has always been known to mystical thinkers and is symbolized in the 'tau' cross: T. This figure indicates that the area above the horizontal line is undivided, whereas that below is bisected by the vertical into the pairs of opposites. The horizontal is the Barrier. Another version is to be found in the ancient Egyptian *ankh*: ☥. Here the loop at the top is a distorted circle, signifying the sphere of undifferentiated totality; the figure appears again in the astrological symbol for Venus: ♀.

Mental progress is achieved by 'raising' contents from the undifferentiated area into the light of consciousness, thereby assimilating them into the personal world-picture or personality and subjecting them to the control of the Ego. In this last analogy the undifferentiated area is seen as lying 'below' that of consciousness: it is the universal or collective unconscious seen as the sea, the mother of all things, the contents of which are captured and brought up into the light by the function of intuition just as the fisherman catches and lands fishes. With the symbol of the fisherman we shall be concerned again. The three symbols illustrated above, on the other hand, show the undifferentiated area lying 'above' the differentiated: there it is regarded as 'the realm of spirit' from which divine inspirations and revelations 'descend' into the world below. The difference is only one of viewpoint.

As we shall see later the admission of contents to consciousness is controlled by a selective mechanism, itself unconscious, which has been built up by the individual, and arbitrarily so constituted that it excludes whole categories of experience from consciousness. We cannot go further into the matter at this point, but any reader of maturer years will probably be able to remember how in the course of his life the area of his consciousness has from time to time expanded, revealing to him whole departments of mental experience of which he has hitherto been completely unaware: it may have been music, or other people's feelings, speculative thought, religious experience, or something more concrete such as the delights of gardening, the refinements of cooking, the joy of possessing exceptional or beautiful objects, or the practice of some art or handicraft. Looking back it is hard to realize how one had hitherto lived in total ignorance of all the richness of experience and the living implications of one's 'discovery': how all awareness of them had apparently been witheld from the mind without one's knowledge or consent.

These are cases of spontaneous and felicitous adaptations to the mind's inherent tendency to expand the area of consciousness by assimilating contents of the unconscious: cases, however, often arise in which the conscious attitude opposes obstinate resistance to such assimilations. The reasons for this will appear later; for the present we must be content to accept the fact that the situation occurs, and that the result is an internal conflict between the principle of the selection of conscious contents and the class of content thereby denied admission: it is as though a doorkeeper who had received orders to exclude all candidates for admission having certain characteristics were fighting with an indignant mob of such people clamouring to be let in. The doorkeeper, and the authority which has issued the orders which he obeys—in other words the mechanism governing the admission of contents to consciousness—are themselves unknown to the conscious mind: the conflict, in fact, is taking place wholly in the unconscious. The conscious mind is not aware of the existence of a conflict, for the latter exists only in a latent or potential condition, only becoming manifest in the state of tension and exhaustion which it produces. Here we have the explanation of that atmosphere of depression and drained vitality which we have noted, and which provides the incentive for the venture into the hinterland beyond the Barrier in search of the Treasure of renewed life, energy and decisiveness which has disappeared into it.

Such a penetration of the Barrier implies the direction of the light of conscious discrimination into dark regions normally inaccessible to it, and the effect of such illumination is that the opposites, hitherto concealed in the unconscious, immediately become apparent and fly apart. All the latent tensions and hostilities inherent in the situation flare up and become actual, leading to a savage battle in the conscious mind. Such penetrations of the Barrier, therefore, are dynamic and often agonizing experiences; they are also dangerous, and that is the basis of the theme of the forbidden door in the fairy-tales:[1]

[1] Familiar in Germanic folk-lore; an example taken at random from a remoter world is to be found in *The Tale of the Second Kalandar* from the Arabian Nights.

the hero always opens it, thereby falling into great danger and suffering, but he sometimes succeeds in securing the Treasure.

For if the conscious mind is strong and adaptable enough to retain its identity and sense of orientation in the midst of the turmoil of the great forces which it has unleashed, their confrontation and coming to grips with one another acts as a discharge of tension. Even if the Treasure is not secured and slips back, like Eurydice from Orpheus' arms, into the darkness, there is at least temporary relief from the longdrawn devitalization of suppressed conflict. Something has been achieved in the uprush of repressed forces, and it often takes the form of a creative work. If, however, the conscious mind fails to contain and master the powerful figures which erupt into it from the unconscious, some form of personal catastrophe ensues. The subject becomes 'possessed' by blind forces which usurp the control of the conscious will, and he is either driven to symbolical and ultimately self-destructive actions or succumbs to suicide, neurosis, or at best neurotic collapse. Creative work is a dangerous activity, but needs must when the devil drives.

FATHER AND MOTHER

John Blandish and Ma Grisson are the remote focal points of the two opposing factions. It is noticeable that they never meet; they never even encroach on one another's territories, for Ma throughout the story never leaves her premises, and when Blandish wishes to join in the pursuit of his fugitive daughter and her lover he is turned back by Fenner.

Both are Archetypal figures: Blandish is the King, for the local millionaire in the world of *No Orchids* is no less, and he is specifically described as 'the meat king'—and essentially the Father. Ma is no less a queen, for she has carved out a kingdom for herself in the underworld. She has created the gang which controls it: 'The Grisson mob was the most vicious murder machine in the State. Ma had built it up and she was proud of it.' And of course she is essentially the Mother—the mother of Slim, the villain-hero.

We do not see very much of Blandish personally, but throughout the story we are aware of his authority. Right from the start it is of him that the gangsters are afraid, for the police are no more than his agents: 'He (the gangster) began to realize that this job was going to be big. . . . He could imagine how tough Blandish would get with the cops'; or: 'If we rub her out her old man will spend every cent to catch up with us. The amount of heat that old guy could dig up would make us dizzy.' And Blandish himself is implacable in his hatred of the underworld: ' "I think my daughter is dead," Blandish said quietly. "I hope she is, otherwise. . . ." ' And immediately afterwards: ' "I want those men caught. I don't want them to get away with this. I should be more satisfied if they were killed than arrested." ' His daughter's honour—that is to say, his own honour—is dearer to him than her life, but his hatred of the underworld is the strongest motive of all.

In his person Blandish represents the grim world of the industrial West. Its moral virtues are those of the godly, righteous and sober life: industry, respectability, purity, toughness and a shrewd common sense: a successful ideal, but a narrow one. We see it all expressed in his portrait: 'Just above middle height, a thin face, clean-shaven, and heavy jaw. His eyes gave his face its extraordinary power and character. Deep-set, in dank sockets, they were hard, shrewd and vital.' He is 'cold, impersonal and unfriendly'. One imagines him dressed in rusty black, a Bible under his arm: the personification of sour Puritan intolerance.

Ma resembles him in many respects: grim, unscrupulous, authoritative, determined and power-loving, she is his replica. Only in the activities they favour are they diametrically opposed, for Blandish represents respectability, chastity and orderliness whereas Ma cultivates licentiousness, lawlessness and all the vices. Some of these characteristics are not revealed in their own persons but in those of their minions: Fenner, for instance, displays orderliness and chastity, for he has an office in which he sits during the conventional hours, whether he has anything to do or not, occupying himself by repulsing the advances made by Paula his glamorous secretary: on one occasion he explicitly declines to make love to her 'during office hours'. This chastity of Fenner's is important: we have seen that it enables him to stride past the barrier in the night-club without succumbing to the blandishments of the blonde who guards it. He is the one character who is free of both worlds, it being explained that in his previous career as a journalist he had got to know all the hoodlums. He has the right of entry, which Blandish and the police have not, but he can enter freely only when he goes alone: as soon as he comes accompanied by the police army the underworld resists, and although the resistance is eventually overcome, the effort, as we have seen, is fruitless, for when the victors at last penetrate to the innermost citadel they find that Miss Blandish, the Treasure, is no longer there. Nevertheless, by his impregnability to the advances of the Blonde, and by his determination and toughness, Fenner is able to preserve himself in safety in the underworld, and it is he who discovers the Treasure although he fails to secure her, for, like Eurydice, she slips back into the darkness.

Ma, likewise, is not personally given to any kind of licentiousness, but apart from racketeering she runs a night-club in which every kind of luxurious dissipation is practised; it is she, also, who brings about Miss Blandish's debauch by Slim.

Now in stories which we shall examine later we shall find this theme of the estrangement and conflict between King and Queen, or Father and Mother, recurring. In Rose Macaulay's *The World my Wilderness* we shall find the couple playing exactly the same roles, the father representing conventional rectitude while the mother personifies the amoral, orgiastic principles; but in Dickens' *Great Expectations* the roles are reversed. We must, therefore, be on our guard against ascribing the roles of arbiter of rectitude and of anti-moral rebellion to Father and Mother respectively as representatives of the male and female sexes. We have noted that the similarities in character between Ma and Blandish outweigh the differences; confining ourselves, therefore, carefully to the deductions permitted by our material we are entitled only to the following conclusions. First that this couple, as man and woman, represent a pair of opposites which are capable of union; secondly that instead of being united by love they are separated by hatred; thirdly that they are powerful and authoritative figures —in fact parents. But it seems probable that in the specific roles they play as leaders of the warring factions they may be interchangeable. This point may perhaps be explained if we turn to the instinctual basis of the images.

THE GREAT ADULT

Unlike a foal, a lamb or a duckling, an animal which, like the human baby, is born in a helpless condition, is under no necessity to identify its mother. The young animal does not have to follow the mother about; the mother either carries it with her or deposits it in a safe place and visits it in order to feed it. It is safe to assume that an instinct which is entirely valueless to a species will not be found to exist in it (unless, of course, the loss of value is due to an artificial change of environment): it is therefore highly probable that the human mind is not equipped with any innate mechanism designed to identify any single being as 'mother', that is to say as the protective, nourishment-providing centre of youthful existence. By the time the child has grown sufficiently to get about on its own its intelligence has developed to a stage which enables it to identify a number of beings as such, its mother among them; by then, of course, if she does happen to be the being who exclusively cares and provides for him she will have come to occupy a special place in his world, but only as one person among others; there is no justification for assuming any inherent tendency to make a 'mother-projection' as such, in the way that the duckling and the foal do.

We are, moreover, far too apt to assume that the artificial picture of 'the family' consisting of mother, father and children is something fundamental. Human beings have always lived in communities, and pre-human beings almost certainly in herds; the primitive household, moreover, is generally a large one, accommodating several generations. When the primitive human child was old enough to move independently, and hence to get into trouble, the relationship of greatest importance in preserving it from danger would be that to other members of the herd in general rather than to its two specific parents. It is, therefore, a fair conjecture that the child would be equipped with an innate instinctive impulse to imitate, follow and obey any adult human being, with whom it would tend to take refuge when afraid. This surmise seems to be supported by the actual behaviour of young children, who are extremely accommodating in the matter of attachment, being prepared to accept the ministrations and authority of almost anybody who approaches them in the right way. Unfamiliarity may for a moment arouse their mistrust, but they very soon habituate themselves and are often no more and no less attached to nurses, servants, aunts and others with whom they are familiar than they are to their own parents. As a contrast to this it should be observed how a lamb which has wandered away from its mother will, if frightened, run back to her across a whole field, passing numerous other ewes without a glance, or how the foals, in a herd of horses on the move, remain close to their own mothers.

If this is a true picture of the human instinctual pattern in the matter we may assume the existence of a single mental figure of a very indeterminate nature towards which the child would tend to manifest the reactions of seeking protection, imitation and self-subordination. Such a figure would necessarily possess the quality of authority which would evoke the related feelings of trust and dread, submissive love and its converse, rebelliousness; it would be experienced both as the terrible arbiter of rectitude and the incitement to sin, as loving protector and stern judge. As to its external characteristics, it need only be human and large: its sex, in particular, would be indeterminate.

Here, evidently, we have something which might have served as the nucleus around which there crystallized the figure of the Semitic 'paternal' deity and his counterpart Satan, originally seen as two manifestations of a single essence.[1] He is not, moreover, truly 'paternal', but rather 'parental', for the feminine element in the composition of Jahweh is revealed in the symbolism of the Ark and the Mercy Seat; subsequently it splits off into the independent figure of 'Wisdom' or Sophia in the later Hebrew canonical scriptures, and of the Glory of the Lord, or Shekinah, of the Kabbalists, who is seen in female form.

I shall call this figure the Great Adult. In my opinion it provides the basis of all superordinated or authority-deities who, as a class, are distinct from the deities based on other inherent images, such as those of the mating and other patterns to which humanity is predisposed. I must, however, make it clear that I do not for a moment advance this theory as an 'explanation' of the nature of Deity or Divinity as such: to do

[1] Cf. Dr. R. Schärf in Jung and Schärf: *Symbolik des Geistes.*

so would be to adopt the typical superficial 'reductive' attitude. But to advance a theory designed to explain why human beings experience the principle of divinity in particular forms is no more an explanation of the ultimate nature of that principle than a theory concerning the mechanism of the eye and its effect on the images which we see is an explanation of the nature of light. We are concerned for the moment only with the nature of the human mind which interprets the essence or principle in the form of images with particular attributes. A differently constituted mind would form different images of the same essence or reality, just as an abnormal or differently constituted eye would do.

When the figure of the Great Adult is brought to consciousness it is necessarily split into pairs of opposites, and this dichotomy appears to tend to follow one of two planes of cleavage: that between male and female and that between good and evil, or constituted authority and rebellion. The former produces the Father and Mother images, the latter those of God and the Devil. The second of these dichotomies may produce a pair of deities of equal status, as in the Ormuzd and Ahriman of the Zoroastrian system: these I shall call the Upper and Lower Gods, both of whom may be seen as belonging to the same sex, in which form we shall meet with them later.

The Father and Mother form of dichotomy involves the sexual images, which have basically nothing to do with the Great Adult. The resultant figures are therefore composite: Authority *plus* Man (King) and Authority *plus* Woman (Queen) respectively. As such they give rise to mixed and unsuitable projections in which elements pertaining to the relationship between the sexes are entangled with others belonging to the relationship to authority: in the subsequent course of this study we shall find examples of the troubles to which this confusion may lead. The theory, incidentally, offers an alternative explanation of those phenomena which the Freudians have interpreted as 'fixations' on the figures of the personal father and mother.

In *No Orchids* both forms of dichotomy have taken place: Father and Mother, or King and Queen figures have appeared and have been allotted arbitrarily to the opposing factions of upper world, representing constituted authority, and of underworld, representing rebellion. Dickens, as I have mentioned, made the opposite allocation. It is possible that personal factors play their part in the choice, but if so they are accidentals and we need not trouble with them. For the time being we must assume that Father and Mother are interchangeable.

THE TERRIBLE MOTHER

The question still remains why Ma, whose prototype in *Sanctuary* is more of a humorous sketch than a vision of horror, should have become something so very repulsive, evil and dangerous. The explanation is to be found in part in the nature of an Archetypal figure to which Jung has drawn attention, giving it the name of Terrible Mother. Out of deference to the conventional attitude towards motherhood she is more commonly seen in the role of Wicked Stepmother, or, even more closely disguised, as a monster, dragon or wild beast with which the hero must do battle. Jung has given a large number of examples in his *Wandlungen und Symbole der Libido*,[1] and others will appear in later chapters of this study, in which the significance of the figure will be further discussed. For the moment we may regard her simply as the shadow side of the image of motherhood.

The light side of the Mother, the guise in which we like to see her, is that of a protective, lavishing, nourishing, wise, provident, guiding and prolific principle, but this representation necessarily implies its opposite, the shadow side. This negative or dark aspect of motherhood derives from the awareness of individual separateness, of the position of the living organism over against its non-individualized environment. Physical life represents a perpetual effort on the part of the individual organism to maintain itself in a state of differentiation from the great inorganic world. Let the effort once fail and the physical body loses its coherence: its carefully regulated temperature equalizes itself with that of its surroundings; the complicated and unstable molecules of its chemical constitution break down into simpler forms; the law of Entropy asserts itself and the few pounds of matter that had borne a living intelligence merge back into the millions of tons of unintelligent matter from which they were once drawn. Dust to dust, ashes to ashes.

It is precisely the same with mental life: consciousness arises

[1] English transl., *The Psychology of the Unconscious.*

from the great undifferentiated mass of the collective unconscious; it burns more or less brightly for its allotted time and finally decomposes into the materials from which it was drawn, which return whence they came. Its maintenance is a perpetual effort, from which we find relief in sleep, and at last release in death. Thus the Mother, from whose body we once drew the constituents of our own, stands for the great earth from which all living bodies are formed (And the Lord God formed man of the dust of the ground, and breathed into his nostrils the breath of life; and man became a living soul).[1] She is also the great sea of the collective unconscious, in which the individual consciousnesses swim like fishes. To return to her is rest for the weary, but it implies also extinction for the spark of consciousness. In the last resort the personal self is nothing but a coherent stream of consciousness, and what we fear in death is its termination—it can be nothing else. Therefore we also fear the Mother, for she is the Abyss and the darkness which comprehendeth not.

In this respect, therefore, the Mother is an object of fear, and in another she is an object of loathing. The Blonde is an artificial synthesis of all the elements which are erotically pleasing in woman and I have already indicated that such a selection leaves a number of other constituents of the inherent image of the opposite sex unaccounted for. These consist of those elements of the mating pattern which have no direct erotic value, and which, from the erotic point of view, are irksome and undesirable. These, being excluded from the conscious ideal, sink into the unconscious where they tend to crystallize into a shadow image of womanhood, representing her as possessive, exigent, tyrannical, parasitical and so forth. Personal, objective experiences of women are similarly divided, attractive elements being incorporated in the conscious ideal while everything distasteful and repulsive is relegated to the unconscious, where it associates itself with the shadow image, thereby adding to it the images of the hideous old hag and other distasteful aspects of femininity. Ma Grisson, therefore, is the shadow side of the Blonde, as repulsive as the latter is beguiling, as harsh and intractable as the Blonde is amenable, as overbearing as she is submissive.

We have seen how Chase, evidently with an uneasy feeling

[1] Gen. ii. 7.

that the blonde in black pyjamas lacked something of full femininity, experimented, in the person of Anna, with some of those less welcome characteristics which, as of course he knew, do occur in objective women. Anna is not entirely submissive: she has a temper; and she is not satisfied with endless sterile couplings with her lover: she begins to hanker for some more binding arrangement. But then the author begins to have misgivings and has Eddie ruthlessly reduce her to order. The most revealing episode, however, is that in which the Blonde makes her brief appearance as a fat girl. Here the writer, feeling that the unbroken succession of perfect figures was perhaps becoming unrealistic, not to say monotonous, has forced the Blonde to accept a typical feminine shortcoming: the tendency to run to fat. The consequence is startling, consisting in the sudden materialization of Ma with her tommy-gun. Evidently the insistence on the anti-erotic quality of fatness has activated the shadow image, and the fat girl is virtually transformed into Ma, thus revealing their underlying identity. Thus it becomes apparent what the quest of the complete nature of the Blonde entails: it is nothing less than reconciliation with Ma Grisson. That means not only the acceptance of the less enjoyable, even the less edifying aspects of femininity, but a coming to terms with the whole collective unconscious with all its terrors.

Before leaving this figure I wish to emphasize again how easy it is to fall into error by presuming the existence of parallels between the inner and outer worlds before it has been conclusively shown that they exist. It is clear that the complex figure of Ma Grisson contains an element of motherhood and, proceeding from that point, it is all too easy to attempt an explanation of all her characteristics on the basis of the particular, characteristic relationship of the child to its mother in the outer world. But this relationship, as we have seen, has virtually no counterpart in the inner world, since the human child is almost certainly not equipped with any innate mother-identification pattern. The characteristics of Ma derive partly from the relation of the conscious to the unconscious, partly from that of man to woman as mate, and partly from the innate tendency of subordination to authority. The element of motherhood occurs only in the first of these, and then only indirectly, in symbolical form.

DEADLOCK AND RELEASE

The latent conflict between the opposites personified in Blandish and Ma which cast its shadow over the opening scene amounts to a mental deadlock. The position, as already indicated, is that the conscious attitude, represented by Blandish and the principle of constituted authority, is obstinately refusing to allow the assimilation into the conscious mind and personality of a whole category of experience. The explanation of the nature of this discrimination must be left till later; for the moment we must be content with indicating that in the present case it is connected with the feeling life. That is why the courtship, matrimonial and parental elements of the mating pattern are unacceptable: they are matters of feeling relationship as opposed to erotic attraction.

Jung, on the basis of clinical experience, tells us that this situation is the essential cause of neurosis. It derives from the fact that the conscious attitude (which, as we know, is itself unconscious until the attention of the conscious mind has been drawn to it by an outside agency) has built up a set of prejudices against certain categories of experiences and functions which are inherent in the mind. These it sincerely regards as inferior, unreliable, misleading, dangerous and repulsive: at best trivial and foolish and at worst definitely evil. Consequently it rejects this type of experience, flees from it, combats it and attempts to suppress it altogether. But its efforts are worse than useless, for the functions and modes of experience in question are as much an integral and inherent part of the mind as the digestive system is of the body: it is impossible to eliminate them, and the attempt to do so only arouses inner resistance: in a serviceable analogy which must not be taken as a scientific statement, we may say that this attitude 'provokes' the elements discriminated against to hostile activities. These may take the form of obsessions, compulsions and similar neurotic symptoms, or simply of devitalization, depression and general misery.

When this situation obtains Jung shows that the conscious mind is not only helpless, but that its attempts to deal with the condition can only aggravate it. Every conscious effort implies an intensification of the repressive conscious attitude and hence an added provocation of the repressed elements, which react with increased hostility. The action of the conscious mind is essentially discriminative, and therefore the more the problems in question are revolved in consciousness the more widely are the opposites sundered and the greater grows the tension between them: the possibility of reconciliation grows more remote than ever. In these circumstances a solution can only be provided by the unconscious mind, and Jung has found from practical experience that it does offer suggestions which, if accepted by the conscious mind and followed in practice, do in fact cure the condition. He has named this mode of activity of the mind 'the transcendental function' because it transcends the strife of the opposites and thereby brings about reconciliation and the restoration of the lost unity of the personality. Its working may be visualized as a direct intervention by that Centre of being which must of necessity remain intact for as long as individual life lasts. The schism between the opposing and sundered halves of the personality may go very deep, but if it is followed downwards far enough the point of union in the Centre must at last be reached, and from this point it is possible to take a truly impartial view of the conflict which does justice to both sides and from which it is therefore possible to formulate a solution which satisfies both of them.

The solution, however, is not produced by the conscious mind except in so far as it makes itself receptive to it by establishing contact with the Centre. The Centre lies, so to speak, in the innermost recesses of the unconscious: it cannot itself by any possibility become conscious since its essence, being absolute unity, precludes the differentiating function which is the essence of consciousness. It is That regarding which we can predicate nothing and which is therefore always inaccessible to our thought. This matter will be considered in closer detail later. The solution emanating from the Centre, therefore, always appears to consciousness as coming from outside itself: it may be in the form of an inner image appearing in a dream, vision or fantasy, or which simply 'writes itself into' a story or other work, or it may appear in the form of a projection on to an outer object which suddenly acquires significance of an unexpected kind. But, whatever the form of its appearance, it is certain to give the impression of something new and unfamiliar, or something demanding a fresh approach, hitherto untried;

for its very essence is change. In consequence it will evoke an initial mistrust: the conscious mind will at first be reluctant to accept it, but everything depends on its finding the insight and adaptability to overcome this reluctance. Frequently the new departure demanded of the conscious mind takes the form of the acceptance of something hitherto despised or feared, and of this we shall find numerous examples.

Maud Bodkin, in her *Archetypal Patterns in Poetry*, draws attention to the exposition of this situation in Coleridge's *Rime of the Ancient Mariner*. The Mariner, having committed the crime of shooting the albatross, is becalmed: he has, in fact, reached the condition of deadlock and is stuck fast. In this situation he is in danger of dying of thirst, as his shipmates in fact do: in other words he is cut off from the 'waters of life', an old and fundamental symbol of the life-giving powers of the unconscious with which we shall meet again. Attention has already been drawn to the condition of being parched and exhausted in connection with the opening scene of *No Orchids*, and the theme is the same as that of Demeter's denial of vegetation to the world during her daughter's absence; it occurs again in a slightly different form in Wagner's *Ring of the Nibelungs* which will be considered in a later volume. As the Mariner suffers the torments of thirst among his dead companions he sees loathsome creatures in the sea, from which he averts his eyes in disgust:

> The many men, so beautiful!
> And they all dead did lie:
> And a thousand thousand slimy things
> Lived on; and so did I.
> I looked upon the rotting sea,
> And drew my eyes away. . . .

Then the moon rises and he is overcome with a sudden love for the creatures of the sea:

> O happy living things! no tongue
> Their beauty might declare:
> A spring of love gushed in my heart
> And I blessed them unaware:
> Sure my kind saint took pity on me,
> And I blessed them unaware.

After this reconciliation he finds himself able to pray again, the shameful corpse of the albatross, which had been hung about his neck,[1] falls off into the sea and he sinks into a deep sleep. While he sleeps it rains and he is refreshed; then the wind springs up and the ship moves once more.

Maud Bodkin, in a detailed analysis of the emotional effect of the various passages, states that several readers of the poem have confirmed her own impression that the atmosphere of hopelessness and depression which pervades the account of the becalming is suddenly lifted by the line which tells of the moon's rising: it is in fact the appearance of the feminine principle in her pure and celestial form which breaks the deadlock. Coleridge, in his marginal notes, places this matter beyond doubt. These are the relevant items:

(The Mariner) despiseth the creatures of the calm,
And envieth that *they* should live and so many lie dead.
In his loneliness and fixedness (i.e. the deadlock) he yearneth towards the journeying Moon. . . .
By the light of the Moon he beholdeth God's creatures of the great calm.
Their beauty and their happiness.
He blesseth them in his heart.
The spell begins to break.
By the grace of the holy Mother, the ancient Mariner is refreshed with rain.

Here, evidently, we have a complete account of deadlock broken by the love and acceptance of something hitherto despised and rejected, and it is 'the holy Mother' who reveals to him the unsuspected virtue, grants him the power to love and to pray, and at last restores to him the waters of life and the ability to move onwards.

No Orchids is a very different story, and yet, as we have seen, it is the appearance of Miss Blandish which brings new life to

[1] This symbolism of carrying an animal or corpse, etc., is cited by Jung as representing the *transitus* or difficult passage between two stages of mental development. It is to be found also in the medieval romances, in which knights are frequently condemned to carry the head of a person shamefully slain, about their necks, until it falls off of its own accord. An instance is also to be found in the Arabian Nights, in the image of the Old Man of the Sea whom Sindbad cannot remove from his shoulders, until at last he falls off when drunk.

the situation and transforms the trivial tale of a jewel robbery into the fantastic epic of the rape of Persephone or Helen and the siege of the Paradise Club. Her relationship to 'the holy Mother' will shortly become apparent.

V The Reconciler

THE VIRGIN

I HAVE already spoken of the way in which Miss Blandish outgrows her prototype, the shallow and vicious girl of *Sanctuary*, and of the strange respect with which her creator handles her. It would, perhaps, be too much to say that something of the *numen* of divinity surrounds her, but there are moments, as when Rocco penetrates to the upper floors of the Paradise Club and finds her in her luxurious prison, which have at least fairy-tale magic about them. They are followed by such brutal scenes as Slim's coupling with her on the bed in Rocco's flat while the owner's freshly murdered corpse lies on the floor beside them, but that again leads to the unexpected moments of pathos in the epic flight and Slim's last stand. The writer has left the painstaking realism and the subtleties of *Sanctuary* far behind, and, in a way, has risen above them. Miss Blandish's sordid humiliations somehow acquire dignity as essential constituents of a high destiny.

Miss Blandish's superior status is expressed in a symbolical form: she is habitually to be found upstairs, and, as I have already mentioned, Slim is constantly to be found climbing stairs: in two cases in order to reach her. And we may note a second point: for so long as she remains upstairs peace reigns, but as soon as she is brought down the killing starts. It is worth giving a summary of these descents and their consequences. When she is first abducted she is taken by her captors to an upstairs room in their hide-out: they try to conceal her there, but Slim arrives and orders her down. Her descent is vividly visualized, and it is followed immediately by the killing of all three members of the first gang. The Grisson mob then remove her to their headquarters, where they hold her captive in an upstairs room, and for so long as she remains there, which is for a considerable time, virtually no killing takes place. On the contrary, Slim, instead of ordering her down to him, begins his career of stair-climbing, and eventually wins her love (even though it is only with the aid of his mother's drugs and rubber hose). Then she is removed to the new Grisson premises, the Paradise Club, the topography of which is described in some detail. First there is the steel barrier, guarded by Maisey, the blonde, and beyond it are the club rooms, the scene of the luxurious debauches which characterize the underworld and culminate in Anna's strip-tease act. 'Upstairs,' in the author's words, 'was nobody's business.' There, in a private room, Miss Blandish is held captive. Every night, in the small hours, Slim brings her down for a walk, and for so long as she is in his company all is well. But one night he is away and one of the minor gunmen deputizes for him: he is promptly murdered by Rocco, who removes Miss Blandish to his own flat, and there he, in turn, is murdered by Slim. Slim's ascents to Miss Blandish's room in both houses are described with a wealth of detail altogether disproportionate to the outer significance of the act, and in order to gain access to Rocco's flat he has recourse to the service lift, which is a peculiarly striking visualization of the theme of ascent; twice, moreover, we see him going upstairs in hotels, but nowhere is he seen coming down: there can be no doubt that the theme of ascent is intimately associated with his figure. From Rocco's flat he takes Miss Blandish down for the last time, and the final battle begins. They escape in a stolen car, and after various vicissitudes we find them trudging together up a mountain road. They rest together at the top, exhausted and woebegone, sitting side by side at the road's edge—an unexpectedly touching spectacle —and then they set off down the other side to their deaths. At last they are cornered in a barn, and Miss Blandish, upstairs again (this time in the loft) watches Slim below her as he exchanges shots with the police. Suddenly she retires from the trap-door, and it is then that Slim virtually commits suicide. He marches out into the open and is shot down.

The inference to be drawn from this pattern is that Miss

Blandish belongs on a higher plane than the rest of the characters. She descends to their level for a reason which we have yet to discover but which, we may already surmise, has something to do with Slim. This descent, however, implies the dragging down of the ideal to a lower level and it is followed by suffering and strife; worst of all, the majesty of John Blandish, the King, is dishonoured and his authority defied, and that entails the mobilization of all his powerful forces of repression. The better solution is for Slim to struggle upwards to Miss Blandish's level.

We have now to ask what it is about Miss Blandish that sets her in so high a place. In the first place, of course, she is the King's daughter, a princess and the heiress to all the power and riches of the upper world. But there is something else which is even more important, and it is revealed at her first appearance. Here is the description of her impact on the gangster Bailey on that occasion: 'She was unspoiled. That was what got him more than anything else. She wasn't like any of the girls he had run into before. She had everything they had and then a lot more.' What she had is shortly revealed by Eddie, reporting to headquarters: 'She'd a lot of red hair, a figure like a bra. advertisement and enough oomph to give a corpse wicked thoughts.' Except for the red hair it is simply the picture of a super-glamorous blonde; yet she had 'a lot more': she was unspoiled—in other words a virgin.

The Glamorous Blonde has never been a virgin: her first experience of love, whenever we meet her, always lies far behind her in a nebulous past. In Kafka's *Trial*, which we shall consider later, she appears on one occasion as a misshapen little girl of whom we are told that in spite of her youth she had already been debauched. As Athene was born fully armed the Blonde comes into the world already soiled. She is also sterile, for the element of motherhood has been carefully excluded from her composition. Miss Blandish, therefore, is something new: as a virgin she is potentially a mother, and it is a mother, to bring forth new life, that the situation requires. With her appearance the vicious circle of endlessly repeated sterile matings with the incomplete Blonde has been broken. Miss Blandish is complete because she has not yet been touched, and now she is in search of a lover.

THE SPLENDID TALE OF PRINCE DIAMOND

We have noted that bloodshed ensues whenever Miss Blandish comes downstairs, and now we may note another form in which this fatality which attends her is revealed, and that is that every man who comes into contact with her is killed. To begin with it is the playboy who was her escort on the occasion of her first abduction, then her three captors, then the gunman who deputizes for Slim as her escort for her nightly exercise, and who is killed by Rocco, and finally Rocco himself. Only Slim is exempt until the very end, and then it is not until Miss Blandish at her trap-door withdraws from him that he is killed. By then, as we shall see shortly, he had already accomplished his destiny: Miss Blandish's withdrawal, otherwise unmotivated, may be taken as confirmation of the fact. Slim, evidently, is her fore-ordained lover, and for him she is reserved: every other man who seeks to take possession of her is destroyed.

The theme of the princess whose unsuccessful suitors lose their heads is a familiar one in the legendaries of all peoples. We may now examine one such tale as a reassurance that we have not gone astray in our exposition of the universal elements in *No Orchids*. It is taken, once again, from the Arabian Nights, and is called *The Splendid Tale of Prince Diamond*.

The story is presented in that vein of ribald bawdiness which is typical of so many in this collection, but the elements of the original legend are clearly discernible. It relates how Prince Diamond hears that the hand of a beautiful princess is offered to the royal suitor who can answer a riddle which she has propounded. Although the penalty for failure is decapitation, and innumerable suitors have already suffered it, he resolves to try his fortune, and he refuses the offer of his father the king to send him with an army with which to take the princess by force. Here, already, we have a parallel with *No Orchids*, for we have seen that the attempt to win the Treasure with the aid of the forces of constituted authority is useless: she, and the kingdom which goes with her, can only be secured with her consent, won by the merits of her lover alone.

Diamond immediately penetrates the Barrier, in the form of the wall round the palace garden, by means of swimming under it through a conduit—a striking image of the passage 'downwards' into the waters of the unconscious; inside he meets the princess and her girls, and both she and her favourite attendant fall in love with him. The latter offers herself in marriage, which he promises, but only after he has successfully answered the riddle; in return she informs him that a negro is concealed beneath the princess's bed, that it is he who has propounded the riddle, and that its answer is to be learnt only in his remote homeland.

Diamond therefore sets out for this distant kingdom, and on the way penetrates into no less than three successive walled gardens, each inhabited by a princess of ravishing beauty who offers herself to him; in each case he promises marriage, but only after he shall have succeeded in his quest. One of them, a Circe figure, transforms him into a stag, and he has difficulty in escaping from her garden; his attempts to do so by jumping over the wall are fruitless, for he always finds himself inside again, and it is not until he discovers the door through it that he is successful and is restored to human form. This theme of the difficulty of returning from the Other Side will concern us later. In the course of the quest Diamond slays numerous negroes.

At last he successfully discovers the answer to the riddle, which concerns the estrangement of a king and his queen; retracing his steps he marries each of the girls as he passes, and on reaching the palace of the original princess he marries first her favourite and then the princess herself, although she is discredited by the discovery of the negro under her bed. The latter, needless to say, is slain by Diamond.

It is probable that the numerous marriages have been added, in a late recension, for the sake of the opportunity they offer for salacious descriptions of their consummations; the essential is that Diamond refuses all the advances of the Blonde in her various embodiments until he has completed his quest.

The parallels with the theme of *No Orchids* are obvious: apart from the quest itself and the penalty for failure we have the repeated penetrations of the Barrier and the invariable discovery of the Amorous Blonde behind it, the necessity of abjuring dalliance with her until the whole quest has been completed, and the theme of the estrangement between king and queen which lies at the back of the whole complex. A characteristic of the underlying Persephone situation is to be found in the princess's bondage to the dark figure under her bed: the legend as a whole, however, is inferior to the others which we have discussed in that no attempt is made to deal seriously with the implications of this awkward element, which is simply brushed aside in the conventional happy ending. It is in points such as this that we are justified in discriminating between superior and inferior versions of a mythical theme in the matter of their faithfulness to the matter of symbolical truth. Judged from this point of view *No Orchids* must be rated high, whatever its defects from the aesthetic or moral viewpoints may be, for its author never defers to the conventions or to sentimentality by distorting the situations which his intuition presents. We cannot say the same for some among even the greatest masters of literature: in our study of Dickens, for instance, we shall find constant evasions and distortions of unpalatable truths; we shall see, moreover, how the attitude of mind which led to such inner untruthfulness revenged itself in the disfigurement of his personal life.

The story of Prince Diamond, therefore, although it is no more than a superficial and perfunctory tacking together of symbolical elements into a salacious romance, is of value as showing how, in an environment as remote from that of *No Orchids* as the Islamic culture of the middle ages, the identical symbolical elements have coalesced into the theme of the Quest.

THE DYNASTIC UNION

The male is not without the female, and conversely the female is not without the male: the very existence of Miss Blandish presupposes that of her lover, and we have already seen how he was, as it were, drawn up out of the darkness of nonentity by her appearance. The essence of Miss Blandish, however, is that she is singled out as one partner in a very special and fateful union. The casual copulations of the Blonde have always been a superabundant feature of life on the Other Side, but they are unsatisfactory because they are both unworthy and sterile: now a longing is making itself felt for something higher. The new union must be fruitful, which means that it must be complete and must therefore embrace those elements which are lacking in the nature of the Blonde, and these are symbolized in the first place by the high origin and the purity of Miss Blandish, the virgin princess. But if the fruit of this union is to fulfil the great demands which are made of it, which are nothing less than the resolution of the conflict which is devastating the inner world, the princess's partner must be no less carefully selected than the princess herself. The project contemplated is no less than the reconciliation of the irreconcilables, and in order to bring it about the partners in the union must each embody and personify one of the contending factions. That is the reason why Miss Blandish's lover can be nobody else than Slim, for if she is a princess, the heiress to the upper world, he is no less a prince and the heir to the lower: only through the union of these two can a total and complete reconciliation be effected. The theme is the old one of the Dynastic Union, once again a familiar pattern in fairy tales, and one which forms the basis of *Romeo and Juliet.*

But Montague and Capulet, in conformity with most of the fairy-tale versions of the contending factions, are seen simply as antagonists in a traditional feud: there is no disparity between them in status or worthiness of aim, and the conflict between them has no material basis. In order to reconcile them it is only necessary to transform their traditional hatred into love, and thereby to show them that they have no real grounds for contention: they have only to forget old scores in order to realize that it will be more beneficial to both of them to live in amity and concord.

This problem is difficult enough, but it is overcome by a device of the psyche with which we shall meet again: it consists of the evolution of what might be described as a special organ of attractiveness by the offending or repressed principle, which is thereby presented to its opponent in a beguiling and desirable form which disarms him and causes him to seek union with it instead of attacking it. This, in the last resort, is what the Blonde herself is: she represents the bait held out by the spurned and neglected Other Side, or collective unconscious, in order to persuade the self-obsessed personal mind to approach it in a conciliatory spirit. This device, however, is not proof against the selective powers of the conscious mind, which may succeed in nibbling off the bait without swallowing the hook:

137

it concentrates on those aspects of the Blonde which are compatible with its purposes and ignores the rest, which are relegated to the unconscious where they build up into the threatening figure of Ma.

In order to free itself from the unsatisfactory situation which ensues it is necessary for the personal mind to undertake the quest of the Blonde's full nature, or in other words to make a determined effort to unearth the roots of the conflict. Passing through the Barrier and ignoring the Blonde in her familiar incomplete aspect it must penetrate into the interior of the Other Side, where it discovers the contending factions. This is already an advance, for it is now apparent that the trouble lies in the strife of these equally matched opponents: neither will ever succeed in permanently suppressing the other, so the only solution lies in reconciling them. The means to this end also lie to hand, for now the Anima appears in the fuller and higher form of the virgin princess, heiress to one of the kingdoms. Reconciliation can therefore be achieved by her union in love with the prince, heir to the opposing party, who is her fore-ordained lover and who must necessarily exist by virtue of her existence. The venture is a difficult one, for it is essential that none but the right lover shall take her. He must, therefore, first be found and identified, and then prove himself worthy of her, and it is for this reason that such difficult conditions are attached to the suit and that the penalty for failure can be nothing less than elimination.

If the personal mind accepts this situation all is well. The conflict is seen as a futility which it is only necessary to halt in order that it should disappear, and it is taken for granted that the prince should be in every way worthy of the princess: handsome, brave, highly born, virtuous and wise. Union in an ideal love then follows as of necessity. But if the personal mind takes sides in the conflict the problem remains unsolved. The opposing factions, in this case, no longer appear as of equal status and worth, and one or other of the lovers is consequently seen as inferior to the other. Their love is no longer an ideal union hindered only by the prejudices of the older generation: it becomes something dangerous and wrong, involving the risk of the victory of the inferior faction. Nevertheless it has to take place because it is dictated by forces in the collective mind which the personal mind is powerless to circumvent: it runs its course, therefore, in face of the horror and misgivings of the latter.

It is clear that this is what has taken place in *Sanctuary*, and the theme was taken over in *No Orchids*. The prejudices of the conscious attitude have proved too strong: they have caused the personal mind to side with the Father, whose regime, although recognized as oppressive, harsh and intolerant, is still seen as essentially right and superior. There is nothing at all to be said for the other side, which appears solely vicious and evil: no compromise with it can possibly be considered. The longed-for reconciliation, therefore, does not appear in the form of a happy union between two idealized lovers, but as the sordid humiliation of the princess by a loathsome ravisher. No good could possibly come of such a union, which is accordingly abandoned in despair. Yet, if her creator could only have brought himself to see it, Miss Blandish, in her short sojourn in the underworld, gives considerable proof of her powers of ennoblement and reconciliation. She succeeds in inspiring pity and admiration in the hearts of several of its inhabitants, and in the heart of Slim she inspires love. Only Ma remains implacable in her hatred, and it is of course her figure, in its reciprocity with that of Blandish, which is the cause of the failure of the venture.

The root of the trouble is that the figure of the Father is still too strong. In this story he represents constituted authority, or authority imposed from without and accepted simply because it has always obtained, and it is not until that force has been overthrown that the mind is free to take a truly impartial view of the conflicting factions and thus to allow the lovers to fulfil their destiny of reconciliation without interference. To accept an ethical system, or any system of values, uncritically and without question is to deliver oneself into the power of John Blandish, and that implies the adoption of a prejudiced and intolerant attitude towards Ma and her faction. If authority is thus vested in any one-sided system which fails to take due account of inherent tendencies in the mind of a nature which happens to be uncongenial to it, then the authority principle (the Great Adult) will be split into light and dark halves and will manifest itself through both. The dark half will enforce its inherently superordinated or dominant nature by compelling the subject against his will to adopt types of behaviour which are directly opposed to the dictates of the light half, and he will fall into the unpleasant and dangerous situation of being in conflict with himself. The further implications of this complex matter must be left until later; we may anticipate here, however, by stating that emancipation from this condition of servitude is symbolized by the weakening of the authority and finally the death of the father and mother figures. We shall meet with examples of this in works to be considered later; in *Sanctuary* and *No Orchids*, however, we find both figures still in their prime.

THE PRINCIPLE OF EQUAL AND OPPOSITE REACTIONS

The principle of the Opposites, which shows the manifold nature of the phenomenal world as deriving from the division of an ultimate unitary essence (τὸ ἄπειρον, the Indeterminate or Infinite) into contrasting pairs or opposites was first introduced into Greek philosophy by Anaximander around 600 B.C. although its appearance in oriental thought is probably earlier. Such images are Archetypal: they symbolize fundamental mental patterns and will be found reappearing in various forms and contexts throughout the history of thought. A striking example of such a 'reincarnation' of an idea is to be found in the modern scientific principle of equal and opposite reactions. When we fire a rifle the bullet is projected in one direction with a certain momentum, and in consequence the rifle recoils with an equal momentum in the opposite direction; when we concentrate an electrical charge in one plate of a condenser an equal and opposite charge is automatically induced in the opposite plate. Precisely the same law applies to mental life: whenever we make a conscious effort in one direction a precisely equal reaction is produced in the unconscious in the opposite direction. The harder we try to be good the more insistently does the devil tempt us; the more we force ourselves to be gay the gloomier grows the background of our thoughts; if we compel ourselves to be hard-headed and tough in the world, we develop an indulgent sentimentality in our private lives. The comedian who is so melancholy at home, or the unscrupulous financier whose mistress or daughter can twist him round her finger are well-known figures; so also is the high-minded philanthropist with the unedifying private life. If our conscious attitude is too one-sidedly based on principles of Christian love and forbearance we shall provoke an unconscious reaction in the form of unadmitted impulses of hatred and vindictiveness and shall begin to persecute and oppress, or at best to call down the wrath of Heaven on the heads of those of whom we disapprove.

This melancholy frustration of our best intentions is not only occasioned by excessive devotion to principles consciously chosen; it can also be brought about by the intolerance of that attitude of consciousness of which we are not conscious because it is itself the censor and selective filter which controls the contents of the conscious mind. The functioning of this selective mechanism constitutes in itself an act of dichotomy, a violation of the primal indeterminate unity which calls forth its equal and opposite reaction. An explanation of the peculiar savagery of Ma and her minions may be sought in this process: they represent the equal and opposite reaction to an excessively civilized outlook, based on the principles of reasonable restraint, forbearance and the absolute and unconditional rejection of violence in all its forms. Such an outlook, while it may or may not be characteristic of this author's personal attitude, is evidently typical of our international life, with the notorious contradiction which it displays between its professed aims of pacific collaboration and its overmastering proclivity towards quarrelsomeness, persecution and violence. *No Orchids*, in its sure intuitive correspondence with Archetypal situations, is a portrayal of the mind of our times; its author, in grappling with his personal problems, whatever they may have been, has risen above them and presented us with a picture and a diagnosis of the ills of our whole civilization. It tells us that our conscious aims have reached a state of inflation which has cut them adrift from the roots of our humanity, and that the resistances which we have thereby provoked are ineluctably undermining and frustrating our misdirected efforts towards the conquest of the material universe and the regimentation of the soul.

We shall be more closely concerned with this matter in later chapters; for the present we may note that violence begets violence and the orderly and disciplined world of John Blandish is compelled to defend the position which it has usurped, by the employment of henchmen like Fenner and the police, whose methods are hardly superior to those of their opponents. It is immaterial 'who started it': all that matters is that hatred reigns and has given rise to a conflict which in its bitterness descends to the employment of progressively ever more ferocious methods.

I do not speak of outer-world movements, of the battle between the Haves and the Have-Nots, the Capitalists and the Workers or between any opposing movements or political systems. It is immaterial, as we shall see later, on whom the image of the Adversary is projected. Humanity can be, and has been, divided and brought to bitter strife on the basis of distinctions between religious confessions, racial cultures, and national policies, no less than on that between political and economic ideologies. All that is required in order to set men at one another's throats and degrade them to a level lower than that of simple, unadorned barbarism is that the natural impulses towards hatred and fear should be canalized, concentrated and projected on to an arbitrarily chosen figure, be it that of international Jewry, Communism, the coloured races or religious dissidents. War and persecution are psychological phenomena and we have to seek their roots in the study of the mind, not in that of material conditions. If another man is richer and more privileged than I am I may accept the relative position as being justified, or I may set out to equalize it by methods which we both accept as permissible; in either case I may legitimately envy and dislike him, but that is quite a different matter from giving rein to a savage hatred which impels me not only to hang him from a lamp-post, but to cut the throats of his wife and children as well. The difference is obviously purely a psychological one.

THE REDEMPTION OF SLIM

In no character is the functioning of the principle of equal and opposite reactions more evident than in that of Slim. Fundamentally, as we have seen, he fills the role of Prince Charming, the princess's fore-ordained lover, yet he is portrayed as a loathsome monster of ferocity and unnatural viciousness. That, in the first place, is because he is contaminated by his underworld origins; but in his case there is an additional factor, and that is the reaction which he represents against the element of purity imposed on the Blonde in order to create the figure of Miss Blandish. The traditional fairy-tale prince and princess—Florizel and Perdita, for instance—are quite simply and naturally virginal and chaste because they are no more than the embodiments of the organs which their respective factions have, so to speak, developed for the purpose of reunification in love: they are the Lovers and nothing more. But into the figure of Miss Blandish there enters an additional element which complicates the situation: she had all that the other girls had *but* she had a lot more, for she was unspoiled. She is developed out of the impure figure of the Blonde, and her purity is therefore something positive, something arbitrarily imposed. Just as the selective concentration of erotic charms in the figure of the Blonde herself produced its equal and opposite reaction in the repellent characteristics of Ma, so does the selective imposition of purity on to the figure of Miss Blandish produce its equal and opposite reaction in the viciousness of Slim, who is unequivocally portrayed as a sadistic pervert.

This hypothesis is substantiated by the fact that the Blonde, in her original unimproved form, also has a partner, but he is far less repellent than Slim. This is Eddie, the gay philanderer of the Grisson mob. He never commits any atrocities—he does not even kill anybody in the course of the story—and for a gangster he is really quite an acceptable person. I think that he represents the Blonde's partner in the process of her rehabilitation, and this is probably why he is the only gangster to survive the story. He suffers for his membership of the underworld by undergoing a severe third-degree treatment at the hands of the police, but he is allowed to survive because the process of the Blonde's rehabilitation is not yet complete. The major venture, Miss Blandish's attempt at a total reconciliation, failed, and she was lost as Eurydice was lost; but the more modest enterprise of the Blonde's rehabilitation has shown some solid gains by the time the story reaches its tragic end.

The psychological process whereby the underworld lover has

to take upon himself the vices corresponding to Miss Blandish's virtues had already taken place in the creation of Faulkner's Pop-Eye who, we know, evidently served as the inspiration for Slim. It is therefore interesting to note in what respects Slim's picture and development differ from those of his prototype.

Pop-Eye was irremediably impotent, yet his impotence did not prevent his debauching and degrading, by indirect means, the unfortunate girl who had aroused his lust. The meaning of the parable is evident: it is that the image of the pure princess can be besmirched and degraded by impure sexual practices and fantasies. Such sexuality remains impotent, even if it finds expression in normal sexual activity, for it is incomplete, lacking the true essence of virility, which is to vitalize and fructify. It is no more than what James Joyce, in *Portrait of the Artist as a Young Man*, describes as 'cold lust'.

Slim begins by following his model faithfully: he too is a sadistic killer, and whereas Pop-Eye is armed with a pistol he, more ferocious, has a knife. His impotence, however, is not irremediable, his reason for never having had anything to do with girls being only that 'he was afraid they might laugh at him'. Miss Blandish, by inspiring his passions, gave him not only his physical virility but his manhood also, for it was in defence of her that he first dared to defy his terrible mother. He, moreover, indubitably inspired an answering passion in her.

Chase, true to his model, depicts this love in a revolting form, yet he cannot prevent elements of devotion and protectiveness from slipping in. Not only does Slim protect Miss Blandish from his mother, but in the end, when destiny is closing in on him, he does not seek to save his own skin in solitary flight: he takes Miss Blandish with him. That makes death inevitable, but he will not give her up.

Miss Blandish's task in the underworld thus becomes clear: in order to achieve the reconciliation which is the main purpose of her mission she has first to redeem Slim, her fore-ordained princely lover, who has been degraded by his environment and brutalized by the reaction from the very virtues which she herself has assumed. Here we find another familiar fairy-tale theme: that of Beauty and the Beast. It is to be found in a number of forms in the Germanic folk-tales, in which the lover appears in a variety of ignoble shapes, such as that of a frog, from which he is released by the love and devotion of the princess; in order to demonstrate the universal nature of the theme it is worth mentioning that it is common also in the Arabian Nights, in which we find the enchanted lover in the forms of dog, ape and even he-goat. In one of them, which reveals similarities to the Lohengrin myth, to be discussed later, he is even confined in an underground cavern into which the princess must descend in search of him.

THE RIVAL

In dealing with the images in which the Archetypes express themselves in consciousness we have to beware above all of the besetting danger of facile identifications. The inner world is quite unlike the outer in that it is not inhabited by identities strictly circumscribed and separated from their environment and from other identities by a physical envelope, as appears to be the case in the outer world. I say 'appears' advisedly, for the more closely we study the outer world the less definite and strictly circumscribed do we find these identities to be: the human body, for instance, is made up of individual cells, each of which has its independent existence and life-history, and some of which, such as the phagocytes, behave almost autonomously. Where, then, does the identity lie? Are the cells separate identities or merely parts of the whole? And what becomes of the undoubted identity of a drop of water when it falls into the sea? The question of identity, with which we shall be concerned more closely in later chapters, is a difficult one, even in the material world; in the world of the mind it is infinitely more complex. Having identified a mental tendency, therefore, and discovered its identity with some typical fantasy-figure, we must be cautious about assuming without further consideration that the latter derives solely and exclusively from the former, for the image may well be a composite one in which two or more heterogeneous elements are confused and combined. Striking examples of such figures are those of the father and mother which we have identified in John Blandish and Ma Grisson, the composite nature of which has already been discussed. Another case is to be recognized in Slim. We have already identified the Prince or Lover element in his composition and noted how it tends to assert itself, forcing its way through the repellent exterior derived from another source, so that Slim, under the beneficent influence of Miss Blandish, begins to acquire the rudiments of the nature of the Lover. The repellent exterior we have derived from the equal and opposite reaction to the purity imposed on the Blonde in order to form Miss Blandish, and to the rectitude and propriety of the upper-world system. There remains, however, one element, symbolized by his knife, his sadism and the general feral quality of his nature, which has still to be accounted for. Its explanation, I believe, is to be found in another Archetypal figure, namely that of the Armed Rival.

In discussing the mating pattern we identified one element to which we have devoted no further attention: that is the masculine impulsion to drive away rivals. There can be no question whatever that this element exists in the human species, for it is universally recognized that men become pugnacious and cantankerous when their sexual interest is aroused. Since the same tendency exists in animals it may be taken as a true instinct: in other words man possesses a special neuro-sensory mechanism for recognizing members of his own sex exactly as he has one for recognizing his mate. Normally this image is only activated in conjunction with other elements of the mating pattern of which it forms an integral part: in other words it is associated with the image of the mate. Obviously in a gregarious species it would be disastrous if all males invariably attacked one another on sight: the predominant impulse in normal circumstances must be one of trust, friendliness and attraction in order to hold the herd together. It may therefore safely be assumed that the image of the male's own sex receives its hostile and menacing colouration only when that of the opposite sex as such has been activated. The two form a pair, closely associated and imbued with opposite emotional tones.

Now we have seen that the image of the mate may be activated and appear in consciousness in the absence of the appropriate external stimulus, and in the circumstances we are justified in expecting that when this happens her appearance might be followed by that of the subject's own sex in the guise of a hostile and menacing rival. This we find in fact to be the case. The figure in question I have called the Armed Rival, for he is almost invariably equipped with some weapon, and the hero is compelled to do battle with him. The Rival's weapon plays a double symbolical role: in the first place it represents his hostility and dangerousness, and in the second it symbolizes his sexuality. 'Weapon' is a familiar colloquialism for the penis in more than one language, and it has been demonstrated that weapons, and particularly weapons which shoot, such as the pistol and the bow, frequently represent the physical element of virility in dreams. The Rival, in fact, is man in his sexual aspect, not simply man as a fellow-member of the species.

We shall meet the Armed Rival in a number of exemplars as this study progresses, and I shall therefore postpone a more detailed consideration of his attributes and trends of development; for the present one classical example may be quoted: he is Gretchen's soldier brother Valentin, with whom Faust is compelled to fight a duel. The relationship of brother to the mate image which, beside the more obvious one of wronged husband, the Rival habitually favours, will also be explained in its place. Another very striking example is worth quoting at this point: it occurs in a film, *Les Belles de Nuit*, directed by René Clair, which appeared in the early 1950's. The plot is briefly as follows.

A poor young teacher of music has a series of dreams in which he is involved, in turn, in fantastic romances with all the pretty women with whom his profession and his daily life bring him into contact. There is a theme-song to the words 'I shall be thine, but only at night'. But in each adventure his love-making is interrupted by the Armed Rival: husbands, fathers, brothers, equipped with every kind of weapon, make their appearance, and the dreams culminate in a nightmare flight from a crowd of pursuers threatening him with pistols, clubs, rapiers, muskets and even a gigantic pair of scissors. These last, incidentally, are first produced when he is trapped in an oriental harem, and are introduced with the sinister intimation that the outraged brothers of the lady intend to keep a souvenir of the dreamer's visit. When he attempts to defend himself with a sword the great scissors snap it off at the hilt, which is an evident allusion to the symbolic penalty for trifling with the Blonde.

It is worth noting that the Rival has his counterpart in the feminine psychology, but needless to say she is not armed. She may appear as a seductress, but more commonly she is portrayed as an insensitive, practical, managing type of woman who ensnares the heroine's true love into matrimony. She 'makes him a good wife' from the worldly point of view but is seen as destroying his soul; the latter, needless to say, is truly understood by the heroine alone. Examples are to be found in the Rebecca in Daphne du Maurier's novel of that name, and the wife in Margaret Kennedy's *The Constant Nymph*. This element in the mating pattern, however, has almost certainly less force at the instinctual level in woman than in man; the feminine Rival, therefore, plays no such important role as her masculine counterpart.

Returning to the male pattern it is easy to see that this particular element may be unacceptable to the typical civilized conscious attitude, which deprecates all forms of violence and enjoins courtesy and brotherly love in all circumstances. The highly civilized man, although he may welcome and approve of the impulse which he discerns in himself to seek and win a mate, is apt to look with distaste on the concomitant desire to commit physical violence on other males, for which purpose he may, in any case, be ill suited by temperament, physical endowment and training. If he is of a retiring and self-conscious disposition he may even deprecate any tendencies which he discerns in himself to clear the field of rivals by means of an assertive and masterful demeanour; he considers such behaviour in bad taste, and in any case, being imperfectly identified with it by reason of the critical attitude of his conscious mind, which insists on pointing out to him that it is not objectively justified, he lacks the confidence to carry it off. If he attempts to do so he is apt to collapse in a humiliating manner and becomes obsessed, like Slim, with the fear that girls will laugh at him.

He therefore finds the aggressive side of the mating pattern unwelcome and attempts to suppress and ignore it. He cannot, however, get rid of it because it is rooted in an innate mental pattern, and the attempt to ban it from consciousness merely results in its building up in the unconscious, where it takes the form of archaic urges towards the most primitive forms of violence. The distinction between subject and object and that between self and not-self is by no means clear in the unconscious, and impulses which ought properly to be realized by the action of the subject may very easily be interpreted, in fantasy, as influences acting on him from an external source, as, indeed, in a sense, they really are, since his instinctual disposition is external to his conscious mind. Hence the figure of the Armed Rival represents not only the danger inherent in the mating pattern of possible attacks from outer, objective, rivals, but also the danger which the subject feels as emanating from an uncongenial aspect of his own sexuality. This may manifest itself in the form of alarming and distasteful archaic representations of violence which are none the less filled with an unholy fascination.

This image is clearly one of the principal ingredients in the figure of Slim. In the conventional love-story, such as that which we have seen in the tale of Prince Diamond, and of which we shall meet with further examples later, the Rival appears as an evil and inferior opponent whom the Lover must overcome, but in Slim the two roles are merged and combined. In the former case the union of the lovers is regarded as an ideal possibility which can take place in all chastity and purity once the impediments represented by undesirable archaic elements have been removed: the conflict with these elements is indeed seen as an integral and indispensable part of the pattern. The difference between this view and that found in *Sanctuary* and *No Orchids* can be attributed to a fact to which attention has already been drawn, namely that the conscious mind of the narrator has taken sides with one of the opposing factions, which it sees as superior to the other. This leads to the stigmatization of one of the pair of lovers as inferior and unworthy, and hence to the denial of the possibility of an ideal union. What is far worse, it leads to conscious interference with the natural process of reunification which, if left to itself, would follow its own proper course.

Slim, therefore, like Ma, is a composite figure made up of heterogeneous elements. The appearance of such a figure in consciousness implies that mental contents of a disparate nature have been left to languish too long in the unconscious and are in need of raising to the conscious level where their ingredients can be analysed and separated. Until this is done it is impossible to adopt the correct attitude towards any aspect of life in which the complex in question is concerned, because the mixed projections which it engenders provoke incompatible and often mutually contradictory reactions. The process of mental development, therefore, and the progressive adaptation to a growing field of conscious experience which it implies, may be seen in terms of a continual raising of such composite figures to consciousness and of their analysis into their separate constituents. Such an analysis, of course, does not consist of a merely intellectual process but of an actual sorting out of the impulses, feelings, etc. in question in terms of life; this process constitutes one of the principal themes of this study.

THE ANIMA

In Miss Blandish herself we have a representation of an Archetypal figure which Jung has identified and named Anima. The Latin word, of course, originally meant 'breath', hence 'life', and finally acquired the meaning of the 'animating' or life-giving principle, a concept which is commonly called 'soul'. But ancient philosophy generally regarded man's constitution as threefold, consisting of spirit, soul and body. The body it recognized as being like in nature to the inanimate substance, the 'earth', 'dust' or 'clay' into which it decomposes when it loses the anima or breath of life. The best known formulation of this doctrine is the passage from the second version of the Creation myth in Genesis quoted above, which, in the Vulgate, reads as follows :

Formavit igitur Dominus Deus hominem de limo terrae, et inspiravit in faciem ejus spiraculum vitae, et factus est homo in animam viventem.

God takes the clay, breathes life into it, and man 'becomes a living soul' (anima). From this passage it is apparent that the soul, which man actually 'is', results from the impregnation of the lifeless clay by the life-giving breath of God; the 'breath' here is not the anima but something else: it is the impersonal, divine essence commonly called 'spirit', a word which is of course also derived from another name for 'breath'. Spirit was thought of as an essence, fire or energy without form, variously conceived, but never regarded as personal, which it could not be because of its formlessness and universality. Both the two elements which went to the making of man, therefore, were impersonal: universal earth and universal spirit; between these two the soul was a connective medium which, on the one hand, held or contained the formless universality of spirit, thereby enabling it to manifest itself in a particular form, and on the other 'animated' lifeless matter, transforming it into a living, individual body. Soul was therefore at the same time personal, when seen as the particular soul inhabiting a particular body, and universal, when seen as the world-soul or vessel of the spirit.

It is only in more recent times that the dichotomy between spirit, or 'mind', and 'matter' in the modern scientific sense, has been developed. Until about two centuries ago no precise dividing line between the two was recognized, the difference being regarded rather as one of degree. Spirit and soul were regarded as 'substances' which differed from what we now call matter only in the degree in which they possessed an attribute described as 'subtlety'. According to the modern way of looking at things, on the other hand, everything is either matter or not-matter; spirit and soul, therefore, fall together into one group, standing in contrast to its opposite, which includes the body as matter. The Church almost seems to have anticipated this development, for it has long ago reduced the ingredients of human nature to two: soul and body. Spirit has apparently disappeared as a separate constituent, being seen as a Divine Substance external to man, and in which he has no part. The various theological dogmas concerned represent a complicated subject on which I am not qualified to speak, but the ordinary current beliefs in this matter are certainly that man consists of an immortal soul inhabiting a material body, and that there is no third element in his composition. But such beliefs as that of the threefold nature of man are precisely of the type to which reference has already been made as 'psychological truths': they have been held for a long time and by many people and it is certain that they are no mere idle speculations, but represent some inner-world reality. In confirmation of this it may be mentioned that Berdyaev,[1] himself a mystical Christian, comments on the regrettable fact that the concept of a spiritual ingredient in human nature has disappeared,

[1] N. Berdyaev: *Freedom and the Spirit.*

leaving us with the confused notion of a soul which embraces the whole non-material nature of man. There exists, in short, a definite need for a fresh analysis of man's mental or inner nature which takes account of the fact, long recognized, that it contains two separate and contrasting elements, once distinguished as 'spirit' and 'soul'.

Jung has made a beginning in this formidable task by his identification of the Archetypal figure of the Anima. This figure, like most of his discoveries, was not the outcome of theoretical speculation *in vacuo*, but of the empirical observation of his material, consisting of the fantasy-products of his patients, which he found confirmed in legends and works of poetry and fiction. The Anima has virtually no connection with the current conception of 'soul' described above: she is a psychological fact, an image in feminine form which he has identified in the masculine psyche and which does actually constitute a kind of mediating link between the two worlds of the personal mind and of the universal Archetypes: this, evidently, is why we have found her guarding, and personifying, the door through the Barrier. He has named her the Anima for this reason, for she is both the personal soul and the world-soul, and thus pre-eminently the bridge over which we may pass into the Other Side.

The Greek word psyche, which means literally 'butterfly' and has come to mean something similar to soul (providing, of course, the root of such words as psychosis and psychology) he uses in a sense almost exactly equivalent to the English word 'mind', for which there is no exact equivalent in German: it embraces the whole mental, spiritual and 'psychic' nature of man (for English, in turn, has no equivalent for the German *seelisch*, the adjectival form of *Seele*, the soul) both conscious and unconscious; it includes the typical contents and patterns of the mind and has a dynamic as well as a static aspect. The Psyche, as the word is used by Jung, is a world in itself and corresponds approximately (but only approximately) to what I have described as the inner world. The Anima is one of the Archetypal contents of the Psyche, and as such a living, objective reality with her own characteristic tendencies, which become manifest not only in the images of fantasy but in actual human behaviour.

Jung, taking the existence of the Anima as an empirically established fact, explains it as deriving from three sources: (*a*) the actual relationships of the individual with women in his personal life; (*b*) the natural 'feminine' characteristics in every man, repressed and confined to the unconscious as a result of his conscious and unconscious striving to shape his character and behaviour in accordance with a 'manly' ideal; and (*c*) as a hypothetical mental heritage from man's experience of woman in all her roles and aspects in the course of past generations.[1]

It will have become apparent from the foregoing that I would add to these sources the innate mate-image determined by the special neuro-sensory mechanism of the instinctive mating pattern. As to the element described in (*c*) above, I regard it as an accretion, embodied in the collective unconscious, in which all individual minds are contained and in which they participate at their more primitive levels, not ordinarily accessible to personal consciousness. It is at this level that such images as those of the Queen or Mother are to be found. We have, moreover, already seen that variants of this image may be of a composite nature, and here we come up against one of those problems adumbrated in the introduction to this work: what, exactly, are we to define as the identity in question? Ma Grisson, Miss Blandish and the Blonde are all variants of a figure which falls under Jung's comprehensive definition of the Anima, yet we have already established the fact that each of these contains ingredients which are absent in the others. We have, moreover, noted that each of them is liable to transform herself suddenly into one of the others, and additional evidence of the same phenomenon will shortly appear. We are therefore faced with the problem of deciding whether to place the emphasis on the common elements, thereby building up the picture of a single underlying identity, 'Anima', which exhibits different attributes when exercising different functions and when seen from different viewpoints, or, alternatively, emphasizing the diversity of elements and defining 'Anima' as no more than the form resulting from a particular combination of these elements. As I stated in the Introduction the material

[1] C. G. Jung: *Beziehungen zw. d. Ich u. d. Unbewussten*; English transl. in Vol. 7 of Collected Works.

available and the present development of the terminology and definitions of the science of the inner world are not as yet adequate to permit of a final decision being reached in this matter; for the time being we must accept a considerable degree of uncertainty and imprecision. We shall be concerned with this important figure, or figures, at considerable length in later volumes, and perhaps it may be possible, after considering the additional material which will be adduced, to reach some more precise definition; the reader, however, is warned that the study of the Anima, as of all the inner-world figures, will inevitably reveal much that is irrational and contradictory. This difficulty is inherent in the task of raising the contents of the unconscious, a region of the mind in which thought is still at what Lévy-Bruhl[1] describes as the 'pre-logical' stage, to the light of consciousness.

It is worth mentioning at this point that according to the theory there should exist a corresponding male figure in the feminine Psyche, and this is found to be true in fact. Jung has called him the Animus, and in our study of *Wuthering Heights*[2] we shall find him dominating the scene.

THE FAILURE OF THE VENTURE

The basic theme of *No Orchids* is the attempt to achieve the reconciliation of the irreconcilables by means of the age-old device of the Dynastic Union. For this purpose the Anima who, as the soul, is of divine origin (Persephone is represented by most mythographers as the daughter of Zeus) is compelled to descend into the underworld in order to unite with, and if necessary to redeem, its ruler or heir. In the face of all opposition the union takes place, but only at the cost of unleashing a titanic conflict in which most of the contestants, and the lovers themselves, are annihilated. In this respect the story resembles that of the rape of Helen and the Trojan War.

I have suggested that the cause of this failure lies in conscious interference, in that the conscious mind of the narrator cannot restrain itself from siding with one of the parties in the conflict, or in other words from identifying itself with one of the opposing

[1] L. Lévy-Bruhl: *Les Fonctions Mentales dans les Sociétés Primitives.*
[2] In a later volume.

principles. Instead of encouraging all efforts directed towards the attainment of reconciliation, peace and harmony, which is the true desideratum, it views the prospect of any concessions to the underworld with such horror and misgiving that it secretly connives with the Blandish faction, thereby frustrating the efforts of the Psyche towards the desired end.

In order that the reconciliation may succeed it is necessary for the lovers to be left alone in trust and confidence to fulfil their inherent destiny. But to do this requires considerable courage and insight, and in this case they were inadequate. Insight is necessary in order to perceive that no reconciliation is possible for so long as Blandish upholds the harsh intolerance of his attitude, claiming the sole and exclusive right of defining good and evil; courage is required to defy his authority, which is the authority not only of the universally accepted social code but also of those sacred principles and values on which the individual has built up his own personal code. Unless Blandish is held in check with both firmness and clarity of vision he will find means of frustrating the attempt to overthrow his tyranny. These means are personified in the detective Fenner. It has already been pointed out that he is a kind of offshoot of Blandish's, sharing the latter's rectitude and coercive respectability and adding to them a knowledge of the underworld and the ability to penetrate unharmed into the dangerous region of the Other Side. Once he had been a journalist, that is to say an impartial observer and reporter of the doings of the underworld, and hence an invaluable function in the mind; now he has sold himself to constituted authority. He is no longer impartial, and he treacherously exploits the knowledge and the connections which he had formerly acquired in order to subserve the cruel tyranny of Blandish. It is he who tracks down the lovers and is responsible for their destruction.

The figure of Fenner is also a composite one. In his aspect of former reporter and penetrator of the Barrier he represents the mental function of intuition, which as we shall see later is the means whereby the contents of the unconscious are revealed to the conscious mind; he is the faculty which enables the author to draw on his creative fantasy for the making of this story. In his invincible chastity, however, and in his inveterate hostility to the unfortunate lovers, he represents a far more powerful figure with whom we shall be very much concerned in the next volume: it is that of the Child-Hero.

The beginning of the trouble lay in the escape of the princess. She is, to begin with, an empty-headed little thing who, like Persephone, is given to running around innocently plucking flowers in the neighbourhood of the gate to the underworld, without an idea of the existence of anything so dangerous. But on account of her exalted origin and her virginity she is the focus of great forces and the bearer of a great potentiality. Like Emma Bovary she has always had callow dreams of a great love, but she is innocent of any conception of the realities of lust and passion. And although she has no knowledge of the fact, her fore-ordained lover exists, and he is very close to her, namely just below her feet. The unalterable law of her nature, moreover, is that once she has seen him she will be his for ever. All this is only too well known to her father, and for this reason he generally keeps her immured in a tower and closely guarded: examples in myths and fairy-tales are innumerable: the classical type is Danaë, and several examples are to be found in the Arabian Nights and in Germanic folk-tales. But love always finds means of circumventing the father's most careful precautions, for the drive to reunification is a necessity of spiritual survival and emanates with irresistible force from the Centre of the individuality. It is to this drive that the princess owes her very existence, and she is its principal instrument. The lover, therefore, succeeds in penetrating to the princess, or else she escapes and flees with him, and this is the first step on the road to reconciliation. In *No Orchids* the theme of escape is spread over two episodes: the visit to the night-club which leads to her abduction, and the flight with Slim at the end. In the latter case, although the stronghold from which she escapes is her underworld prison, it is with her lover that she flees, and it is from her father that she is escaping.

But although this event is full of high promise for the total individuality it represents a disaster for her father, the upholder of the established regime whose oppressive tyranny has brought about the conflict which his daughter was born to reconcile. He, therefore, remorselessly pursues the pair (unless, as in some cases, his natural affection triumphs over his prejudices) and in doing so he sometimes, as in *No Orchids*, makes use of another fanatical upholder of the *ancien régime*, the Child-Hero Fenner. We must postpone consideration of this figure until later. Sometimes we shall find him in notable opposition to the Father, for, like those of all Archetypes, his nature is full of inherent contradictions; but when he allies himself with him the two make a very formidable combination which may easily succeed in frustrating the budding romance. This is clearly what happened in *No Orchids*.

RENEWAL

Since the Anima, by definition, embodies all that woman represents to man without exception, she must in particular combine in her single figure the four cardinal roles of mother, sister, mate and daughter. This is a matter of vital significance, and we shall have ample opportunity to consider its implications in a variety of situations during the further course of this study.

At first sight this statement might appear a truism or a matter of merely academic interest. It is obvious that many women combine all these roles, but of course in outer-world fact they stand in each relationship to a different man; we can, of course, also construct an abstract notion of 'woman' which embraces all these mutually exclusive practical relationships in just the same way as we can form a notion of, say, 'state', which embraces mutually exclusive forms, such as those of absolute monarchy and democratic republic. But we are dealing with an inner-world, not an outer-world entity: the Anima is a pattern of the mind, and as such is perfectly capable of combining attributes which, in the outer world, are mutually exclusive.

The importance of this consideration lies in the fact that if one of these attributes is touched upon or activated the others tend to present themselves: the relationship to the mother image (i.e. the collective unconscious) involves those to the sister, mate and daughter images, and the same applies to each of the others. In the world of the mind there is no harm in this: the recognition and acceptance of the identity of the Anima, as soul, behind all these forms is, indeed, a necessary stage in the process of self-realization. Difficulties, however, arise when mixed projections are made on to individuals in the outer world: a man's relationship to his wife, for instance, will obviously be falsified if elements proper to the relationship to the mother creep into it, his relations with his daughter will suffer if they are contaminated by elements belonging to the relationship with the mate and so forth. It is an obvious and well-known fact that such confusions constantly do take place, and that alone affords considerable support for the hypothesis of a single underlying image.

The fourfold nature of the Anima is also constantly to be found in symbolical form: some random examples will illustrate this. First there are the four Marys of the Gospels: their exact identity is a matter of some uncertainty, but the number four is associated with them with the same insistence as that of twelve is associated with the Apostles; just as the Virgin, moreover, is essentially the mother, Mary Magdalene, as harlot, obviously plays the part of mate, and Mary and Martha are a combined type of sisterhood. Again, in Bernard Shaw's *Pygmalion* Higgins and Pickering, on learning Liza's name, declaim the following poem:

> Eliza, Elisabeth, Besty and Bess
> They went to the woods to get a bird's nes':
> They found a nest with four eggs in it:
> They took one apiece, and left three in it.

To this Liza retorts 'Oh, don't be silly'—a very appropriate comment, since the interpolation has no purpose whatever. It is neither funny nor apposite, nor does it add anything whatever to the story, nor characterize the situation: it is completely pointless. The only explanation of its presence is that it is a piece of Anima symbolism which has crept in with Liza in exactly the same way as the image of water crept in with the Blonde: Liza is the Anima, and she is four-in-one. As I have already observed, the next thing which happens to her is a bath: the image of water has also crept in.

Finally we may take Evelyn Waugh's *Put out More Flags*, which is a story of the four women surrounding Basil Seal: his mother, his mistress, his sister and a young girl evacuee who is entrusted to his charge and thus stands in the relation of daughter to him. Of the four three are unequivocally stated to be in love with him and the fourth, his mother, is seen entirely in the light of her preoccupation with him: it is once again a picture of the fourfold relationship of woman to man, and it indicates the possibility of confusion between the various roles.

The complete picture does not appear in *No Orchids*, but we have already seen how the image of the virgin or daughter grows out of that of the Blonde or mate. Now, at the end of the book, we find the third element, that of motherhood, insistently presenting itself.

When Slim has been killed and Fenner has rescued Miss Blandish he takes her to a hotel and conducts her to a reserved room. She walks to the window, where she stands 'looking out at the white clouds that piled up in the blue sky', and she tells Fenner that Slim is still with her—that he always will be. Attention has already been drawn to the vividness with which the significant scenes in *No Orchids* are visualized; a suscepti- bility to the beauties of nature, on the other hand, is not one of its characteristics. This image of the clouds, therefore, is all the more striking, and we are justified in looking for some sym- bolical significance in it. The clouds are 'piling up': the wind is penetrating their swelling forms. One is reminded of Titania's 'to see the sails conceive And grow big-bellied with the wanton wind'; the Wind, the Breath, the Spirit as fecundating power is an image as old as mankind (it is *animus*, the counterpart of *anima*). Then Miss Blandish says that Slim is still with her and always will be. The inference that she is pregnant is inescapable, and it is perhaps worth mentioning that in my first draft of these chapters I drew attention to it. It was not until later that I had the gratification of finding my conclusion confirmed in a sequel, *The Flesh of the Orchid*, of which I had no knowledge at the time: it centres round Carol Blandish, Miss Blandish's daughter by Slim, it being explained that Miss Blandish had survived her attempted suicide for long enough to give birth to this child. Orwell also, in the article referred to earlier, mentions parenthetically that there is 'another possible con- clusion' to the story, namely that Miss Blandish was pregnant; but whether he too had interpreted the image of the clouds, or whether he had knowledge of the sequel we shall never know.

The notion of the pregnancy, then, was certainly present in the author's mind when he brought his story to its dramatic close. To what extent it was conscious only he himself could say. We may conjecture that it had presented itself to him as a possible further development, only to be dismissed, mainly, perhaps, because his story had reached the requisite length and seemed to have arrived at its fitting and dramatically inevitable conclusion in the death of Miss Blandish, including that of any possible unborn child. But it is typical of the Archetypes, as we already know, that they take no account whatever of the decisions of the conscious mind. Anybody who has written fiction will know this: if a situation which has spontaneously presented itself is arbitrarily altered in such a way as to suppress any essential content, then the suppressed element will soon present itself again, either in the same or in some alternative symbolical form. It was Miss Blandish's destiny to become a mother, and a mother she became.

The attempted suppression of Miss Blandish's motherhood frustrates the entire venture which the story represents. That venture was to bring about reconciliation through dynastic union, and the union is not complete until the heir is born. He, or she, is the heir to both worlds: it is only in the person of the heir that the irreconcilables can be truly reconciled, for this paradox can only become truth in the creation of a new individuality.

In the sequel Carol Blandish, the daughter, is portrayed as half heroine, half maniac, and in this combination we may trace an additional reason, possibly more cogent than the mere desirability of bringing the story to a close, for the initial rejection of Miss Blandish's motherhood. The conscious mind has taken sides: failing to understand that Miss Blandish had been drawn into the underworld in a mission of redemption and reconciliation, it insisted on regarding her abduction as a tragic disaster. Failing to perceive that Slim is Prince Charming transformed by enchantment into the Beast, it persists in portraying what was really an ideal of devoted love in the light of a foul debauch. It categorically refuses to admit that the offspring of such a union could be the Divine Child, born to inaugurate a new era of peace and concord: Slim's child, on the contrary, is seen as inevitably tainted by her heredity.

Another significant point is that the child is a daughter. We shall find later that this automatic and uninterrupted self-renewal is typical of the feminine principle known as the Anima. The situation with which *No Orchids* ends is precisely the same as that which divides *Wuthering Heights* into two halves, when the elder Catherine in dying reproduces herself in the younger. Mother and daughter are one, each for ever transforming herself into the other. It is the male, not the female principle that must pass through the maternal darkness on the way to self-renewal.

It is therefore true that the venture failed. The story contains the statement of a problem and the suggestion of its potential solution, but that solution cannot yet be realized on account of certain impediments in the mind. Therefore the cycle, having reached its conclusion, which is also its beginning, without breaking away on to a new plane, simply recommences: Miss Blandish renews herself as the daughter of the virgin. If the problem had been solved the child would have been a son.

ELEUSIS

The mysteries of Eleusis played a very important part in later classical times. Thousands, from the Emperors downwards, yearly attended the ceremonies, in which they were initiated into some secret which, on the testimony of several reputable authorities, possessed a high spiritual content and served as an inspiration and a solace to many. Speculation concerning the nature of the secret imparted to the initiates has naturally been prolific, but no adequately authenticated evidence on the subject has ever been discovered. There are, however, grounds for supposing that the identity of Demeter and Persephone constituted one ingredient: an inscription has been discovered in which Demeter is celebrated as both mother and Kore, or maiden.[1] One point, however, which deserves attention is that only in one rather unreliable reference to the Mysteries is there any reference to the birth of a child to Pluto and Persephone.[2] This, to say the least of it, is surprising, since the pair are represented as living in wedlock for a part of every year. Only two inferences are possible: either the union is seen as inherently sterile, or else there is some mysterious reason for hushing up

[1] See Jung and Kerenyi, *op. cit.*
[2] See L. Farnell, *Cults of the Greek States.*

the birth of an heir. The former possibility receives some slight support from the detail, related in one version of the myth, that Persephone, who had gone out to pick flowers, was admiring a narcissus at the moment of her abduction. Sterility is of course inherent in narcissism, a theme with which we shall be concerned later. The alternative supposition, however, is suggested by a certain dark rumour which became current regarding the rape. Persephone, in some versions, is Zeus' daughter; Pluto or Hades is invariably his brother, the two having agreed to divide the sovereignty between them, Zeus ruling the upper, Hades the lower world. Hades, in other words, is Zeus' other self, his dark half, that part of the authority principle which resides in the unconscious.[1] With this couple, the Upper and the Lower God, we shall be concerned later, and shall find them appearing spontaneously in widely diversified contexts: they are, in fact, Archetypal images. Now a number of mythographers have suggested that there was some secret connivance between the brothers in the matter of the rape of Persephone, and this can only mean that it had become necessary for Zeus to seek union with his own daughter. This supposition is lent some colour by the fact that there exists another myth concerning one Klumenos who committed incest with his daughter Harpalyke; concerning this legend Farnell[2] states that it probably arose 'from a forgotten Hades cult contaminated with Orphic-Zagreus elements'. The theme of incest between father and daughter seems therefore to have been associated with this complex, but it is important to realize that the vital point is not the incest, but the fact that the male principle seeks union with a female principle which it has itself engendered: the notion of incest as such arises only from the transposition of this theme into a human, outer-world context.

It was, of course, out of the question for even Zeus to carry out this scandalous project openly: he could not, indeed, even

---

[1] There were of course three brothers, the third being Poseidon who ruled the sea; his connection with a variant of the myth, in which he rapes Demeter and becomes the father of a child by her, presumably to be identified with Persephone, has been mentioned above. The theory that Pluto was a derivation of Zeus and represents his dark counterpart is put forward by Farnell, *op. cit.* In the Iliad (IX, 454) he is referred to as 'the underworld Zeus'.

[2] *Op. cit.*

admit it to his own consciousness. In consequence he was compelled to carry it out, apparently by proxy, through the mediacy of his lower or unconscious counterpart. Yet in fact, without admitting the damaging identity to himself, he did ravish his own daughter, who thus became his wife. Supposing that there was issue of this union Zeus would be both the father and the maternal grandfather of the child: he would, in fact, be its male progenitor on both sides, making use, for the purpose of engendering it, of a female principle which he had himself produced. To put this situation in another way the Deity, having separated off the femine side of his own nature, proceeds to unite with it, thus procreating himself in renewed form. This theme of self-renewal or rebirth is one with which we shall be concerned throughout this study, and for the moment we must postpone a more detailed consideration of it; as we shall see later it is by no means incompatible with the theme of narcissism.

In the light of the above it is a not completely unfounded conjecture that some intimation of this mysterious relationship may have formed part of the Eleusinian secret. Farnell discusses the possibility that the theme of a 'mystic birth' may have formed part of the mysteries, a suggestion for which ancient authority exists; while leaving the question open, however, he inclines to doubt the reliability of the evidence. Thus, while the matter is by no means proved it is not impossible that there may have been some suggestion that the Heir, the reconciler of two worlds, had been engendered and was born, or about to be born, in the hearts of men. The connection of this theme with that of the regeneration of the Deity will become apparent later in this study; in the closing centuries of the classical era it was very much in the air.

THE STORY OF NUR EL-DIN, SHAMS EL-DIN AND HASAN BADR EL-DIN

At this point we may once more have recourse to the remote world of the Arabian Nights for confirmation and reassurance. The story named above relates how Nur el-Din and Shams el-Din, sons of the old wazīr, become, on his death, the joint wazīrs of a certain sultan. In consequence of a trivial quarrel, however, Nur el-Din goes away in a rage; arriving in a distant kingdom he becomes wazīr to its ruler and never returns to his home. This situation of the two brothers separating and each ruling his own territory shows an obvious parallel with that of Zeus and Pluto.

The quarrel which causes the separation arises in the course of a discussion in which the two brothers agree that they should marry on the same day, that Nur el-Din's wife should give birth to a son, Shams el-Din's to a daughter, also on the same day, and that the pair should eventually marry. Here we already find the longing for reunion between the two sundered halves of the original unitary principle. But this very longing for union implies the consciousness of dichotomy: hence the antagonism between the opposites is intensified and the estrangement becomes complete. The project of reunification now crystallizes into the picture of the pair of predestined lovers.

The events predicted duly come to pass, the two brothers, having married on the same day, being presented by their wives with a son and a daughter respectively, also on the same day, but of course without one another's knowledge. When Shams el-Din's daughter grows up, however, his sultan, enraged by the wazīr's refusal to grant him her hand in marriage, condemns her to marry a repulsive and ignoble hunchback. Nur el-Din has in the meanwhile died, and his son, Hasan Badr el-Din, has fallen into misfortune.

An ifrīt now takes a hand in the game, substituting young Hasan for the hunchback on the bridal night. At the wedding ceremonies the two men stand side by side, and later the ifrīt removes the hunchback and stuffs him down the privy—a characteristically Arabian Nights variant of the theme of the transformation of the Beast into Prince Charming. After the consummation of the predestined union the ifrīt removes Hasan, whom he accidentally leaves in a remote spot, where he is compelled to remain. A son is born of this union, but of course nobody knows who the bridegroom was, and the latter, ignorant of the bride's identity, has also no knowledge of the existence of his son. The boy is therefore brought up in the belief that Shams el-Din, his maternal grandfather, is his father. This is that same mysterious relationship to which I have drawn attention in the case of Zeus and Persephone on the supposition that the latter had given birth to an heir, and the situation is evidently basically the same. Shams el-Din and Nur el-Din are two halves of the same identity who desire reunion but cannot achieve it except by producing a mediating feminine principle. One half produces this principle and the other half unites with her, albeit under the polite veil of a rejuvenated version of himself, for Nur el-Din is dead and consummates the union in the person of his son. All the participants in this rather questionable procedure are ignorant of exactly what has happened, yet the underlying purpose is achieved in the birth of the reconciling principle in the person of the heir. The true situation is revealed in the explanation given to the boy that Shams el-Din is his father: the latter is thus seen as the husband of his own daughter and the procreator of his own rejuvenated self, or, more precisely, of the totality which had existed before his division into a pair of brothers.

The name of the heir is Ajīb, which means wonder or marvel: he is the Divine Child born to reconcile the estranged parties, and this he eventually succeeds in doing by discovering his lost father. Before being restored to his bride of one night, however, the latter, who had fallen to the low estate of a pastrycook, has to go through a process of regeneration or rebirth symbolized by his being shut up for long periods in a chest: here we have the image of the self-renewal of the male principle, which necessitates passing through the maternal darkness.

THE CHRISTIAN PARALLEL

It is evident that this light-hearted and rather indecent little fantasy contains the essential elements of the birth story[1] in the

---

[1] This element, which is to be found only in the third Gospel, was evidently a late accretion. The second Gospel, indisputably the oldest, leaves the question of the origins of Jesus unexplained, while the first opens with 'The book of the generation of Jesus Christ, the son of David, the son of Abraham', which consists of a long genealogy, beginning with Abraham, including David, and culminating in 'Joseph the husband of Mary, of whom was born Jesus'. Since Jesus was 'the son of David' the implication that Joseph was his immediate father cannot be escaped; it is thus clear that to

Christian legend. There are plenty of parallels for the theme of the mysterious and supernatural factors involved in the paternity of the Divine Child: the story of King Arthur's origins, as related by Mallory, may serve as an example. The interesting point about the Arabian Nights parallel, however, is that it goes further, incorporating the question of the origins of the Divine Mother. This matter has been formulated by the Roman Catholic Church in the dogma of the Immaculate Conception of the Virgin Mary; although this tenet was not promulgated until 1870 and has never been accepted by the Protestant churches, it did no more than sanction a belief that had been widely held for centuries: it is, in fact, a psychological truth, and it clearly implies that the Mother of God is his daughter as well as his wife. This complex relationship, hinted at in the Persephone legend, is, we saw, unequivocally revealed in the symbolism of the Islamic legend in the suggestion that Shams el-Din was the father of his daughter's child.

The parallelism substantiates the point raised in the Introduction, namely that if the Gospel stories are of universal psychological significance it is unlikely that they will be found to be unique, since the basic symbolical truths which they embody will almost certainly have been discovered by other people at other times and places as well. The recognition of this fact does not in the least detract from their value to an unprejudiced mind; rather, on the contrary, it enhances it, since it demonstrates the universality of their content.

Nevertheless the idea will come as a painful shock to many people, and the reason for this is twofold. First there is the unpleasant contrast between the two treatments of the theme: the cynical, lewd frivolity of the Arabic story on the one hand and the deep reverence associated with the Christian legend on the other. This is certainly distressing, and the juxtaposition of the two stories undoubtedly does do violence to feeling values; I am aware of this fact and regret it, but I am writing for like-minded people who are in search of psychological and intellectual truth and who insist on the right to state it as they see it without fear or favour. If, in the process, we wound the feelings

the author of the first Gospel the theory of the Virgin Birth was unknown. St. Paul, whose epistles are the earliest writings in the New Testament, also reveals no knowledge of it.

of others not so minded we can only be sincerely sorry; we can, however, comfort ourselves with the reflection that it has often happened before and that the devout, once having recovered from the shock, have succeeded in accommodating their beliefs to the new outlook without their suffering any real damage in the process. Darwin's refutation of the Biblical legend of the Creation is an obvious case in point.

To quote Jung: 'The man who simply believes and does not reflect always forgets that it is *he* who is continually exposed to the attacks of his own specific enemy, namely *doubt*; for where faith rules doubt always lurks. To the man who reflects, on the other hand, doubt is always welcome, for it serves him as the most valuable step to better understanding. People who are able to believe[1] should be somewhat more patient with their fellows who are only capable of thinking. For faith anticipates thought by reaching in one bound the heights to which thought seeks painfully to climb. The believer should not project his own familiar enemy,—doubt—into the mind of the thinker, thereby attributing destructive motives to him.'[2]

The second cause for the revulsion experienced by many people against theories of this nature lies in the failure to discriminate between the differing natures of the two worlds, and the consequent tendency to interpret symbolism in terms of fact. The stories in question are purely symbolical: they are concerned with the renewal in the mind of a unitary principle of individuality which has become split into two conflicting halves or opposites by the excessive activity of the conscious mind. The conscious mind is itself incapable of bringing about this reunification because it is itself indissolubly identified with one of the pair of conflicting and irreconcilable opposites; it is therefore necessary for the principle of unity, the Centre, the Self, God, or whatever we choose to call it, to step in. This Centre can only act on the conscious mind through the un-conscious, and the unconscious disposes only of a symbolical mode of expression: it is simply incapable of thinking in

[1] In another passage in the same work he says, 'Faith would be enough if it were not a divine gift (*Charisma*), the true, as opposed to the forced possession of which is a rarity. If this were not so we doctors would be spared much grim work.'

[2] C. G. Jung: *Symbolik des Geistes.*

abstract terms—of dealing with such abstruse concepts as 'reunification', 'principle', 'factor', 'mind' and so forth. It is therefore compelled to present its message in terms of parenthood, the fruitful union of the sexes, birth, death, and similar images which have held profound significance for humanity from time immemorial. It is the task of the intellect to accept these messages and interpret them in its own abstract terms, which are free of the emotional irrelevancies which cling to the archaic symbols.

Virgin births simply do not occur in the outer world; consequently the symbol is not associated for us with any strong emotional implications, and we can accept the story that one once occurred, very long ago and far away, without doing any violence to our feelings. It was a miracle: something manifestly impossible which nevertheless happened—once and once only. Any attempt to prove that the story was not impossible in the outer-world sense at once destroys its value, for if it was possible according to the laws of the world we live in today, then it was not supernatural and it might happen again, and this time in trivial, everyday circumstances. Incestuous relationships, on the other hand, do sometimes occur in the world we live in, and they are regarded with horror; the symbol, therefore, is associated in our minds with a powerful negative emotional reaction. We must, however, learn to free ourselves of this prejudice when we are considering what is purely symbolical; we must remember that the incestuous relationships which form an ever-present background to the myths of all peoples in all ages have absolutely no connection with the sexual relations of individual men and women in the outer world: they are simply the expression, in archaic symbolism, of certain processes which take place unconsciously in all minds.

Where there is only one male and one female principal there can be no question of incest, since these two must necessarily stand in every possible relationship to one another.

The last thing we should do is to attempt to discover a factual basis for the symbols by asserting that they are generalized formulations of 'real' incestuous impulses between actual, outer-world people: such thinking is not only embarrassing and repulsive, but 'reductive', regressive and misleading as well.

VIRGIN AND MOTHER

In all this some adumbration of the mysterious totality of the Anima is discernible. She is the mother who is celebrated as a virgin, the virgin who becomes a mother and whose virginity is perennially renewed. She is the daughter who becomes her father's wife and mother, the indwelling feminine essence who is mother, wife, sister and daughter to the principle of identity in the mind. She is at the same time the dark origin of our individual being, the incentive and the goal of our striving, the fruit of our labours and the means of our regeneration.

This totality, as I have said, is no mere intellectual abstraction: it is a living force which is continually acting in the mind, presenting itself to consciousness at all times and in all places in images of the type which we have been considering. If any one of these partial representations is pursued to its origins on the Other Side, other aspects of the totality of the Anima will inevitably come to light. One such eventuality we have seen in *No Orchids*, where the pursuit of the Blonde (the mate) led to the discovery of Miss Blandish the daughter and Ma Grisson the mother. These discoveries are often perplexing and disquieting, not to say painful; this is not only because of the repellent implications of such identities as those of mate and mother when transposed into outer-world terms, as the Freudians have transposed them, but because of the association of heterogeneous elements with some of the Anima's forms. An example is to be found in the authority aspect of Ma Grisson which, in the classical Persephone myth, is more correctly seen as belonging to Pluto, the Lower God, who has no connection with motherhood. The Mother, it is true, must always be connected with the image of the Abyss, but not necessarily with any compulsive authority emanating from the darkness. This confusion was evidently one of the impediments which frustrated the attempt of Miss Blandish and Slim to achieve reconciliation and regeneration; the other was the identification of Slim, the princely lover, with the menacing figures of the Rival and of another Archetype with whom we shall meet presently, namely the Shadow.

Thus another potent reason for hurling Miss Blandish, the daughter, back into the depths rather than admit her motherhood was that to acknowledge it entailed acceptance of her identity with the repellent figure of Ma.

This monstrous figure, like that of Slim, arises from false identifications of disparate elements in the unconscious: they form the basis of those troublesome phenomena colloquially known by Jung's designation of 'complexes'. The mental process of self-realization cannot proceed to fruition until these images have been broken down into their constituent elements. But intellectual understanding is only the first stage in disposing of them: the understanding thus achieved must then be lived out in the pattern of individual life.

THE DESTINY OF PERSEPHONE

We set out to answer three questions: who Persephone was, why she was carried off to the underworld, and why she was compelled to divide her life henceforth between the two worlds. With the help of *No Orchids* we are now in a position to offer tentative answers.

Persephone is the Anima, the soul in the sense of the mediating principle between various pairs of opposites. The most important of these from our present point of view is the polarity particular—universal: the mind of civilized man has become split into these two halves, seen as This World and the Other Side, and it is sometimes urgently necessary for him to restore the primal unity between them. If he fails to do so he is liable to be deprived of the Waters of Life, which are available only on the Other Side, and he becomes parched and exhausted in his life in This World. In order to divide them he must pass through the Barrier, and it is the Anima who incites and enables him to do so.

But the Anima, in her personal aspect, actually is the individual himself as he exists on the Other Side: when he passes through the Barrier he becomes identified with her. This matter of the mystical change of sex we must postpone for later consideration: all that we can say for the moment is that Persephone's disappearance into the underworld represents the passage of the Barrier by the individual himself. One of the few things which we know with comparative certainty about the Eleusinian Mysteries is that the initiate carried out certain ritual acts in which he personified the goddess: even though he was a man, in fact, he was identified with her, and he regarded this identification as subsisting throughout his life. The Emperor Gallienus even had coins struck in commemoration of his initiation on which he is referred to as 'Galliena Augusta' in allusion to this idea.[1] It represented, in short, the assertion and acceptance of the individual's identity with his soul.

Thus Persephone is in fact the type of every human individual in one of the most important aspects of his life. She shows the division between the two halves of the mind, and their fundamental identity; her destiny of dividing her life between two worlds is the universal, inescapable destiny of humanity. The proportions of two thirds above and one third below into which the myth divides that life has surely less correspondence with the cycle of vegetation than with the traditional division of the day between sleeping and waking. We are always, throughout our lives, compelled to spend one third of our time in the darkness of unconsciousness: that is the most familiar form of the pattern, but the coming and going of Persephone is also concerned with a greater rhythm. The whole of life, as we shall see later, can also be divided into three periods, and Persephone's descent into the underworld and her return are images of the transitions between them. The second descent represents the conclusion of personal life, and there can be little doubt that the final secret of the Eleusinian Mysteries concerned the promise of resurrection, for it is that promise, and that only, which can give solace to all, from Emperor to beggar.

RECAPITULATION

This concludes the analysis of *No Orchids*, and before turning to the wider significance of the main theme which we have discerned in it, it will be advisable to summarize the conclusions which we have reached up to this point.

(1) The extraordinary popularity of *No Orchids for Miss Blandish* cannot be adequately accounted for by its sensationalism or by any other superficial characteristic; the story must therefore be regarded as a contemporary myth, the figure and

[1] See Jung and Kerenyi, *op. cit.*

destiny of Miss Blandish having become embedded in the collective mind in the same way as those of Sherlock Holmes, Alice, etc., in modern times, or those of Hercules, King Arthur, etc., in the past.

(2) This acceptance of an image in the collective mind implies that it has fitted into and filled a place there: in other words that it brings to expression some pattern which is active in the unconscious mind, but for which the conscious mind has not yet found a rationally intelligible formulation. Thus it provides the generality of people with a form for the expression of something which they 'sense' but cannot express for themselves.

(3) The basic forms which appear in such cases are the symbols of the Archetypes, which are the fundamental structures or patterns of the mind. They present themselves to consciousness in the form of characteristic symbols, consisting of typical figures, situations, etc., and their typical activities or developments. Hence their behaviour appears autonomous, since the activities of the figures and the development of the situations are inherent in them and cannot be arbitrarily changed. Any attempt to coerce them into a form incompatible with their inherent nature is a falsification of psychological truth exactly equivalent to a falsification of factual truth. Hence the 'creative' artist or thinker does not really 'create' his material—*ex nihilo nihil fit*—for it exists already, and his task is to render it in an intelligible and acceptable form. When he succeeds in doing so he has produced a formulation which is universally valid, because he has found the solution of a problem which exists unconsciously in the collective mind of his time and therefore in every individual mind; hence its universal appeal.

(4) *No Orchids* is evidently such a successful formulation. It falls short of the criteria by which we adjudge a work a masterpiece, because its presentation is inferior and unacceptable from the aesthetic and ethical points of view; but in respect of its symbolism—i.e. its presentation of the bare bones of psychological truth—it must be rated more highly than many works which are superior in other respects.

(5) If we analyse its plot in the light of these considerations we find the following outstanding features.

(*a*) Its basic theme is of Two Worlds divided by a Barrier.

(*b*) The dichotomy is seen in the following two characteristic forms:

(i) The division between This World and the Other Side, or between fact and fantasy, realism and romance, conscious and unconscious, particular and universal.

(ii) The conflict between two factions: on the one hand the upper world of constituted authority and rectitude, ruled and personified by John Blandish, on the other the underworld of the rebellious dispossessed and of vice and licentiousness, ruled and personified by Ma Grisson.

(6) The division between This World and the Other Side is expressed by an awareness of unseen presences, who communicate symbolically by telephone from a Somewhere Else, or become visible in emerging out of the darkness of the night. Figures which have appeared in the light in this way may be banished when they become inconvenient, but they always reappear, although sometimes disguised—usually thinly enough.

(7) The separation between the Two Worlds leads to an impoverishment and devitalization of This World, and this to a longing to penetrate the Barrier in order to experience the richer life of the Other Side, and to recover some of the vitality, life-force or libido (in the sense of that which confers value) which has vanished into it.

(8) This lost vitality, etc., is seen as the Waters of Life, an age-old symbol for the life-force residing in the unconscious or generic part of the mind. Its absence is symbolized by the parched and exhausted conditions of This World, as revealed in the opening scene in Minny's hash-house, or by the danger of dying of thirst, as in the *Rime of the Ancient Mariner*.

(9) Water is associated with a female figure who, in *No Orchids*, is always found guarding the door through the Barrier; in other legends she is found residing in the garden which it encloses.[1]

(10) Another form, in which the goal of the quest into the world beyond the Barrier is seen, is that of the Treasure, which

---

[1] Further examples of this symbolism will appear in later volumes.

is an object of supreme value. This treasure may be seen in the crude materialistic form of an object of pecuniary value, a piece of information conferring power, the rulership of a kingdom, etc., and in this form it constitutes the nucleus of every 'thriller'. In superior versions of the theme, however, the Treasure appears in human form, signifying that it represents the voluntary allegiance of a free agent. In *No Orchids* the Treasure is first seen as a diamond necklace but transforms itself into the person of Miss Blandish, who has a will of her own and insists on accomplishing her inherent destiny. In this transformation we may see a deeper penetration behind the Barrier, with a consequent raising of the standard of the symbolism, taking place as the story progresses.

(11) In the last resort the Treasure represents the capacity for free and independent decision residing in the individual. So long as this remains inaccessible in the unconscious the individual is not really free, but remains in the status of the Treasure in inanimate form, which is the helpless object of the contention of forces external to itself. This is because we can neither accept nor reject tendencies and impulses of which we are not conscious, i.e. which we do not see and understand as forces acting on us from within according to their own peculiar nature and laws. Instead of this we are either identified with them, seeing them as manifestations of our own individuality, or else we project them, seeing them as emanating from the outer world which is not subject to our volition. In consequence we 'cannot will', and either relapse into a supine condition of dependence, or else are driven by forces which we cannot control to commit actions which are contrary to our superior understanding. The nature of the forces in question, and the manner in which they act on us, are matters which remain for later investigation.

(12) The only solution to this state of deadlock is to adventure into the dangerous world of the Other Side into which the Treasure has vanished, as the author of *No Orchids* did when he wrote this story. This is the explanation of what we call creative activity.

(13) The consequence of such a venture is that the discriminating light of consciousness is brought to bear on a number of mental contents which had hitherto been hidden in

the darkness of the unconscious. The result is that the potential opposites contained in a latent state in them become apparent and fly apart, creating new conflicts and problems in the conscious mind. These have now to be dealt with, which is a difficult and dangerous process, entailing an adjustment of the conscious attitude to enable it to deal with the new and unaccustomed contents and problems. If it fails in this task the consequences may be serious, but with luck it is generally possible to break off the experiment temporarily, in time to avoid serious trouble. If, on the other hand, it is successful, a work of creative value will be produced, even if it is only in the form of an enrichment of the subject's personality. In any case some of the life-force incarcerated in the unconscious will have been released, and the condition of devitalization will have been at least temporarily relieved.

(14) This process is revealed in the state of war between the kingdoms of John Blandish and Ma Grisson which gradually pervades the scene as the story progresses, culminating in the great battle for the Paradise Club: this exhibits a parallelism with the legend of the rape of Helen and the Trojan War. At the beginning the conflict was only latent, but the resolve to pursue the Treasure brings it to actuality.

(15) It is discovered that each of the rulers of the two irreconcilable factions has a child and heir, and these two fall in love and eventually consummate a forbidden union which ought to produce the heir to both worlds. This happy outcome is thwarted by the scruples of the author, who is prevented by a number of mental impediments from accepting it; the venture is therefore temporarily abandoned, but the Archetypal symbols, undeterred, continue to force the outcome demanded by the inherent laws of their nature into consciousness; the author therefore eventually writes a sequel in which the birth of the heir is admitted and her mixed inheritance unequivocally accepted.

(16) This theme of the Dynastic Union is familiar in the legendaries of many peoples in various epochs, and it illustrates the only possible solution to the condition of deadlock entailed by the conflict of the Two Worlds. Neither can ever eliminate the other, since both are inherent parts of the mind; the only possibility of progress therefore lies in reconciling them, and

this is symbolically achieved in the triumphant and fruitful union of the opposites which is represented by the union of the sexes and the resultant procreation of a new individual who combines the opposites in himself. Only thus can the self-perpetuating vicious circle be broken and a fresh start made. For this purpose the two factions present themselves in the form of the pair of idealized lovers through whom alone reconciliation and reunion is possible.

(17) The theme is characterized by the care necessary in selecting the pair: this is usually symbolized by the arduous tests and ordeals which the male lover must successfully undergo, and the penalty for failure in which is death. The point, however, is not so much that he should prove his merit as his inherent right to the hand of the princess: the fairy-tales do not see the situation as a mere competition in strength and prowess, and the hero is generally assisted by supernatural means which are anything but 'fair'. The meaning is that the hidden agencies which are directing the play are insistent that he, and he alone, should win her. This theme is also illustrated in *No Orchids* in the fatality which befalls every man who comes too close to Miss Blandish, saving Slim alone, for whom she is reserved. No attempt to fob off on the Princess any lover acceptable by ordinary standards must be allowed to succeed, for the whole point of the undertaking is that she must be united to the one lover who is utterly unacceptable to her faction, namely the representative of their opponents. ('O Romeo, Romeo! Wherefore art thou Romeo?')

(18) A successful outcome implies the termination of the rule of the Princess's father, the king of the upper world; knowing this, he therefore first attempts to preclude her foreordained love-affair altogether, by shutting her up, or by imposing, or allowing her to impose, apparently impossible conditions on all suitors; then, if these expedients fail, he remorselessly pursues the pair. This theme is embodied in *No Orchids* in Blandish's pursuit and eventual destruction of his daughter and her lover through the agency of Fenner. ('I think my daughter is dead . . . I hope she is . . . I would rather (these men) were killed than arrested.')

(19) The meaning of this paternal opposition is that the existing conscious attitude, the one-sided intolerance of which

has brought about the trouble, is not prepared to make any concessions to the innovations demanded by the attempt at reconciliation: it seeks to maintain its supremacy even at the price of sacrificing the only chance of regeneration. If the subject is unable to break his identification with his now outmoded conscious attitude he surreptitiously sides with Blandish and assists him to thwart the venture. This has evidently occurred in *No Orchids*, as in *Sanctuary*, which provided its inspiration; the fact is revealed in the hostility displayed towards the male lover and in the ugly colours in which his love is portrayed; nothing could be further removed from the idealized union of the fairy-tale prince and princess, such as Florizel and Perdita, yet the underlying theme is the same.

(20) The means of attaining this end in *No Orchids* is the venial treachery of Fenner, once a free agent, who had obtained access to the underworld, but who now sells himself to Blandish and makes use of his privilege of entry to pursue and destroy the lovers where Blandish and the police, unaided, would have failed. The nature of this figure, and of the subtle and treacherous methods by which the conscious mind is prepared to thwart the projects of the unconscious, will be the subject of later investigation.

(21) Turning to the female figure who guards the Barrier, we approached her from two different viewpoints, those of symbolism and of the scientific study of instinct. The former revealed that she may be identified with a figure which has haunted the minds of creative artists throughout history. She appears for preference as an incomplete female figure, generally of aqueous origin, whose lower half is either concealed or is represented in non-human form. She seeks the love of men, and her purpose is to win a soul. In *No Orchids* she appears at the gateway through the Barrier, and it is evidently her function to lure men into the Other Side beyond it. If, however, they succumb to her charms and dally with her at the gate they achieve nothing; in order to win the Treasure they must resist her blandishments and press on into the world beyond, as Fenner does.

(22) The investigation of her instinctual background revealed that she is a development of an inherent image of the mind, namely that by which man recognizes his mate. Pursuing

this line we concluded that she is a partial representation of a more generalized figure of wider import, which Jung has named the Anima, and which represents man's 'soul': she symbolizes that side of his nature which has become lost to him through his concentration on his individual consciousness. In this capacity she is more or less equivalent to the world of the Other Side, since she embodies those richer experiences of which he has deprived himself by concentrating on his conscious existence in this world and thereby delivering himself into the power of John Blandish, the intolerant and one-sided conscious attitude which condemns and rejects whole categories of experience to which he has an inalienable right. She is also the dispenser of the Waters of Life.

(23) We noted that in *No Orchids* the Blonde displays a spontaneous tendency to widen and enrich her nature by developing characteristics of temperament and feeling which run counter to her apparent function as a mere 'wish-fulfilment' or appeaser of lust. This tendency we traced to the fact that in her original form as the hash-house waitress or the anonymous blonde in black pyjamas she represents an incomplete and distorted version of the image of woman inherent in the mind of man. In this guise she is no more than a pin-up girl, or an exaggerated representation of the mate-recognition image to which male lechery has been artificially added. The elements of the total image which have been rejected and ignored in making up this incomplete image belong to the courtship stage of the mating pattern, and to the feeling elements demanded by the specifically human components of the relationship between the sexes. These latter are not solely contemporary conventions, but contain a large ingredient from the image of womanhood that has grown up in the course of the centuries of human history. This has become embodied in the collective system which shapes so much of our thoughts and values that no individual is free of it; any attempt to ignore or defy it therefore produces a reaction in the unconscious mind. This reaction is expressed by the Blonde's tendency to fill out her character by the acquisition of feeling values, and by the mermaid's search for love. The essence of the matter is that in the guise of the Blonde she is incomplete, which means not only that the sexual life of those who see women in this light is defective,

but that they are not in possession of the totality of their souls. If they are to fulfil themselves they must seek to complete her image.

(24) The repression of feeling values is by no means solely a matter of sexual behaviour or standards: it reaches into every department of life, and the contemporary cult of the Blonde or pin-up girl is no more than a special symptom of the general tendency to neglect the feeling life in favour of the intellect. A further elucidation of this matter had to be postponed for the present.

(25) Finally the Blonde, as the guardian of the gate through the Barrier, personifies that gate and all that lies beyond it, for it is in her figure that it first becomes apparent. The Other Side is the lost side of our nature—the side that transcends personal limitations and the viewpoint bounded by the ego. It is to this that the Blonde beckons us in the challenge to undertake the quest of her full nature, which is the missing component of our own full nature.

(26) The Anima has a variety of roles at her disposal and has favoured different ones at different periods of history. The reason why at the present time she favours that of the Blonde is that it has become vitally important that she should attract attention to herself. Her purpose in doing so is to persuade man to turn his attention to that which he has lost: sound feeling values (which, for instance, include the ethical sense as opposed to intellectual principles and legalism) and the supra-personal, universal side of his nature.

(27) The penetration of the Barrier and the refusal to dally with the Blonde which are symbolized in the early part of *No Orchids* do in fact lead to the discovery of both a completer form of the Anima and a superior apperception of the Treasure. Both are embodied in the person of Miss Blandish: as a virgin she is untouched and complete, and therefore potentially capable of filling all the Anima's roles (which the Blonde, as such, is not) while as a human being she adds to the conception of the Treasure the element of freedom of decision.

(28) It becomes apparent that her mission is to descend into the underworld and to stay there, despite all opposition and the suffering entailed, until she has redeemed her bewitched and degraded lover: she must transform the Beast into Prince

Charming. When an attempt is made to restore her to the upper world before this mission is completed she resists vigorously.

(29) A distinct parallelism is discernible between this story and the myth of Persephone, which formed the central theme of the Eleusinian Mysteries. The latter evidently contained a spiritual message of great importance, and their central theme appears to have been the identity of Demeter the mother and Kore, the maiden, known as Persephone the daughter. Behind this again lies a mysterious relationship between her and the father who is the husband of his own daughter and at the same time her son: the son is the Divine Child who is his own father ('I and my Father are one').[1]

(30) This latter theme has nothing to do with incest, but is a symbolical intimation of the totality of the Anima, who is at the same time mother, sister, daughter and wife to the male principle (and of the Animus, who is father, brother, son and husband to the female principle). The male and the female, or creative and receptive principles, necessarily stand in every possible relationship to one another. The regeneration of the lost unitary principle in the mind takes place by means of a process of rebirth which involves union with the Anima or soul, who also stands in the relationships of mother, sister and daughter to that principle; the process is represented symbolically in myths and legends which necessarily seem to imply incest, but that is only because of the archaic symbolism which is the only language at the disposal of the unconscious mind.

(31) This matter of the multiple relationship of the Anima to man, and the incompatibility of her various roles with one another, finds its place in *No Orchids* in the development of Miss Blandish the virgin daughter into the mate and finally the mother. It was the last identification from which the author drew back in alarm, for the figure of the mother was identified with Ma Grisson, the Terrible Mother, which is another of the Anima's roles; the fundamental identity of the figure of Miss Blandish, with its almost divine implications, and this loathsome and frightening image, is one which is very hard to accept—a fact which we shall find confirmed in the analysis of other works. Nevertheless its acceptance is unavoidable in the quest of the totality of the Anima's nature.

[1] John x. 30.

(32) One of the most characteristic and significant elements of the Persephone myth is Persephone's participation in two worlds and the consequent necessity of her dividing her life between them. In this she typifies the human soul, which is both particular or individual, and universal or generic, and is compelled to live concurrently in these two contrasting and incompatible modes. These are the Two Worlds between which we are condemned to share our lives; we cannot afford to neglect either, and we must at all costs learn to distinguish between them. Their natures are irreconcilable, and it is our task to reconcile them in our lives. This can only be accomplished by participating in the destiny of Persephone.

I have referred repeatedly to the Two Worlds but have only given vague indications of what they mean in terms of life. It has seemed preferable to begin with the symbolism of the theme, rather than with a reasoned disquisition, because the living symbol acts directly on the intuitive mind, engendering a sense of conviction in its own right. It is only those who set some store by intuitive perceptions who will be interested by a book of this nature—I am convinced that anybody not so minded will have laid it down in disgust long before reaching this point—so that nothing will be lost by appealing to the intuitive faculty first. At the same time it is advisable to seek confirmation of the conclusions of intuition in a more logical approach; abstract statements, moreover, are apt to remain empty formulae unless their application to what we call 'real life' is directly experienced. This consideration is in itself a differentiation between the two worlds, for, as we shall see, what we mean by 'real life' is the outer world. A theory is constructed in the inner world and applied in the outer, which explains why theory and practice do not always correspond; each world is incomplete without the other, and a careful distinction must be made between the two. This particular distinction, however, does not exhaust the differentiation between them, which is a complex one, and difficult to formulate clearly. An attempt to do so must nevertheless be made, and it will form the Second Part of this volume.

PART II
THE TWO WORLDS

The Dream

ONCE upon a time, I, Chuang Tzu,[1] dreamt that I was a butterfly, fluttering hither and thither, to all intents and purposes a butterfly. I was conscious only of following my fancies as a butterfly, and was unconscious of my individuality as a man. Suddenly I awakened, and there I lay, myself again. Now I do not know whether I was then a man dreaming I was a butterfly, or whether I am now a butterfly dreaming I am a man. Between a man and a butterfly there is necessarily a barrier. The transition is called metempsychosis.[2]

(*Chuang Tzu*, translated by Herbert A. Giles.)

---

[1] A leading Taoist, or follower of Lao Tse, who flourished during the fourth century B.C.

[2] This late Greek term, commonly translated 'the transmigration of souls', was of course not current in Chuang Tzu's time and environment in which, to the best of my knowledge, the relevant concept did not exist in the crude form which it later assumed—i.e. that the individual principle of one being 'migrated' after death into the body of another. Richard Wilhelm, a later translator, renders this last sentence, 'Thus it is with the transformations of things.' This question will be elaborated later.

I Walter Mitty

A FIGURE which has gripped the popular imagination in the same way as Miss Blandish's did, taking its place in the second rank behind such leading personalities in contemporary mythology as Sherlock Holmes, Jekyll and Hyde, Alice, Tarzan and Peter Pan, is that of Thurber's Walter Mitty. The pathetic, ineffectual, hen-pecked little man who is perpetually losing himself in dreams of glory is a figure of whom almost everybody has heard, even if he has not read the original sketch: Mitty, in fact, has been accepted as a formulation of something real in the collective mind. His function, I think, is much the same as that of the poignant figure created by Chaplin in his earlier films: he serves as a harmless, because wryly humorous, release for our self-pity.

Self-pity is a dangerous weakness, which may easily degenerate into a victimization complex and a permanent grudge against the world, but this occurs only when it is repressed. In itself it is a natural reaction, for we try so hard, and the intentions of most of us are so good—but we are for ever being frustrated and misunderstood by an obtuse, perverse and intractable world which goes its own way, refusing to accommodate itself to our good intentions. If we take the trouble to think about it we know perfectly well why this is so: it is because good intentions are not enough. It is necessary to learn in the hard school of practical experience how they can be made effective in a refractory world which was not made to our order. There is a danger, however, that we may not take the trouble to think about it: instead we build up a private system of self-justification based on the feelings of resentment and humiliation occasioned by our failures. As soon as we

186

become aware of this tendency we are, to be sure, fore-armed: we can catch ourselves in the act of cherishing feelings of self-pity and resentment; we can point out to ourselves that they are foolish and unworthy, and dismiss them without more ado. But unfortunately this course, apparently so sensible and full of insight, represents the essence of that mental pattern which we have seen symbolized in Fenner's subservience to Blandish, and the latter's exploitation of the ex-journalist's right of entry to the underworld in order to frustrate the attempt at regeneration. The intuitive faculty—Fenner—provides the conscious mind with information concerning what is going on in the unconscious, but it is essential that that information be utilized in a tolerant and conciliatory spirit, and not perverted by the conscious attitude to subserve its own despotic repression of all that is uncongenial to it in the unconscious. If the subject's situation evokes a feeling-reaction such as self-pity or resentment, then that feeling must be accepted and faced as a reality possessing its own inherent justification, irrespective of what view the conscious mind may take of it. If it appears unworthy and unsuitable to the circumstances it must, certainly, be prevented as far as possible from affecting the subject's actual behaviour in important matters, but it must on no account be brushed aside as unworthy of consideration. The latter course evokes in the subject even more unsuitable and unadmitted feelings, this time of superiority and self-righteousness, which will colour his attitude and affect his behaviour without his realizing it: his last state is therefore worse than his first.

There is an anecdote of a man—I think George Moore—who had been unintentionally but culpably injured by another; when the latter came to apologize, the victim, instead of concealing his resentment behind the conventional, and therefore expected mask of magnanimous forgivingness, greeted him with the words 'Go away! I never want to see you again!' This reaction may appear—and indeed it was—pettish and self-indulgent; yet if forgiveness did not spring spontaneously from the heart the outburst was in many respects better than a false and hypocritical pardon, which would have poisoned the relationship between the two men indefinitely, and left the injured party wallowing in unadmitted self-adulation. The childish outburst was, perhaps, reprehensible, yet it finished with the matter once and for all, and was much fairer to the culprit. This trivial story illustrates, by the censorious criticism which it evokes in most people, how apt we are to judge our feelings according to principles, and therein lies a danger of disowning them, which may develop into an ingrained and vicious habit which distorts the whole personality.

Feelings cannot be reasoned out of existence: if we refuse them consideration, for whatever reason, however praiseworthy in itself, they descend into the unconscious, where they accumulate and fester. In the end they find means of evading the repression of the conscious attitude and of expressing themselves in ways which are far more objectionable, and generally more harmful, than a little spontaneous self-pity and resentment. Therefore we must learn to accept our self-pity and live it out, because we cannot get rid of it in any other way.

In this connection such figures as those of Mitty and the early Chaplin are helpful (Don Quixote is another example, on a more heroic scale), for they evoke a compassionate pity for the absurd, well-intentioned little man who is for ever being made a fool of in his attempts to bring a little kindliness, or some colour and excitement, into a hard-headed, tough, unsympathetic, humdrum world which is ruled by mean trivialities. Their function is cathartic, for they release feelings which most of us really entertain about ourselves but disown as unworthy.

The essential point is that Mitty's position is a universal human one, for even the toughest and most hard-headed individuals suffer in some way from this distressing paradox: we all live in two worlds and often have difficulty in reconciling the two. The only difference between individuals in this respect is that some are more conscious of the fact than others.

To put the matter in its most prosaic terms: things are not always as we should like them to be or think they ought to be, and we are faced with the problem of either changing the outer world to accord with our desires, or of adapting our requirements to it as we find it. Conversely, of course, things are not always as bad as we feared they might be, in which case we are thankful; but in either case we are faced with the contrast between two conceptions: of things as they are and things as they might be.

THE 'REAL WORLD'

For so long as we concern ourselves merely with concrete cases the problem seems simple and obvious enough: we live in a 'real' world which exists independently of us, having its own characteristic nature and following its own inherent laws; in our minds we imagine situations concerning which we believe, rightly or wrongly, that they exist, or could exist, in the 'real' world. If we are right in our supposition, then the 'real' world behaves as we expect it to behave when we apply our ideas to it, and we thus succeed in our purpose; if, on the other hand, we were wrong, and the situation we have imagined does not exist, or is incapable of existing, in the 'real' world, we receive an unpleasant shock when the two are confronted. Our task, therefore, would seem to be simply to discover as much as we can about the 'real' world and the laws according to which it operates; once we have succeeded in understanding it fully we shall no longer make mistakes, because we shall no longer attempt things which are impossible, or at any rate unsuited to the circumstances of the moment.

When we look a little deeper, however, we find that the position is not quite so simple. In the first place our thoughts and imaginings are by no means confined to the 'real' world, for we are also interested, not only in abstractions which have only the remotest connection with it (if they have any at all) but also in situations in fiction, legend and fable which are frankly impossible in the context of the outer world and which we freely admit to be so. These matters undoubtedly have value for us, for humanity has always prized them, and there can be no question that they exercise at least an indirect effect on our outer lives. There must, therefore, exist what we may describe as an inner world—a world of thought and imagination which exists separately from the outer world which we call 'real', and is in many respects independent of it.

APPARENT SUBJECTIVITY OF THE INNER WORLD

At first we are apt to assume that this inner world is 'merely subjective': everybody, we think, has his own, which need have no connection with that of anybody else, whereas the outer world is the same for everybody. This assumption, however, is also open to question; the matter will be elaborated as we proceed, but we have already adduced a considerable quantity of evidence which suggests that certain basic images such as that of Miss Blandish-Persephone-Helen have a habit of appearing spontaneously in the minds of the most various individuals at the most diverse times and places; when these Archetypal images appear, moreover, they tend to behave autonomously, in accordance with ascertainable laws which are in many respects equivalent to the laws governing the phenomena of the outer world, although differing from them. It thus appears that there is a definite objective element in the inner world, which is to some extent the same for all individuals in the same sense as the outer world is.

THE SUBJECTIVE ELEMENT IN THE OUTER WORLD

Turning now to the outer world, we are compelled to admit that although it appears to be completely objective, i.e. the same for everybody, this common element is confined to its basic principles, for each individual experience of it is essentially different from any other. Even if two people are looking at the same object at the same time they cannot see exactly the same picture, if only because they are necessarily looking at it from points of view which are different, however slightly. Each, to be sure, normally constructs from his visual impression a mental picture of a three-dimensional object which he can imagine from any point of view, and thus, so long as the object is familiar and can be clearly seen, both observers will draw identical conclusions from what they see. But such conclusions exist solely in the mind: they are interpretations of sensory data which each observer makes on his own account, and it is easy to imagine cases in which their interpretations may differ materially. If, for instance, they are looking at an unfamiliar object from opposite sides they may come to very different conclusions regarding its three-dimensional form, and when we go on to consider their conclusions as to the nature, purpose and potentialities of the object, it is obvious that their conclusions may differ even more widely: the conclusions of a savage and a civilized man, for instance, may be imagined when they observe a television set in action.

It is thus evident that the outer or 'real' world exists very largely in the mind of the individual: he draws conclusions from his immediate sensory experience—i.e. from the images on his retina, the vibrations of his ear-drums and the pressure on the skin of his fingers—in accordance with pre-conceived images in his mind. In other words he recognizes what he sees, hears, feels, tastes and smells by comparing the immediate data with mental images, most of which are built up from experience, but some of which, as we know, are innate; he then interprets what he has recognized in accordance with his individual, subjective knowledge and understanding of the outer world, the objects it contains and their relationships with one another. It is on this complex and largely subjective basis that the conclusion regarding what he is experiencing rests, and this conclusion is probably the only part of the whole sequence which reaches consciousness.

It may justifiably be objected that the outer world must be completely objective after all: astronomers, for instance, predict an eclipse years in advance, and at the due moment it is visible to every single observer in the predicted area, and in absolutely identical form; the phenomenon, moreover, may be photographically recorded and the individual impressions of the observers confirmed by comparison with the picture. It is perfectly true that an absolutely objective element in our experience of the outer world may be determined if we take enough trouble to circumscribe it, and we are apt to assume on that account that if only we took enough trouble and had enough understanding we might succeed in reducing the whole of outer existence to objective terms. Even scientists, however, are beginning to discover limits to this process of objectivization, within their own most special spheres.[1] The same consideration, moreover, undoubtedly applies to the inner world: we are already beginning to discern objective elements in it, and we have not as yet devoted to this sphere of experience one ten thousandth part of the attention that has been devoted to the outer world in the course of the last two centuries.

[1] E.g. in the 'principle of indeterminacy' and the 'Heisenberg limits'.

EQUIVALENCE OF THE RELATIONSHIP OF THE SUBJECT TO INNER AND OUTER WORLDS

If we accept the hypothesis that the individual does not independently create his thoughts and imaginings, but simply perceives what is presented from an 'inner' source in exactly the same way as he perceives the data of the senses or 'outer' source, it will become apparent that his relationship to the inner world is basically the same as his relationship to the outer: neither is inherently more nor less 'objective', nor universally true, than the other, any apparent disparity in these respects being almost certainly attributable solely to the difference in the amount of attention which has been directed in modern times to the two spheres. Thus if the subject bases his interpretation of his 'inner' experience on the methods which he is accustomed to use in interpreting 'outer' experience he will be just as certain to make mistakes and experience disappointments as he will if he does the reverse.

THE TWO WORLDS AS MENTAL SYSTEMS OF INTERPRETATION

There are thus sufficient grounds for assuming *a priori* that two alternative, contrasting, largely incompatible modes of experience are universal in the civilized mind, and that each individual builds up, on the basis of his experience of each of them, two separate bodies of knowledge, or systems of principles and values, which he uses to interpret his actual experiences. It is in these complex images, not in the immediate perceptions themselves, that his true experience of life, i.e. of meaning, is to be found. Thus, if he hears a speech in an unknown tongue he experiences nothing but sound, but if it is in a familiar language he already possesses a complex mental image of sounds, words and syntax with which he can compare the sensory data from his ears: thus he 'hears' not sound but meaning.

Similarly, when a certain pattern is projected on to the retina of his eye he sees, not forms and colours, but, let us say, a chair or a human being;[1] but that is only because he knows what these

[1] The ordinary individual in a highly civilized community is not conscious of forms and colours as such at all, unless they are exceptionally con-

objects are and recognizes the essential features characteristic of the visual impression produced by them when seen from a variety of different viewpoints. When the viewpoint is unfamiliar—e.g. a human being seen directly from above—he may have difficulty in identifying the image. In the same way, once he has become familiar with, for instance, the characteristic impressions produced by the symbol which we have identified as the Anima, he will be able to identify it as it is presented from a number of different individual viewpoints—in fiction, in his dreams, etc. In both cases he is comparing a particular perception with a generalized image pre-existent in the mind.

If all the images connected with, and derived from 'outer' experience are brought together, classified, and arranged in a coherent, consistent and intelligible system, they constitute the subject's individual picture of the outer world. But this, it is found, leaves a certain amount of material unprovided for: this is of an irrational symbolical, mystical, occult, coincidental and obscure nature. It is my contention that it is possible to arrange this material into a corresponding and opposed pattern

spicuous, or unless he has some extraneous reason for concentrating on them; what he 'sees'—i.e. what reaches consciousness—is a conception or notion, such as 'chair', 'old man', etc. This fact becomes apparent when he approaches works of art: he 'reads off' a picture in the same way as he is accustomed to 'read' the illustrations in the newspaper, interpreting their notional meaning and no more. In order to learn to appreciate works of art most people have to undergo a course of instruction in 'what to look for', which means rather what to ignore: they have to learn that the painter is not concerned simply with producing a reproduction of, say, an apple, which is recognizable to anybody as a kind of fruit which he commonly eats, but with communicating a particular visual impression in terms of form and colour, which has little or no connection with the 'meaning' of the apple as an edible fruit. Experiments with schoolchildren have shown that true appreciation of artistic values is considerably lower in highly civilized communities than in more backward ones; this is because the highly civilized children have already carried the process of interpretation of the original sensory data to a higher degree of selectivity in one particular direction; their images of the outer world are more highly developed in a one-sided 'thinking' pattern which screens and rejects the 'straight' response to the sensory stimulus as such, proceeding instead direct to the conceptual notion 'that's meant to be an apple'. The typical contemporary mind, having reached this point, sees no possibility of proceeding further and asks 'So what?'

of the 'inner world'; this can be just as coherent, consistent and intelligible as that of the outer world, although the system of classification and reference required to make it so differs widely from that which is appropriate for outer-world material.

The reason why so few people nowadays make any serious attempt to do this is simply that the contemporary outlook is so strongly prejudiced in favour of the outer-world system that we take it for granted that it is the only possible one: material must either be fitted into our outer-world picture or, we believe, it cannot be fitted into any intelligible picture at all. Consequently, when we meet with anomalous material we either do violence to its inherent inner-world nature by forcing it into the Procrustean bed of an outer-world system, or we attempt to explain it away as 'merely subjective', or in other words unreal.

At this point I am begging the question of the possibility of two alternative and intrinsically opposed and incompatible methods of interpretation, each of which can produce a coherent and intelligible system. It is a hypothesis, and we have yet to discover to what extent it is capable of explaining the phenomena which we actually experience.

These two systems, or complex images by the aid of which we interpret life are, if taken as wholes, of unimaginable intricacy and scope, and it is justifiable to call them worlds: they are, in fact, the only worlds we know, for our conceptions of any world or part of a world 'outside' our own minds are only projections of the images 'inside' them. Very often we do not realize that there are two of them: the outer world, we believe, is the only one which 'really' exists: everything else in our minds is just nonsense, or fancy, or superstition, or psychology. But in fact, as will shortly become apparent, we do constantly discriminate between the two, and this implies the existence of an image of the inner world, however nebulous and incomplete it may be in comparison with our rich and highly-developed image of the outer. The contemporary mentality, in fact, is strongly prejudiced against the inner world in all but one respect—that of rational thought—which simply means that we are incapable of making sense of it, just as we are incapable of making sense of speech in an unknown tongue.

This study is mainly concerned with the manner in which the awareness of this duality of experience works its way into consciousness, of how the images of the two worlds are built up, and of the respects in which, when fully developed, they are found to differ.

THE MIND AND THE BRAIN

We think that we know where the outer world is, and it is hardly necessary to warn the intelligent reader against the ingenuous assumption, common in more primitive thought, that the inner world is in another place, e.g. above the sky, or beyond the sea or the mountains; it is, however, perhaps advisable to make it clear from the start that one is not 'inside our heads' and the other outside.

This is the basic misconception against which we have to fight, and the background and causation of which will become apparent as we progress. The contemporary picture of the world, which is accepted as self-evident by even the majority of leaders of thought, is that of a host of individual minds, often confused with brains, each confined within its own individual skull and all contained in a common outer world which exists in its own right, independently of them, and is the same for all of them. At least it would be the same if only they could understand it properly, for the sole function of these brains is to form a picture of the outer world, as revealed to them through the organs of sense, which shall correspond as closely as possible with its workings, again as revealed by the organs of sense. It is generally assumed, and often expressly stated, that the only things which the subject can 'know' with certainty are those which have been revealed to his brain as a result of sensory experiences, and the sole purpose of knowledge or understanding is seen as the correlation of the sensory experiences of the past in such a way that those of the future can be predicted. The consequence of this attitude is that mind comes to be regarded as a mere function of the brain, and it is this misconception which gives rise to most of our difficulties.

The brain is a physical object, situated at a precise point in time and space. It possesses extensions, in the form of the organs of sense, which provide it with information regarding the position which it occupies in relation to other material objects, thereby defining that position and giving it a central or nuclear quality. The mind, on the other hand, although in its personal aspect it is linked to one brain or another, is by no means exclusively confined to any point in time and space. *Time, space and material objects, including the brain and the sense-organs, are contained in the mind, not the mind in them.* (Time and space, of course, cannot be perceived in themselves, but only as relationships between objects, states or situations.)

While personal consciousness is normally very largely determined or shaped by the precise position in time and space of the brain with which it is associated, it is perfectly capable of escaping from this bondage and turning, instead, to the other aspects of mind which are not so confined. This latter aspect of mind is commonly unconscious—i.e. personal consciousness is averted from it—but it is always available as an alternative mode of experience, and some individuals who are gifted in this respect make use of it frequently and are even capable of making the transition—passing through the Barrier—at will.

This matter will become clearer as we progress; the contemporary prejudice against accepting mind as something separate from, and to some extent independent of the brain is, however, extremely hard to eradicate and cannot be attacked too often. Let it then be repeated: the inner world is not confined within our heads, nor is the outer world confined outside them. Both are aspects of the mind.

THE TWO WORLDS OF WALTER MITTY

Yonder see the morning blink:
  The sun is up, and up must I,
To wash and dress and eat and drink
And look at things and talk and think
  And work, and God knows why.

Oh often have I washed and dressed
  And what's to show for all my pain?
Let me lie abed and rest:
Ten thousand times I've done my best
  And all's to do again.[1]

Most people must have felt at some time or other the tragedy

[1] A. E. Housman: *Last Poems.*

and horror of the daily return to the bondage of This World
—that misery immortally rendered in terms of the human body
in Michelangelo's figure of Dawn on the Medici tombs. 'She
doesn't seem to be very happy about it,' somebody seeing a
picture of this reluctant awakening for the first time once said
to me. Indeed she does not; but how many people have seen
the point?

Reference has already been made, in connection with *No
Orchids*, to the delights of the Other Side and the cheerlessness
of This World when contrasted to it; one more example of the
expression of this feeling, taken this time from a highly reputable
source, may complete the picture.

> Be not afeard: the isle is full of noises.
> Sounds and sweet airs, that give delight and hurt not
> Sometimes a thousand twangling instruments
> Will hum about mine ears; and sometimes voices,
> That, if I then had wak'd after long sleep,
> Will make me sleep again: and then, in dreaming,
> The clouds methought would open and show riches
> Ready to drop upon me; that, when I wak'd
> I cried to dream again.[1]

This inner world, which is in some respects so much pleasanter
(although in others so much less pleasant) and nearly always
so much more exciting, colourful and full of meaning than the
outer, cannot be simply dismissed as the expression of longings
for pleasures which we have once enjoyed but lack at the
moment in the outer world: it is no mere substitute for 'real'
experience but a complete alternative to it, existing in its own
right. It is true, of course, that we are often led to turn to it as
a refuge from an unsatisfactory outer life, but on the other hand
it often forces itself on us, not infrequently in unpleasant forms,
quite of its own accord. This, incidentally, is the difficulty with
which Freud was confronted, and which he attempted to
explain away—in my view quite unsuccessfully—in *Beyond the
Pleasure Principle*.

If we are open-minded we are compelled to admit that
virtually everybody is more or less distinctly aware of an

---

[1] Caliban, in *The Tempest*. Prospero's island, as we shall see when we
come to analyse the play in a later volume, is a symbol of the inner world.

alternative mode of experience in which things have a totally different significance from that which they have in the outer world, and in which they conform to totally different laws. They long to hear of arduous journeys to fantastic places, of catastrophic loves and even of extravagant torments, not because they have ever experienced anything even remotely resembling these situations in their personal lives, but simply because the stories have symbolical significance. They are enabled to experience the symbolical pattern in imagination, and the symbol, being a living force and no mere allegory, acts on the mind, relieving tensions and showing the way out of deadlocks. When, on rare occasions, such symbolical patterns do appear in their outer lives they experience them, of course, with even greater intensity; but on such occasions the very intensity of the experience produces repercussions, in that part of the mind which is orientated towards outer experience, which are so powerful that they tend to be overwhelming. Hence such experiences are invariably disturbing, and are generally unpleasant rather than pleasant. In the end the clear-cut symbolical significance tends to be lost, becoming overlaid by the multitude of practical repercussions which it engenders, and very few people who have gone through really dramatic experiences have any desire to repeat them—although they will talk of them endlessly. An outstanding example of the overpowering and crushing effect of such coincidences of the two worlds will be seen when we come, in a later volume, to consider the case of T. E. Lawrence. It is only the tough and insensitive who are capable of enduring much symbolical content in their outer lives.

Thus fantasies, and an interest in the inner world in general, are not to be regarded as morbid symptoms of maladjustment to the outer world: on the contrary, they are the signs of a very healthy adjustment to it. An understanding and objective interest in the fantastic, the dramatic and even the sensational are evidence that the subject is aware of mental needs which cannot possibly be satisfied in his outer life without disrupting it completely: he therefore very wisely satisfies them in the inner world. He recognizes the primary necessity of maintaining himself as a responsible and productive agent in the outer world, and he knows that this task is a difficult one which can only be accomplished by a patient and persevering concentration on his outer life: there is no scope there for the volcanic and shattering manifestations of the spirit, which is the pure essence of the active power of the inner world. But such a concentration on the harsh and dreary necessities of the outer life leaves something in the mind uncatered for, and he experiences a craving for the wider horizons and the intenser, more dramatic life of the Other Side. If he is wise he will not dismiss this craving as a temptation to waste time and energy in escapism, but will offer it the expression and the scope it demands: when he finds waking unbearable and cries to dream again he will allow himself to dream; or, if he lacks talent for it, he will participate in the dreams of the story-tellers.

He must, however, beware of one mistake, which is the mistake of Walter Mitty: that is to identify his outer-world personality with his inner-world experiences.

The Secret Life of Walter Mitty is Thurber's masterpiece, but its theme is by no means unique in his writings, many of which hinge on this contrast between fact and fancy. Generally Walter Mitty appears as the writer, who never tires of presenting the unworldly, unpractical, fantasy-ridden personality (which, he implies, is his own) in its humorously painful collisions with the prosaic outer world of machinery, policemen and domestic servants. Yet behind the wry self-depreciation may be discerned an insistence, sometimes gentle but at times almost arrogant, on the fundamental superiority of this incompetent and in-decisive, yet poetic figure, which he makes himself out to be, over all the hard-headed and efficient persons who form his environment, and who think so highly of themselves.

But he has also another vein, in which he mildly ridicules all that is pretentious, or that lacks a sense of proportion, or that 'horse-sense' which spontaneously discriminates between the factual and the fanciful.

His insistence on the compensatory superiority of the Mitty type and its justification in its own right is wholesome, for the contemporary world is inclined to accept extravert values too uncritically. Hard-headedness, efficiency and competence are its gods, and it is all too apt to overlook the fact that these virtues, valuable though they undoubtedly are, tend to crush and suppress the delicate growths of the mind. Life, the Tao

Teh Ching[1] says, is soft, tender and fragile (like the bud); it is death which is hard and tough (like the seasoned timber). The success of a Thurber suggests that contemporary people are in need of some little comfort and reassurance in face of the harsh demands of the Blandish system.

This unworldly trend in Thurber is at first sight hard to reconcile with the insistence on realistic common sense and sobriety of statement—the tendency to 'debunk'—which we have also noted. If he insists on the value of fantasy and of the irrational over against the intransigently practical, utilitarian standpoint, then why does he so subtly attack (with a trenchancy graciously concealed by his mild and almost apologetic tone) such extravagances as Salvador Dali's auto-biography, and the theses of those purveyors of popular psychology who attribute road accidents to the idea that a motor-car is a sexual symbol ('because of the mechanical principle involved')? The answer is that he makes a fine distinction between two worlds: those of fancy and of fact. Probably he does not visualize the matter in these terms, yet his writings are a perpetual affirmation of his intuitive apperception of the truth that two worlds exist. Fantasy, he asserts, has value, however irrational it may be—or, rather, precisely because of that irrationality. It is the enemy of the factual, down-to-earth, practical attitude which is perpetually trying to suppress it; the man who is gifted with fantasy and who lives a part of his life in a world of imaginings is for ever at loggerheads with the outer world of facts and its ineluctable demands. He makes a fool of himself when faced with the simplest practical problems (Mitty cannot even park his car efficiently) and is despised by his fellows and his wife, yet he feels superior to those who lack his gift, for he knows that his inner values are real.

Yet at the same time those who possess the gift of changing the scene of consciousness from the outer to the inner world —from the realm of fact to that of fancy—must for ever be on their guard against the danger of overlooking and under-rating the requirements of the former, and of distorting their

---

[1] The basic work of the Taoist movement, traditionally ascribed to Lao Tse, but in the opinion of modern scholars a compilation from various writers (including Lao Tse) probably made in the third century B.C. See Sir Arthur Waley: *The Way and Its Power.*

perception of its true nature in accordance with the requirements of fantasy or theory. Thus Thurber insists that facts and
the world of practical living have their own validity and obey
their own laws, which are totally different from those obtaining
in the world of fancy. These laws, and the pattern of this outer
world, must be recognized and respected; that is why he is
moved to scornful attacks against those who impose their
theories and their fantasies on to factual material in defiance
of the totally different patterns of the factual world; it is also
the reason why he is for ever describing the absurd predicaments
into which he, and those like him, are constantly falling when
they come into contact with the intractable world of matter,
and of human prejudices and presuppositions. Fact and fancy,
he inferentially insists, must be kept strictly separate, for they
are irreconcilable. Seeing himself in the unpleasant situation
of living at the point of collision of these two powerful and
irreconcilable forces he is a little sorry for himself and makes
a determined effort to overcome his sufferings (which, like
those of all such people, are real enough) by laughing at
them.

Humour is an invaluable aid in smoothing over the minor
frictions of terrestrial life, yet it must not be allowed to obscure
basic problems, and the irreconcilability of the two worlds is
a very real problem which must be tackled in all seriousness.
A valuable first step in escaping the dilemma in which we find
ourselves is precisely this, of visualizing these two modes of
experience as two separate worlds which, while they interpenetrate, are of two diverse and incompatible natures. (This
is the symbolism of the two interpenetrating triangles called
'the Star of David': ✡). This conception is of course no more
than a heuristic aid towards understanding the problem: the
two worlds are neither of them objective facts, although many
of their contents are, and every entity which is perceived by a
consciousness exists concurrently in both of them. What we are
concerned with is the form in which anything appears in consciousness, i.e. the manner in which it has been shaped and
interpreted in those levels of the mind which select and form
the objects of consciousness. The nature of the ultimate image
in consciousness, which is what we conceive the external object
to be, depends on (among other things) whether outer- or

inner-world principles have been employed in its selection and shaping.

The story of Walter Mitty is a brilliant exposition of this theme. Its most striking feature is that the passages of the conscious mind from one world to the other are made without transition or indication of the change: at one moment we are being told of the thrilling experience of a naval commander taking a giant hydroplane through a hurricane, and in the next paragraph, without a word of explanation, we find poor Mitty being reprimanded by his wife for driving the car too fast; he passes the hospital and suddenly we are in the operating theatre, with Mitty performing prodigies of surgery. If told conventionally, of course, the narrative would contain explanatory transitions: 'The sight of the hospital evoked pictures in Mitty's mind of what was going on inside. Probably, he thought, an operation was in progress at this moment; a human life lay in the balance: everything depended on the surgeon's skill. Suddenly the scene took shape before him: he saw himself, etc.' The result would be a trite description of a 'pipe-dreamer's' fantasies, but Thurber's method leaves the reader, with a delighted thrill of perception, to make the discovery for himself: 'Of course! He's imagining all this!'

It is in gratitude for that thrill of triumphant understanding that the reader remembers the story with pleasure; it is unlikely that he realizes that he has been put in the way of understanding far more. For the point of the story is not the fact, which everybody knows, that people in general, and more particularly, perhaps, the ineffectual and unsuccessful, are given to seeking compensation for the poverty and disagreeableness of the experiences afforded them in the outer world by availing themselves of the richer and more colourful experiences provided by fancy; it is far rather that the consciousness of Walter Mitty, which is no more than an artistically exaggerated type of human consciousness in general, exists alternately in two modes, and that, so far as that consciousness is concerned, there are no grounds for saying that either of them is more 'real' than the other.

This question of 'reality' is of the essence of the problem: it will form the subject of the next chapter, and for the moment we may content ourselves with noting that the exclusive reality of the outer world, by which, for the moment, I mean 'that which we may touch or see', is by no means so self-evident as it might appear at first sight. At other times and in other places, indeed, the prevailing prejudice has been of the opposite nature: the civilization of ancient India, for example, was founded on a philosophy of life which insisted that the material universe was a mere illusion, and that reality was to be found only in the mind; even in our own Middle Ages the inner life (often seen as the 'after-life' of the soul) was definitely valued more highly than life in this world.

It may at first sight appear absurd to see such abstruse philosophical ideas in the humorous little sketch of Walter Mitty; but philosophical ideas need not necessarily be expressed in philosophical form. Or, to put it in another way, the philosophical is only one of the possible forms in which an idea can be expressed: it is essentially an academic and intellectual form, from which all but logical and conceptual elements have been rigorously excluded. But the idea (in the Platonic sense) being a reality on the Archetypal level, is a pattern which embraces aesthetic, symbolical and feeling values besides the intellectual, and it may be brought to expression in any of these media just as well and as truly as in a philosophical dissertation. The Archetypal 'idea' of the Two Worlds is clearly expressed in Beethoven's music, and there is no reason at all why it should not become manifest in a humorous sketch by Thurber.

The basic pattern is there, to be seen in the insistence on the equal validity of Mitty's two modes of experience. The conventional novelist describing Mitty would have used some such forms as I have indicated above: taking the outer-world Mitty as the point of reference he would have insisted that here was the reality; the excursions into the world of fantasy would have been described as thoughts produced by this character, precisely on a par with his thoughts about his wife or his car. But Thurber shows us that there are in fact two separate Walter Mittys, united, like Jekyll and Hyde, only by the fact that they share a single stream of consciousness and must therefore alternate in their possession of it.

For the inner, the secret Mitty is always the same, no matter in which of the trite heroic roles from film or thriller he appears, and the situations in which he finds himself, varied as they are, have the one characteristic in common, that they are as exciting and dramatic as Mitty's outer life is dull and prosaic. The picture of the two contrasting lives and of the two contrasting personalities who live them is brilliantly worked out, with an extraordinary economy of means, and the final impression is that, of the two, the inner is the more real: Mitty regards his outer life as no more than a series of vexatious and incoherent interruptions in his far more vividly experienced heroic career. That is why he devotes so little attention to it, and is for ever making a mess of his outer-world activities: he does not build a fantasy-world for himself as a compensation for his incompetence in the outer world: he is incompetent in the outer world because, for him at least, the world of fantasy is so much more real than the world of fact.

Here we reach the point mentioned earlier: Mitty's mistake lies in his inability to distinguish between the contrasting natures of the inner and outer worlds, and of the two selves who experience them respectively. It is for this reason that he is a pathetic and, in the last resort, contemptible escapist, who flees from the difficulties of the outer world by taking improper advantage of the facilities of the inner. If he understood the problem he would be able to appease his unsatisfied craving for the symbolical, the dramatic and the colourful elements in which his outer life (like most outer lives) is deficient, by the perfectly legitimate and harmless means of imagining exciting situations without seeing his outer-world self as their central character and hero. This is the form of imagining of which the creative artist makes use, and Mitty is potentially creative; his only trouble is that he stands in his own light. It is a sufficiently common weakness, and it is because most people know the creative fantasy only in this distorted form that it is commonly regarded as inferior and even harmful. Thurber himself, of course, is perfectly well aware of this fact.

And when we turn to the consideration of actual cases, do we really find that it is only, or even predominantly, the incompetent, the unsuccessful and those who lead dull lives who indulge in fantasies? From my personal experience I should say it was rather the reverse, for I have known several individuals whose lives were full of interest and excitement and who, in their way, were far from unsuccessful, but who none the less indulged in fantasies to a pronounced degree. Such types reveal certain weaknesses in face of outer-world problems, being generally undependable, lacking in consistent application, and liable to act on occasion with a hair-raising irresponsibility and ineptitude; they may, however, learn to overcome these shortcomings. Often they exhibit outstanding enterprise and determination, and the urge to translate fantasy into fact may provide the incentive to sensational performances: in the study of T. E. Lawrence a case in point will be considered. Imagination, after all, is indispensable to greatness, and it may well be that the idea that fantasies are 'nothing but' inferior and infantile substitutes for 'real life' activities is only another product of the contemporary prejudice against the inner world.

Fantasies, nevertheless, as the study of Lawrence, and, still more, of Hitler, will show, may be dangerous, or even catastrophic: this is the case when the subject fails to appreciate the contrasting natures of the two worlds and attempts to coerce the outer world to comply with the pattern of the inner. It is impossible to elaborate this thesis until we have progressed considerably further in the study of the characteristic patterns of the two worlds and their contrasting natures; for the moment we must content ourselves with the observation that Walter Mitty's dual mode of experience is universal, in a greater or lesser degree, in all human beings; the difference between one individual and another in this respect lies in the degree to which the two modes are brought to consciousness and their irreconcilability appreciated.

VARIATION IN THE RELATIONSHIP TO THE TWO WORLDS AS BETWEEN INDIVIDUALS

This is a vital point, because, as we shall see, there is no universally valid dividing line between the two worlds. They consist, as we have noted, of mental systems, according to which diverse experiences are interpreted: the difference lies not in the material itself but in the manner in which it is, so to speak, 'processed' and given significance in the mind. Thus, to take a simple example, one man will interpret a feeling of depression and malaise in outer-world terms, attributing it to his digestion or to the weather, whereas another will see it at once as the symptom of an inner-world disturbance, such as dissatisfaction with his progress in life, or even, if he has psychological insight, of the conflict between two purely mental factors. Inner and outer must be regarded as directions, like East and West, rather than as fixed areas: no matter where we start we can always move either eastward or westward, and the line dividing the two depends solely on our position at the moment. Thus regions which to one individual are 'the East' are to another, living further eastward, 'the West' (we must overlook the convention whereby even Americans refer to Japan, which lies westward of them, as 'the Far East'; New York, to an American, is 'the East', whereas to a European it is 'the West').

Thus each individual has a mental 'residence' or habitual point of departure in the matter of discriminating between the two worlds, and what is 'inner' to one is 'outer' to another. This analogy, however, must not be pursued too far, for the mind is inherently so constituted that it must work in both directions: it is, however, open to the individual to concentrate his consciousness on either the inward or the outward tendency at the expense of the other, and this process results in the relegation of the neglected tendency to the unconscious, where he is not aware of its functioning and loses control of it.

Thus the inner world, for instance, affects different individuals in different ways. In the unimaginative materialistic type it barely reaches consciousness at all: he is unaware of inner problems and sees everything in outer-world terms. This, up to a point, simplifies life for him: his inner life is embedded in the collectivity and thus conforms to patterns which, in a stable society, have been evolved through centuries of trial and error and suffice to canalize the impulses emanating from the inner world. These are the mores[1] of his community: the collective ideas and ideals, customs and values in which he has been brought up and which (except, perhaps, in matters of detail) he accepts as unquestionably right. Personally, of course, he is convinced of his own absolute freedom of action and independence of judgment, but in fact most of his actions are dictated and his opinions and judgments formed for him by collective patterns, the action of which he does not perceive.

[1] Plural of the Latin *mos*; usage, custom or conduct; adopted in English as a translation of the German *Sitte*, for which there is no exact equivalent.

This condition implies that he is entirely dependent on the undisturbed and satisfactory functioning of his community, and on the continuing efficacy of those collective forms which shield him from personal contact with inner-world forces.

Collective, systematized religion provides a good example of such a shield: as Jung has demonstrated in his *Psychology and Religion* its purpose is not to bring man into direct contact with God, but to protect him from it. The direct action of the spirit is a dangerous and disruptive influence which few individuals are fitted to control: when it strikes those who are incapable of dealing with it, excesses and enormities are the inevitable consequence. Communalized religion therefore imposes on the faithful beliefs and ideals, and, above all, symbolical observances, which possess the property of canalizing and regularizing their chaotic religious impulses and guiding them into beneficial channels.

Such a shield may break down either individually or collectively. Individuals who develop their inner-world consciousness to a degree which frees them from the collective bondage find the collective religious forms no longer efficacious and are henceforth compelled to find their own individual way of coming to terms with those inner-world forces from which they had been hitherto shielded. These, of course, emanating from deep and archaic levels of the unconscious mind, are apt to take forms which are anything but 'religious' in the conventional sense. Or the shield may break down in the collective sense if the current religious system is for any reason discredited: this may occur as a result of abuses, or of some advance of consciousness in another sphere which makes the traditional beliefs or observances no longer acceptable. When this occurs the masses are at the mercy of any prophet who succeeds in activating and gaining control of the inner life of the collectivity.

Examples of this process are numerous in history: the most recent was the Nazi episode, which was the outcome of the system devised by the prophet Hitler to fill the vacuum left in Germany after 1918 by the discredit into which the pre-war collective system had fallen. This, of course, was not merely a question of religion: monarchy, capitalism, the military system —all the pillars on which the Second Reich had been built— had collapsed as well as Christianity in its communal aspect.

The latter, however, has long been losing its efficacy as a social force in the more advanced communities, and whatever its importance in the minds of isolated individuals, it is no longer capable of canalizing and directing the forces of the collective unconscious, as it did in the Middle Ages.

Thus although, as I observed above, life is considerably simplified for those who never come into conscious contact with the inner world, the price which they pay for this alleviation of the human lot lies in their dependence on the collectivity and their vulnerability to the dangerous side of the mass unconscious.

To the Walter Mittys, on the other hand, the inner world is more conscious, and hence more 'real' than the outer. Their outlook is predominantly orientated by what they know and experience of it, and to them it is the outer world which lacks reality and inherent validity. When the two come into conflict it is the outer world which they see as 'wrong', and instead of adapting their ideas to what they have discovered about it in the course of the collision, they either withdraw from it or seek to alter it in accordance with their ideas of what it ought to be. In the latter case, of course, they may be successful, but only to a limited degree. With their particular capacities and problems we shall be concerned later: we may, however, note at this point that although their attitude complicates life for them in some respects it may give them, in others, greater adaptability, and certainly greater insight than their outer-world-orientated fellows.

EMPHASIS ON THE REALITY OF THE INNER WORLD

My basic purpose is to insist on the reality of the inner world, not only in the abstract sense in which we say that a star, for instance, is real, although the fact has absolutely no effect on our lives—which would be exactly the same if it were an illusion —but in the sense that it contains forces which do act upon us, and sometimes in a most drastic manner. I am not, of course, contending that the inner world is any more real than the outer, but merely that it is no less real. So great, however, is the contemporary prejudice in favour of the exclusive reality of the outer world that there is no need to emphasize that it does possess reality: rather is it necessary to depreciate and disparage its importance in order to make a little room in people's minds for the acceptance of the reality of the inner. If A stands in the middle of the hearth, taking all the warmth of the fire for himself and depriving B of his share, then it is necessary to push A aside in order to make room for B; A is still entitled to his half-share, but in order to satisfy B's legitimate requirements it is necessary to start by attacking A.

This undertaking is no less necessary for the Walter Mittys than for the extraverts and materialists, for although Mitty in fact undervalues the outer world he does not understand what he is doing and has nothing adequate to put in its place. Being indoctrinated from his earliest years, like everybody else, with the belief that only the outer world is real, and having acquired from his environment a far richer and completer picture of it than he has of his own province, the inner world, he inevitably tends to interpret the latter in terms of the former, and this may lead to very serious trouble. As we shall see when we come to study the Conquerors, the really dangerous men are not the practical and worldly self-seekers, but the doctrinaire and the fanatic who refuse to admit the difference between theory and practice: they are Mittys of a more aggressive and positive type who are impelled to force their theories and their dreams on an outer world which they neither value nor understand.

Now that the forces of the inner world—the dreams and theories, fears and suspicions,—have thermo-nuclear bombs at their disposal, the question of controlling them has become the question of human survival. The thermo-nuclear bomb is being developed as a deterrent, on the assumption that those who have control of them will never be so utterly deficient of a sense of outer-world reality that they will make use of them when they are assured that the inevitable consequence of doing so will be retaliation in kind and the possible destruction of the human race. But can we be assured that those in power inevitably will possess such a well-developed sense of outer-world reality? Sir Winston Churchill, in the course of rather complacently announcing to the Commons his government's decision to manufacture such bombs, admitted that the doctrine of the unchallengeable deterrent broke down in face of the mentality of a Hitler, and certainly there can be no doubt that if this weapon had been perfected ten years earlier Hitler would have made use of it, even if he had been assured of the inevitability of retaliation. For in his last months he was bent on destroying as much as he could, inside Germany no less than outside, and he expressly and repeatedly stated that there was no purpose in the German nation's surviving defeat.[1] When we come to examine his motivation we shall see that it was basically suicidal from the outset, and what could have been a more effective way of achieving a truly gigantic self-immolation?

Paradoxical though it may seem, Hitler was a characteristic Mitty, although of the aggressive type. 'Should anyone say to me,' he proclaimed in a speech in 1940, ' "These are mere fantastic dreams, mere visions," I can only reply that when I set out on my course in 1919 as an unknown, nameless soldier I built my hopes for the future upon a most vivid imagination. Yet all has come true.'[2] And Field-Marshal Guderian, Chief of Staff of the Army during the last phase of the war, relates that when he attempted to point out the dangers of the situation to Hitler at a conference on 9th January, 1945, he was met by a hysterical outburst of rage, for, he says:

He had a special picture of the world, and every fact had to be fitted into that fancied picture. As he believed, so the world must be: but, in fact, it was a picture of another world.[3]

When we come to examine the career and personality of Hitler in a later volume we shall see that there was nothing very extraordinary about him until he began making political speeches, and it was the modern apparatus of power which eventually unhinged his mind by finally destroying his always weak sense of the independent reality of the outer world. He, and together with him the German nation and most of the rest of the world, was thus left at the mercy of his personal interpretation of the images of an inner world, the nature of which he did not understand. Is there any guarantee that the same thing will not happen again?

I am not advocating that any nation should unilaterally dis-

---

[1] See Alan Bullock: *Hitler, a Study in Tyranny.*
[2] *My New Order.* Speech of 10th December 1940. Quoted by Bullock *op. cit.*
[3] Quoted from the same source.

continue the manufacture of thermo-nuclear bombs: apart from the fact that in the present psychological situation any such exhortations are a pure waste of time, it is my conviction that since these devices exist it is better to be numbered among those who possess them than among those who do not, for if they are used nobody will be saved by the fact that he is defenceless. But I do maintain that our only slender chance of survival lies in learning to understand and appreciate the factors at work in the inner world, for it is by this means alone that mentalities of the type of Hitler's may possibly be prevented from developing and attaining power. The two factors, as I have suggested in connection with Hitler, work together, each reacting upon and intensifying the other: power-fantasies lead to a bid for power, and the experience of power encourages (in this type of mind) the indulgence in yet more grandiose fantasies, which induce a bid for further power, and so on. This question, however, must be postponed for later consideration.

The inner world, then, possesses a very high degree of reality in its own right. *Wirklich ist was wirkt* Jung says—'that is real which acts', or 'which has consequences'. In illustration of this he points out that if a man shoots me because he believes that I am his worst enemy, the fact that his belief happens to be mistaken does not make me any the less dead. The notion in his mind, in fact, was 'real' enough to cause my death, although it bore no relation to the factual situation. Similarly Hitler's special picture of the world brought about at least twenty million deaths, as well as untold suffering and material losses which have not yet been made good twelve years after his death: it was 'real' enough for that.

We shall not succeed in avoiding a repetition of this catastrophe, on a still larger scale, by the simple expedient of saying that Hitler was mad, for, in the first place, the ability to win, and to hold for twelve years, the allegiance of a great and highly civilized nation, and to carry out, methodically and consistently, a preconceived plan for the conquest of Europe, cannot be covered by any reasonable interpretation of the word 'mad'; and in the second, even if we substitute the more appropriate term 'irresponsible', we have to accept the fact that if one leading contemporary state can be carried away by such a wave of irresponsibility we are not justified in assuming, without more ado, that it could not happen to our own, or to any other. Germany is not unique.

However improbable it may seem that 'it might happen again' we simply cannot afford to take for granted the supposition that it will not do so, until we have at least made a serious attempt to identify the background and causes of the last outbreak, as we should do in the case of an epidemic of physical illness, and thereby assured ourselves that we understand its causation and can master any tendency to a recurrence. Such an attempt will be made in a future volume: in the meanwhile I put forward the hypothesis that the question is connected with the contemporary ignorance of the nature of the inner world and its forces.

A study of the inner world reveals that its nature can be analysed and understood, and that its contents are objective and obey laws in exactly the same way as those of the outer world. The phenomena of Hitler and of Nazism are perfectly intelligible by reference to those laws and may be regarded as no more anomalous, and about as unusual, as an epidemic of cholera used to be. By a concentrated study of the laws of the outer world we have learnt to understand the nature of cholera and have largely eliminated it in civilized countries. Why should we not achieve the same control of inner-world epidemics?

There is no reason why we should not do so, but if we are to be successful two conditions are indispensable. First we must persuade ourselves to believe in the reality of the inner world to the extent of being prepared to act upon our conclusions with regard to it with the same conviction and determination as those with which we are prepared to act upon our conclusions regarding the outer world. In other words we must accept its reality whole-heartedly, and without any tacit reservations of the 'no more than' type. Secondly we must appreciate the fact that it has its own laws, which have little or no relation to the laws of the outer world with which we are so obsessed. Instead of attempting to interpret it in accordance with the latter, which are totally alien to its nature, we must start with a clean slate and an unprejudiced mind to collect appropriate material and to formulate the patterns and tendencies which it reveals.

APPROACH TO THE PROBLEMS OF THE INNER WORLD

To begin with we must humbly accept the fact of our complete
ignorance and ineptitude in this strange world; we must make
a modest start by considering in all seriousness what the writer
of a disreputable thriller has been able to discover about it. We
may reassure ourselves by noting that the conclusions he has
reached show significant parallels with stories and myths
originating in very different circumstances; from this discovery
it is legitimate to infer that he is dealing with basic problems
which have concerned humanity in many different ages and
places throughout history. It is true that our material consists,
so far, only of one personal rendering, originating in a mind
apparently not particularly profound or widely informed—
and presented in a manner which inspires anything but a serious
reception—of a theme of exceptional profundity and scope;
nevertheless it is a mind which has adventured into distant
regions to which the majority of us lack the enterprise, or perhaps the courage, to penetrate; we must therefore accept what
its owner has to tell us of his experiences in the same grateful
spirit as that in which we accept the information brought back
by travellers into distant lands of which we have little knowledge. However ignorant or superficial they may be in themselves, theirs is the best information available to us.

I imagine that Hadley Chase (regarding whose outer-world
existence and personality I possess no information whatever)
is by no means as superficial as a casual reading of *No Orchids*
might suggest; at all events, as I have remarked, there is reason
to believe that he is honest about his inner-world experiences,
for he shirks no unpleasant issues and is not concerned to foist
any false picture of his personality or his values on the reader.
The same cannot be said of many novelists, even among the
greatest. And finally there is the richness of symbolical forms
which distinguishes his work and reveals the parallels which
lead over to other versions of the same theme.

No Orchids therefore presents an acceptable starting-point for
an investigation of the laws and patterns of the inner world. Its
comparatively low status in the literary scale increases rather
than diminishes this suitability, for its popular success demonstrates that its subject-matter has made an immediate appeal to

the contemporary collective unconscious. A classic from the past, or a superior work of fiction of the present, the popularity of which was confined to the appreciative few, would lack this advantage, since it might be held that its appeal was based, at least to some extent, on formal literary or intellectual values, or on prestige. These last are matters with which we are not concerned from the point of view of this study, except as a secondary consideration.

The study of *No Orchids* revealed not only the basic theme of the two worlds themselves, but led also to a number of conclusions regarding some of the figures inhabiting the inner world—in other words its contents—and their typical manner of behaviour. Therewith we have taken the first steps in the vast field of study which the inner world represents. A great deal of further investigation, involving many other products of the creative fantasy and the lives of their progenitors, will be required before we can fill in even the broad outlines of the picture thus glimpsed. This work will be the subject of future volumes of this study: for the moment we are still concerned with the contrast between the two worlds themselves, and with the first of the conditions essential for the mastery of the inner world which I mentioned earlier; namely the acceptance of a force of 'reality' in the inner world no less than that which we habitually take for granted in the outer.

This question of 'reality' lies at the root of the matter. Our attitude towards the inner world is very largely determined by the extent to which we are prepared to accord the property of reality to its contents. No reasonable person can deny reality, in the sense in which the term is commonly understood, to the outer world and its contents, and civilized thought has succeeded in constructing from them an intelligible, consistent and serviceable system which excludes that material which I have described as belonging to the inner world. If, therefore, we are to accept reality in the latter we have to consider the question whether there may exist two different forms of reality, an inner and an outer, in the same way as I have suggested that there are two different forms of truth, the factual and the psychological, which are completely independent of one another. In order to do this we must first examine the nature of the criteria on which we base our normal, everyday discrimination between the 'real' and the 'unreal', and secondly what conscious, half-conscious or unconscious prejudices we may have in the matter of what we are prepared, on reflection, to accept as 'reality'. This will be the subject of the next chapter.

II *The Problem of Reality*

ON the 10th November 1619 René Descartes, being then a young gentleman of twenty-three soldiering in the Bavarian service, retired to rest in his overheated[1] quarters at Neuburg on the Danube and was visited by three dreams which made a deep impression on him. The content of the dreams need not concern us: the really important thing about them was evidently their vividness for, as we shall see, Descartes was certainly left with that impression, which everybody must have experienced in similar circumstances at some time or other, that although he had indisputably been dreaming, something had 'really happened'.

Ordinarily, on our awaking after a dream, the sense of the reality of the outer life flows back with such overpowering force that we are immediately aware of the less substantial nature of the recent experience: recognizing at once that it was 'only a dream' we dismiss its implications as unworthy of further attention. If, for instance, I dream that I have returned to boarding-school, my first mental act on awaking is to compare this situation with the picture of my present, outer-world condition which is always at the back of my mind, and to realize that the two are incompatible. I have long since achieved adult

---

[1] The expression which he uses is *dans un poêle*, and this has generally been taken to refer to the physical circumstances. But he also tells us that at the time he was immersed in his thoughts, grappling with freshly emerging ideas, and it is possible that he used the phrase in a figurative sense. Allusion has already been made, in connection with the overheated atmosphere described in the opening scene of *No Orchids*, to the symbolism of heat as it appears in the Indian notion of *tapas* or creative effort, and in the 'cooking' of the Alchemists. Jung also states that the image of a pot on the fire indicates that the unconscious process of integration is in progress.

status and am free of the petty restrictions of school discipline and the subordinate position of the pupil; it is an unheard-of and virtually impossible thing for a man of my age to find himself suddenly returned to the situation of boyhood. Furthermore, I realize, such a change could not occur without previous preparation, and a hurried examination of my memories of the immediate past discloses (to my relief) that no such preparations have taken place. These processes of thought, of course, occur so rapidly and with so little conscious elaboration that I am hardly aware of them: I am conscious only of the immediate conviction that my recent experience was impossible and absurd and cannot, therefore, have been 'real'.

What has happened is that I have re-orientated myself rapidly in accordance with my picture of the outer world and my situation in it, and before I accept the 'reality' of any experience I demand that it should be compatible with this picture and should fit into it without violating any of the rules of logic or any of my convictions regarding what is possible; if it fails to satisfy these requirements I regard it as a delusion. Since I am familiar with dreams and their disconnected and irrational nature I can immediately and easily account for my recent experience by classifying it as a dream, and thus as lacking any practical importance or implications; I can, in fact, discount it as a 'real' experience from which it would be necessary to draw conclusions regarding my relationship with the outer world, and thus need trouble my head no more with it. This attitude is of course necessary in order to enable me to deal with my life in the outer world, for on awaking I have immediately to concern myself with a host of problems connected with the latter, even if they be no more than those of getting up and dressing; if I were to devote my attention to the dream experiences, regarding them in the same light as those of waking life, I should not only waste a great deal of time, but should also begin to base my behaviour on false premisses. If I went so far as to abandon all discrimination between these two modes of experience I should become totally incapable of coming to terms with the outer world and should have to be certified insane and placed under restraint. When, in a later volume, we come to consider the case of Nietzsche, we shall see this process exemplified.

This brings us to the first important conclusion regarding the two worlds or two modes of experience, namely that *the ability of the individual to lead a rational, independent life in civilized surroundings is dependent on his maintaining a modicum of discrimination between the two.* For everybody has dreams, no matter how little importance he attaches to them, or how quickly he succeeds in forgetting them: dream experience, or an 'inner life' which manifests itself in other forms besides dreams, is universal in humanity, even though in many individuals—in fact in the great majority—it barely reaches consciousness; it is only by segregating it strictly from all those other experiences which conform to his picture of the outer world (which he calls 'reality') that the individual is able to maintain himself as a responsible, independent person. This is the purpose of the Barrier.

But there are occasions when the reorientation in accordance with the outer-world picture does not take place with the usual ease and spontaneity. This occurs when dreams possess such a degree of vividness and intensity, or are accompanied by so powerful an aura of importance, that the dreamer, on awaking, cannot rid himself of the conviction that something has 'really happened'; alternatively the memory of the dream situation may recur later in the day (or even after a considerable interval) in the guise of a factual memory, in which capacity the subject for a moment accepts it, only to realize with something of a shock that it was not factual at all, but 'only a dream'. These are what Jung characterizes as 'great dreams', in contrast to the small dreams of every day; he gives examples from the cases of patients, in whom the occurrence of such great dreams heralded the attainment of some important stage in mental progress, and states also that the distinction is recognized by primitives.[1] Among the latter the dreaming of great dreams is the province of the chief or medicine-man,[2] and when such an event occurs a tribal council is called and the dream related and discussed as an important happening. The distinction, of

---

[1] See Jung: *The Integration of the Personality*, and *Modern Man in Search of a Soul*.

[2] The importance attached to the dreams of leaders persisted into early civilization: e.g. Pharaoh's dream in Gen. xli, and Constantine's dream (*in hoc signo vinces*) before Pons Mulvius.

course, is mainly a subjective, and entirely a relative one, for it is mainly the incommunicable intensity of his experience which enables the dreamer to decide when a dream is great: yet, in the last resort, it is often the intensity of an experience which serves as our criterion in deciding on the degree of its 'reality'. Objectively speaking there is no difference of kind between great and small dreams, but only one of degree; there is, however, an objective element which makes comparison possible, and it is to be found in the proportion of universal or Archetypal as against personal and particular elements, by which the content is characterized.

Even more convincing, of course, are what are colloquially called 'visions', which are, in effect, dreams which occur when the body is in a 'waking' condition. Here the ready explanation 'it was only a dream' is inapplicable, since the subject knows from experience that mental states of the kind in question do not normally occur during waking life. He therefore feels it necessary to fit the content of the vision into his picture of the outer world: in other words he attributes what he calls 'reality' to it and seeks to discover causes and antecedents for it in the outer world, which he would feel under no necessity of doing if the same experience had occurred at a time when he knew himself to have been asleep. In consequence he usually concludes that supernatural forces have been at work.

These considerations lead to a second important conclusion regarding the Two Worlds: *that we are in fact so familiar with the duality of experience that we accept it without question*, provided only that the two forms occur in situations with which we are familiar. This familiarity may be at second hand, for if we are assured that we were under the influence of a drug, or of an abnormally high temperature, at the time of the vision, or even of acute emotional stress, we are also prepared to accept its incongruity without further question, since the effects of these conditions on consciousness are familiar to us by report.

At all events it is clear that the dreams of Descartes were great dreams in the subjective sense, for the starting-point of his whole system was the question of the reality of dream experience. He states that in the period before the dreams he 'was filled with enthusiasm, and discovered the foundations of a wonderful new science';[1] exactly what his line of thought previous to the dreams may have been we do not know, but his *Principia* opens with the following argument. His purpose was to elucidate the nature, limits and validity of knowledge in general, and his method was to start by questioning the reality of everything which we habitually take for granted. We believe, he says in effect, in the reality of the outer world which, we assume, is revealed by our waking experiences; but this reality is incompatible with the reality of the world which we experience in dreams: if the one is real then, it seems, the other cannot be. Yet we do experience a world in our dreams, and sometimes with a vividness no less than that with which we experience things in our waking life. If there is no reality behind the dream experiences, to what can they be attributed? Assuming, for the sake of argument, that there is a demon who produces the dream-images and displays them to us, how can we know that it is not this demon, or another, who similarly creates and displays to us the images of waking experience? The fact that other people confirm the objective validity of the latter is of course no proof, since those others may themselves be a part of the delusion; dream characters, moreover, behave in exactly the same way.

The demons are obviously not intended literally:[2] the point is simply that all we know consists of our individual experiences and what we can deduce from them, and there are no grounds for assuming that there is any greater reality behind the experiences of waking life than behind those of dreams.

The only thing we know for certain, Descartes continues in effect, is that there is experience, or that experience exists, and that therefore somebody must be experiencing it. That somebody is 'I', the subject: in it resides the only reality of which we can be certain. *Cogito, ergo sum*, which, in modern termino-

---

[1] The dreams are related in a short manuscript entitled 'Olympica', which starts: 'X Novembris 1619, cum plenus forem Enthousiasmo et mirabilis scientiae fundamenta reperirem . . .' (see Haldane: *Descartes*). The 10th November was the Eve of St. Martin, an occasion when heavy drinking was customary. It has accordingly been suggested that Descartes was probably drunk when he went to bed, but this is entirely beside the point, which is what he made of his experiences afterwards.

[2] He admits that he uses the term in order to avoid imputing such trickery to God (*Principia*).

logy, might be freely translated, 'I experience, therefore I am
certain that I, at any rate, am real.'

Descartes was, I believe, the first critical western philosopher
to arrive at this central conclusion of philosophy. I should not,
however, be in the least surprised if confronted with evidence
that some other modern European had anticipated him, for the
idea is as old as speculative thought: one of its most beautiful
and striking statements is to be found in Chuang Tzu's 'Butterfly Dream',[1] which was written nearly two thousand years
before Descartes came into the world. It is also the central
theme of Indian thought, but that was not imported into
western philosophy until the days of Schopenhauer, two
centuries later. We Westerners must not forget that we are
barbarian upstarts, and that in many respects we still lag far
behind the maturer civilizations of the ancient East.

The central point at which Descartes had arrived was the
recognition of the fundamental significance of the subject-object
relationship. He had reached the conclusion (although he did
not succeed in finding a complete formulation of it) that everything we commonly believe was open to question except the
one, ultimate, unquestionable fact that something was going
on in his mind. Whether that something did or did not represent
something else, i.e. some 'reality' outside his mind, on which
that which was in his mind, i.e. that of which he was aware,
depended, was open to question, but the fact that he was aware
of something was not so open. He perceived that that awareness
demanded a subject, and this conclusion he expressed in the
famous *cogito, ergo sum*.

It is worth going into this formula a little more closely. In the
first place we may note that *cogitare*, which nowadays we should
render 'to experience', since it must cover feeling, sensation and
any other forms of awareness besides 'thinking' in the narrow
sense, is the real nucleus or starting-point of the argument: it is
that 'something going on in the mind' which we cannot deny.
We can therefore start with the statement 'there is experience':
it is impossible to deny this, but that is all that we have yet
established as our starting-point.

The next point is that we cannot conceive of any happening
without a subject: 'doing' is meaningless without something

[1] See p. 185.

which 'does'; 'being', even, is meaningless without something which 'is'. Experience, being a happening, therefore demands somebody to experience: we may say 'Descartes experiences' or 'I experience', but the use of the pronoun 'I' is no more than a grammatical convenience, and if, in the latter case, the speaker is Descartes himself, the statement could equally well be made in the form 'Descartes experiences', just as a young child says 'John wants' instead of 'I want'. Thus *cogito, ergo sum* need mean no more than 'René Descartes thinks, therefore he is'. But is that really what Descartes meant? We may doubt it. What he was trying to say was 'a subject experiences', or 'this experience, which we have agreed to accept as the central, unquestionable fact from which to start our enquiry, demands a subject: since there is experience there must also be a subject'. But who is this subject? As soon as we name René Descartes we have an *object* of experience which possesses a number of particular attributes. René Descartes was a certain definite person, possessing a body, a past life, a father and mother and so on, and in naming him we imply the existence of these things. That, however, is by no means justified by our proposition, for the fact that there is experience does not in itself imply that there must be a René Descartes: it merely implies that there must be a subject of experience. This subject, therefore, must be distinguished from the personal René Descartes: we shall discover more about it shortly, and in the meanwhile I shall distinguish it by referring to it as the Subject, with a capital S. All that we know about it so far is that it is that which experiences.

But how does René Descartes, or the Subject—whichever of them it may be that is making the statement—know that it experiences? The answer can only be that it experiences something other than itself. By this means it knows that it experiences, and therefore that it is, or exists. An experience of nothing is not conceivable, and the Subject cannot experience itself. There must then be an Object which the Subject experiences: the one demands the other, just as the male demands the female and the buyer the seller: neither is possible without the other. We must not jump to the conclusion that this implies that there must be material objects, or objects of any kind outside the mind: that which the Subject experiences need be no more than the substantive 'experience'. The essential nature of this we have not yet discovered in the course of our argument, and it was in effect what Descartes proposed to find out: he called it 'knowledge' and embarked on a critical investigation of its possibilities. For the time being I shall call it the Object, which may be taken as a generalization, without specific attributes, denoting that which is experienced by the Subject.

From this point it is possible to proceed in two directions, towards the Subject or the Object respectively. Oriental thinkers have tended to follow the former line, concentrating on the ultimate reality of the Subject and brushing the Object aside as a mere delusion. Pursuing the nature of the Subject they have reached Chuang Tzu's position, namely that we cannot tell 'who' the Subject is: sometimes it appears to be the man Chuang Tzu, and sometimes the butterfly. The Indians, going farther, perceived that both Chuang Tzu and the butterfly are in fact objects, which can be known to the Subject when it breaks its identification with either of them: thus, looking through the eyes of Chuang Tzu it sees the butterfly as a separate entity, but looking through those of the butterfly it sees Chuang Tzu. Normally these two modes of experience of the one Subject are distinct and separate, but we are all capable, on occasion and in varying degrees, of seeing 'ourselves' 'from outside', or of alternating between the viewpoints of the butterfly and of Chuang Tzu, as we do between dreaming and waking; and yet we retain the contrasting modes of experience in a single stream of memory. Who is it, then, who can see 'ourselves'? It can only be the Ultimate Subject (called, in the Upanishads, *Atman*, the 'Self') who is neither you nor I, nor Chuang Tzu nor the butterfly, but all of them together, and at the same time none of them. In the formula of the Upanishads, 'looking through our eyes It sees; listening with our ears It hears; perceiving our thoughts It knows; but It can in no wise be seen, or heard, or known'.[1]

The final stage is the recognition of the fact that Subject and Object are contrasting modes of an ultimate ONE (the Sphere of indeterminacy or totality) concerning which, however, nothing whatever can be predicated, since It is neither knower nor known, but both. It is neither existent nor non-existent; It is at the same time all that is—and nothing. This concept is

[1] See Paul Deussen: *Allg. Gesch. d. Philosophie.*

already inherent in that of Atman, the great Self as opposed to the limited personal self, and Atman is often interpreted in this sense. With the further implications of this matter we shall be concerned in later volumes of this study; for the present we may content ourselves with recognizing it as a possible line of speculation.

Descartes, in conformity with the prevailing stream of western thought, proceeded in the opposite direction. Having intuitively reached, thus early in life, the crucial point of mystical philosophy, namely that all existence exists solely by virtue of the existence of an absolute Subject in correlation with an absolute Object—which latter was implicit in his assertion that the Subject 'thought', and was later to be identified by Kant as the Thing-in-itself (*das Ding an sich*)—he seems to have overlooked the line of speculation opened by the recognition of the unique position of the Subject and his own mysterious identity with it. It does not seem to have occurred to him that the entity in question in any way transcended the phenomenon known as René Descartes, who had been born in Touraine on 31st March 1596, the third son of Joachim Descartes, and who was at the time experiencing the world from the viewpoint of a mercenary in the Bavarian army. Assuming, apparently, that the identity of this young man with the Ultimate Subject was self-evident and required no qualification, he turned to the consideration of the Object, to which he devoted the remainder of his life.

He had tacitly and implicitly presupposed the real existence of an object of some kind as his starting-point, and was only concerned to find out what it was 'really' like; in other words, as he put it to himself, he embarked upon a critical investigation of what it was possible to know. His speculations led him to discoveries in the spheres of mathematics and logic which have served as the foundations of most of modern thought, but with these we are not concerned here. The points which do interest us are the following four:

(*a*) Descartes was the first (or among the first) of the representatives of the stream of European thought to formulate an idea long familiar in the Orient, namely that all that we can be said to know is what we experience (or, as he put it, what we 'think') and that there is no justification for assuming the existence of a world, or a class of objects, concealed behind our direct experience and possessing a greater degree of 'reality' than those experiences themselves.[1] Hence the 'world' apparently revealed in a dream has no more and no less 'reality' than that apparently revealed by our waking experiences. The latter are found to be more coherent and more rational, but that is all.

(*b*) Proceeding from this conclusion he recognized that the Subject exists independently of the nature of Its experiences (*cogito, ergo sum*). It may be immersed in the world of a dream or in that of normal waking experience, but it is the same subject even though the implications of these two modes of experience are incompatible. In other words two separate and irreconcilable worlds of experience do not demand two separate subjects.

(*c*) The orientals proceeded from this point to the logical conclusion that there can be only one absolute and ultimate Subject which transcends the individual personal subject. Individual subjects are merely separate modes of experience of the one Subject. These individual modes are normally segregated from one another by the fact that none of them has direct knowledge of the experience of the others. Chuang Tzu's statement of this fact is translated by Wilhelm as follows:

Now I do not know whether Chuang Tzu dreamed that he was a butterfly or whether the butterfly dreamed that it was Chuang Tzu, although there is certainly a difference between Chuang Tzu and a butterfly. Thus it is with the transformations of things.[2]

[1] He did in fact go on to postulate an independent, objective reality, not in material objects but in notions which, he maintained, presented themselves with an inherent force of conviction; he saw these mainly as logical propositions, but in the last resort they are equivalent to Plato's 'ideas' or to Jung's Archetypes. Philosophers, as Jung says, generally end by writing about their own psychology, and Descartes was in fact describing the constellation of his own mind, which was ruled by thinking. To a musician the qualities of chords present themselves with the same unquestionable certainty as logical propositions did to Descartes: it is a matter of the projection of an Archetypal image, which might be described as that of Truth, or of the Absolute Object, into different classes of experience. The pattern of this Archetype confers the property of unquestionability on its recipient and hence endows it with the power of conviction.

[2] Dschuang Dsi: *Das Wahre Buch vom Südlichen Blütenland*, transl. by Richard Wilhelm (introduction dated 1912). My translation from the German.

Giles, however, translates:

Now I do not know whether I was then a man dreaming I was a butterfly, or whether I am now a butterfly dreaming I am a man. Between a man and a butterfly there is necessarily a barrier. The transition is called *Metempsychosis*.[1]

The Barrier mentioned by Giles we already know, and have defined it as that which separates the Two Worlds. We may now give the definition in a more philosophical form, saying that it is that which segregates the various individual modes of experience of the universal Subject from one another. We know also that there is always a door through the Barrier, enabling the individual subject to pass in full consciousness from his normal waking mode of experience into another, which we have designated the Other Side. This duality of experience in the mind of the single individual, the commonest form of which is the alternation between dreaming and waking, is the exception to the law of the total segregation of different individual modes of experience by the Barrier.

The essential point about this duality is that the two modes are united in a single stream of memory, for the waking man remembers his dream, and the dreamer commonly has some knowledge, albeit confused, of his waking life. It is not, therefore, excessively difficult to accept the identity of the subject in this particular dichotomy of experience; to accept its identity

---

[1] Chuang Tzu: transl. by Herbert A. Giles, 1886 (both translations are now unobtainable and it is high time that one or other was republished; the German version appeared in 1940 and at least 9,000 copies were sold). In view of the nature of ancient Chinese, which lacks tense-forms, personal pronouns, etc., there is no reason to regard either of these translations as more accurate than the other. Wilhelm, while implicitly accepting Giles' qualifications as a translator, criticizes his version on the grounds that it is 'strongly subjectively coloured' and that 'in various difficult passages he offers conjecture rather than translation'. The translation of ideograms which are neither concrete nor abstract (but serve for both) into a modern European language, however, evidently cannot be done without a good deal of 'conjecture', and in my view where the two translations differ materially Wilhelm's tends to be obscure and meaningless. Giles' version, on the other hand, brings out a perfectly definite system of thought, which is coherent throughout and not inconsistent with that revealed by Wilhelm's; the version which offers the lay reader some intelligible interpretation of the 'difficult passages' therefore seems to me preferable.

in two entirely distinct individuals, however, requires a considerable effort of the imagination. In his parable Chuang Tzu leads us gently from the one to the other; it is a parable because he could not, of course, really have dreamed that he was a butterfly in the sense suggested, since a butterfly's outlook and mental processes could not be embodied in a human memory. What he is really saying is, 'Chuang Tzu and the butterfly are, in one sense, One; in another they are Two; 'I' am both and neither; this fact is demonstrated in the phenomenon of dreaming.'[1]

Descartes, however, failed to reach this stage of understanding because, like most of us, he was too closely identified with his memories. He was prepared to admit that the personal subject embodied in René Descartes could live in two entirely separate and incongruous worlds without forfeiting its underlying identity, but he failed to take the further step of visualizing an impersonal and absolute Subject, lying behind the personal René Descartes and experiencing in every mind, according to its degree, without forfeiting Its supreme unity and identity. It was left for Schopenhauer, basing himself on the Upanishads (translations of which had in the meanwhile become available) to take this final step two centuries later. Nevertheless Descartes' idea represented a great advance from the confused thought of the Middle Ages: it disclosed a first stirring of the perception of the duality of experience—of the existence of Two Worlds—in the modern European mind.

(d) After reaching this crucial perception as a result of a violent upsurging (in the form of his 'great dreams') of contents from the collective, Archetypal layer of the unconscious mind,[2]

[1] It is worth noting that at about the same time the Greeks were adopting the butterfly as the symbol of what we now call the 'soul' or Psyche.

[2] The contents of the dreams may be summarized as follows:

(1) He is fleeing from certain ghosts. A great wind forces him to bow to the ground as he goes. He decides to enter a church, situated in his path, to pray, but as he passes through the courtyard somebody calls him; desiring to turn back, he is seized by the force of the wind and turned about again. Awakes in fear.

(2) On falling asleep again is awakened by a terrifying clap of thunder, the 'sparks' of which he still sees in the room on opening his eyes.

(3) Concerned with a Latin text he is studying. He comes to the question *Quod vitae sectabor iter?* (What course shall I follow in life?) whereupon somebody presents him with a paper on which is written *Est et non* (Yes and no—

Descartes virtually abandoned it by ignoring its implications regarding the nature of the Subject-Object relationship and of the Subject Itself, embarking instead on an intensive study of the nature of the Object. In so doing he virtually set the course followed by European thought up to the present day, and which will, no doubt, be followed for some centuries to come. This must not, of course, be regarded as his own unaided performance; others were already working in the same direction, and if there had been no Descartes his discoveries would, sooner or later, have been made by somebody else. Nevertheless he is typical and representative of modern western thought: we are the heirs of Descartes.

His conception of the Object was an advanced one, and superior to anything which had gone before. He saw it as a coherent and logical system, all tending towards, and deriving from, an Ultimate Perfection which, of course, he called God. This is characteristic of our western outlook, which seeks the Absolute, whether we call it God or not, in the Object and not, like the orientals, in the Subject; it insists, moreover, that the Absolute must be of a rational and coherent nature. The Absolute, the Prime Cause, the Eternal or whatever we choose to call It, is an Archetypal image which the human mind is compelled to project into some form or other: the westerner seeks It in an Absolute Object, that is to say a system of thought of such complete 'objectivity' that it remains the same from every conceivable viewpoint, or in other words is independent

a faint suggestion of 'it is and it is not'). (See Louis Dimier: *La Vie Raisonnable de R.D.*)

Reference has already been made to the symbolism of the wind as the power of the spirit, and the thunderclap has the same significance. In the *I Ching* it is said of the trigram Chen, Thunder or the Arousing: 'God comes forth in the sign of the Arousing.' The image is used in a very similar sense by Giordano Bruno (1548-1600—a similarity between whose system and that of Descartes has been discerned, although the probability of the latter's having read his works is slight). These are therefore pure Archetypal symbols of the power emanating from the Self, and Descartes experienced them in a manner which induced powerful feelings of awe, fear, and helplessness in face of a superior power (the force of the wind which turned him round against his will). These manifestations can be very shaking. He therefore showed perfect insight in interpreting the dreams as manifestations of God. The paradox *Est et non* is a further allusion to the mysterious and unfathomable nature of the Self.

of every possible individual subject; he visualizes the Subject as an infinity of separate, distinct and virtually worthless particular entities—in fact as 'unreal'. The oriental, on the other hand (or at any rate the oriental civilizations of the past) seeks It in an Absolute Subject which shall be free of all dependence on any object: the Object is seen as a heterogeneous collection of accidentals—'the ten thousand things' of the Chinese—which are no more than an illusion, hence worthless and 'unreal': in very much the same light, in fact, as the westerner regards the Subject.

'Reality' is a purely relative term: both outlooks are of course fundamentally incomplete, and the most profound minds (not necessarily the formal philosophers) of both East and West have transcended both in the form of intimations of an ultimate ONE which at the same time is and is not, is possible and impossible, is all things and nothing—is, in short, unknowable. On this basis, of course, no formal, consistent system can be constructed, since everything is seen to be self-contradictory and all truths are paradoxes.

This is not the place to go further into this matter, which leads directly to mystical speculation. We shall be concerned with some of its implications later in the course of this study, and I mention it here solely to indicate that there is some kind of Middle Way, as the Taoists call it, in which the polarity of Subject and Object is transcended.

Thus we see that in the phenomenon of dreaming man has always recognized the existence of an alternative form of experience enjoyed by that same subject which apprehends the more coherent and familiar experiences of waking life. This profound and vital understanding has, unfortunately, become largely lost to the contemporary mind as a result of the thinking derived from those current psychological systems which seek to 'explain away' dreams as mere distorted interpretations of the sole 'truth' of waking life. This development, I believe, made it clear once and for all that the modern western trend of rationalization and objectivization had reached the point of no return: no further progress is possible in that direction: we can advance only if we reverse it.

The more penetrating and intuitively gifted minds of both past and present have further perceived that there are no

229

grounds for attributing any greater theoretical 'reality' to the one mode of experience than to the other: either both are real or neither is. Since the two are in many respects incompatible, if we are to accord any reality to experience at all we must recognize that there are at least two (if not more) distinct and separate modes of reality: two at least are universally experienced by every individual. This pattern, being universal in the human mind, is Archetypal, and its Archetypal symbol is the image of the Two Worlds.

Everything is thus seen to hinge on what we regard as 'real'. There are two ways of approaching this question: we may either proceed theoretically, attempting to equate the concept of reality with others, such as those of invariability, universality, absoluteness or what not, and then denying the attribute of reality to any entity or phenomenon which lacks these properties; or alternatively we may adopt the empirical standpoint, maintaining that 'real' is merely an epithet describing a certain manner of experiencing phenomena, which we apply by extension to the phenomena themselves.

'Thus do I refute Bishop Berkeley,' cried Dr Johnson, giving the kerbstone a violent kick. This characteristic outburst illustrates the conflict between the two opposing viewpoints described above: Berkeley had maintained that the objects of experience existed only as images in the mind, and therefore, at least by inference, that they were not 'real';[1] Johnson, who lacked philosophical perception, insisted on the 'common sense' viewpoint that anything which produced an intense sensation in his toe, accompanied by a sound audible to others as well as himself, could not be denied the property of reality. What he overlooked was that his toe and his ears were as much part of the unknown outer world as the stone: all that his consciousness experienced on this occasion was something mental, compounded of what it interpreted as the product of sensations of impact in his toe and of sound in his ears, and it was from these that it constructed the image of the solid kerb-stone. But that

---

[1] I have not scoured the texts in order to ascertain whether the Bishop actually makes use of the word 'real' in this connection; the formulation given above represents the purport of his theory, and it was that which incensed Dr. Johnson.

image existed in his mind, and whether it corresponded to anything 'outside' his mind—i.e. unknown to him—cannot be ascertained. It certainly did correspond both to the sense-impressions and to the vast complex pattern made up of his previous sensory experiences of a like nature and classified by him as 'solid objects'; but all these things were in his mind, so that all that could be said was that he had recognized an experience as corresponding to others which he had made previously and in which he had discerned a certain pattern. Others, it is true, presumably heard the sound produced by the kick, and, if they followed the Doctor's example, could be relied on to confirm that they also experienced a sensation which they recognized as that of impact in the toe; but, as we have already noted, the same thing occurs in dreams, in which other persons appearing in the dream confirm that they share the experiences of the dreamer.

Berkeley, on the other hand, seemed to the Doctor to be denying reality to the kerb-stone; what he actually said was that he had no direct means of ascertaining its existence other than by sensory experience, and that, for all he knew, when he could neither see, feel nor hear it, it might have ceased to exist. We shall go into this matter in greater detail later; for the present it is sufficient to point out that Berkeley, whatever his theories on the subject, must certainly have conducted his life on the assumption that such things as kerb-stones were 'real', since otherwise he would frequently have found himself prostrate on the pavement.

What it comes down to is simply that the two men were using the word 'real' (or its equivalent, if they chose another terminology) in completely different senses. Berkeley was insisting that reality implied certain properties (of universality, etc.) which were lacking in the image of a kerb-stone constructed in the mind on the basis of sensory impressions, while Johnson was retorting that the experiences connected with kerb-stones, whatever the ultimate nature of the latter may be, were so intense, and of such immediate importance in the practical conduct of life that they could not be ignored. That was what he meant, and what most people mean, by 'reality'.

SUMMARY

The conclusions which we have reached so far may be summarized as follows.

(1) All that we know is what we consciously experience, which is what may be described as 'in our minds'. Experience may take various forms, e.g. sensory impressions, such as that which Dr Johnson recognized as impact in his toe, logical propositions, such as that twice two makes four, feelings, such as anger, shame, etc., and possibly others as well.

(2) By classifying various items of experience according to properties which we perceive that they possess in common, and by bringing them into association with one another, we form coherent patterns, to which we find that they invariably conform. E.g. visual experiences which we classify as images of the type of that which Dr Johnson recognized as a kerb-stone, are associated with tactile sensations. Virtually all the experiences of waking life can be fitted together into an immensely complex but coherent and intelligible system centred round the individual's awareness of his own particular identity. This pattern is not subject to his volition—i.e. it remains the same whether he wishes i⁺ to or not—and if he forgets about it, it will assert itself unexpectedly in a manner which, he realizes on reflection, he might have foreseen if he had devoted due attention to it. He therefore regards it as an outer world, existing in its own right 'outside' his mind and independently of him. If he is of average intelligence and leads an average life he finds that concentration on this pattern enables him to maintain a satisfactory existence, whereas neglect of it is followed by unpleasant consequences; therefore he attributes paramount importance to it.

(3) When he is asleep, and sometimes on occasions when he is awake, however, he has experiences of a nature which does not fit into the pattern. He soon learns to identify these as anomalous and finds that neglect of them is apparently (I say 'apparently' advisedly) not followed by any recognizable consequences, unpleasant or pleasant. He therefore concludes that these experiences do not represent any outside world, existing independently of him; since they do not appear to have any further significance he discards them as insubstantial rubbish—

as 'unreal' in contrast to the 'reality' represented by normal waking experience.

(4) Descartes and the Oriental thinkers, however, discerned that there are no adequate grounds for making this differentiation. The fact that we see no significance in dream experience does not mean that it could not have significance for us if we understood it; they thought, indeed, that they could discern considerable significance in it. Similarly the fact that we think we understand waking experience does not necessarily mean that it 'represents' any independent 'reality' in a manner which the dream experience does not. They accounted for the incompatibility of the two modes of experience by the theory of the universal Subject which is capable of experiencing in more than one 'world', i.e. according to more than one of the systems or patterns which are characteristic of each individual world or stream of experience.

(5) Thus when we say that anything is 'real' in the ordinary sense (as distinct from any special sense demanded by a particular philosophical theory) we are referring to the nature of an experience, concerning which we believe that it has, or potentially could have, importance for us, and of which we must therefore take account. We reach this judgment either on the basis of the intensity of the direct experience (as in the case of Descartes' dreams) or, more frequently, on that of the compatibility of the particular experience with a system or pattern existing in our minds but which, we believe, represents an independent outer world which is the same for all possible subjects.[1]

The general picture which thus emerges has already been adumbrated in connection with the mind and the brain: it is that of the mind as a mere emptiness contained within a substantial outer world—something like a bubble in a liquid—its exclusive function being to recognize or 'know' that outer world, which is revealed to it by means of the senses. It is in fact nothing but the picture of an animate body seen from

[1] This is the basis of what Kant called 'synthetic judgments', in which something is *added* to the evidence of the senses on the basis of a logical deduction. What he overlooked was that the evidence of the senses is itself in the first place interpreted and judged in accordance with that same system, based largely on the laws of logic, which provides the additional element.

outside. We see how the animate body adjusts itself to its environment, and how it is separated from it by the principle of identity or individual life, which permeates it but does not extend to the environment. The skin, the envelope of the body, seems to be a barrier separating two absolutely distinct entities: inside it, all is sentient life, unified and coordinated by the purposeful identity which permeates it, while outside, completely cut off from it and apparently of an entirely different nature, is the non-sentient outer world which goes its own way and is not subject to the life-force within.

This picture we transpose, quite without justification, to the mind, confusing it with the brain and imagining it as a kind of localized space, outside which is the material world, as we imagine it would be seen by a hypothetical, absolutely objective, external observer, while inside it is an insubstantial picture, more or less correct according to the capacity of the particular brain, of that independent outer world. The picture 'inside' the mind is seen as unreliable and unreal: the best we can do is to check it at every possible opportunity against the external 'reality'. But how are we to discover what that 'reality' is? From the foregoing it has already become evident that the task is not so simple as it might at first sight appear. The evidence of the senses is our usual standby, but it is not considered completely reliable, since in various abnormal conditions, and above all in dreams, we experience sensory images which we subsequently reject as incompatible with 'reality' and therefore as erroneous and misleading. Hence we must admit that we have a second criterion of 'reality' which is to be found 'inside' our minds; as has already been indicated, moreover, the raw material of sense-impressions has no meaning for us until it has been interpreted by comparison with images in the mind. Our judgment of reality therefore essentially consists in comparing items of experience with a criterion or complex image in the mind: if the experience corresponds to it we accept it as real; if it is incompatible, as in the case of most dream-experience, we reject it out of hand. It is therefore of the utmost importance for our enquiry to ascertain how this criterion or image of reality is built up, and of what elements it consists.

III *On the Existence of Mermaids*

THE belief in the exclusive 'reality' of the outer world which we associate with normal waking experience is so deeply ingrained that it requires a great deal to shake it. Since it is our purpose to do so we must pursue our investigation further, and it now leads to another term extensively used in this connection, namely 'existence'.

I find a difficulty [Sir Arthur Eddington writes in *The Philosophy of Physical Science*] in understanding books on philosophy because they talk a great deal about 'existence', and I do not know what they mean. Existence seems to be a rather important property, because I gather that one of the main sources of division between different schools of philosophy is the question whether certain things exist or not. But I cannot even begin to understand these issues, because I can find no explanation of the term 'exist'.

The word 'existence' is, of course, familiar in everyday speech; but it does not express a uniform idea—a universally agreed principle according to which things can be divided into existing and non-existing. Difference of opinion as to whether a thing exists or not sometimes arises because the thing itself is imperfectly defined, or because the exact implications of the definition have not been grasped; thus the 'real existence' of electrons, aether, space, colour, may be affirmed or denied because different persons use these terms with somewhat different implications. But ambiguity of definition is not always responsible for the difference of view. Let us take something familiar, such as an overdraft at a bank. No one can fail to understand precisely what that means. Is an overdraft something which exists? If the question were put to the vote, I think some would say its existence must be accepted as a grim reality, and others would consider it illogical to concede existence to what is intrinsically a negation. But what divides the two parties is no more than a question of words. It would be absurd to divide mankind into two sects, the one believing in the existence of overdrafts, and the other denying their existence. The division is a question of classification, not of belief. If you give me your own answer, I shall not learn anything new about the nature or properties of an overdraft; but I shall learn something about your usage of the term 'exists'—what category of things you intend it to cover.

Later, after qualifying his attack on the philosophers by admitting that 'in the more recondite works the meaning of the term (existence) is sometimes discussed' he continues

For me (and, it appears, also for my dictionary) 'exists' is a rather emphatic form of 'is'. 'A thought exists in somebody's mind', i.e. a thought is in somebody's mind—I can understand that. 'A state of war exists in Ruritania', i.e. a state of war is in Ruritania—not very good English, but intelligible. But when a philosopher says 'Familiar tables and chairs exist', i.e. familiar tables and chairs are . . . , I wait for him to conclude. Yes? What were you going to say they are? But he never finishes the sentence.

THE COPULA

Here Eddington, although he fails to draw any clear conclusions from his discussion, has intuitively hit upon a matter of some importance, namely that something is inferentially implied by the use of the terms exist and existence, although people rarely trouble to work out what it is. Before going into this question we may first dismiss a purely grammatical matter which has confused Eddington, namely the use of the verb 'to be' as a copula. As he discovered in his dictionary, 'to exist' is virtually a synonym of 'to be', but as he does not appear to have realized, 'to be' is employed in two quite different manners. The common use is as a copula, in which it merely serves to connect the subject of the sentence with the predicate, as for instance when we say 'the boy is good'. In this employment it is no more than a grammatical formality and adds nothing to the meaning of the statement (except in respect of the tense used), and in some languages it is dispensed with. In Arabic, for instance, no copula is used (the past tense being indicated by a non-verbal particle); thus the statement 'the boy is good' is rendered simply 'the boy good'; when 'the good boy' is intended it is rendered 'the boy the good'. In English various synonyms are used for 'to be' in similar cases, but purely for stylistic reasons: thus, as Eddington points out, we may say 'A state of war exists in Ruritania' in place of 'is in Ruritania', because the latter, as he says, is 'not very good English'; we may, moreover, equally well say 'a state of war prevails' or 'obtains' in Ruritania: the meaning is precisely the same in each case, and the choice of words is merely a matter of usage or euphony.

In this usage, therefore, 'to be', 'to exist', 'to prevail', 'to obtain', 'to be found', and any other synonyms, are mere grammatical conventions without any significance whatever— in a telegram, for instance, they may be omitted without any loss of intelligibility resulting—and this aspect of the terms in question can be dismissed without more ado.

'To be', however, may be used in a different manner, without a predicate. It is not usual to say 'God is', but the sentence will be understood by everybody as the equivalent of 'God exists', or 'there is a God'. The latter form, of course, is no more than a grammatical rearrangement of 'God is', for the word 'there' has no meaning and is described by grammarians as a 'notional subject', demanded solely by the English grammatical rule that finite forms of the verb (other than the imperative) must be preceded by some word acting as subject. Hence the fact that we say 'there is a God', in preference to 'God is', is purely a question of usage and has no further significance. Since 'to exist' is a synonym of 'to be', we may express exactly the same meaning by either 'there exists a God' or 'God exists', only in this case the latter form is the more usual.

In so far, therefore, as ordinary usage is concerned, Eddington's objection that the statement 'familiar tables and chairs exist' is incomplete and demands a predicate, is unjustifiable, since if we wish to substitute the synonym 'to be' we need not use it in the form 'tables and chairs are', which in common usage demands a predicate, but can substitute 'there are familiar tables and chairs', which demands none. In other words, we are normally quite content to use both the verbs 'to be' and 'to exist' in this absolute sense. Eddington is, however, perfectly justified in demanding to know what we mean when we do so, and we must now turn to this question.

THE USE OF 'TO EXIST' AND 'TO BE' WITHOUT PREDICATE

When we use other verbs in this way, they themselves constitute the predicate, which is thereby attributed to the subject of the sentence: in other words by naming the subject the speaker evokes a mental image of something (which may be either a concrete object or an abstraction) and then by adding the verb he evokes that of a state or activity which, he maintains, applies to the subject; if the negative is used the suggestion is that the image evoked by the verb differs from that of the subject. Thus when I say 'plants grow' I am associating the generalized concept of plants with the generalized concept of becoming larger, and when I say 'this water does not boil' I am asserting the difference between the concrete image of the water in question and a generalized image of boiling water. Thus, if the statement is to convey anything, two mental images are necessarily always involved.

But, Eddington insists, when I say 'tables and chairs exist', what is the second image implied? There are two possible answers: either nothing additional is implied at all, in which case the word 'exist' (or any synonym which may be substituted for it) is as meaningless and superfluous as it is when used as a copula; or else something definite is implied, in which case it must be possible to find some alternative manner of formulating that something so that we may recognize its nature.

If the first answer is correct the statement means no more than that the image of tables and chairs has occurred to me— i.e. that it is present to my consciousness—but that I do not associate it with anything else. In everyday life it does sometimes happen that an image spontaneously presents itself to consciousness without the subject's being able, for the moment, to associate it with any of his current concerns. Such phenomena are frequently reminders from the unconscious mind of something which has been forgotten, and when they occur the subject may name the image in question as a kind of exclamation, without adding any predicate. Thus, for instance, he may suddenly exclaim 'the car!' and if questioned what he means will reply that there was something he had to do about the car, but he can't remember what. He may also, in the course of a discussion, say 'Well, there is the car', but in such a case the predicate is assumed as understood in the light of the matter under discussion: e.g. the car can take you to the station.

It is only in cases such as these that the mere naming of the subject without any additional predicate is conceivable, and it is obvious that they cannot apply to a formal philosophical treatise. When the philosopher affirms that tables and chairs exist it is inconceivable that all he means is 'the image of tables and chairs has occurred to me, but I don't know in what connection', or even 'in the light of the foregoing you will know what I mean when I draw your attention to tables and chairs'; he must, evidently, mean something more, and the question of what he means still remains unanswered. The fact that, whatever his additional meaning may be, the irreducible minimum significance of the statement is that the image of the subject of the sentence is present to his consciousness, should be noted for future reference.

THE SPECIAL USE OF THE TERM IN PHILOSOPHY

With respect to philosophical writing a limited answer to the question may be suggested: it is that the predicate 'in this system' is implied. When a speculative thinker sets out, as Descartes, for instance, did, to construct a critical and logically coherent system embracing all knowledge, he begins by wiping the slate clean of every preconception. People believe an incredible amount of nonsense, he says, and if we are to begin by questioning each of their beliefs one by one we shall never get anywhere: the only thing to do is provisionally to deny everything. Then we can look about for a starting-point which is absolutely certain and reliable, and from this we can proceed step by step, examining each new element which we admit to our system, in order to ensure that it is compatible, according to the laws of logic, with what we have already admitted. If it is not so compatible we must exclude it: it is something which some misguided person has thought up at some time or other, but it is irreconcilable with the demands of the system by which I seek to offer a logical explanation of the nature of knowledge, or of the universe. It cannot form part of this system, which must remain coherent and interrelated in all its parts, and since this system contains everything necessary to explain the universe there is no place in the universe for this superfluous idea.

In such a process it is customary to use the word 'exists' in order to imply that a new element conforms to the system and may be admitted to it, or, conversely, to say that it does not exist if it is incompatible. Thus, when I say 'if the Subject exists, then the Object must also exist', or conversely that if the one does not exist then the other does not exist either, I mean that if the one is to be admitted to or excluded from my system, then the other must of necessity be admitted or excluded also, for the rules of logic will not admit of the acceptance or rejection of the one without that of the other.

This usage is permissible provided that it is confined strictly to circumscribed arguments of this kind. Danger, however, arises when the terms 'existence', etc., are loosely used outside such a limited and connected argument: such assertions as, e.g., that tables and chairs exist, or that God exists, when made out of the blue, are, philosophically speaking, reprehensible, since it is not clear what they imply.

In so far as the strictly specialized and circumscribed sphere of philosophical thought is concerned, therefore, we may answer Eddington's question as follows: when the philosopher says that something exists he means that it is logically compatible with, and therefore a necessary, integral part of the system he is developing. As a philosopher he has no right to imply any more by the statement, although, of course, he is at liberty to use the term in any other way he chooses, provided that he explicitly states what he intends it to mean.

ITS USE IN EVERYDAY SPEECH

But Eddington poses the question in a wider context, for he brings in the use of the term in everyday speech, and adduces the example of the overdraft. Here it is necessary to proceed very carefully, bearing two points in mind: (a) that the meaning attached to any term 'in the market-place' often differs from that assigned to it by specialists—e.g. philosophers; and (b) that if a term is widely and currently used, that fact alone denotes that the meaning assigned to it in the colloquial usage must be basically the same to all users, since otherwise obvious mis-understandings would soon arise.[1]

(a) The first point requires no further elucidation, for it has already been shown that the term 'existence' is used by philo-sophers in a special sense; further obvious examples are the use of such terms as debtor and creditor by accountants, which differs in some respects from what the ordinary man under-stands by them, or that of such words as collapse and intoxica-tion by doctors.

(b) The second point has been overlooked by Eddington when he maintains that if the question of the existence or non-existence of bank-overdrafts were put to the vote a difference of opinion would become apparent. In fact there would be none, for the man who 'would consider it illogical to concede existence to anything that was intrinsically a negation' could only be a philosopher actually in the process of developing a particular logical system, and therefore using the term 'exist-ence' in the special sense peculiar to philosophers: his system would have to be based on the principle of including only elements that were affirmations, or positive quantities. In other words he would have equated the property of existence with that principle, in the same way, as I have indicated above, that some philosophers equate that of 'reality' with some other abstract principle. But the very fact that he had worked out such a system implies that he must be aware of its difference from 'market-place' notions, and if the question were actually put to him his reply would take the form made famous by the late Dr Joad in 'Brains Trust' sessions: 'That depends on what you mean by existence'; and he would explain, 'In the sense in which you and all of us use the term in everyday life an overdraft certainly exists, because it is a factor in life of which one must take account. But in the special sense demanded by my system (or the system of So-and-so) it may be said not to exist because, etc. etc.' There would, in fact, be no significant disagreement on the answer, unless it came from somebody who, like Eddington himself, was making pronouncements on

[1] E.g. an American who asks for 'suspenders' in an English shop will soon discover the difference in usage. As regards abstracts, greater variation is possible, yet people in the market-place understand one another very closely, although they may be unable to define what they mean.

philosophical questions which have just come to his notice for the first time, and without having devoted much deliberation to them.[1]

The philosopher in question would obviously, if he received a letter from his bank informing him that 'an overdraft existed' in his account, understand the statement and react to it in exactly the same way as anybody else, and in ordinary conversation, when no questions of philosophy were involved, he would use the term in the ordinary way, because it has a meaning which is understood by everybody in a practical sense, and he would find it very hard to dispense with it. It is in this ordinary, practical meaning of the term, according to which an overdraft exists as a grim reality, that we are interested, because it indicates the prevailing attitude towards certain important matters.

WIDESPREAD AGREEMENT ON THE SIGNIFICANCE OF THE TERMS

If, then, we ignore specialists who are deliberately using the word in a peculiar sense, we shall find (at least among civilized western people) that in practice the field in which general agreement regarding existence and non-existence obtains immeasurably exceeds that in which a significant body of disagreement is to be found. Nine hundred and ninety-nine people out of a thousand will agree that, e.g., tables and chairs exist whereas mermaids do not. In those cases in which a significant degree of disagreement is found, it is again, in nine hundred and ninety-nine cases out of a thousand, only on the value of the evidence that opinions differ, both parties understanding 'existence' in the same sense and disagreeing only as to whether the existence of the particular entity in question can be adequately established: this applies, for instance, to such

[1] In fairness it must be admitted that in spite of lapses when the author adventures rashly into the field of pure philosophy, in which his background is inadequate, and attempts to solve all problems by the use of the mathematical type of thinking to which he is accustomed, and which, like that of Descartes, tends to overvalue the object, the book in question contains some very valuable ideas. I am particularly indebted to it for the emphasis which it lays on the importance of the concept of pattern.

problematical phenomena as the abominable snowman, ghosts, flying saucers, telepathy and the like. There remains only a narrow field in which disagreement is found to be fundamental —i.e. based on a difference in what the disputants understand by the term 'existence': this covers such concepts as the soul, spiritual forces, Archetypal figures, free will, etc.

RELATIONSHIP OF EXISTENCE TO THE HYPO-THETICAL INDEPENDENT OUTER WORLD

If we now compare the three categories of object to which, in the common opinion of the contemporary market-place, the property of existence is (*a*) generally admitted, (*b*) generally denied, and (*c*) its admission or denial is the subject of a significant degree of disagreement, we may reach some understanding of what is at the back of the ordinary man's mind when he uses the term.

In the first place there is universal agreement as to the existence of material objects as a class. This is not such a truism as it may appear, for we must remember that in the civilization of ancient India, for instance, the material world was held to be *maya* or illusion. This was no mere academic foible, for, although certain minimum concessions to the illusory world of which our bodies form a part were recognized as unavoidable, those individuals at least who aspired towards spiritual progress were exhorted to devote as little attention to it as possible, concentrating instead on the real existence of its opposite, namely the images of the mind which are divorced from outer appearance, and some of them did in fact carry this precept to extraordinary lengths. The contemporary bias is obviously in the opposite direction, for we are urged to concentrate on 'real life' to the exclusion of fancy and fantasy, the contents of which are generally regarded as being non-existent (i.e. the equivalent of the Indian *maya*) and attention to them being branded as harmful 'escapism'.

When anybody makes the statement '*x* exists' he means, as we have already decided, that the image called *x* is in his mind, and that it possesses the attribute of existence. But he may equally well assert that *x* does not exist, and we have to discover on what grounds he makes the discrimination when he is using the term in the ordinary market-place sense. If x has the form of a material object, then, to the contemporary western mind, there is no *a priori* reason why it should not exist. On what grounds, therefore, can the negative statement be made?

Let us take an example. 'When I tried to find the address he had given me I discovered that the house did not exist.' The address had evoked in my mind the image of a house with a certain number in a certain street; since a house is a material object of a familiar type I was prepared, *a priori*, to concede it the property of reality or existence, but on searching I was unable to find any house bearing the appropriate number in the street in question. In other words *the image in my mind was not confirmed by sensory evidence.* My deduction from this is that the house in my mind does not form part of the outer world which is revealed by sensory investigation, *and it is in this latter that the property of existence resides for me.* Therefore when I say that something exists or is real I may mean that the image in my mind, which, by my naming it, may be presumed to evoke a similar image in the mind of my interlocutor, is not confined to our minds but is also to be found somewhere else—in the hypothetical outer world—where its presence may be confirmed by sensory investigation.

But it is not possible to confirm everything by sensory investigation. It is, for instance, generally believed that the moon is a sphere which revolves round the earth in such a way that the same area of its surface is always turned towards us, for nobody has ever seen any other part of it. How, then, do we know that the other side exists—that the moon is a complete sphere, and not a hemisphere, or even a hollow hemispherical shell? We are convinced of the fact because astronomers have calculated that if its shape were anything other than spherical it would not behave in the way it does. In this case, therefore, our belief in the real existence of the moon's remote hemisphere is based on our confidence in the calculations of the astronomers, which means in the laws of logic and dynamics on which they are based. We are therefore confident that although it has not yet been possible for anybody to confirm the presence of the remote hemisphere of the moon by direct sensory evidence it is none the less there, waiting to be seen by the first human being who succeeds in transporting himself to the necessary position in space: in other words we are confident that it 'exists'.

DENIAL OF EXISTENCE TO CERTAIN CATEGORIES OF OBJECTS

If, now, I am asked whether mermaids exist I shall unhesitatingly reply that they do not. On what is this denial based? I have never seen a mermaid with my own eyes, but that in itself is no insuperable obstacle to my believing in their existence, since I believe in the existence of many things, which I myself have never seen, on the evidence of others who claim to have seen them. Many mariners of past ages have claimed that they saw mermaids, yet I do not believe that they 'really' did, for I am not only convinced that mermaids do not exist today, but also that they never did exist; yet I am quite prepared to believe in the past existence of the Colossus of Rhodes and of the Hanging Gardens of Babylon on the authority of evidence intrinsically no more reliable.

The reasons for my disbelief are based on my knowledge of physiology, anatomy and zoology, for I know that no creature with the attributes claimed for the mermaid is possible according to the well-established principles of these sciences; for, to take but a single instance of the impossibilities involved, such a creature would have to be warm-blooded in the upper half and cold-blooded in the lower. Even if I were myself to see something which appeared to conform exactly to the conventional picture of a mermaid I should still refuse to believe in the real existence of the species: I should explain away the evidence of my senses by supposing either that a deception was being practised on me or that I was suffering from a hallucination. The evidence of the senses, therefore, is not the sole criterion on which we base our acceptance or denial of the reality or existence of anything: that evidence must be compatible with our convictions of what is possible.

THE CRITERION OF POSSIBILITY BASED ON A MENTAL SYSTEM

Our views on what is possible and what impossible constitute a coherent, logical system or pattern (according to which, for instance, no creature equipped with ordinary human lungs could survive under water, etc.). All the parts of this system are interrelated, and to question any single detail of it would imply questioning the whole; since I find it extremely serviceable in accounting for the great majority of observed phenomena, and base the conduct of my life, in an environment of which this system is the formative principle, very largely on my understanding of it, I am naturally extremely reluctant to undertake anything so alarming as a revision of the basic principles on which it rests. Accordingly I reject the real existence of mermaids out of hand, or at least, before I allow myself to be convinced of it, demand very cogent proof.

Thus, in the long run, we find that the meaning which the ordinary man assigns to the terms 'existence' and 'reality' in everyday speech is basically the same as that assigned to them by the philosopher in his special usage: their basic meaning is that *the nature of the subject to which they are attributed is compatible with the scheme or system according to which the speaker understands experience and orientates himself to life.*

The scheme or pattern in question is obviously what I have designated the complex image of the outer world. The contemporary bias is to equate this with reality and existence: that which forms a part of it exists and is real while that which is incompatible with it is impossible, and is therefore seen as unreal and non-existent. The outer world is visualized as an 'existence' outside the mind and independent of it: when the contemporary westerner says that something is real or exists he means 'this image, which is in my mind and which, by naming it, I am evoking in your mind, is not confined to our minds *but is also part of the outer world*'; when he says that it is unreal or does not exist he means that he is referring to an image which has no counterpart in the outer world, and he bases this denial on one of two facts: either that the attributes of the image demand that it should be possible to confirm its nature or presence by sensory experience at a certain place and time (as with the house) and that this confirmation is not forthcoming, or alternatively that the attributes in question are irreconcilable with the universally accepted nature of the outer world (as with the mermaid).

ABSENCE OF JUSTIFICATION FOR THE BELIEF IN THE EXCLUSIVE VALIDITY OF A SINGLE SYSTEM

Following Descartes, however (as well as the Orientals), we have concluded that there is no possibility of knowing anything 'outside' the mind: both the sensory experiences, with the laws to which we expect them to conform, and the complex image of the outer world, are parts or contents of the mind. They are independent of our volition, which inclines us to believe that they are external to our minds, but that is a mistake, for there is no reason why everything in the mind should be subject to our personal wills. The phenomena of hypnosis, delirium, insanity, hallucination and hysteria, moreover, not to mention dreaming, demonstrate that the mind is perfectly capable of manufacturing sensory impressions, possessing the complete power of conviction, which nevertheless do not conform to the familiar outer-world pattern. Hence it follows that *normal waking sensory experiences are only a special case.*

They are, it is true, by far the most important class of sensory experience in the life of the individual, yet they represent only one of the manifold potentialities of the mind in this connection, and they should not be regarded as intrinsically more significant than any other.

Returning now to the mermaid we may ask why, if such creatures are and always have been impossible, anybody ever came to imagine them. The answer, obviously, is that sailors, suffering from prolonged celibacy, projected the mate-recognition image into the forms of breaking waves, leaping fishes, glimpses of submerged rocks and the like. The image of the mermaid, in fact, arose from hallucinations produced by the psychological process of projection, and differed only in degree from the normal projection which confers, in the eyes of her lover, qualities of such extraordinary fascination and desirability on any very ordinary girl. Projection affords complete conviction if the subject is not aware of its workings, and the sailors of old, lacking our contemporary understanding of the laws of the outer world, saw no reason to doubt the outer-world reality of what they saw—for they did see it, exactly as you or I might have seen it in similar circumstances; the only difference is that they interpreted the image on their retina as a female form, whereas we should have interpreted it as that of a breaking wave which resembled a female form. The image which presented itself to consciousness would be exactly the same in either case—a female form; the difference would lie solely in the deductions subsequently drawn from it.

The mental world-picture of the ancient mariner permitted of the existence of creatures, half human and half fish, which lived in the ocean and which he might conceivably catch in a net; the mental world-picture of the contemporary man rejects such a possibility—but is the difference so important? Our understanding of the biological impossibility of the mermaid has not eliminated her from our minds: it is a fair bet that out of one hundred comic cartoons in the contemporary press at least one will contain a mermaid; as a Nereid her figure in stone or bronze adorns our fountains, and in her own or closely allied forms she is, as we have seen, a familiar figure in fiction and legend; recently the lower half of a lady was squeezed into a reproduction of a fish's tail in order to make a film about a mermaid. Evidently this figure complies with Jung's definition of a 'psychological truth'; the reason for our pre-occupation with her has already been indicated: she is an Archetypal symbol, and as such she constitutes, in her own right, a part, or a universal content, of the collective mind. Her figure may appear in any individual consciousness spontaneously and without the volition of its owner, in exactly the same way as that of a material object with which he is confronted: it comes, in fact, from 'outside' his individual mind and persists whether it is present to any personal consciousness or not. In these circumstances is there any justification for saying that it does not 'exist'?

Where, after all, does the bank overdraft exist if not in the mind? It is, of course, recorded on a piece of paper, but that is not its essence, which lies in the interpretation of the marks on the paper: it is a debt, and a 'debt of honour' which is un-recorded is no less real; an unwritten law 'exists' no less than a written one, and so does a traditional song which has never been written down. Surely the poem 'exists' in the poet's mind before he has committed it to paper. And does anybody doubt the 'real existence' of his job? Yet the job consists solely of ideas in his mind and in those of other people: he is expected to appear at a certain place at a certain time and to carry out certain activities, in return for which figures are written down which, when interpreted, allow him the right to enjoy the amenities of life—and, what is often more important to him, to be treated with proportionate respect by his fellows. Why, then, should he refuse to admit the real existence of mermaids, which are no less familiar to him and his environment than the ideas which constitute the situation in the world which is so important to him, or the laws which he unquestioningly obeys?

The answer is that people once believed in the presence of mermaids in the outer world, but have now, owing to the advance of scientific knowledge, ceased to do so. To believe in them therefore seems to the contemporary mind to be a regression to barbarism. But the modern civilized man demonstrates the superiority of his world-picture over that of the old-time sailor in two ways: when each of them sees a female form in the sea the latter concludes that a flesh-and-blood creature is actually swimming there, whereas the former (a) objects that no such creature is possible, and (b) explains the hallucination by pointing out that such things are commonly 'imagined', or in other words that images in the mind are often projected on to sensory data to which they are unrelated. In his conclusion, in fact, he is making use not of one but of two complex images in his world-picture, those of the outer and inner worlds respectively. These were lacking in the world-picture of the sailor, or were but primitive and confused compared with the development to which one of them at least—that of the outer world—has been brought in the mind of the modern. The availability of the two images in the mind of the modern does constitute a real superiority, in that it equips him far better to deal with the outer world, the nature of which he understands; but it may represent a compensating inferiority if it leads him to admit reality to one system only and deny it to the other. In order to achieve real superiority he must learn to value each system equally.

IMPORTANCE OF THE NATURE OF THE CATEGORIES TO WHICH EXISTENCE IS CONCEDED OR DENIED

The importance of this matter lies in the fact that the use of the terms existence and reality implies not only intellectual belief but a strong feeling relationship with the objects to which they are attributed. The real and existent—for the two terms are used in virtually the same sense—are important to us: they are things which must be taken seriously, and according to which we must orientate ourselves in life; the unreal and non-existent, on the other hand, can be passed over and brushed aside. Hence the question of what we believe to exist and to be real, and what the opposite, is a vital factor in our attitude to life.

Eddington says that 'it would be absurd to divide mankind into two sects, the one believing in the existence of overdrafts and the other denying their existence'. If the distinction were strictly confined to the specific matter of overdrafts it would of course be as absurd as Swift's satirical division of humanity into big-endians and little-endians, according to which end of a boiled egg they began with; but the absurdity derives solely from the triviality of the example chosen. A man's beliefs concerning any specific object are an index to the nature of the system on which he founds his beliefs in general, and that is anything but unimportant. (Eddington says that this is a question not of belief but of classification; but what is the difference?) If we choose less trivial examples the fact at once becomes apparent: it is obviously possible to draw significant conclusions regarding a man's attitude to life from his assertion that God, or altruism, beauty or justice do or do not exist.

The question of the belief in the real existence of God provides an important example in this connection. Nowadays there is very considerable disagreement regarding the existence or non-existence of God, and this is because in past ages, when the nature of the outer world was less perfectly understood, claims were made for him, as for the mermaid, which are irreconcilable with what we have subsequently discovered about it. A personal God endowed with conscious purpose and volition, who acts directly on the material world, is certainly impossible, but that does not mean that God does not exist as a reality of the mind. Such a mental reality may be described as a pattern, factor or influence that affects us in its own right in the same way as our physical appetites, or our impulse to learn or to imitate, affect us. We have already seen that such universal images, or structures of the mind—the Archetypes—act spontaneously and purposefully according to laws which can be ascertained, and the image which we call God has demonstrably manifested itself in humanity at all times and in all places; its underlying attributes have always been the same, although it has been seen in a variety of forms, dependent on the mental level of any particular community. The theological doctrine of Progressive Revelation is, in fact, perfectly reconcilable with the psychological interpretation of this matter. If, out of deference to any one-sided intellectual system, we attempt to ignore the real influence which such images exert on us we shall only compel them to act through the unconscious mind, which they will do as a protest (in the sense explained earlier) and consequently in unpleasant ways. The image of God, as we shall see in the later course of this study, is apt to be particularly troublesome in these circumstances.

As we have already noted in connection with the Anima, the Archetypes are apt to present themselves to consciousness in the archaic forms of primitive symbolism, and it is one of Jung's most important doctrines that we must not only accept these forms without prejudice, but that we must also adopt towards them the attitude which we should adopt towards autonomous beings—for they are not subject to our volition, and their purposefulness is as real as that of our physiological processes. But such an attitude smacks of regression to the past, and it is the cause of much misunderstanding, such as that expressed in the protest quoted in the Introduction, to the effect that Jung's teaching is no better than 'a fresh bunch of superstitions'. But this is only a prejudice which we must overcome. Jung and his followers do not believe that it is possible to catch mermaids in nets, or that God performs outer-world miracles entailing an abrogation of the laws of nature. Such claims were made in the past, and since it has been proved that they were impossible, superficial minds have jumped to the conclusion that God and the mermaid do not 'exist' at all: it is as though we were to deny the existence of the laws because it was demonstrated that Justice, in the form of a blindfolded female holding a sword and balance, did not exist in the flesh.

THE ATTRIBUTION OF EXISTENCE TO BOTH
OUTER-WORLD AND INNER-WORLD CATEGORIES

How, then, can we recover our belief in the reality and existence of such things as God and the mermaid without swallowing
all the absurdities of ancient myth and legend? Simply by
discriminating between outer-world and inner-world existence
and reality. *The two are complementary, and neither is more valid,
nor more intrinsically important than the other, but their characteristic
laws and patterns are entirely different.* Tables and chairs are outer-
world realities which have no significance, and virtually no
existence, in the inner world; mermaids have inner-world
existence and reality but are not to be found in the outer world;
the human individual is inescapably concerned with both, for
both worlds are a part of the mind in its universal, supra-
personal aspect. The universal aspect of mind, in fact, does
represent something in the nature of a surrounding 'world', in
which our individual conscious minds are contained, just as
our bodies are contained in the physical universe, but that surrounding world of universal mind presents itself to consciousness in two distinct ways, which lead to the construction in the
individual mind of two distinct pictures: those of the inner
and the outer worlds.

DIFFICULTIES IN THE WAY OF ACCEPTING THE
HYPOTHESIS

It is terribly hard to accept the hypothesis that the vast and
intricate system of the outer world as revealed to us by modern
science exists 'in the mind' in exactly the same way (although,
so to speak, in a different department) as mermaids do, but
that is only because the contemporary conception of mind is so
inadequate. This matter will be discussed in closer detail in the
next volume; the arguments adduced above should suffice to
demonstrate that a *prima facie* case for the hypothesis does exist,
but in face of the powerful and deeply ingrained prejudice to
the contrary which permeates the mental environment of today,
nobody whose mind has not been prepared by years of reflection on the subject can be expected to accept the full implications of the theory on first acquaintance with it. The way to

understanding is an arduous one, entailing considerable mental effort and many disappointments when false trails end in the wilderness.

DIFFERENTIATION BETWEEN INTELLECTUAL
DEFINITION AND FEELING ATTITUDE

Before leaving the subject it is advisable to reiterate that we are dealing with two separate matters: the intellectual meaning assigned to a terminology, and an attitude towards experience, or in other words towards life. So far as the intellectual meaning is concerned anybody is at liberty to attach any meaning he wishes to any given term; in order that discussion with others may be fruitful, however, he must obviously define precisely what he means. There is therefore no theoretical objection to anybody's insisting that he intends to confine the terms reality and existence to those things which form part of his picture of the outer world; in that case, however, he must (a) admit that this category does not cover everything which may affect the course of his life, and of which he must therefore take account, and (b) suggest some new term to cover that attribute of validity and efficacity when it is found in factors to which he denies the properties of reality and existence. For he cannot get away from the fact that the terms in question have arisen as the expression of a universal feeling value attaching to those things which people believe that they must take seriously and cannot ignore, and that some term is required to express it: if he restricts the meaning of the terms reality and existence in such a way that they do not cover everything which possesses this attribute, then he must offer alternatives. Since, however, we already possess these terms, and they are generally used in the sense indicated, to change their use thus arbitrarily is an unnecessary complication, and one which, furthermore, is liable to lead to misunderstanding and confusion. Not only will those whom he is addressing be liable to receive the impression that when he says that something is not real, or does not exist, he means that it has no significance and can be ignored, but his own conclusions will also tend to be coloured by the feeling connotation which unconsciously attaches to the words, and from which he can never be sure that he has completely freed himself. Thus, while there is no theoretical objection to such a use of the terms (provided that it is clearly defined) it is practically unsuitable.

The undeniable difference between the type of reality and existence discernible in tables and chairs and that attaching to the mermaid can, as I have already suggested, be recognized by differentiating between outer-world and inner-world reality and existence respectively.

THE ABSOLUTE AND THE RELATIVE MEANING OF THE TERMS

Finally it may be suggested that if we attempt a definition of the only absolute theoretical meaning of the terms which will cover every possible case, we must admit that everything which ever has been, or ever will be experienced is real, and exists. Every experience is an act of relationship, a contact, between the ultimate Subject and the universal Object, both of which transcend our comprehension. From the highest or most absolute viewpoint which we can conceive it is immaterial whether any item of experience is sense or nonsense—i.e. whether it can or cannot be fitted into any coherent pattern—true or untrue, sublime or ridiculous, or whether it is universal or confined to one single individual consciousness: in all cases it is a perception of an aspect of the Object by the Subject, and nothing, in the last resort, is more than that. When used in this absolute sense the terms can have no negative: nothing is unreal, and nothing is non-existent.[1] Thus the terms become superfluous, for by naming anything the speaker proves that whatever he understands by the name is present to his consciousness: it is an aspect of the Object which the Subject is experiencing: therefore it IS. If he wishes to state any more about it he will have to provide a predicate.

[1] This, of course, does not apply to the numerous uses of the word 'exist' as a copula. 'Poverty does not exist in Ruritania' simply means that it is not to be found there, although, by implication, it is to be found elsewhere; often, moreover, the predicate, although not stated, is implied by the context. The only exception to the inadmissibility of the negative use of the term existence in this absolute sense is with regard to the ultimate ONE in which both Subject and Object are included. Of this it may be said that It is both existent and non-existent, which, of course, remains a paradox.

Practically, of course, such a definition robs the terms of all usefulness; but we need them, and therefore we must go on using them, although in the clear understanding that their significance in any practical context is only relative: they mean 'this is important to me because it is part of the mental system according to which I understand life'.

Thus in any particular connection, or as seen from any particular viewpoint, some things may be said to exist, or to be real, while others are non-existent or unreal, whereas from another viewpoint the same things fall into the opposite categories. From the viewpoint of the biologist bacteria exist and mermaids do not; from that of the student of symbolism mermaids exist and bacteria do not. To the artist, irrespective of whether he admits the fact as an intellectual proposition or not, beauty and aesthetic values exist and have reality, whereas to the philistine they do not.

This relativity is particularly noticeable in the matter of the feeling-relationship of reality which different individuals entertain towards various objects. Thus, to return to the overdraft, the degree of 'grim reality' which different individuals feel in it will vary: one will not be able to forget his overdraft for a moment: it will induce in him feelings of insecurity, anxiety and even guilt, and he will remain worried and unhappy until he has paid it off. To another it will mean practically nothing: he will continue to draw cheques undisturbed until Nemesis overtakes him, and when that happens it will only be the policeman, and still not the overdraft, that is 'real' to him.

IMPORTANCE OF THE FEELING ELEMENT

This matter is particularly important, because it is useless to persuade anybody to accept the reality of something as an intellectual proposition if that acceptance is not confirmed by his feelings, or is opposed by contrary feelings. (This distinction is presumably what Eddington means when he says that the distinction between existent and non-existent is a matter of classification and not of belief. As a matter of 'belief', he implies, everybody would accept the existence of the overdraft as a 'grim reality'—it is only on the question of 'classification' that they will be found to differ. The word 'belief' is badly chosen, for what would be the purpose of making a classification in which one did not believe? It might, however, perfectly well be opposed to one's feelings.)

Intellectual theories which lack the backing of feeling are for the most part no more than empty words, for the individual's attitude towards any problem in life, as opposed to theory, is inevitably to some extent affected by his feelings about it. The importance assumed by the two factors—intellectual conviction and feeling—varies of course both as between individuals and according to the nature of the problem involved, and in the event its workings are often surprising. Those intellectuals, for instance, who are boldest in their theories are often the most helpless victims of feelings which completely belie the latter, and which had remained unrecognized until special circumstances brought them into play. Thus Nietzsche, the stern progenitor of that Superman who knows neither scruple nor pity, was in fact a timid and soft-hearted individual: he could not screw himself up to the point of proposing marriage to a girl who had given him every encouragement, and his last act, before he became irremediably insane, was to throw himself, weeping, on the neck of a cab-horse which was being maltreated by its owner. The acceptance of the inner world as a reality, which is what the times demand of us, is a matter which transcends mere intellectual conviction. We must start with the intellect because the prejudices which oppose us are largely of an intellectual nature and can only be combated on intellectual ground. But if the acceptance is to be effective it must be translated into terms of life, and that entails a long, patient and at times disagreeable reorientation. Such a process can never be carried through in the face of prejudice, derision and obstructionism, both from without and within, if it is opposed by contrary feeling values, of the nature and power of which the subject is not fully aware. We cannot reason away our feelings, but if we bring them to full consciousness we can confine them to their proper sphere, and are fore-armed against them when they run counter to our purposes.

SOURCES OF THE FEELING ELEMENT INVOLVED

Hence it is necessary for us to devote very careful attention to those feelings which are liable to oppose us in our attempt at reorientation. They derive from two sources: from the authority value of the prestige enjoyed by the scientific outlook, and from the most powerful of all sources: instinct.

The scientific outlook is, unfortunately, one of our greatest enemies, for, as will be explained in a subsequent chapter, the overwhelming success of the mental attitude which lies behind this outlook, in enriching us and improving the conditions of our outer lives, has been the principal cause in producing the contemporary prejudice of confining 'reality' to the outer world. So long as our belief in the primacy of the outer-world pattern remains merely relative, and is confined to low-grade practical details, it is solely beneficial, and in better balanced ages this indispensable, utilitarian, down-to-earth attitude has been offset and compensated by universally accepted religious or speculative systems, and by customs which have emphasized the mystical, symbolical and irrational forms through which the other side of man's life and nature — the inner world — can find expression. But the contemporary scientific outlook is more than a mere guide in practical matters: it has set itself up as a universal philosophy, thereby encroaching on provinces of the mind with which it is not fitted to deal. It would, I repeat, be absurd to deny its enormous value — so long as it is confined to its proper sphere; but since it has dangerously overstepped the limits of its usefulness, and is threatening to usurp an unqualified supremacy in our view of life, it is necessary to begin by attacking it in order to reduce it to its proper place.

The vital sphere in which the prestige enjoyed by this attitude is supported by the immense power of instinct lies in our attitude to the evidence of sensory experience, and it is to this matter that we must now turn.

IV The Role of the Senses

THE question of the role played by the senses in the determination of our picture of the outer world may be approached from two sides: first the investigation of the causes behind that spontaneous, normal, universal reliance on sensory experience as a confirmation of outer-world reality which we have already noted, and secondly the consideration of the role which it plays in scientific method. It will be convenient to take the latter first.

THE ROLE OF SENSORY EXPERIENCE IN SCIENTIFIC METHOD

Ever since Galileo dropped his two stones from the leaning tower in Pisa, demonstration by sensory experience has been the keystone of scientific method. Nothing, the scientist insists, may be accepted as true simply because we believe it, however strong our conviction; nor because it has been reported to us, however great the reliability of our informant: it must be demonstrable in the form of a sensory experience which can be reconstructed by anybody at any place or time.

The so-called scientific 'experiment', if it is successful, is in reality the demonstration of the truth of a hypothesis; the demonstrator, in effect, says to the world at large: 'Observe that when I do this and this something definite happens: the pointer moves on the scale, the bell rings, the liquid changes colour, the mouse dies, or whatever it may be. You have seen or heard it yourself: you cannot deny it. If you still don't believe me you can try for yourself, anywhere and at any time. If you do exactly as I have done you will end with the same sensory experience, or its equivalent. It therefore follows that the conditions in question always produce the like results, which may be formulated thus and thus. This is a scientific law.'

The simple type of the scientific demonstration is Dr Johnson's attack on the kerb-stone: there the proof of the hypothesis by the sensory experience is obvious, and the same applies to the simple demonstrations which we are shown at school. The results of more complex experiments, on the other hand, may be presented in some indirect form, such as a table of figures or a graph, and the chain of reasoning by which the results are connected with the hypothesis may contain many stages in which scientific laws and principles are assumed without demonstration. To the layman, therefore, the universality of the sensory confirmation may not be apparent: to him the scientist appears to reach his results principally by way of arcane computations in his mind, and he accepts them as established truths solely because of the prestige which the scientist enjoys in his eyes. The scientist himself, however, never loses sight of the necessity of sensory confirmation at every stage of his reasoning, and every law and principle which he quotes must have been the subject of a demonstration which he has himself carried out, or seen carried out, in the course of his training. Sensory confirmation remains indispensable to scientific method, however much it may be overlaid by symbols on paper: so far as science is concerned it is the sole and exclusive criterion of truth.

This matter is important, because nearly every inhabitant of a civilized country nowadays has some acquaintance with scientific method, and the basic ideas of science are so much 'in the air' that they tend to colour all our thinking. People have, of course, always relied on the evidence of their senses above all else, but hitherto they have been prepared to accept the truth and reality of many other things, not demonstrable by sensory experience, as well. They have believed in some kind of 'invisible world' and have been encouraged to do so by teachers who recognized in such beliefs an indispensable counterpoise to the crass materialistic attitude which the struggle with outer circumstances tends to induce in most people. Nowadays, on the other hand, although a few teachers of religion and of the humanities still insist on the reality of the incorporeal and imponderable, a greater number of authorities, whose prestige stands higher with the general public, are, at least inferentially, proclaiming that nothing is real or true which we cannot touch or see. I have even read the assertion by a distinguished scientist that nothing should be accepted as true that could not be made the subject of an experiment, and that it was scarcely ever permissible to make generalized statements about classes of objects—e.g. 'horses', or 'the horse'—but only particular statements about individual exemplars. This is no more than a crude form of medieval nominalism. Such ideas are not usually stated or accepted in so many words, and a great many people, if asked, would sincerely assert that they believed in the reality of things not demonstrable to the senses; when it comes to decisions affecting their conduct, however, they generally tacitly assume the contrary.

Thus nowadays the tendency to attach a disproportionate, almost exclusive, reliance on the evidence of the senses is no longer, as it used to be, merely a weakness of the unreflecting man, adequately counterbalanced by the united voices of the intelligentsia; it has grown into an elaborate theoretical system, sponsored by a great part of that very intelligentsia, whose proper and indispensable function should be to direct the thoughts of their fellows into less materialistic channels.

I have said that for science sensory demonstration is the sole and exclusive criterion of truth, but this naturally does not mean that science, as a system of thought, or that scientists as individuals, necessarily deny the validity of other matters altogether. The difference is commonly formulated by saying that science has no concern with 'values', the validity of which is accepted as something universally experienced which is not susceptible of proof or demonstration by scientific methods. If people consistently maintained this distinction all would be well, but unfortunately the enormous prestige enjoyed by science today has the inevitable effect of depreciating the importance, and, above all, the reality, of everything which is not susceptible of scientific demonstration; scientists, or pseudo-scientists, moreover, are tempted by the success which has attended their method in its proper sphere to attempt to apply it in spheres which are in fact alien to it. Attempts are for ever being made to establish material or concrete causation for mental phenomena: it is, for instance, suggested that the visions of the mystics were due to vitamin deficiency and so forth. The point here is that while it cannot be denied that vitamin deficiency, the action of drugs and other physical causes may affect the condition of consciousness, thus making available to it regions of the mind which are normally inaccessible, yet the contents which consequently appear in consciousness are themselves purely mental phenomena, and are in no way dependent on the nature of the physical cause which makes them available to consciousness. Descartes was possibly drunk on the night of his great dreams; St. Paul was conceivably an epileptic; Coleridge took laudanum and St. Antony of Egypt and the children at Fatima were probably suffering from vitamin deficiencies; are we to suppose that if Coleridge had suffered from vitamin deficiencies, St. Paul had taken laudanum and Descartes had been epileptic, the consequences would have been any different? The content and nature of the visions of the mystics, as well as of other people, are found to conform to their own laws and patterns, no matter by what physical means consciousness is predisposed to perceive them. It is, once again, a question of distinguishing between the Two Worlds.

We have now to ask the reason why the scientific outlook is so insistent on the sensory confirmation of all hypotheses. What is there about sensory experience that gives it such a particularly high value? The first thing to be noted is that although the scientist insists on a sensory experience of some kind as the criterion of truth he is not interested in the sensory experience in its own right, but solely in something that it represents. The sphere of mental activity which is devoted to sensory material in its own right is the aesthetic, for it is only there that sensory experience is evaluated, differentiated and studied according to its own nature, and without diversion of interest to any extraneous considerations. To those who have developed aesthetic discrimination a sensory experience has value in itself, quite apart from what it may represent, but this attitude is completely alien to the scientific viewpoint. The scientist, as an individual, may of course appreciate aesthetic values just as well as anybody else, but as a scientist he is not concerned with them. This is one of the reasons for the deterioration of artistic

taste in modern highly civilized communities: the scientific outlook and all that it implies has developed the interpretative
approach to sensory experience to such a high degree that, in
the average mind, the direct appreciation of the material itself
is almost totally suppressed and can only be brought to the
surface by means of a sustained course of study. We shall be
concerned with this matter in the next volume of this series:
for the moment our interest lies in that which the sensory experience is regarded as representing, and in terms of which it
is interpreted.

To the scientist, of course, and to nearly any contemporary
mind, the question does not appear in this light at all. As he
sees it the sensory impression is tantamount to 'reality': if, like
Dr Johnson, he kicks a stone, he believes that he is directly
experiencing the real, independent, outer world through the
medium of the nerves of his foot, and it is in that supposed outer
reality that he is interested. He is, in fact, identifying himself
with his foot, just as we commonly identify ourselves with our
eyes and ears, or at least with our brains, regarding the whole
organism as identical with the self, and the area outside it as
the not-self or outer world. But, as we have seen, this position is
untenable; for all practical purposes it is serviceable, but if we
wish to look more deeply into the processes of the mind we must
abandon it. The contents of consciousness arise from various
sources, and sensory impressions are only one of them; therefore, in order to reduce them all to a common denominator, we
must treat the sensory material solely as a mental content,
equivalent to any other; we know that it is found to conform to
its own specific laws and patterns, but so do thoughts and
feelings, and there is no reason why we should accord a superior
validity to one pattern than to another.

In the light of this consideration the question takes on a new
form: we are not so much concerned with the nature and
intrinsic values of the sensory experience, for that, we saw, is a
question of aesthetics, with which science is not concerned.
What we are concerned with is the pattern to which certain
elements of sensory experience conform, and which is commonly
regarded as being the reflection of an independent outer world.
In order to understand this we may turn to our second question, namely why, quite apart from scientific theory, sensory

experiences should produce in us such a particularly strong sense of conviction and reality.

THE INSTINCTIVE BASIS

'Seeing is believing'; 'I could hardly believe my own eyes'; these are familiar phrases which illustrate the profound reliance which we place in our sensory perceptions. Yet experience, or 'the stream of consciousness', consists of a medley of conceptual thoughts, words, feelings, and sensory images—some of which are derived from memory while others present themselves spontaneously to the imagination—as well as 'present' sensory experience. We have demonstrated that there is no adequate reason for attributing any intrinsically greater degree of 'reality', importance or validity to any of these elements of experience rather than to any other; nevertheless we cannot help ourselves: argue as we may, we cannot free ourselves of the conviction that what we 'see with our own eyes', or touch or hear, is in some mysterious way a more reliable guide to reality—or in other words that it possesses greater validity and importance—than anything apprehended in any other way. Some people trust logical deductions, others their feelings, others again 'hunches' or flashes of intuitive insight, as guides sufficiently reliable to base their actions upon, but those who place reliance on one of these will almost invariably be found to mistrust the others; yet everybody, without exception, places reliance on the evidence of his senses. Why is this so?

I have suggested above that the vividness or intensity of any experience is often our criterion as to the degree of its reality: on reflecting on it afterwards we may come to deny it reality in the outer-world sense, because it fails in some way to fit into our picture of the outer world, but our immediate reaction to a vivid experience is normally to regard it as 'real', and if we can see no objection of the kind indicated we will accord it outer-world reality. Secondly, I pointed out that our instincts are still the source of many of our most intense experiences: it may, therefore, be worth looking for the explanation of our problem in our true instinctual equipment.

It is immediately evident that sensory stimuli cause the release of nearly all instinctive reactions in the animal world, and man is obviously no exception. Here, then, would appear to be the answer to our question: the spontaneous intensity of our reaction to sensory experience is simply instinctive. But we have noted that instincts consist solely of specific and highly specialized responses to very narrowly circumscribed stimuli, and it is doubtful whether a heterogeneous collection of such separate, limited and very specialized reactions could become generalized into the kind of attitude which we are considering. It is necessary, therefore, to carry the investigation further.

The explanation, I think, is to be found in one particular instinct, that of curiosity, or the tendency to investigate the unfamiliar. This tendency is to be found in varying degrees in most of the higher animals and is, of course, particularly pronounced in the primates, and presumably in man: the inquisitiveness of monkeys is proverbial, and it appears beyond question that the same tendency, carried to an even higher degree, must have been one of the most important factors in the development of the human mentality.

This instinct is peculiar—perhaps unique—in that it is activated, not by the presence of a particular sign-stimulus but rather, apparently, by the absence of any. A great deal of experiment would be necessary in order to elucidate its exact workings, and we must of course beware of imputing our own motivations to animals: the animal, presumably, does not experience curiosity in the human sense, namely the desire to know and understand, but it is undeniable that a great many animals, and particularly young animals, are impelled to approach and investigate unfamiliar objects. When this occurs two tendencies may be observed working in opposite directions: on the one hand fear, or apprehensiveness, impelling to flight, and on the other the impulse to approach. This combination would obviously have survival value in those species capable of learning from individual experience, since the unfamiliar object might be dangerous or might, on the other hand, be beneficial: an example of the latter is to be found in the tendency of some small birds—notably robins—to follow larger animals (including human beings) because the latter often disturb the surface of the earth and thereby expose grubs, etc.[1] In this case it is probable that a positive sign-stimulus is involved, i.e. the bird

[1] See Lack, *op. cit.* Any gardener can confirm the fact for himself.

is impelled to approach the object, not because it is unfamiliar, but because it is a large moving form. The recognition of unfamiliarity, indeed, implies mental powers which are probably not to be found in any but the highest animals, since before an object can be recognized as unfamiliar it must first be identified as an individual entity, separate from its environment, and its image must then be compared with all the categories of familiar objects. Accurate investigation would therefore probably disclose that animals are impelled to approach and investigate by certain positive sign-stimuli—e.g. movement of a rapid and irregular nature, bright colour, etc.—rather than by the negative quality of unfamiliarity.

However this may be there can be no question that most animals are instinctively impelled to approach and investigate certain classes of object, of the nature of which they are uncertain—i.e. such as are not immediately recognizable by comparison with one or other of the stock of innate recognition-images, such as those representing its food, its enemies, members of its own species, etc.[1] When an object is recognized as one of these latter the reaction is swift and certain; the impulse to approach the unknown, however, being held in check by apprehensiveness, is uncertain, which is an unusual feature in animal behaviour. This uncertainty is the key to the whole pattern: it must be the rudimentary form of what we know as doubt, and it demands alleviation by reassurance. It is probably this function of reassurance by sensory investigation which forms the basis of our picture of the outer world.

The majority of animals reassure themselves by the use of the sense of smell: in mankind the corresponding role is played by that of touch, and it is in tactile sensations that we seek our final confirmation of outer-world reality. There can be no doubt that the human impulse to pick things up with the hand, or to finger, grip or shake them is a true instinct: we can observe its irrational working today in the inveterate tendency of sightseers to finger anything which excites their wonder—even a picture. (Is it really real?) Obviously, to an animal which uses its hands to the extent which man does, the 'feel' of an object is of vital importance: the questions whether it is fixed or loose, hard or soft, rigid or pliable, light or heavy are constantly

[1] For examples of such images, see Tinbergen, *op. cit.*

requiring answers. When instinctive man is in doubt, therefore, he touches, just as a dog smells.

In this connection it is interesting to consider our attitude to the everyday hallucination of the senses in dreams. The most commonly involved, of course, is vision: dreams are commonly experienced as something seen, and although a great deal of them is made up, similarly to the experiences of waking life, of a direct experience of the meaning of what is going on, while the visual elements remain in the background, we can generally, although by no means always, say what the characters in our dreams looked like; frequently, moreover, visual images occur in their own right and are experienced with considerable intensity: we are suddenly confronted by a vividly seen landscape, the image of an animal or object or whatever it may be. Auditory images are less common, for although dream-characters commonly speak we are normally aware, as in waking life, only of what has been said, and not of the sound of the voice as such; when a disembodied voice speaks, or the voice of a visible speaker is distinctly heard as a sound, the impression of 'reality' is considerably heightened, and, as Jung says, when this occurs it is evidence that the dream in question is unusually important. The tactile sense, however, is scarcely ever involved —a fact which is substantiated by the familiar phrase 'to pinch oneself to make sure that one is awake'. I have, however, experienced one very vivid tactile sensation in a dream—a bird perched on my hand, and the characteristic light, cool, hard feel of its claws on my skin has left an ineradicable impression on my mind. This was, needless to say, a 'great dream', full of pure Archetypal symbolism, but it was the rare tactile impression which gave the crowning touch to its unforgettable 'reality'.

Thus we do not place complete confidence in the evidence of vision and hearing, because even in waking life they are fallible on account of the stupendous demands we make of them: sometimes, at a distance, we mistake a stranger for a friend, or the sound of a bicycle-bell for the ringing of the telephone. With regard to touch, however, from which we expect no such prodigies of fine differentiation, we are completely confident: sight or hearing, we know, may on occasion betray us, but touch, we believe, never can. It was by the sovereign evidence of his sense of touch that St Thomas finally allowed himself to be convinced of the reality of the resurrected body of the Saviour.

The strongest reassurance of all is obtained by the confirmatory evidence of two or more senses, in particular vision and touch. It is on this combination that our conception of material bodies is founded, and the expectation that the confirmation of one by the other will be forthcoming is so profoundly embedded in our picture of reality that the mere notion of not being able to feel something which we see in the form of a material object is enough to plunge us into a panic horror: the idea, of course, is the standby of ghost stories.

This generalized image of material objects as things which may be both touched and seen is so basic to our thinking that its importance cannot be exaggerated. Any suggestion of a doubt of its validity is equivalent to a threat to remove one of the most indispensable—perhaps the most indispensable—of all the props on which our picture of the world is supported, and consequently it induces a panic terror, or at least an angry outburst of the type of Dr Johnson's attack on the kerbstone; for anger is often a reaction to fear.

This is one of the earliest discoveries about the world around us which we made in our infancy, and on it we have based an incalculable amount of the subsequent accretion of knowledge, and rules for our guidance, which enable us to hold our own in a dangerous world. The threat of removing it seems to imply plunging us back into the darkness from which we once emerged at the cost of so much arduous labour—the darkness of the unknown, the unintelligible and the unconscious: the darkness that comprehendeth not.

In the next volume an attempt will be made to reconstruct some parts of the process whereby the infant builds up an intelligible picture of the world—virtually, in fact, creates a world—and painfully achieves full consciousness. It is a far more complex and arduous process than is generally realized, for we adults take so much for granted that we project a large part of our mature understanding into the baby's mind. To us, for instance, it is so self-evident that certain visual patterns represent material objects—things that are permanent, that occupy space, that continue to exist when we cannot see them, that can be moved about in their entirety, that present a different aspect when seen from different points of view and so on—that we assume that all this is immediately self-evident to the infant. But this cannot be so: it all has to be learnt, and until it has been learnt the world of sensory experience is unintelligible: visual and tactile impressions succeed one another without rhyme or reason. But once it has been learnt every human attainment becomes potentially possible. It is one of our most invaluable possessions. But as is the way with invaluable possessions we generally take it for granted, and fail to appreciate its worth until we are threatened with losing it.

Around this nucleus, or concomitantly with it, there grows up the wider picture of the world of material objects arranged in time and space. This again appears to the adult as either so self-evident that it must be immediately obvious to the baby, or else, if he devotes his developed intelligence to the matter and begins to concern himself with such things as the four-dimensional continuum, as so abstruse that it cannot possibly have anything to do with the infant mind. But the truth is that it is not self-evident to the baby: he has to find out about it, and although of course such abstract concepts as those of space and time do not exist for him, he has to build up his own picture of that universal arrangement which appears to us so obvious that we do not even trouble to think about it.

The baby's problem is to understand the visual images of which he becomes aware—which, in the first place, are mere patches of different colours and tones—by constructing a picture of the world in terms of material objects with intervals between them, and this he can only do by learning first to confirm the evidence of sight by that of touch, and later by himself moving about among the objects of which he becomes aware. His conclusions, of course, are not formally expressed in words: they must consist of a multitude of small empirical discoveries: for instance that if you stand in one position an object may be obscured by another, but if you move to the side it emerges, that a small object near at hand appears larger than a big one at a distance, and so on. These again, of course, are not consciously formulated but simply learnt as a picture by means of constant repetition of the experiences concerned. Anybody who takes the trouble to work out the mental processes involved in the picture which he makes of the shape and arrangement of a room and its contents in the course of a single glance, having regard to the shapes of the further sides of three-dimensional objects which cannot be seen, the position of each object with relation to the others, etc., will be astounded by the complexities involved in producing all this from a coloured pattern on the retina. Nevertheless the ordering principle of intelligence in the mind of the infant is already capable of collating the disjointed material provided by his eyes and constructing from it a generalized mental picture which enables him, in a year or two, to master such complicated three-dimensional problems as that of getting to the other side of a table by crawling under it if it is not possible to walk round, and so on. All this is based on the existence in his mind of a coherent system which, for want of a better term, we may call a complex image: the image of the world in space.

To what extent this image may be regarded as instinctive and to what extent it is learnt is a moot point—it would be necessary to conduct a large number of experiments in order to determine the matter—but at any rate it is fundamental to a very large part of our mental activity; it must certainly, in any case, be regarded as Archetypal, since unless there were some kind of pre-existent nucleus around which the baby could begin to arrange his original incoherent sensory impressions it is hard to see how he could so infallibly construct this very complex image long before he has conscious continuity to aid him.

We implicitly and confidently rely at all times on the expectation that our sensory experience will invariably conform to this image, or at least to the various laws and relationships which make it up, and when we occasionally meet with an experience which appears anomalous we are not only surprised, but concerned and distressed as well, and do not rest until we have discovered an acceptable explanation for the anomaly. For the prospect of never again being able to rely on these fundamental presuppositions, on which we base our greatest and our smallest actions, is too appalling to contemplate. The explanations which we are prepared to accept in order to set our minds at rest in face of an anomaly vary, of course, with our individual intelligence and knowledge: the primitive is quite content to put anything of the kind down to witchcraft, and civilized people will accept almost anything on the word of a doctor or a scientist; on the basis of empirical experience, moreover, all of us are content to dismiss the most outrageous violations of our world-picture with complete equanimity, if only we are satisfied that we were properly asleep at the time.

Later, when the child becomes aware of his own continuity as the subject of experience, he begins to appreciate the element of time. Here again the complex image built up in the mind is no more than the sum of a multiplicity of small empirical discoveries: for instance, that two objects cannot occupy the same space at the same time, and that one object can only be in one place at one time: if an object is at one place now, but was earlier somewhere else, then it must have passed through all the intervening space in the interval, and in doing so it cannot have passed through any part of space occupied by another object. The surprise produced in our minds by the arts of the conjuror is of course in almost all cases the result of his apparent violation of this last law, and until we have become accustomed to the spectacle it is followed by a feverish search for the explanation.

This deeply ingrained picture of the immutable laws governing the relationships of material objects in space and time probably forms the nucleus of our picture of the outer world. To it are added a number of other empirical discoveries, such as the characteristics of the animate and the inanimate, mechanical causation, the possibilities of changes of form in material objects and so on. Later it becomes elaborated by abstract ideas, and the picture of the outer world in the mind of an educated and well-informed man includes such purely abstract elements as the laws of science, economics and even psychology.

To return to the child: when consciousness has achieved a certain degree of differentiation and independence he discovers an alternative mode of experience, which is to abstract images from their space-time-conditioned situation in the outer world and do things with them in his imagination. This saves him a great deal of trouble and represents an enormous increase in his mental powers, for now, in order to discover that a round peg will not fit into a square hole he no longer needs to procure the objects in question and make the experiment in the outer world: he has simply to visualize the two in order to assure himself that they cannot fit.

This represents the discovery of the inner world as distinct from the outer, for the direction of abstraction is inwards, that of concretization outwards. It will be remembered that inner and outer are relative terms, and we cannot describe any given mental content as belonging exclusively to either the inner or the outer world: everything depends on how we look at it and what we are doing with it. Thus the imaginary picture of a round peg and a square hole belongs to the inner world when contrasted with the 'present' sensory experience of them, on the other hand it belongs to the outer world when contrasted with the higher degree abstracts of roundness and squareness, from which it may have been concretized for the purpose of investigating the practical application of a theory. The latter operation is of course beyond the mental powers of a young child: to him any imaginary picture may be described as inner. To the adult, on the other hand, an imaginary picture may be part of the outer world, for we must not forget that both worlds are contained in the mind. Even the most materialistic people constantly imagine things, but their tendency is always to concretize, and their purpose is to put their imagining into practice, or at least to consider whether it is possible to do so.

Until the child has consciously perceived the difference between the two worlds they do not exist for him as two contrasting and alternative modes of experience: he does not, in fact, discriminate between fact and fancy. Only one world exists for him, in which anything is possible, for the type of experience which in the adult falls into the category of fancy is of course familiar to the child from the start: nothing could be more mistaken than to regard it as a mere second-hand derivation of 'reality'. For the child, however, the two modes of experience are mingled, and merge one into the other, the various contents, values, etc., which the adult so carefully segregates from one another existing side by side without distinction.

The differentiation comes gradually, and it is true to say that it is never completed. Throughout life we continue to confuse the two modes of experience: everybody has his 'blind spots', concerning which he is strangely incapable of discriminating between the possible and the impossible, the factual and the imaginary. But intelligent people continue throughout life to enrich the image, applying the distinction between inner and outer to ever wider spheres of experience.

It is almost certainly with regard to the scheme of material objects in space and time that all of us first learn to make the distinction, for any discrepancy in that field between the imaginary and the actual sensory experience is obvious—sometimes painfully so. Long after he has learned to discriminate between the imaginary picture and the material presence of such things as round pegs and square holes, however, the child continues to overlook the difference between inner and outer in such matters as the difference between the animate and the inanimate. It is not that he fails to see the difference—he understands it perfectly well, for he knows a 'real, live' animal when he sees one—but he prefers to ignore it, and in his games he is free to do so without incurring any vexatious consequences. When a little girl insists that her doll is a 'real baby' it is sufficient indication that she knows quite well that it is not, for otherwise she would not use that significant word 'real'. If the doll began to kick and scream she would certainly be very alarmed. Officious adults and malicious elder brothers, however, should refrain from pointing this fact out to her, for to do so causes mental distress. She will recognize the distinction of her own accord when she is ready to accept the mental strain that it incurs.

For the moment, however, we are not concerned with these later accretions to the complex image representing the outer world, but with that picture of the world as a collection of material objects arranged in space and time, which is its nucleus and its essence. One of the principal contrasts between the two worlds is to be seen in this respect: that whereas the outer world is essentially concerned with space and time the inner is characteristically free of them. Complete freedom from space and time of course implies the elimination of all form, change and number. In this condition no conscious experience is possible, and only the ultimate ONE, which is indeterminate, undifferentiated, unchanging and unknowable, can exist. (Yet this 'existence', being a negation of all experience, is equivalent to non-existence.) This ultimate condition is not attainable by the individual consciousness until its final merging with the universal in death (unless it be in the temporary union with the universal, and the consequent release from the bonds of time, space, and particularity, which is claimed for the Beatific Vision of the mystics). The inner world, however, is a direction of thought or experience: it is the direction towards the universal aspect of the ultimate ONE, just as the outer world is the direction away from this, and towards Its particular aspect. The nearer the former is approached, the more universal grow the contents of consciousness, and the weaker and more indistinct the bonds of space and time. The awareness of particular identity also grows concomitantly weaker, and there is a danger as we shall see, that it may be permanently lost. This results in insanity.

This consideration leads to a further basic conclusion regarding the nature of the distinction between inner and outer: *the inner is the direction of attention towards the universal element in phenomena, the outer towards the particular element.* Absolute universality and absolute particularity represent the projection of the concept of the Absolute—which is one of the forms under which we attempt to visualize the ultimate ONE—into this particular polarity. They are unattainable, in the phenomenal world, in a pure state, just as absolute Good and absolute Evil are unattainable; they represent the theoretical concepts of that which is all-embracing and from which all forms proceed—i.e. the Universe in Its transcendental aspect—on the one hand, and on the other that which is finally indivisible and therefore contains no parts, being nothing beyond Itself—i.e. the 'atom' in the classical sense, the Leibnizian monad, or the principle of absolute individuality, uniqueness and particularity.

Consciousness moves between these two, directing itself first towards one and then the other. The pattern of the contemporary conscious attitude accepts the direction towards the universal only in the sphere of thinking: in other spheres it is prejudiced against it and sees significance only in the direction towards the particular or concrete.

Thus, although the inner world, as it manifests itself to a particular consciousness, cannot be absolutely free of space and time, their importance in this mode of experience is far less than when consciousness is directed towards the pattern of the outer world. Consequently many of the laws of outer-world logic do not apply to it: in the inner world, for instance, a single identity may exist in two or more exemplars at the same time, or a single image may embody two states which, in the outer world, are necessarily separated by an interval of time.

The picture of the world as a multiplicity of objects arranged in space and time is based in sensory experience and in a powerful instinct—that of investigation for reassurance—concerned with our use of the senses. Being connected with instinct it is universal in the species and therefore Archetypal; in other words it is an inherent structure of the mind in accordance with which we are compelled to interpret our experience: we cannot do otherwise. More than that: it is one of the agents which actually make our experience, determining the form in which it reaches consciousness, which is all that we know. Yet it is not the sole manner in which experience can be interpreted, nor the sole agent which forms it, for it has its opposite and counterpart in the alternative mode which in this study is called the inner world, and which other writers have called the inner vision, the creative imagination, the sense of poetry, the world of the Aeons, the Other Side and many other names.

In an earlier chapter I asserted that when we get into chronic mental difficulties it is due to the fact that our conscious attitude has grown one-sided and intolerant, and is repressing and neglecting categories of experience which are produced by patterns which are inherent in the mind and therefore cannot be eliminated. I further pointed out that since the mind is bounded by its Archetypal structures any such consistent and general attitude adopted by the conscious personality must itself be Archetypal: the trouble arises from the over-valuation of one Archetypal pattern at the expense of the others. Here we may perhaps discern the basic cause of the troubles from which civilization is suffering today, and which threaten to annihilate it—perhaps once and for ever. If it is so, it is clear which Archetypal pattern we are over-valuing: it is that which sees the world exclusively as material objects arranged in space and time and regards sensory experience as the sole criterion of reality. This is the root of the scientific outlook.

We are now in a position to answer the question posed earlier: we recognized that the scientific method demanded a sensory experience as the indispensable demonstration of the truth of any hypothesis, but we noted that the scientist, as such, has no interest in the sensory experience in itself, as the artist has, but in something which it represents, and we set out to discover what that something was. It is, evidently, an event, consisting of the states or situations of material objects in space and time, which the sensory experience fixes. The scientific method has eliminated all other considerations: everything which is non-corporeal (energy, being transformable into mass, and being identifiable only in its action on material bodies, can be subsumed under the heading of corporeal) and which is not bound by space and time, is intentionally left out of account.

I am not decrying the scientific method in itself, the enormous value of which no reasonable person could deny, but only that attitude which sees in the scientific outlook the sole and exclusive truth. The scientific outlook is a magnificent servant, but servants do not make good masters. It is vitally, urgently necessary that we turn our attention, before it is too late, to the alternative outlook, namely the inner-world pattern. If we are to give this unfamiliar manner of looking at things a chance to find a place in our minds, cluttered and obsessed as they are by the picture of the outer world, it is necessary to make a start by attacking the scientific outlook in order to reduce it to its due place.

THE SENSE OF INNER AND OUTER

It is interesting to note that Jung, in a late work,[1] describes sensation as *la fonction de réalité*. This term was invented by the psychologist Janet,[2] evidently in order to designate the mental activity of distinguishing between what in this study are called the Two Worlds; when anybody suffers from delusions, for instance, his reality-function has broken down and he is unable to distinguish between 'fact' and 'fancy'. When Jung identifies sensation with this hypothetical function it is evident that he must be on the track of that role of the senses in identifying the outer world which is the subject of this chapter; his definition, however, is inadequate and to some extent misleading. I have

---

[1] *Antwort auf Hiob.*   [2] My authority is Jung.

already quoted the definition of reality which he gives else-where—everything is real which acts, or which has conse-quences—together with his own illustration demonstrating the 'reality' of a delusion, and it is evident that he cannot under-stand Janet's term in this sense. In the absence of any explana-tion (the statement in question is made parenthetically) we can only assume that in equating sensation with *la fonction de réalité* he is using the word 'reality' in its normal colloquial sense, i.e. as denoting outer-world nature. If this is so he is at variance with his own assertion, in *Psychological Types*, that sensation can be introverted, for there, after stating that introverted sensation is characterized by the predominance of the subjective element of sensation, he goes on: 'Subjective perception differs remark-ably from the objective. It is either not found at all in the object, or, at most, merely suggested by it.' This, evidently, is no *fonction de réalité*.

The confusion appears to arise from two sources: the first is that Jung does not appear to have freed himself completely from the common delusion that material objects somehow 'exist' in a more valid form than anything else: the consequence is that he identifies sensory experience with the functioning of the organs of sense, and presupposes a hypothetical 'reality' which gives rise to it, and in which the organs themselves par-ticipate. But, as we have seen, sensory experience which possesses the full force of conviction normally occurs to everybody in dreams, when the organs of sense are not involved, and it is only after he has woken up that the dreamer convinces himself that the experience lacked the artificial quality of 'reality' which he accords to waking experience alone. In the study of instinct we have also seen that the mind inherently possesses its own stock of sensory images, associated with the 'special neuro-sensory mechanisms', which can become conscious spontane-ously, without the participation of the organs of sense. Hence sensory experience is by no means limited to the hypothetical outer-world 'object', but is simply a mental function, equivalent to thinking, feeling, or any other.

The second cause of confusion is Jung's lack of understanding for the arts. In the section on introverted sensation from which I have quoted he refers repeatedly to them, but it is evident, both from these passages and from other references to the arts which he makes elsewhere, that his conception of painting, for instance, is confined exclusively to its representational aspect, and, even more mistakenly, that he believes in the possibility of a hypothetical, objectively 'correct' manner of reproducing the appearance of nature: this misconception, for which photography is largely responsible, is of course widespread nowadays. This is not the place to go into theories of art, but anybody who has any acquaintance with the subject will appreciate the point that painting, so far as it is representational at all, is largely concerned with the values and nature of visual experience in itself, and not with either the properties of natural objects as they might be determined by scientific measurement, or with the uninstructed layman's idea of 'what things look like'. Music, of course, is almost exclusively concerned with the direct perception and evaluation of sensory experience as such, quite irrespective of either intellectual 'meaning' or of any similarity to natural sounds. When sensory experience is approached from this viewpoint it is evident that its function in revealing that arrangement of material objects in space and time which forms the nucleus of our picture of the outer world is only one limited aspect of its totality. As we have seen, moreover, other things, such as bank overdrafts, which are wholly independent of sensory experience, are normally accepted as 'real'.

Nevertheless Janet's idea is valuable, for it emphasizes two things: first that it is by no means so easy as we commonly suppose to distinguish between the inner and outer worlds, and that, as we have seen, the attempt to reach a definition of their natures is beset with difficulties; and secondly that we constantly do discriminate none the less, although not always successfully. As I have already pointed out, anybody whose power of discriminating between them is seriously defective is incapable of coming to terms with civilized life and has to be certified insane and put under restraint.

Janet, therefore, identifying the outer world with 'reality', and recognizing that there is no simple rule for distinguishing it from the inner, postulated a special mental function to account for our ability to do so. Here lie the two objections to his choice of terminology: first that he confines 'reality' to the outer world, whereas we have agreed that if the word is to have any meaning in terms of life it must apply to the inner world also; and secondly that he presupposes a special mental function, equivalent to, e.g., thinking, feeling or memory, where, according to our theory, the process in question involves no such special function. The differentiation between the Two Worlds is solely a matter of classification, individual items of experience being placed in one category or the other with the aid of the normal mental functions of thinking, feeling, sensation, etc. We do exactly the same in distinguishing between good and evil, beautiful and ugly, abstract and concrete, or any other pair of opposites, and we do not see any necessity for postulating special mental functions for all these. We do it with the aid of complex images, the nuclei of which are instinctive or Archetypal. Around these nuclei, in the course of our personal experience (which includes reflection), we build up an intricate system of principles, values and concrete examples, one or other of which can be relied upon to offer a common factor with any item of experience with which we meet, thus enabling us to classify it as belonging to one group or the other.

Two points emerge from this definition: first that, apart from the Archetypal nucleus, there is nothing absolute or universal about our various personal conceptions of the inner and outer worlds: they vary from one individual to another, just as our conceptions of good and evil, beautiful and ugly vary. It is true that in any given community a number of collective ideas and values are normally embodied in these complex images, which therefore tend to correspond very closely in average people; the difference between the prevailing pictures of any of these polarities obtaining in different communities is, however, striking: what is good to the savage, for instance, may be evil to the civilized man, and even between a Frenchman and a German, an Englishman and an Italian material differences may be discerned. And even within the same community we frequently find exceptional people who disagree on one point or another.

An almost universal standard in the matter of any such distinction is, however, possible: it may be attained by those gifted with the power of insight, which enables them to penetrate to the Archetypal nuclei of the various patterns and to judge according to them without regard for relative or superficial standards such as the conventions of the community. Thus there is a genuine ethical sense, which judges without regard for legalism or other intellectual principles, for religious precepts or for empty conventions; and there are universal aesthetic standards, on which all those who have devoted themselves with perseverance and insight to the study of artistic matters will be found to agree very closely.

The second point is embodied in the last consideration: it is that all these complex images are capable of being enriched and perfected. They are enriched by widening their scope—by bringing them progressively into association with wider and more various categories of experience; they are perfected by approximating them as closely as possible to their Archetypal nuclei, which constitute the absolute and 'true' element in their composition. It is to be observed that this last process is not to be achieved solely by thinking: the importance of the function of thinking varies in the different polarities. As regards inner and outer, for instance, a good deal can be achieved by it, but the ethical sense is mainly a matter of feeling, and aesthetics of developed sensory values: neither can be satisfactorily exercised by principle alone, or adequately formulated in conceptual terms. It therefore follows that although anybody may have a highly developed working understanding of any of these polarities he may be unable to offer any adequate definition of it: the definition of good and evil, for instance, is notoriously difficult, yet all of us apply it after a fashion, and some with conspicuous success.

When anybody possesses a developed and effective pair of complex images of such a nature we say that he has a 'sense' of beauty, of good and evil, or whatever it may be, and we speak of the ethical and aesthetic 'senses'. I therefore propose to rename Janet's *fonction de réalité*, as I understand it, as *the sense of inner and outer*. It undoubtedly exists, in the sense that people habitually make the distinction spontaneously and some more aptly than others, and this designation obviates both the objectionable implication about the nature of reality and also the unjustifiable assumption that a special mental function is involved.

The sense of inner and outer, then, is the means which we normally and habitually employ in discriminating between the outer- and the inner-world elements in any experience. As explained above it functions by comparing the concrete case with two complex images, one representing the outer and one the inner world; in the normal contemporary mind, however, the former is rich and highly developed, while the latter is at best nebulous and primitive. Hence only a negative identification of inner-world elements is generally possible: we see that they do not fit into the outer-world picture and are therefore impossible, or at best highly improbable, but with a few superficial exceptions we do not recognize them positively as belonging to the inner-world system. Since, moreover, when we have identified them we have no adequate system into which we can fit them, as we can in the case of the outer-world elements, we cannot make use of them, and nothing remains but to discard them as meaningless and worthless. Thus, in the contemporary situation, the employment of the sense of inner and outer results in a progressive enrichment of the outer-world picture but contributes little cr nothing to that of the inner world.

Since we know from experience that this inner world has a tiresome habit of projecting itself from the unconscious into outer-world situations and masquerading as fact (as seen, for instance, in the growth of rumours), we are, or should be, always alert to sharpen and intensify our sense of inner and outer in order to arm ourselves against deception. It is from this that our interest in the extraordinary and the improbable arises: it is the criterion of 'news value' in the sense of the man biting the dog, and the Press thrives on its exploitation. When we read of such a thing we say to ourselves 'so things like that *can* happen!' This enriches our outer-world picture by drawing our attention to the fact that such things very rarely do happen; it is evident that they are not impossible, but our sense of their extraordinariness and improbability is heightened. In certain cases, moreover, such strange reports do a little to develop our inner-world picture, for we may recognize the kind of thing which ought to happen but so rarely does.

These fine distinctions can be carried to a high degree of subtlety for which some people have a talent. They are for ever playing on the borderline between fact and fancy: their reminiscences acquire in the re-telling every kind of whimsical 'twist', more or less subtle according to their talent, and the most prosaic events are embellished with fantastic accretions and exaggerations; yet the results are never obviously impossible.

Such a talent undoubtedly constitutes a social asset, and we may be grateful for the pleasure and stimulation which it contributes to life; yet it has, of course, its dangers, for the success which it earns him may lead the amateur story-teller from the mere choice of words and invention of amusing details which enliven a dull conversation, by way of 'leg-pulling' which may have a malicious trend, to outright imposture. When we come to the study of T. E. Lawrence we shall find a case in point, in which a talent for the facile invention of such conceits led as far as the falsification of official reports and the building up of a largely mendacious legend around the figure of their author.

What happens in such a case, of course, is that the sense of inner and outer has become too flexible: the subject no longer takes the discrimination between the two worlds with sufficient earnestness, and thus loses his sense of responsibility for his statements. For what we call the sense of responsibility is in large measure equivalent to the sense of inner and outer in this special application, and it is apt to be weak in those who, like Mitty, constitutionally undervalue the outer world. (The opposite type has of course corresponding vices: the attitude which regards anything as justified if it gets 'results' is a typical one.)

It is vitally necessary that we should direct our attention to the inner world, but when we do so we must never for a moment forget that it differs from, and is in many respects diametrically opposed to the outer: the great danger is always that of interpreting inner-world contents in outer-world terms. Thus the dividing-line between the harmless and stimulating use of the talent for imaginative story-telling, and its malignant aberrants, is the degree of the subject's consciousness of its implications.[1] I would not for a moment advocate that all conversation

[1] I recently listened to a commercial traveller in a bar attempting to entertain some colleagues with the tale of a car that had been stolen while containing the dead body of the owner's mother-in-law. He insisted that the story was 'gospel', and adorned it with all manner of circumstantial detail designed to heighten the factual impression, but his friends, whose sense of inner and outer was no doubt sharpened by their calling, were not satisfied. 'The dead body in the car,' one of them said—'there's something *about* it . . .' He had placed his finger unerringly on the central image, around which the remainder of the story, which took some ten minutes to relate, was built up. There is in fact a symbolical, inner-world element involved, which I am unable to interpret but do not altogether like, for an

should take the form of pedantically accurate, pedestrian accounts of fact, for the really gifted narrator can exert a genuinely beneficial, vitalizing effect on his hearers: he is dispensing the Waters of Life which are only available in the inner world. This is a function which we shall find being exercised in a high degree by Oscar Wilde, who excelled in 'taking people out of themselves' as a conversationalist and entertainer. But Wilde's sense of inner and outer, like Lawrence's, broke down under the strain and became so elastic that it ceased to function adequately even for his own requirements.

The proper sphere for the exercise of the talent for clothing inner-world contents in outer-world forms is, obviously, the writing of declared fiction, and in this connection it is interesting to find Thurber, in whom, as I have pointed out, the sense of inner and outer is strongly developed, consistently diverting himself and his readers on the borderline between the two worlds. Most of his writing is presented in the form of reminiscence, yet, among the elements which bear the stamp of factual exactitude, fantastic details are constantly appearing which tax the reader's credulity and thus stimulate his sense of inner and outer. To take two examples at random, there is his friend in Ohio named Harvey Lake, concerning whom we are told that 'When he was only nineteen, the steering bar of an old electric runabout broke off in his hand, causing the machine to carry him through a fence and into the grounds of the Columbus School for Girls. He developed a fear of automobiles, trains, and every other kind of vehicle that was not pulled by a horse.' There is nothing intrinsically impossible in this story, yet it is of the type of a fantasy, and is intended to be recognized as such because the writer is making fun of the popular psychologists. Anybody who is acquainted with the symbolism of fantasies will in fact recognize symbolical elements, but these were almost certainly unknown to the writer. No fantasy is without a hidden meaning and Thurber, in inventing this little

entirely different story involving a dead body in a car was 'going the rounds', both in England and on the Continent, in the period immediately preceding the 1939 war, and it referred to Hitler. The narrator in the present case was probably not clearly conscious of the fact that he was lying (he claimed to have 'checked up on' the story, and to know the man to whom it had happened) but would have broken down under cross-examination.

anecdote, is to some extent destroying his own case against the psychologists, because he is unwittingly revealing something about himself; that, however, is beside the point, which is his ability to invent stories on the borderline between fact and fantasy, the recognition of which as possible fantasies is spontaneously made by a well-developed sense of inner and outer.

Then there is the sketch of the dog which he himself owned as a boy, most of which is obviously 'straight' reminiscence, but in which we are also told how the family was once awakened by the noise occasioned by the efforts of the dog (which was given to dragging large objects about) to transport 'a small chest of drawers' up the steps of the porch. Thurber, in his confidential way, is leaning towards the reader and murmuring 'there's no harm in my embroidering a little on the facts: it makes the story more amusing and you are too intelligent to take everything literally'. And in fact, provided that it is done in this spirit and within these limits, this kind of tight-rope walking between fact and fancy serves a useful purpose, for it sharpens our sense of inner and outer just as the consideration of difficult ethical problems (such as the conflict between love and duty) sharpens our sense of good and evil, or right and wrong.

RECAPITULATION

Before proceeding it will be advisable to summarize our conclusions regarding what we call reality, and our manner of distinguishing between the Two Worlds.

(1) All that we know is the contents of our consciousness. If we regard the individual as a subject, nothing exists for him except what he experiences; it is only if we regard him as an object that he is seen to be associated with and influenced by things which he does not consciously experience. But this demands another subject to make the observation. There is therefore nothing that we know that is not experienced by some subject: no such thing 'exists'.

(2) Nevertheless we commonly believe, and act on the belief, that some of the contents of our consciousness represent objects in an outer world which exists independently of the subject, and 'outside the mind', whereas others do not. The former we

designate as 'real' and the latter as 'imaginary', or by other equivalent terms.

(3) The distinction is valid in that the contents of consciousness can be arranged in various coherent systems or patterns, and have to be so arranged in order that we may understand them. One such pattern is the polarity of the 'inner' and 'outer' systems or complex images, which are opposed in nature. By learning to classify the items of experience under these two headings we are enabled to understand and hence to come to terms with them. A mistake in classification results in confusion and may lead to a false attitude and hence to undesirable consequences. E.g. if I dream that I am a king I must beware of classifying this experience in the outer-world category, in which it would have a certain definite significance which is incompatible, in my case, with the remainder of the pattern. In the inner-world category, on the other hand, it has a totally different significance, the understanding of which is helpful to me in adjusting myself to the influences affecting me from the inner world.

(4) We are at liberty to define the terms reality and existence as we please, and there is no logical objection to anybody's saying that he intends them to mean conformity with what in this study is called the outer world. The words, however, as colloquially used, do not only denote an intellectual concept, but also an attitude in which feeling values, which are unaffected by logical conclusions, play an important part: this attitude takes the form of a conviction that that which exists, or is real, is important and significant, and that we must take account of it; the non-existent and unreal, on the other hand, lack importance and significance and can be ignored. Such an arbitrary use of the terms, therefore, is inadvisable, because it implies that everything which does not belong to the outer-world system is unimportant.

(5) We have adduced evidence to show (a) that outer-world experience, which we commonly regard as universal and objective, also contains elements which are peculiar to the individual subject, and (b) that inner-world experience, commonly regarded as purely subjective and individual, contains universal elements which are the same for all individual subjects. There are therefore no grounds for discriminating between the two

on this score. A difference undoubtedly exists, but it must be based on other factors.

(6) It is this supposed exclusive objectivity and universality of the outer-world category of experience that gives rise to the notion of an independent 'real' outer world which is represented by them, while no such 'reality' is deemed to be 'behind' those experiences which do not fit into this category, i.e. those of the inner world. Profounder thinkers, however, have always recognized that no such differentiation is justified: if experience represents anything beyond itself—i.e. anything unknown to the subject—there are no grounds for attributing such a background to one form of experience and not to another—e.g. to waking life and not to a dream.

(7) This position leads to the notion of the universal Subject which lies behind and beyond the personal subject and is therefore unknowable. The Subject perceives through the multitude of individual subjects, according to the particular type of consciousness available to each of them, but the experiences of each individual subject are segregated from those of the remainder by the Barrier of the particular individual viewpoint. Each individual subject becomes an individual object when seen from the viewpoint of another individual subject, but the universal Subject can never be an object and is therefore unknowable.

(8) The hypothetical 'reality' lying beyond all experience, of any nature, may be regarded as what Kant called 'the thing-in-itself', or the universal Object, which, like the universal Subject, is unknowable to the individual subject.

(9) Subject and Object are obverse and reverse of the universal ONE which lies behind all experience and existence, containing all things within Itself in a potential form, and each of these two aspects of It exists only as the counterpart of the other. All experience, whatever its form, and irrespective of whether it is 'true' or 'untrue', or whether universal or confined to a single individual consciousness, is equally an aspect of the Object as perceived by the Subject, and none enjoys a greater degree of validity, or of 'reality' in the absolute sense, than any other. In this context it is inadmissible to discriminate between 'truth' and 'reality' on the one hand, and 'illusion' or 'figment' on the other. All that we can say is that certain items of experience are found to conform to familiar coherent patterns,

united and determined by logical principles, sensory experience or whatever it may be, while others are not.

(10) Those items of experience which can be fitted into a pattern are readily understood, and are therefore regarded as important, valuable and 'real', whereas those which do not, being incomprehensible, are ordinarily overlooked, or discarded as meaningless, worthless and 'unreal'. The patterns in question, however, are built up by each individual in the course of personal experience, and his inability to comprehend certain classes of experience may well be due simply to the fact that he has failed to equip himself with a mental pattern into which they fit.

(11) The contemporary western outlook has been built up on the basis of a pattern determined by concentration on the rational, the objective, and certain aspects of sensory experience. It lacks a pattern capable of assimilating material which falls outside these categories and is consequently prejudiced against such material. The scientific outlook is the epitome of this pattern, and, although of great value in itself, is threatening to produce a dangerous psychic disequilibrium through its one-sidedness and its neglect and depreciation of material which is incompatible with it.

(12) Quite apart from the scientific outlook, however, no amount of theorizing can eliminate our universal and spontaneous conviction of the superior reliability of sensory experience as a revelation of 'reality', i.e. of that which is important and, we imagine, exists in its own right, irrespective of our mental processes. The explanation of this is the importance of sensory experience in the instinctive patterns, which are universal in the species and act on every individual with intense and compulsive power.

(13) The most important instinct from this point of view is that which impels the individual to resort to sensory investigation in order to remove doubt regarding the nature of anything conspicuous but not immediately recognizable. In the human species the two senses particularly concerned are those of sight and touch, and on the mutually confirmatory evidence of these two is based the Archetypal picture of material objects, which is basic to all our thought.

(14) A further development of this picture is that of the

world as an arrangement of material objects in space and time, disposed round the person of the subject in the present moment of consciousness. This picture is so fundamental to our thinking that it is almost impossible for us to visualize the world in any other form, although mathematicians are concerned to a considerable extent in constructing 'imaginary worlds' based on other premisses.

(15) So inextricably is our outlook bound up with this picture, and so intimately do all the ideas on which we base our understanding of the world, and the rules by which we guide our conduct, depend on it, that in the ordinary man any questioning of its validity produces a reaction of fear, often followed by an indignant protest. Only those who have accustomed themselves to speculative thought and its implications are able to view with equanimity the prospect of abandoning this picture.

(16) Thus that element in sensory experience which is basic to our picture of the outer world, and on which the whole system of science rests, is solely the aspect of the senses which is connected with the Archetypal picture of the world as an arrangement of material objects in space and time. The pure study of sensory material, according to its own intrinsic nature and values, is aesthetics, and with this subject science is not concerned; it partakes, indeed, rather of the nature of the inner than of the outer world, and is regarded by most people as of small importance.

(17) Although the picture of the world as an arrangement of material objects in space and time provides the Archetypal nucleus around which our picture of the outer world is constructed, a great deal is built on to it by each individual in the course of his personal mental development. The additions vary from one individual to another, although in any community the majority of individuals accept the prevalent collective picture ready-made, and their pictures of the outer world therefore coincide to a considerable degree. The pictures of the outer world in the minds of a savage and of a civilized man, however, differ very considerably.

(18) The correct classification of our experience in the inner- and outer-world categories is of the greatest importance to us, and in our normal daily lives we are very frequently called upon

to discriminate, on the best evidence available, between the two. We have to decide what is practicable, what plausible, what possible and what the reverse. Inner-world elements which are not valid in the outer world are very apt to slip into our estimations, and it is most necessary for us to guard against this danger. This process of discrimination may be described as the application of 'a sense of inner and outer', which is precisely on a par with the senses of good and evil, or of beauty and ugliness. The process in fact consists in the comparison of the image in question with the two pre-existent complex images of the inner and outer worlds, which have been built up in the mind, and the richness and scope of which varies from one individual to another.

(19) The general tendency in the contemporary western world is for the outer-world image to be highly developed, whereas that of the inner world is poor and nebulous. Outer-world elements, therefore, are positively identified, whereas those of the inner world are only recognized negatively, by reason of their irreconcilability with the outer-world picture. Once they have been identified, moreover, no use can be made of them, since we lack any comprehensive scheme into which they can be fitted.

(20) Certain individuals, of the Walter Mitty type, are constitutionally and by habit inclined to undervalue the outer world, living by preference in the inner. If such people possess a developed inner-world picture they are able to make sense of their experience and may succeed in becoming creative. This, however, is seldom the case, for in common with everybody nowadays they are indoctrinated with the belief in the exclusive reality of the outer world, and are taught a great deal about its laws and workings, whereas the interpretation of the inner world, which is so much more important for them, is left to their own unaided abilities, which may not be considerable. Thus they find themselves in the position of a savage left in charge of a power-house, for the inner world contains great forces. Inevitably they interpret their inner-world experiences in outer-world terms, and seek to apply them in this form to their environment. In consequence of the unsuitability of 'raw' inner-world material to the totally different nature of the outer world the Mittys, to begin with, meet with failure and humilia-

tion, whereupon they either withdraw from the outer world in disgust, living in the seclusion of their 'secret lives'—in which case such abilities as they may have are generally lost to the world—or else they persevere until they have found means of forcing their inner-world conceptions on the outer world, irrespective of the consequences. In the latter case they become fanatics and doctrinaires and may do great harm. The elucidation of the nature and laws of the inner world, in order to bring the collective picture of it into something approaching parity with that of the outer world, is therefore a matter of urgent necessity.

V *The Two Worlds Present Themselves*

THE discrimination between the Two Worlds is something really new in the human repertory. People have, of course, always recognized that there was a difference between fact and fancy, but they did not, before the Renaissance, draw many conclusions from the distinction, nor did they accept it as a general guiding principle in the conduct of their lives. Observing the progress of the human mind we find a gradual development of the sense of inner and outer: the primitive, for instance, makes little distinction between dreaming and waking: his world is peopled indiscriminately by factual and imaginary figures. Not only does he regard the great dreams of his chief as actual events, to be considered and acted upon in exactly the same way as the weather or the depredations of a hostile tribe but, we are told, he will assert in all sincerity, and without any sense of the extraordinary, that he has just been conversing with his deceased father in the woods. With civilization a greater degree of discrimination appears, but the ability to distinguish between the two categories grows only gradually. It is, for instance, very probable that the idea behind the elaborate care devoted by the ancient Egyptians to the sealing off of their tombs was motivated less by the fear that the treasures buried in them might be stolen than by dread that the departed might return, as they do in dreams. Having consideration for the mentality of the time it is inconceivable that anybody would have been prepared to incur the awful penalties—in this world and the next—associated with interference with the dead, and it is unlikely that this thought was uppermost in the minds of the tomb-makers. But the dead were immobilized with bandages and encased in heavy stone sarcophagi; everything that they might need was placed around them—even the beasts and the women and slaves of the earlier kings were killed and buried with them. Finally they were deposited in chambers cut deep into the rock, and the tombs were sealed off with wall after wall of solid masonry. Thus it was made as difficult as possible for the dead to emerge, and it was hoped that, availing themselves of the provision made for them, they would lead a contented life underground and not be tempted to do so, for their return, like Finnegan's, would have been unwelcome.

Even that most practical people, the Romans, took auguries before embarking on any important project and allowed their actions to be governed by the conclusions drawn from them, quite irrespective of practical considerations. And finally, even today, many civilized people expect an inner-world Deity to exert an influence on purely outer-world matters such as the weather. Sometimes such confusions result from a genuine inability to discriminate in the sphere of experience in question; in other cases, like that of the little girl with her doll, they are the consequence of a preference for letting sleeping dogs lie.

Yet, although confusions are still common enough, in our scientific methods and our systems of organization and administration based on a careful study of facts, we have advanced considerably further than any previous civilization in the matter of discriminating between the inner and outer worlds. Our attitude, as already suggested, is one-sided, in that we appreciate and value only the outer world, on which we have concentrated our attention sufficiently to understand its fundamental patterns, while we neglect and depreciate the inner, which we do not understand. Nevertheless we have worked out the differentiation to an advanced stage, even though it be only on one side.

Each epoch, perhaps, makes its characteristic contribution to mental development, and if this is so, then our own enduring bequest to humanity may well be this new mental technique. It is likely enough that posterity will not value the systems and technologies which we have developed from it: they may not want such vast and unnecessary material production at the

cost of the regimentation of their lives, any more than we ourselves want to build pyramids at the cost of slavery. The
organization of slave labour which made the pyramids possible
—and they are still the highest stone buildings in the world—
was the triumph of ancient Egypt; the organization of wage and
salaried labour which makes the production of millions of
motor-cars and television sets possible is the triumph of ours.
Posterity may not want the motor-cars and the television sets
any more than we want pyramids, yet they will be able to
benefit from the differentiation between inner and outer which
made contemporary science, technology and mass production
possible. For it is the mental and the abstract, not the material
and the concrete, which endures: Roman roads and aqueducts,
and the specific enactments and procedures of Roman law, are
no longer of any use to us, but the Roman concept of law in
general is an integral part of our civilization.

The essential contributions to the human heritage made by
the epoch which we call classical antiquity (Toynbee's[1] Graeco-
Roman civilization) are to be seen in the development of the
aesthetic and ethical senses. The valuation of beauty for its
own sake was a Greek discovery: other civilizations had concentrated on the symbolical or the emotional (feeling) significance of form: they had built, carved or decorated in order to
express symbolical truths, or to produce an impression of awe,
magnificence or well-being, and it was the Greeks who were
the first (in the western world) to turn their attention to that
aspect of form which is pleasing and 'right' merely as a sensory
experience, irrespective of its symbolical and emotional
associations.

It is the same with the ethical sense. Starting with a conception of 'rightness' and 'wrongness' hardly superior to the taboo
system of the primitive, classical antiquity worked its way
towards the differentiation of an intelligible and coherent
polarity of good and evil, justice and injustice, honesty and
dishonesty; it succeeded, in fact, in building up a pair of complex images by reference to which the ethical value of any
action might be assessed. The process is marked by the intellectual struggles of the Stoics to work out a principle of 'virtue',
and of the Epicureans to formulate an ideal of co-operative

[1] See Arnold Toynbee: *A Study of History.*

happiness, as well as by the official Roman insistence that the law was binding on all men. In the book of Job, which possibly illustrates the impact of Greek ideas on Hebrew theology, we are even faced with the drastic question of whether the ideals of equity and fair dealing may not be binding on the Deity himself.

This is not the place to go further into this question: I wish merely to suggest the nature of possible enduring contributions to the general mental heritage of humanity, and the manner in which they may be made. The parallel in the case of our own civilization is obvious: the only product of our age which is of universal value, and which would be capable of adaptation to the needs of a new civilization adopting a different approach to circumstances differing from those in which our own grew up, is the discrimination which we are learning to make between the inner and outer worlds. Just as classical antiquity failed to find the final and complete answer to the ethical question, so have we failed in the matter of the inner and the outer worlds; nevertheless, just as the classical age discovered that an absolute differentation between good and evil was potentially possible, and that even a nebulous understanding of it could serve as a universal guide to conduct in all circumstances, so have we discovered the possibility of making a universally valid distinction between inner and outer, and of applying it profitably to at least some of the problems of life.

The outer-world proof of this lies precisely in that obsession with the pattern of objects in space and time which threatens to throw us off our balance and thus to bring about our own self-destruction. For, as we have seen, the essence of that outlook which is epitomized in the scientific attitude, and which has led to such unexampled advances in the material sphere, is the ability to distinguish between those factors of experience which fit into the coherent pattern of material objects in space and time, and those which do not. We have concentrated unduly on the former and neglected the latter, and this short-sightedness is liable to lead to our undoing; nevertheless, although we have failed to grasp the full significance of the differentiation we have learnt to make it, and that discovery will not be lost. If humanity survives the downfall of the present system at all, it will in due course achieve a condition of sufficient stability and enlightenment to rediscover its heritage: there will be another Renaissance, once again bringing about a fruitful union of the old and the new. The consequence will not be a reconstruction of the conditions of the present era, any more than the rediscovery of antiquity in the fifteenth and sixteenth centuries led to a reconstruction of those of ancient Greece and Rome. An entirely new culture will inevitably be born of the union, embodying those elements of the old and the new patterns which are both reconcilable with one another and adaptable to the new circumstances, and among these the differentiation between inner and outer worlds, inner and outer truth, inner and outer existence and reality will certainly find a place. It may be assumed that the inherent tendency of the Psyche to seek equilibrium will have brought out impulses, values and patterns of thought which will act as a counterpoise to the obsession with the outer world to which the present age has fallen victim: it will, indeed, have been precisely these re-actions of the Psyche which will have brought about the down-fall of the present system and formed the nucleus of the new. It may therefore be conjectured that the new age will not attach the same importance to material production, and to material conditions generally, as we do; it will be content with a simpler outer life, and perhaps with more limited numbers, but it will devote more of its energies to the cultivation of those aspects of experience which we neglect.

I have no wish to construct a Utopia, which would inevitably be no more than the expression of my own views on the Good Life. Posterity will no more resemble me than contemporary man resembles Plato, whose hopelessly wrong-headed idea of a state ruled by philosophers is, incidentally, a characteristic illustration of an absolute lack of understanding for the nature of the outer world, or of even a suspicion that such a thing exists. Plato's contribution to thought lies in his understanding of the nature of the inner world: the outer he ignored, for what practical man could doubt for a moment that there is nobody less suited than a philosopher to rule the smallest village, let alone the state?[1] Those whose business lies predominantly in the inner world are almost invariably inept in the outer.

[1] The newly formed state of Israel asked Albert Einstein to become its first president, an honour which he very wisely declined on the grounds that he lacked abilities in the sphere of human relationships. If more dis-

The practical men of the future will have to find practical solutions to practical problems, and I can have no more idea how they will do it than Plato had of parliamentary democracy; it is, however, fair to conjecture that posterity will not reconstruct our technocratic system, for they will see no value in doing so, any more than we see any in the building of pyramids.

We have seen how Descartes, having arrived through a flash of intuitive insight at the central point of philosophy, which is the interpretation of experience as a particular mode of the universal relationship of the absolute Subject with the absolute Object, subsequently abandoned the subjective side of the formula in favour of the objective, on which he based a rational system which claimed to account for the whole of knowledge. In this he was representative of the new thought of his day, which, since the Renaissance, had been concentrating on the discrimination between the two classes of element which were confused in the amalgam of medieval thought, namely on the one hand that which was rational and objective, and on the other that which was irrational and subjective. The rigid segregation of these incompatibles led to the conscious intellectual discrimination between the Two Worlds and between inner and outer truth and reality, and hence to revolutionary conclusions strongly at variance with traditional beliefs. This conflict came to light in such dramatic climaxes as the collisions of Galileo with the Inquisition, or of Darwin with the Bishops; the nature of the new thought is revealed in that unqualified refusal to accept any standards of truth except the rational and the sensory-objective which forms the basis of the scientific outlook, and which is epitomized in such extremes as the categorical denial of a Hegel that anything which was not rational could be real.

Science, however, was not the cause of the new outlook, but one of its products. The causation is hard to elucidate, and we must be satisfied with noting that the new attitude was a generalized phenomenon which became apparent at the Renaissance. It was by no means confined to philosophy or

tinguished people realized their own limitations in this way the world would be saved a lot of trouble.

natural science, for, as Toynbee points out, the modern system of efficient administration made its first appearance in the chanceries of the Italian despots and republics of the Quattrocento: it was there that, for the first time in history, adequate accounts were kept, returns demanded and analysed, and statistics compiled. Italy in the fifteenth century was, of course, the cradle of the Renaissance, which was far more than the scholarly and artistic movement as which it is commonly regarded; administration based on accounts and statistics is a striking example of the new thought which discriminated so rigidly between facts and pious aspirations. In its subsequent developments, of course, the new administration has grown into a system of incredible complexity and scope which now permeates and dominates our lives; its tendency, if left to itself, is to attempt the complete regimentation of the soul.

Science and technology, those two lusty children of the new outlook, have in the meanwhile progressed from strength to strength, and in the space of the last two hundred years have succeeded in transforming the face of the world, and the outer pattern of the lives of a considerable proportion of its inhabitants, to an extent far greater than was possible in the entire preceding five millennia of civilization. Today they enjoy an unassailable authority, for how could anything which has been so successful possibly be wrong? The error will not become apparent until they have broken down the very structure on which they have been built up.

The contemporary situation, then, may be seen as the product of a new attitude towards experience in general—or in other words towards life and thought—which originated at the time of the Renaissance. The attitude is characterized by a growing discrimination between those aspects of experience which may be contrasted under the categories of inner and outer, and by a concentration, amounting to an obsession, on the latter at the expense of the former. The polarity in question has an Archetypal basis—in other words this manner of classifying experience is based in an inherent pattern of the mind—and consequently we may expect it to present itself to consciousness in a characteristic symbolical form. This Archetypal symbol is the picture of the Two Worlds, and we may now turn to some examples of the way in which it has presented itself through the creative fantasy in the course of history.

The picture of the Other Side has presented itself to humanity ever since man, by concentrating on personal consciousness, has cut himself off, as an individual, from his generic roots. Thus in the Babylonian legend of Gilgamesh, which may have originated as early as 2,000 B.C., we find the hero departing on a long and arduous journey to the remote home of Uta-Nepishtim (the prototype of Noah), whence he brings back a miraculous herb, and later we have the Argonauts setting out for distant Colchis in search of the Golden Fleece. This, evidently, is the quest of the Treasure to which reference has already been made, and it is at once apparent that this theme is incalculably older than the situation with which we are momentarily concerned. The image of the Other Side, in fact, does not correspond exactly with that of the Two Worlds; it may, and in later examples it often does, embrace the latter, but in itself it represents something more fundamental, or at least something which has represented a pressing problem to humanity for far longer.

This consideration leads to the important distinction between the polarities outer-inner and conscious-unconscious. These two may be regarded as two possible bisections of the sphere of totality along two different planes which, although divergent, are still close enough to produce two pairs of hemispheres which possess considerable areas in common. Thus the inner world corresponds to the unconscious, the outer to personal consciousness in some, but by no means in all respects. The uniqueness and particularity of the individual are largely based on the unique position of his body in time and space, and in so far as personal consciousness is confined to matters immediately pertaining to this point of reference it corresponds exactly with the outer world; the generic and universal aspects of the mind— the instinctive and Archetypal patterns—on the other hand, being entirely independent of the individual and his particular location in space and time, are to some extent incapable of assimilation in the personal consciousness; to this extent they are purely unconscious, and in so far as the contents of the unconscious mind are confined to elements of this nature it corresponds exactly to the inner world. This is the essence of the distinction between This World and the Other Side: This World consists of the finite, limited, precisely positioned personal life of the individual, whereas the Other Side contains all those elements which he shares with all other members of his species or even, in the last resort, with the whole of living creation; through it access to the personal experiences of other individuals even becomes possible (for they are all experiences of the same Subject).

As we have seen, however, individual consciousness is a selective process in which only a proportion of the experience available to the individual, even in his personal, particular capacity, is accepted, the remainder being rejected and thus confined to the unconscious part of the mind. Thus, for instance, any given mental stimulus, whether it be an immediate sensory experience, a conceptual thought, a 'fancied' image emanating from the generic depths of the collective unconscious or whatever else, may give rise to, say, five different associations in some or other of these various mental spheres. If consciousness is to remain clear and coherent the individual can accept only one of these for consideration, while the remainder must be excluded, at least temporarily. Theoretically he is at liberty to choose whichever he pleases, and even, having considered it, to pass on to the remainder; in practice, however, the amount of material clamouring for admission at the doors of consciousness is far greater than it can possibly master; one association, moreover, having been admitted, leads to others of its own kind, and already in childhood the intelligent individual discovers that it is only by following such a connected train of conscious contents, whether it be in the sphere of logical thought, feeling, sensory impressions or whatever else, that he can make sense of life and deal with its problems. In consequence he invariably tends to concentrate on a single class of content to the exclusion of the others, and thus builds up a screening system which automatically carries out the selection of that class of content which he favours. This screening system constitutes the conscious attitude: it is itself largely unconscious, since consciousness confines itself to the consideration of those contents which have been admitted by it, ignoring the existence of what has been excluded, and hence of the agency which has excluded it. The conscious mind thus tends to assume that only that class of content which is habitually admitted to it has any existence at all: everything else is confined to the unconscious part of the mind and is therefore unknown to it, or in other words has no existence for it.

This matter will be the subject of more detailed consideration in the next volume: for the present I wish merely to indicate that the unconscious mind does not only contain those generic patterns which are in no circumstances assimilable to personal consciousness, but also a large body of experience which could perfectly well have been admitted to it, but which has been excluded purely through the prejudice of the conscious attitude. Since the conscious attitude works on definite principles, accepting, let us say, contents and associations of the nature of logical thought while excluding those connected with the feelings, these additional unconscious contents will conform to a definite pattern: in the case suggested, for instance, they will consist predominantly of contents associated with feeling.

A number of such different patterns is possible, and various characteristic forms are in fact found among individuals: the nature of the contents of the unconscious mind, or, broadly speaking, the Other Side, is therefore not invariable. Superimposed, so to speak, on the basic layer of generic or Archetypal patterns unassimilable to consciousness there is a layer of rejected personal experiences which may conform broadly to one or another of several different possible patterns.

The nature of the conscious attitude depends in the last resort on the individual: it is he who has built it up and he is free to change it, although the process is a difficult one. Nevertheless, although an infinite variety of individual conscious attitudes is possible, in practice they all fall roughly into a limited number of types, determined by those structures or patterns of the mind which can be employed as guiding principles in the process of selection. The complexity of civilized life, moreover, is so great that no individual can discover everything for himself; as a child he instinctively follows the lead of his elders, and at school he is deliberately taught to use his mind in certain ways, and to avoid using it in others. Every community possesses a collective conscious attitude, without which its members could never come to terms with one another, and the values, notions, points of view and guiding principles of that collective attitude are so much 'in the air' that no individual can avoid absorbing them in childhood. Later in life the individual is generally too deeply absorbed in the struggle to hold his own, and to win and consolidate a position in the community, for it to be possible for him to spare any thought for the critical consideration of the attitude in which he has been brought up: he accepts 'what everybody knows' as self-evidently true, and values what everybody values as unquestionably good. Only exceptional and basically abnormal individuals question these things and seek to construct an independent system for themselves.

Thus, although in theory the possible varieties of conscious attitude are infinite, in practice those of the great majority of individuals in any given community conform very closely to the collective pattern; it follows, therefore, that the contents of their unconscious minds are also similar in nature. The collective conscious attitude of the contemporary civilization in the West is, we have seen, characterized by an obsession with the sensory-objective, which is the essence of the outer world, and by the rational. Hence the collective unconscious of the times is characterized by a predominance of contents of an opposite nature, namely intuitive-subjective elements, which constitute the essence of the inner world, and of all that is irrational.

It is for this reason only that in our own civilization we find the Other Side full of inner-world, irrational elements: the fact is determined solely by the prejudices of the contemporary conscious attitude. In other civilizations, such as those of the ancient East, the collective conscious attitude has been biased in the opposite direction, and with them we find the atmosphere of the Other Side completely different: it is characterized on the one hand by lucid, crystal-clear symbolical forms, and on the other by a multitude of vexatious but not very formidable dragons, demons and bogeys: the manifold and heterogeneous problems of the outer world which they dismiss—under the contemptuous designation of 'the ten thousand things'—in their preoccupation with the eternal and the infinite, which are not concerned with either mundane or rational considerations. Western fantasy has long ago abjured bogeys:

it has evolved the far more sinister figure of the Miltonian Lucifer instead.

Thus the polarities inner-outer and conscious-unconscious must be distinguished. The bias of our own contemporary collective attitude results in the relegation of the majority of the inner-world and irrational elements of experience to the unconscious mind, but this is only a particular case. The two polarities even cut across one another in the contemporary mind, for abstract thinking is the one element of the inner world which we consciously accept and value, whereas we reject and deprecate even the outer-world aspect of the irrational, designating it chance, superstition or coincidence and refusing to attach any importance to it. Hence our addiction to gambling.

Returning to the ancient world, we may note that the two examples quoted do not suggest any considerable tension between the images of the two worlds in the minds of their originators. This is what we should expect, for the ancients lacked our understanding of the laws governing material objects in space and time, and therefore made no such sharp differentiation as we do between what is possible and what impossible in the outer-world sense. They were aware of a Somewhere Else—of that duality of experience of which the pre-eminent expression is the contrast between dreaming and waking—but it did not seem to them that there was any intrinsic difference between dream-happenings and those of waking life. In the case of dreams they knew that their bodies did not participate in the experiences of their minds, but that did not seem to them to denote that the dream-experiences were any less 'real' than the waking ones: their minds had simply journeyed into the Somewhere Else, leaving their bodies behind. As to that Somewhere Else, its existence need be no less factual than that of any remote land: only a very small portion of the world was known to them, and what they knew was surrounded by a mysterious darkness, out of which strange and unfamiliar peoples and creatures were liable to emerge. It is hard for us to imagine, but to the ancient Greek the remote lands of the Scythians and the Nubians must have been exactly equivalent to the lands of dream and fable: anything might exist, or anything happen there. Even the meticulous Herodotus, who travelled widely in search of his material, and investigated what he could for himself, accepted the most absurd fantasies as outer-world truth.

The legend of the Trojan War seems to tell another story. It is likely enough that the war was a historical fact, and that the improbable tale of the rape of Helen, which so strongly bears the Archetypal stamp, was tacked on to it afterwards; the episode of the Judgment of Paris is in any case a product of fantasy, and it is characteristic of the growth of legends that it is impossible to say where fantasy ends and fact begins. From our present point of view the question is immaterial, the significant point being that fantasy is to some extent involved, and that certain inner-world elements were evoked by, and became assimilated to certain significant factual events, thus producing a symbolical whole which has continued to fascinate humanity up to the present day. At all events, the result was a clear picture of the conflict between two worlds, centred, incidentally, round the forcible removal of the figure of the Anima from one to the other. This element provides a parallel with the Persephone myth, which latter reveals a clear perception of the rival claims of the two modes of experience on the individual mind. To the best of my very inadequate knowledge these two stories stand alone in the classical period in their presentation of the theme of the conflict between the Two Worlds; it is, however, noteworthy that it was not until the closing period of that epoch that the Persephone myth, in its connection with the Eleusinian mysteries, played such an important role. There are, therefore, some slight grounds for supposing that as the old era drew to its end a psychic tension of a new and hitherto unknown nature was beginning to make itself felt, and it is significant that this tension, together with the formula for transcending it, is strikingly rendered in the teachings of the Rabbi Jeshu or Jesus.[1] Such sayings as 'Render unto Caesar

[1] There are several references to this probably historical personage in the Talmud. He is presented as a heretical Rabbi with a public following (he 'led the people astray') who was put to death for blaspheming. His execution is alternatively stated to have been by hanging or by stoning, both of which were traditional Jewish methods, and certain indications suggest that he may have lived approximately a century before the governorship of Pilate. The identity of the author of many of the Gospel doctrines —and particularly, perhaps, of those sayings quoted above—with the fiery

the things that are Caesar's, and unto God the things that are God's', 'My kingdom is not of this world', 'The children of this world are in their generation wiser than the sons of light', as well as others which will come to mind, are unmistakable evidence of a clear conscious discrimination between the Two Worlds; they are, indeed, possibly the earliest recorded formulation of such a differentiation.

Such a clear discrimination between inner and outer, however, was far in advance of the times, and Christianity, in order to survive, was compelled to transform itself into an outer-world system, which it eventually succeeded in doing by becoming a department of the Roman administrative structure. The Church, as distinct from the basic teachings of Christianity, is a purely Roman institution.

By the time we reach our own Middle Ages the Church was firmly established as an outer-world institution which, in its teachings and in a considerable part of its activity, asserted the paramount importance of the Kingdom of Heaven, an invisible world, or an after-life of the soul, over against This World, which it represented as real, but fundamentally worthless, and tending towards evil. This produced a sound balance in a society which was painfully climbing from barbarism to civilization, and it resulted in the Church's acquiring a monopoly of the Other Side, which for many centuries it succeeded in keeping under control, regulating its relationship to This World by means of the profound and vital Archetypal symbolism of its ritual and beliefs. This mediating position is symbolized by the two keys of St. Peter, representing the Papacy's control of access to both worlds.

In the later Middle Ages, however, advanced spirits, in the

nationalist who appears, by inference from the Gospel account, to have occupied Jerusalem by force of arms and to have been put to death by Pilate—by the Roman method of crucifixion—for raising an insurrection against the Roman overlordship ('the King of the Jews') appears to me to be open to the gravest doubts. In view of the fact that the earliest of the Gospels, from which the basic material of the others is derived, was not written down until at least twenty, and possibly forty years after the events which it describes, and probably far from the scene, it is not inconceivable that the teachings of the Rabbi came to be attributed, in all good faith, to the leader of the popular rebellion of a century later; possibly he bore the same name. In this connection see G. R. S. Mead: *Did Jesus live 100 B.C.?* and R. Furneaux: *The Other Side of the Story.*

persons of the troubadours and writers of romances, began to discover another aspect of the Other Side which was not countenanced by the Church: namely the province of the Anima. In their hands pre-Christian Celtic and Germanic legends, and fragments of classical mythology, crystallized into romances of a fantastic world centring round profane love; the supreme symbol of this trend was the Mountain of Venus, that scene of extravagant and luxurious pleasures which had its historical counterpart in the eleventh century in the East in the Mountain of Delights of Hasan el-Saba', the Old Man of the Mountain and leader of the Assassins or hashish-eaters. During the same period the cult of the Virgin attained its highest forms and greatest popularity and influence, but it proved impossible to contain the spiritual forces inherent in the emergent Anima-pattern within the framework of orthodox doctrine, and when the Mountain of Venus inevitably evoked its spiritualized counterpart the latter escaped the Church, taking the form of the Mountain of the Graal. The latter is a highly spiritualized feminine symbol, developed from pre-Christian Celtic legend and very inadequately christianized. This question will be examined in detail in a later volume: for present purposes it will suffice to say that the keynote of the period is a battle for the control of access to the Other Side between ecclesiastical and profane forces; the eventual victory of the latter was expressed in that tremendous upsurge of profane values which is called the Renaissance. Since then the Church has been fighting a rearguard action.

In consequence of the preoccupation with this side of the question, which was concerned mainly with the feeling and the sensory aspects of life, the dawning awareness of a possible differentiation between the Two Worlds along the intellectual-intuitive plane of bisection, which had begun to manifest itself at the close of the classical period, sank out of sight. People were concerned with feelings and aesthetic values—with the conflict between 'sacred and profane love', and between the sensuous and the austere—to the exclusion of the intellectual differentiation between 'existent' and 'non-existent':[1] they still

[1] The Nominalist-Realist controversy, around which scholastic thought revolved, is, however, fundamentally an attempt to differentiate between inner and outer.

came and went between the worlds of fact and fancy without much circumstance. Every king claimed descent from Alexander, and thus from Hercules, whom Alexander himself claimed as an ancestor, and they were no doubt as sincerely convinced of the historicity of the claim as of the fact that the kitchen of the Virgin Mary had for some reason been removed bodily from Nazareth by four angels and deposited in Loreto. Many of them, paradoxically enough, were eminently hard-headed practical men, but, like the little girl who insists that her doll is a real baby, they felt under no obligation to force their understanding of the outer world on to matters which had no immediate practical concern for them, and might compel them to draw painful conclusions. They had not yet eaten of the fruit of the tree of the knowledge of inner and outer.

After the Renaissance a colder wind blows: it is apparent, for instance, in Shakespeare's *Tempest*. This play will be the subject of detailed analysis in a later volume, and for the present it will suffice to point out that Prospero's confinement on his island was the penalty for neglecting the outer world in favour of the inner. In the Middle Ages, it is true, Tannhäuser had already become entangled with the Lady Venus and had been unable to escape from her mountain for a number of years, and Thomas of Erceldoune (Tom the Rhymer) had disappeared from This World for seven years, which he spent in the service of the Queen of Elfland. These are references to a specific matter, which, indeed, evidently concerned Shakespeare too, but the spirit in which he tells the story is a very different one. Tannhäuser and Thomas had merely succumbed to the beguilements of the Other Side in a manner which had been well known ever since the companions of Ulysses, in the course of their long voyage, had fallen into the clutches of the Lady Circe; all these men had paid the penalty for an illicit affair with the Anima and had eventually been restored to This World. But Prospero is resentful: he had not been simply self-indulgent: he had been engaged in respectable studies 'of the liberal arts', and was 'dedicated . . . to the bettering of (his) mind', and while thus preoccupied he had been basely usurped by his brother, to whom he had confided the practical government of his dukedom, and who understood the business, as he did not. Here, for the first time in the new era, we find the theme of the irreconcilability of the rival and equally valid claims placed on the individual by the Two Worlds, and the resentment and self-pity of the man suffering from their collision.

My ignorance of the literature of the eighteenth century prevents me from offering more than one example from that period: it is provided by Goethe, who succeeded in understanding the problem intellectually, and presents it in expository rather than symbolical form. He was one of the few creative artists of the first rank who have occupied a responsible worldly position, and although his ministerial duties at the tiny court of Weimar probably demanded no more statesmanlike qualities, and were no more onerous, than those of a contemporary county councillor, his experience sufficed to reveal to him the essential difference between the Two Worlds. There can be little doubt that he found his position a strain, as was inevitable in any man who owed allegiance to the inner world, but he held out for eleven years (his twenty-fourth to thirty-fifth) at the end of which he obtained leave to depart on his famous journey to Italy. On his return to Weimar he did not resume his state duties. A few years later, in the drama *Torquato Tasso*, he produced a lucid and remarkably objective exposition of the irreconcilability of the two worlds of artistic creativeness and mundane affairs; he holds no brief for either, but presents a strikingly fair-minded picture of the complementary virtues and weaknesses of the two mental attitudes which Jung, one hundred and fifty years later, was to elucidate as extraversion and introversion. In my view the subject was unsuited to the medium, and would have been better presented as an essay; nevertheless *Tasso* provides what is possibly the first clearly understood exposition of the theme of the contrasting, irreconcilable, opposed and yet complementary natures of the Two Worlds. Goethe was one of the few who have understood and mastered both, differentiated them fully and reconciled the irreconcilables in one of the fullest creative lives recorded in history. Perhaps Napoleon's famous comment on meeting him —'Voilà un homme!'—was not merely flattery, nor the echo of contemporary adulation, for Goethe was in fact a complete man.

In the nineteenth century the examples, as we should expect, come thick and fast. Towards the middle of the century we have

Dickens' *Tale of Two Cities* and Emily Brontë's *Wuthering Heights*, in both of which the picture is very marked. Both of these works will be the subject of detailed analysis in a later volume, and here it must suffice to say that in both of them the tension between the two worlds is extreme. The striking point about them both is that here, for the first time, the division is not that between This World, the scene of prosaic workaday life, and the Other Side, the world of wonders and delights, but between two scenes of equal status, the inhabitants of which intermingle freely and even intermarry (thus bringing in the theme of the Dynastic Union), yet of opposing and irreconcilable natures, the collision of which brings about the conflict.

In *No Orchids* we have met with these two themes combined: there is the dichotomy between This World and the Other Side, and the conflict, within the Other Side, between the factions of John Blandish and Ma Grisson. The conflict, we noted, does not become apparent until penetration into the Other Side has been effected: this is the full statement of the theme, for the conflict is inherent in the one-sidedness and intolerance of the conscious attitude. It is the arrogance and high-handedness of John Blandish which evokes the rebellion of Ma Grisson and her faction, and until the figure of the former—i.e. the nature of the conscious attitude—has been brought to consciousness, the Ego or conscious subject is not aware of the existence of a conflict. The matter is brought to consciousness in the first place by the rape of Miss Blandish-Persephone-Helen, and by the devitalization of This World which ensues on her disappearance;[1] it is this which compels the subject to undertake the quest of the Treasure, entailing penetration into the Other Side. When this has been effected the differentiating function of consciousness reveals the nature of the conflict in symbolical form: in other words it becomes actual and 'real' to the conscious mind. This has the result of intensifying it and drawing the personal subject into participation in it; but it is only by this means that reconciliation becomes possible for those who succeed in rising above it.

The same picture is presented by Rider Haggard in his

[1] This theme is again very clearly rendered in Wagner's *Rheingold*, which will be analysed in a future volume.

'fantasies'.[1] The emphasis here is on the gulf which separates the Two Worlds, for again and again he describes the arduous journeys of his intrepid explorers in search of the 'lost kingdom' in the African interior; then, when they have penetrated into the Other Side, just as in *No Orchids*, the battle begins. His first fantasy, *King Solomon's Mines*, was written in emulation of Stevenson's *Treasure Island*, in which we find the same combination. Haggard's works, moreover, and particularly *She*, evidently provided the inspiration for a twentieth-century variant in Pierre Benoit's *l'Atlantide*, which contains the lost kingdom but lacks the battle.

This theme of the arduous nature of the way which leads to the Other Side, familiar from ancient and medieval legend (it also occurs constantly in the Arabian Nights, notably in *The Extraordinary Tale of the City of Brass*) and of the strange, contradictory world which it contains, is once again to be found in Samuel Butler's *Erewhon*. Here there is no reason to suspect inspiration by Haggard, for none of the latter's characteristic images appear; *Erewhon*, however, is distinguished from Butler's other works by the earlier passages describing the journey to the Other Side. These latter, and in particular the description of the passage of the tremendous gorge or chasm which separates the Two Worlds, represent a vivid symbolical experience which stands out impressively in contrast to the rather bloodless, intellectual atmosphere of the latter part of the work, and of Butler's other novels. The chasm, of course, is a variant of the image of the Barrier: it is magnificently portrayed in the terrific passage in Haggard's *She* in which the travellers, led by She herself, traverse the bottomless pit in the interior of the mountain (the Mountain of Venus again) on their way to the cavern of the magical fire of eternal youth. The symbolism of this variant image of the Barrier will be discussed in a later volume: at present we are only concerned with noting the symbolical

[1] He divided his works into two classes: novels and fantasies. The former deal with present-day life in actual places, although they invariably include supernatural (e.g. spiritualistic) themes and thus show his constant preoccupation with the Other Side; the latter are set in imaginary places or deal with historical times. The novels are without exception bad: it was only when he allowed his creative fantasy free rein to evoke symbolical forms, without the restraint of outer-world plausibility, that Haggard was great.

rendering of the theme of the separation between the Two Worlds.

The same picture of the remote, contradictory world is to be found in Alfred Kubin's *Die Andere Seite*, from which, following Meyrink, I have taken the designation the Other Side; in this work the *Traumreich*—dream world—is situated in the interior of China and is surrounded by a great wall; the same locality is chosen for his Shangri La by James Hilton in *Lost Horizon*, obviously another version of the same theme. In neither of the latter does the theme of the conflict appear in a marked form, although there are hostile elements which lead to the disintegration of the system of the Other Side, to the departure from it of the principal character, or to both. The dream world of *Die Andere Seite* is eventually destroyed by the appearance of an American business man, evidently representing outer-world values, while the conventional-minded and extraverted young vice-consul in *Lost Horizon* destroys the eternal youth of Shangri La in the person of his princess. Yet in neither of these works, nor in *Erewhon*, does the conflict appear in the straightforward, violent form which it assumes in the other works under consideration; in these three, on the other hand, great emphasis is laid on the fundamental contrast between the values and general attitude to life obtaining in the Other Side and the conventional approach of This World; to this point we shall return.

Die Andere Seite derives additional importance from its influence on Kafka, whose *Trial* is one of the most striking of all the variants of the theme. This work will also be examined in detail in a later volume, and it will suffice for the moment to point out that nowhere are the Two Worlds seen in closer contact: they actually, in a mysterious way, interpenetrate. It is perhaps also worth noting that the awareness of the Somewhere Else is rendered by Kafka in the same symbolical way as by Hadley Chase: by means of the telephone. The central theme of the book is the painful situation of the man who is condemned to share his life between the Two Worlds, and to suffer the collisions of their conflicting claims in full consciousness. It is seen as a tragedy, for men of the calibre of a Goethe, who succeed in coming to terms with both worlds in full consciousness, are rare indeed; today, perhaps, they are even rarer than in Goethe's time, since when the conflict in the collective mind has sharpened appreciably.

Another very striking example is provided by the two 'Alice' books, the theme of which is obviously the Other Side, and both of which, characteristically, are presented as accounts of dreams. In *Wonderland* Alice penetrates to the Other Side by falling down a deep shaft—an obvious symbol of the descent into the underworld—while in *Through the Looking-Glass* she enters it by passing through a mirror; this last is a powerful and apposite symbol with which we shall be concerned later in this study. There is altogether a great deal of symbolism in Alice's adventures, and we shall examine this in its place; the main attraction of the books, however, and that which has won them their universal popularity, is the rendering of the paradoxical nature of the unconscious part of the inner world. Although written for children they can, of course, only be fully appreciated by a mature intelligence, and anybody with a developed sense of inner and outer can rely on finding more in them at every re-reading.

This insistence on the paradoxical—even nonsensical—nature of the Other Side is important. In addition to the Alice books it is strongly marked in *Erewhon*, *The Trial* and *Die Andere Seite*, and is apparent, though less insistently, in *Lost Horizon*. We have noted that in all of these stories the theme of the warring factions which characterizes *No Orchids*, all Haggard's works, *A Tale of Two Cities* and others which we shall consider in later volumes, is absent; in all of them, on the other hand, except the Alice stories—and most markedly in *The Trial* —the conflicting claims of the two worlds on the central character is strongly brought out. The inference is evidently that in the one category the conflict has been recognized—i.e. at least partially understood by the conscious mind—whereas in the other it remains unconscious, or appears in consciousness only in the form of symbolism which is not understood. By accepting and valuing the paradoxical and nonsensical elements in experience the writers of the former category have eliminated the bitter war between the rational and irrational principles in the unconscious mind, and are thus in command at least of that aspect of the situation. They see themselves clearly as Persephone, subject to the claims upon them of two irreconcilable modes of experience, and are thus able to make some sort of a compromise between the two in the conduct of their lives. In so far as they remain—as Kafka, in particular, remained—tormented and unhappy—it is because other elements, generally associated with feeling, have not been accepted.

We shall find yet further examples of the theme of the Two Worlds in fiction when we come, in later volumes, to examine Graham Greene's *The Third Man*, Rose Macaulay's *The World My Wilderness*, Dickens' *Great Expectations*, Meyrink's *Walpurgisnacht* and several works by Helen Simpson. It would be easy to adduce more.

The examples given above suggest that in modern times the age-old picture of the remote land of wonders has given place to something different. Formerly the Other Side was simply a place which had to be visited in order to obtain or to recover the Treasure which had vanished into it; it was inhabited solely by non-human or superhuman figures, and the visitor to it was beset by every kind of danger; once the task was accomplished it was a place from which to return with all haste: not a place to live in. But in many modern examples it is perfectly possible to live there: the two worlds exist side by side and people constantly come and go between them: in Kafka they even interpenetrate, although each retains its own marked individuality. And secondly there is either a bitter conflict going on in the other world, in which the visitor is involved, or else its whole nature is seen as paradoxically, even nonsensically opposed to that of this world, of which it might be described as the inversion, or looking-glass image. These features obviously symbolize the sharpening awareness of the two opposing modes of experience, or systems of interpretation of experience, between which our lives must be shared.

Ever since the Renaissance, when the differentiation of the outer world began to be systematically undertaken, this awareness has been intensifying, and as a result of the fact that we have concentrated to an ever increasing extent on the one world at the expense of the other, the principle of equal and opposite reactions has brought about a building up, in the unconscious mind, of countervailing tendencies of an inner-world—and specifically an irrational inner-world—nature. Hence a state of conflict and tension has arisen between the collective conscious attitude and the collective unconscious of the times: the increasing prevalence of the image of the two worlds at war in fiction is the reflection of this situation, and the growing tendency to neuroses and functional complaints represents its repercussion on the individual. Finally, the glaring paradox of our international relations, characterized as they are by sincere professions of friendliness and pacific intentions on the one hand, and by a simultaneous cantankerousness, suspiciousness and destructiveness on the other, reveals the acute dichotomy of the collective mind. Contemporary nations are perfect examples of the Jekyll and Hyde theme.

At this stage the 'transcendental function' in the collective Psyche has given evidence of its efficacity by producing what was at first a medical interpretation of the image of the Two Worlds, namely the theory of the unconscious mind. This important development amounts in effect to the claim that one and the same subject has two separate sets of experiences: the one in the normal waking life which we call 'consciousness', the other being revealed in the contents of dreams, delusions, hallucinations and in a variety of oddities of behaviour, the motivation of which is otherwise inexplicable. The subject must experience these things in some form or other, since otherwise it would not be related to them; strictly speaking, therefore, the term 'unconscious' is a misnomer, for we are dealing with two different grades or levels of consciousness which are normally segregated from one another: it is the case of Chuang Tzu and the butterfly. It is merely a question of the use of words: are we to describe all forms of awareness, including that of the lower animals, as inferior grades of consciousness, or are we to confine the term solely to that form of awareness which is characteristic of the waking life of human beings above the age of four or five?

This consideration leads to some interesting points which will be discussed in the next volume: for the present we may adopt the arbitrary use of the term consciousness in the second sense described above, designating all other forms of experience as 'awareness'. It must, however, be borne in mind that 'consciousness' is no more than a special form of 'awareness', which latter exists in an infinite number of gradations. The same obviously applies even to 'consciousness' in this limited sense, for there is a greater difference between the intense, razor-sharp mental activity of, say, a mathematician engaged on an abstruse problem, and that of the tired labourer musing over his beer, than there is between the latter and the mental activity which takes place in a vivid dream, or, possibly, even in the mind of an intelligent and alert dog. Consciousness, in this limited sense, is undoubtedly the highest and most differentiated form of awareness, but the difference is one of degree only, not of kind.[1]

If, therefore, it can be demonstrated—and medical psychology undoubtedly has demonstrated it—that the type of awareness revealed by dreams, etc., persists during waking life, concurrently with consciousness but independently of it, and separated from it, we are forced to the conclusion that the same individual subject normally experiences (at least) two entirely separate, and in many senses incompatible modes of awareness at the same time, or, in the terminology adopted in this study, that he lives simultaneously in two worlds. In order to accept this fact we have only to break the normal identification with the personal self: we have to discard the ordinary, superficial notion 'I am Walter Mitty, a prosaic and ineffectual man with a nagging wife, who occasionally imagines that he is a hero living in a more exciting world', and substitute the formula 'This Walter Mitty, with his unsatisfactory life, is only one of the forms in which "I", the impersonal and transcend nt Subject, experience. He, Mitty (not "I"), and his world represent something to which "I" am indissolubly bound for the term of his earthly life, during which "I" can never completely escape from it; nevertheless "I" have alternative modes of experience, most of which are unknown to Walter Mitty; occasionally, when he becomes faintly and indistinctly aware of one or other of them he remembers it as a dream, or he may translate it into terms of his own life, which means that he indulges in fantasies of self-glorification.'

From this position the next step leads to Chuang Tzu's realization of his fundamental identity with the butterfly: in

[1] The relationship of what is commonly called consciousness to the continuity of the Ego is a question into which it is impossible to go at this stage; it will be considered in a later volume.

other words that the Subject is the same in all living individuals, whatever their degree; with this matter, however, we need not concern ourselves for the moment. It is sufficient if we can persuade ourselves, as Descartes did, of the fact that there are no grounds for inferring 'reality' in one of those modes of experience which are known to us, while denying it in another. Consequently there are no grounds for supposing that our waking experiences represent a real, universal world, by which they are caused, whereas our dream experiences represent nothing, except possibly distorted representations of that same waking world. This latter hypothesis might be accepted if it were not for the fact that there are elements in the 'dream' mode of experience which occur spontaneously and universally in a large number of individual cases, and which cannot be satisfactorily accounted for as distorted representations of elements in individual life.[1] These are the Archetypal forms: they presuppose *inherent, universal* contents or patterns of the mind, exactly equivalent to those which we recognize as constituting the hypothetical world 'behind' waking experience, but in many ways fundamentally different from them: in other words a universal inner-world content such, for instance, as that which Jung has designated the Anima, is exactly equivalent to, and no more and no less 'real' than such outer-world contents as mass, energy, income-tax or even the sun. All of them are mental patterns according to which experience may be classified and understood, and in consequence they are seen as independent 'factors' which affect our lives. It is on this fact that the whole thesis of the existence of the Two Worlds hinges.

The discovery that many cases of mental, and even physical, sickness could be traced back to the existence of irreconcilability and conflict between the contents of the conscious and unconscious parts of the mind, and could be cured, or at least alleviated, by bringing those of the unconscious into consciousness, naturally led to an intensive concentration on the nature of the unconscious and its contents. This was what contemporary

[1] The only way in which they can be so accounted for is by adopting such hypotheses as those characteristic of the systems of Freud and Adler: e.g. those of the Oedipus or inferiority complexes, which are claimed as universal in humanity. There are a number of objections to both these theories, which will be examined in a later volume.

humanity required, for it represented a serious and earnest diversion of attention towards those inherent, universal contents of the totality of the mind or psyche which, through our obsession with the prevalent conscious attitude, had been over-laid, obscured, and consequently denied their inalienable right to self-expression. Here the doctors succeeded where the philosophers and the story-tellers had failed: not because they necessarily saw more clearly, but because they treated the problem as *real*, i.e. as an intimate and important concern of individual life, individual happiness and individual success. Furthermore, by applying the scientific methods, developed by the conscious attitude in its concentration on the outer world, to the study of the inner, they constructed a bridge over the chasm that had grown between the two.

Among the pioneers in this new development the two who made the most important contributions were Freud and Jung. Although Freud did not 'discover' the unconscious mind—for precursors had already conclusively demonstrated its existence and the effects of its working—he did lead the way, not only in evolving a technique (psycho-analysis) for bringing its contents to consciousness, but also in making the first important attempt to formulate a systematic theory of its nature and the laws which governed its functioning. Unfortunately he was a super-ficial and extraverted thinker who allowed himself to be deflected from the line of thought demanded by his times, which was the recognition of the equal validity of the two modes of experience, drifting instead into the line followed by Descartes three centuries earlier: he overvalued the conscious, the rational and the objective at the expense of the unconscious, the irrational and the subjective. In Descartes' day this line proved fruitful, since no sufficiently systematic thought had yet been devoted to the rational aspect of the outer world and to the laws of conscious thinking; but in Freud's day it was retrogressive, since humanity already knew far too much about the rational, objective world of consciousness, and was in need of turning its attention in the opposite direction.

For Freud, therefore, the property of 'reality' always re-mained inseverably attached to the personal outer-world life, and to the hypothetical objective world which it appears to represent. Since he undervalued the Subject (or virtually ignored Its existence) he failed to appreciate the equivalence of all modes of experience. For him the Ego's experiences in consciousness were equivalent to reality: they were self-evidently true, and constituted the only possible truth. The alternative mode of experience of the individual subject, therefore—that represented by the activities of the unconscious mind —must be false, or at best a useless and distorted representation of reality. This is the basis of his whole system, and of his method of cure: mental conflicts, he maintains, arise because the unconscious mind, in its inferiority, necessarily makes mistaken interpretations of the truth which is represented by the conscious view of life, and they can be cured simply by revealing these nonsensical ideas to the ego, and demonstrating how absurd they are. It is true that he admits that the original fault may lie in certain concrete details of the communal conscious attitude, such as moral taboos which inhibit the direct satisfaction of instinctual drives, but he never visualizes the possibility of radical errors and shortcomings in the universally accepted conscious view of the world, or of the rebellious manifestations of the unconscious being determined by a purposeful reaction against them. He never, in fact, admits the possibility that the butterfly, seeing the totality of life from a different viewpoint, may discern errors in the basic attitude of Chuang Tzu which are necessarily concealed, not only from him personally, but from all his fellow-philosophers also, by virtue of the fact that they are all unconsciously identified with the principles which determine their thought. For Freud the outer world is always right, the inner always wrong.

It was left to Jung to discover the right path. Insisting on the independent existence and the priority of the unconscious mind —from which higher consciousness is evolved—he demonstrated that in cases of conflict it is invariably the unconscious mind which is right and the conscious wrong. The trouble, he maintains, has been brought about by the one-sided development of a conscious attitude which overvalues certain aspects of life and certain functions of the mind at the expense of others; whereupon the unconscious, stimulated by the danger of disequilibrating the totality of the Psyche which is inherent in the one-sided attitude, reacts in the opposite direction. The situation is similar to that of an enthusiastic young man who has embraced some extremist theory and attempts to base his whole life upon it, contemptuously dismissing the protests and warnings of his parents, whose wider and longer experience of life enables them to appreciate the importance of the factors which the headstrong youth is defying in his obsession with the unique importance and rightness of his theory. Cure, Jung maintains, can only be effected by convincing, not the parents, but the young man of his error; the parents, it is true, may not be capable of fully understanding the nature and importance of their son's theory, but they do know that intolerant and extremist behaviour invariably leads to trouble. When the trouble comes the young man should not abandon his theory completely: if it contains valuable elements he should continue to work at it, but he has to learn to admit that it is not the only thing in life. He must learn to find a compromise between the two factors involved.

Thus Jung claims that such disorders as neuroses are purposeful and basically constructive. They represent the protests of the parents, who foresee disaster for their son and would have him abandon his theory completely. In their ignorance they fail to appreciate the value of the theory, and in view of his particular circumstances, of which they are not aware, the course of action they propose may be impossible for the son to adopt. Nevertheless he must be brought to realize that their protests are by no means unfounded, and in any case they have the power to enforce them, founded or unfounded; the only possibility of a successful outcome, therefore, lies in the adoption by the son of an attitude of realistic compromise.

The essence of all this is that Jung admits the equal reality and validity of the two worlds, but at the same time he draws attention to the differences between them; this differentiation is embodied in his best-known conception, namely the theory of the opposed attitudes of extraversion and introversion. Here again he insists that there is no single standard: neither attitude is intrinsically truer or better than the other, although the standards and values of the two are radically opposed. But it is characteristic of the pattern of contemporary prejudice that even among psychologists extraversion is coming to be regarded as 'normal', proper and wholesome, while introversion is seen almost in the light of an abnormality or failing. The theory in its full development is little known and, where it is known, widely misunderstood, but it is impossible to devote more space to it here, and it will be considered in greater detail in the next volume of this study. Briefly, however, it may be said that Jung defines the two attitudes as the orientation of consciousness towards the outer and the inner world respectively, and in the course of his analysis of the various psychological types which arise from the combination of these two attitudes with each of the mental functions he goes some way towards sketching in the outlines of a picture of the characteristics of these two worlds. To the best of my knowledge, however, he nowhere attempts a final and comprehensive definition.

Lastly, many years later, he formulated the distinction between 'factual' and 'psychological' truth to which I have drawn attention in the Introduction. Here again the image of the Two Worlds lies behind the idea. Truth, Jung says, is a relative concept like any other: as seen from one point of view something may be true, although, from another, it is false, and he draws attention to one particular polarity in which truth appears in entirely contrasting forms. Something may be accepted as true 'psychologically' on the grounds that it has been accepted by a large number of people over a long period and in different places: that can only be because it corresponds to some universal pattern of the mind, since, if it did not, it would have been forgotten or changed into some more accept- able form. Thus, for instance, every widespread rumour must be psychologically true, since, if it were not, people would not trouble to pass it on and would not be believed if they did; it is also a matter of common knowledge that rumours develop as they are passed from mouth to mouth, and if the forms which they take on in the process are examined it will be found that they are not indiscriminate, but tend to bring out definite images, which are, of course, of an Archetypal nature. It is in this way that the great historical myths and legends develop.

When looked at from this point of view it will be seen that the factual truth or untruth of a story is completely without significance. For when we are considering it from this, the inner-world point of view, we are interested only in its signific- ance in terms of the mind, not in acquiring additional informa- tion about the outer world. (I have asserted that the outer world is also a pattern of the mind, but in the present context I am using the terms, for convenience, in their colloquial sense.) This attitude is a powerful stimulus of interest, as may be seen from the characteristics of the popular press, and of fiction. People are interested in reading about incidents, real or imaginary, which conform to certain simple 'dramatic' types, far more than in acquiring factual information, which they reject as dull. This is because a factual truth may be psychologically meaningless, in which case it has no 'news value' and takes no root in the mind: its proper place is in the reference library, where it can be looked up when required for practical purposes.

It is of course obvious that a statement may be both factually and psychologically true, or both factually and psychologically false, as well as true in one sense and false in the other. But in our consideration of it we must adopt one point of view or the other and assess its value accordingly; we may adopt each point of view in turn, as when a news editor considers a story first from the point of view of its news value, and then from that of its factual veracity; but we must not confuse the two. The popular appeal of the story is entirely independent of its factual truth or untruth, and the editor is only compelled to consider it from the factual point of view because his paper also prints items of purely factual interest, and he cannot therefore risk bringing its factual accuracy into discredit in any instance.

It thus becomes apparent that Jung's thought is in many essential respects an intellectual and scientific formulation of a basic theme which, in its symbolical form, has been preoccupying creative writers of the most varied types to an ever increasing extent in modern times, namely the existence of two separate modes of experience in the psyche or mind, of widely divergent and often contrasting natures, but of equal validity and reality. The increasing tension between these two systems constitutes the fundamental problem of our times.

VI   A Tentative Definition of the Two Worlds

I<small>T</small> is impossible to leave this matter without attempting some kind of definition of the nature of the Two Worlds *as they appear when considered from a philosophical angle.* I shall make the attempt for the sake of clarity and completeness, but it should be understood in advance that no such definition can possibly cover all the aspects under which the totality of the phenomenon presents itself. In the same way the definition of poetry in terms of prosody may be a useful aid to our understanding of it, without which no exposition of the subject would be complete, but it will obviously fail completely to cover its all-important emotional and intuitive aspects. The Two Worlds are Archetypal, and as such they embrace spheres of experience which are not susceptible of philosophical exposition, as well as others which are so susceptible. This study is not intended as an attempt merely to explain the Two Worlds, but to present them in as many as possible of the various forms under which we experience them; it would be incomplete and unsatisfactory without some suggestion of a possible logical basis for the discrimination in question, but the discrimination is not confined to its logical elements, nor even built up on them: it is something which evidently exists in its own right. As such it may be partially susceptible of explanation by logical analysis, but no such analysis can exhaust its potentialities.

Before proceeding to the positive task it will be advisable to recapitulate a few negative considerations, i.e. to repeat a few of those points, mentioned earlier, which are liable to give rise to misunderstandings. The prevalent system of thought is so pervasive and deeply ingrained that it is inevitable that the reader should tend to interpret what he reads in its terms unless the different intention of the writer is explicitly and insistently kept before him.

(1) The Two Worlds are not to be visualized as two separate areas, divided one from the other like the sea and the atmosphere above it. From the philosophical viewpoint they must be regarded as tendencies, or as directions of thought, or of experience generally. The differentiation between them may sometimes present itself as the experience of passing from one 'world' or mode of experience to another, entirely distinct from it, as in the transition from dreaming to waking, but this is only a special case. Above all they must not be thought of as existing 'inside' and 'outside' our heads.

(2) It is emphatically not claimed that the inner world is *more* real, important, significant or true than the outer, but that it is *no less* so: we have to accept two distinct and contrasting forms under which truth and reality present themselves, each as valid as the other although incompatible with it.

(3) The distinction between outer and inner is not the same as that between conscious and unconscious: in many respects the two polarities correspond, but not in all. The prevalent contemporary orientation of the conscious attitude tends to concentrate on the outer elements of the polarity while relegating inner elements to the unconscious, but this is by no means necessarily the case, and in some civilizations of the past, as well as in many individuals of the present day, the position is found reversed.

Having cleared the ground so far we may proceed to attempt to elucidate the nature of the discrimination involved.

As I have repeatedly emphasized, the polarity inner-outer is on a par with the polarities good-evil or beautiful-ugly. All these may be said 'to exist' or be 'real' if it can be shown that they represent universal mental patterns which manifest themselves in some recognizable form in all human beings. Nobody will deny that this is the case in respect of the polarities good-evil and beautiful-ugly: the particularities or accidentals of the standards by which these properties are assessed in individual phenomena have varied in different epochs and among different peoples, and they still to some extent vary, particularly among individuals; yet behind all the variants the fundamental nature of the cleavage or dichotomy remains the same. Nietzsche set out to re-value or 'trans-value' (*umwerten*) all values, and set up a system according to which the majority of what are commonly regarded as vices were designated virtues, and *vice versa*; but he was still making ethical judgments in exactly the same way as the most orthodox clergyman: only his particular standards were different. Similarly certain artists, particularly in modern times, have deliberately rejected the categories of form or image (in the widest sense of these terms) which have been traditionally regarded as 'beautiful', seeking their inspiration instead in what is normally regarded as ugly: yet they were still making an aesthetic discrimination.

Such genuine experimentation in the exercise of the mode of discrimination in question, however misguided the particular case may be, stands in the strongest contrast to thought, or artistic work, in which the appropriate mode of discrimination is lacking, or confused with others. Nietzsche's ethics were worse than misguided: they were, as we shall see when we come to consider his case, literally diabolically inspired. Yet his standpoint was a truly ethical one: he was above all concerned with the differentiation between good and evil, and although he went hopelessly astray in his classification we can at least learn a great deal from his mistakes. From the legalist who confuses the ethical sense with the dictates of authority (even if supposedly divine), or from the moral philosopher who attempts to derive it from intellectual concepts,[1] we can learn nothing.

Similarly with the aesthetic mode. We may take the example of a woman choosing a dress: the factors which determine her choice fall into two absolutely distinct categories, namely the utilitarian and the aesthetic. In the first place she must take account of price, wearing qualities, etc., and in the second of appearance, and the extent to which she is capable of differentiating between these two categories, of taking due account of each, and of balancing them one against the other, is an index of her intelligence. It is obvious that any particular dress may

---

[1] But Kant had the insight to assert that 'the moral law', by which he meant the ethical impulse, was a 'categorical imperative', i.e. that it existed in its own right and could not be derived from any logical system.

be ideal from the one point of view and yet unsatisfactory from the other, and it is hardly necessary to point out that any preference which a woman habitually accords to either is significant of her whole attitude to life. The recognition of value in sensory experience for its own sake, quite irrespective of any other value which it may represent, is, in fact, an attitude which is normally adopted, although more pronouncedly by some individuals than by others; we all, moreover, value this attitude, provided that it is not allowed to encroach on matters in which it is out of place, for nearly everybody exacts certain standards of appearance in dress, both in himself and others, whatever their nature may be.

The standards which the purchaser applies to the appearance of her dress, however, may vary widely in nature. She may adhere to precepts: that blue suits blondes, that women over forty should not wear frills, that spots are vulgar but stripes are fashionable this year, or even that a garment which bears the label of a well-known firm, and costs more than the average, must be 'right'. Such criteria, although applied in the aesthetic sphere—i.e. with respect solely to appearance—are clearly not aesthetic in themselves: they are products of thinking—of notions, or what are commonly called 'ideas'—and not of the direct reaction to sensory experience, i.e. to the actual 'look' of the dress. This attitude, which is the best that many people achieve, is a characteristic example of the subordination of one mental function to another—in this case of the sensory to the thinking—and may result in a complete distortion of the values of the subordinated function. If the purchaser's choice is guided solely by considerations of this nature (in addition to those which are admittedly utilitarian) she is not exercising the aesthetic sense at all, and the consequences will be apparent to the discriminating observer.

In the majority of cases the most powerful factor in the determination of the choice will be the search for what is fashionable. The art of being fashionably dressed is definitely of an aesthetic nature, since it is concerned solely with the direct perception of appearances, and with their valuation as such, irrespective of ideas; it is, of course, imitative, but at a fairly high mental level, for each individual does not buy an exact replica of something seen but, from the study of fashion plates, shop displays and the clothes of other women, forms in her mind a synthetic, generalized image of the underlying forms of the prevalent fashion, and uses this abstract image as a criterion with which to compare the dresses she is offered, or even as a guide to making her own. This art has its own objective standards, for women will agree that somebody is always fashionably dressed, whereas another has no 'fashion sense'. Fashion sense is an incomplete form of the aesthetic sense: it can be carried to a high degree of subtlety and sensitivity, but it remains incomplete because its standards have no value in themselves: they are not derived from the ultimate nature of their subject-matter—i.e. forms, colours and textures —but from models arbitrarily set up by somebody in Paris. It is a truism that women are prepared to adorn themselves in the most grotesque and hideous manner in imitation of any fashion that has 'caught on': its ugliness is hidden from them until they look back at their photographs five years later.

Finally, the purchaser may have independent criteria by which she judges appearances, quite irrespective of the dictates of fashion: she may recognize and value combinations of colours, harmonious or otherwise interesting lines, the visual effect of textures, etc., in their own right, applying these standards to her choice of clothes in exactly the same way as in her judgment of a picture or a scheme of interior decoration. This is the introverted or inner-world aspect of the aesthetic sense, and its presence is immediately apparent to anybody who understands it. Its possession safeguards its owner from succumbing to the more grotesque and unsightly of fashionable extravagances, but it carries a corresponding risk of leading her, in her confidence in her own taste and contempt for that of the collectivity, to deviate from the accepted norms to an extent which may reach the proportions of a social solecism. A perfect balance between the two factors concerned—the personal and the collective—is hard to achieve and consequently rarely to be met. This is a contrast between the introverted and extraverted attitudes, with which we are not concerned at the moment; my purpose in introducing the matter is to indicate how the polarity inner-outer is involved in the most varied aspects of life. Similarly, of course, the aesthetic polarity is involved in the discrimination between inner and outer: just as a fully developed aesthetic sense must take account of inner and outer, so must a fully developed sense of inner and outer take account of the aesthetic polarity beautiful-ugly (or, to adopt a more comprehensive terminology, aesthetically superior-aesthetically inferior), for a picture of the inner and outer worlds from which the sensory element is excluded is incomplete. Similarly, again, the ethical sense must be balanced by a due regard for the inner and outer aspects of conduct ('Make unto yourselves friends of the mammon of unrighteousness') for however high the ethical quality of an action may be when judged solely by absolute, inner-world standards, it may still be wrong if it offends and distresses others by flouting harmless conventions.

The position becomes clearer if considered in the light of the symbolical image of the bisection of the sphere. The sphere of indeterminacy represents the totality of undifferentiated experience. It remains unintelligible until it is bisected, by conscious differentiation, into a pair of opposite but complementary hemispheres. Such bisection is possible along an infinite number of planes of cleavage (similar to that of the terrestrial globe along the equator), each of which gives a different result. But although each such bisection is distinct from every other, each is also interrelated with every other, *for every great circle drawn on the surface of a sphere must intersect every other which it is possible to draw, and all have a common centre.*

The polarities good-evil, beautiful-ugly and inner-outer thus represent three of the infinite number of possible bisections of the sphere. Each constitutes *a manner of discrimination* by means of which the conscious mind 'makes sense' (not necessarily intellectual sense) of the unintelligible totality of experience.

The actual discrimination carried out by any particular individual is determined, as I have indicated above, by the building up of a pair of complex images in the mind, to one or other of which he can assimilate any particular experience, thus classifying it as either good or bad, beautiful or ugly, etc. These images vary in composition, comprehensiveness, scope and coherence as between different individuals, yet the universality of their appearance in some form or other implies the pre-existence of a universal nucleus or Archetypal polarity in the mind. *This Archetypal polarity is the essence of the manner of discrimination in question.*

In respect of any particular dichotomy we thus have the picture of an ideal, perfect system of discrimination on the one hand, and on the other of the actual, imperfect systems developed by each individual and by the collectivity, which fall short, in varying degrees, of the perfect system. These inferior, incomplete systems may be visualized as smaller circles drawn on the surface of the sphere in a position parallel to the ideal great circle; for instance, if the perfect dichotomy inner-outer

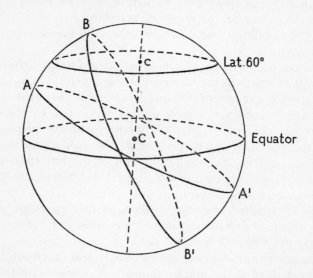

be visualized as the great circle of the equator, then the various incomplete systems correspond to the circles of latitude: they are parallel to the equator, but they do not divide the sphere into equal halves. This picture reveals a vitally important point, namely that although every great circle on the surface of the sphere must of necessity intersect every other great circle, this does not apply to any smaller circles: thus if we draw a great circle at an angle to the equator it must intersect the latter, but if the angle is not too great it may not intersect the higher parallels of latitude.

This situation represents the mentality of an individual or collectivity whose system of differentiation in respect of one of the essential polarities is inadequately developed: instead of visualizing the dichotomy in the ideal position of the great circle of the equator, he sees it at the parallel of latitude of (say) 60°: the consequence is that his reduced circle does not intersect the great circle A–A', which lies at an angle to the equator. In psychological terms this means that the two systems of differentiation in his mind are not brought into relationship with one another, and this represents a deficiency in his attitude to life in one respect or another.

In order to achieve an ideal orientation to life, therefore, it is necessary to widen and perfect the circle representing each characteristic manner of discrimination until it attains its maximum dimension, which is that of the great circle: this automatically ensures that it must intersect—i.e. be brought into relationship with—every other possible great circle, or manner of differentiating experience. The outcome of such all-round development is the achievement of the complete, harmonious and dynamically stable whole—the greatest possible realization of the potentialities of the individual or group—and the age-old symbolism of the search for this condition is that of finding the Centre;[1] for all great circles have a common centre, which is the centre of the sphere itself, but the centres of smaller circles are displaced from the great Centre. This symbolism is brought out by Jung in connection with his theory of the integration of the personality.

My contention is that the circle of differentiation between inner and outer which prevails in the contemporary collective conscious attitude of the West is equivalent to a small circle, such as the parallel of 60° of latitude, which divides the totality of experience into two unequal parts, placing too much in the outer, and too little in the inner. This circle is so oriented that it does intersect the great circle representing logical thought (B–B' in the figure), but fails to intersect other great circles, such as A–A', which may be taken to represent, e.g., aesthetic or ethical discrimination. The consequence is that the potential inner-world aspects of the latter are undervalued and neglected: it is only in the sphere of logical thought that we discriminate

[1] Freemasons will recognize something in this symbolism. The great Centre may also be seen as representing the Self (Atman) or the universal element which is common to all individuals.

with any degree of competence between inner- and outer-world elements, and in which we attach anything approaching an adequate degree of importance to those of the inner world. In order to attain harmony and balance it is evidently necessary to widen this circle, and thereby to bring it to its proper place on the equator: this will result in its coming into relationship with all aspects of experience, and thus restoring the endangered equilibrium of the Psyche. The means of attaining this end are, first to emphasize the reality and importance of the inner world as such, and secondly to devote our attention to those other circles or modes of differentiation which are at present undervalued and neglected.

The essential of each of the 'senses' which we have been considering—the aesthetic, the ethical and the sense of inner and outer—is thus seen to be, not so much the particular elements included on either side of the polarity as the *manner of discrimination* characteristic of it. The question of exactly what things we regard as good, beautiful or 'inner', and what as their opposites, is only a secondary consideration: that which is really significant is the basic pattern on which the principles, points of reference and values, in accordance with which we make the discrimination, is built up. This pattern or manner of discrimination is, in each of the cases considered, different in kind from any other although, in the ideal case, interrelated with all others. In its perfect form it may be visualized as a great circle described on the surface of the sphere of the totality of experience, and in the incomplete forms, which are the best that we can achieve in the sublunar world, as a smaller circle parallel with the great circle of the ideal. The common feature of all such circles relating to any particular manner of differentiation is the *axis* which runs through all their centres, and it is in this axis that we can visualize the essence or Archetypal nucleus of the manner of discrimination involved. It follows that the first necessity in coming to terms with any such system of differentiation is to identify the axis in question, for only when we have formed some conception of its nature, however nebulous, can we orientate our system correctly. Once this is done we can set about describing a circle of discrimination, and then go on to the process of enlarging it until it attains the greatest dimension

—the nearest approach to the ideal great circle—which we are capable of achieving.

In order to illustrate this matter we may return to the example of the woman choosing a dress. If her choice (in respect of appearance as distinct from utilitarian features) is determined solely by precepts or 'ideas' (that blue suits blondes, etc.) then she has not grasped the nature of the axis of aesthetic discrimination at all: her system of differentiation is falsely orientated—according to the principles of thinking instead of to those of sensory evaluation. The woman who is guided exclusively by fashion sense, on the other hand, has orientated her system correctly inasmuch as her criteria are of the nature of sensory experience and not of thinking; but her circle of discrimination is not ideal, being displaced towards the outer-world pole and consequently under-valuing the inner-world standard of what is pleasing in its own right, irrespective of fashion. Her opposite, who is guided solely by 'artistic' values to the extent of ignoring the conventions of fashion to a degree which causes embarrassment in normal society, has displaced her circle correspondingly in the opposite direction.

The foregoing considerations are designed to indicate the nature of the definition which we require: they may be summarized as follows.

(1) The image of the Two Worlds represents a *manner of discrimination* between elements of experience, equivalent in its manner of functioning to other manners of discrimination, such as those between good and evil, beautiful and ugly, etc.

(2) This manner of discrimination is universal in humanity: i.e. it is Archetypal.

(3) It is actually carried out by means of a pair of complex images which each individual builds up in his mind, and by comparison with which he classifies individual items of experience as belonging to the inner or the outer world. He does not, of course, necessarily use this terminology: he normally distinguishes between what he calls 'real' and 'imaginary', etc., but the basis of the discrimination which he actually makes is a more or less adequately understood version of a pattern which is universal and inherent in the human mind.

(4) It is the essence of this pattern which we wish to define as closely as may be possible: it may be visualized as the axis on

which lie the centres of all circles of true discrimination in this mode.

But this axis is Archetypal, and the Archetypes are the formative principles which pervade and actually shape the whole of our conscious experience. They are so much a part of us, and we of them, that it may be assumed *a priori* that individual consciousness can never remove itself sufficiently from them to perceive them in their totality, and thus to be in a position to formulate a fully comprehensive definition of any of them. Nobody has yet succeeded in producing a completely satisfactory definition of good and evil or beautiful and ugly, and I do not believe that anybody ever will. Nevertheless they are 'realities': we all experience them in our manner and degree, and the nearest we can get to understanding them is to study the nature of our reactions to them, to analyse and classify the resultant material to the best of our ability, and then to attempt to derive a general impression from our conclusions.

If we bear all these limitations and qualifications in mind we may attempt to formulate an indication of the essence of the discrimination between inner and outer. I make no claim that it is in any sense a complete and comprehensive definition, since I regard such a thing as *a priori* impossible; much material, even in the foregoing chapters, will be found which cannot be unreservedly accommodated to it; as an intellectually framed formula, moreover, it is by its very nature incapable of embracing many aspects—such, for instance, as the feeling element—which are involved in the discrimination which we actually make.

The point to remember is that we are not setting up an artificial picture of something as it ought to be according to the rules of logic, but attempting to make sense of something which, according to our experience, actually occurs.

The inner seems to be the direction towards that which is universal, the outer that towards that which is particular. The universal tends towards the abstract, and is free of space and time, applying equally at all times and in all places; the particular tends towards the concrete, which is unique in its position in space and time, and has no relevance at any other position. This distinction is not confined to the contents of the thinking intellect, but applies equally to those of all other functions of the mind: e.g. feeling, sensation and intuition.[1]

This is the approximate statement of the essence of the distinction, as it seems to me. In its application, however, a number of complications and side-issues, deriving from its intersection with other patterns, tend to obscure the essential outline, and it is necessary to elucidate some of these.

Individual consciousness is largely defined by its unique time-relationship to items of experience, and by the unique situation in space of the body associated with it, as fixed by the pattern of sensory experience: it therefore tends towards the outer-world pattern. But experience is not confined to the particular: the Subject experiences in a universal mode whether the experiences in question are admitted to consciousness or not. The universal, non-personal modes of experience of the mind are in essence opposed to the personal and therefore tend towards the inner-world pattern.

Personal consciousness is entirely incapable of assimilating many of the aspects of the universal mode of experience, since these are of a nature opposed to its own; these elements must therefore necessarily remain in the unconscious mind for so long as the ego, the subject of personal consciousness,[2] is in control. In certain transitional conditions, however, as when waking from sleep, or in certain abnormal states in waking life, the re-emergent personal consciousness is caught, as it were, before it has set up its defences, and elements from the unconscious process are enabled to slip into the stream of ego-memory. Dreams, therefore (the dreams which are remembered are those which occur during the process of waking), are one of the most

---

[1] The nature and role of the various mental functions, in their connection with Jung's theory of psychological types, will be considered in the next volume of this series.

[2] Ego-consciousness, or the normal waking mode of experience governed by a pattern grouped round the unique situation of the individual, may be regarded as one particular mode of the experience of the universal Subject: the Ego may be likened to an optical instrument—e.g. a telescope—which gives the eye a particular view of the world, but for which another instrument—e.g. a microscope—giving a totally different view, may be substituted. This idea will be given further consideration in the next volume of this series.

important forms in which unconscious contents—hence many aspects of the inner world—reach consciousness. The contents of the unconscious—hence of dreams—are not exclusively confined to inner-world elements, but there are many inner-world elements which can reach the normal man's consciousness in no other way. The dream is therefore pre-eminently a symbol of inner-world experience. Visionary and hallucinatory states have a similar result, but in the normal man they occur so rarely as to be negligible; certain techniques (familiar in the Orient), however, make it possible to establish such states at will, and certain individuals are naturally predisposed to them. The contents of 'visions', or experiences of this kind, are largely of a supra-personal, universal nature and consequently stir the unconscious minds of all men (or the collective unconscious in all men); 'visionaries', therefore, are often prophets or men of genius whose revelations have universal value and exercise widespread influence. Revelations and the like—frequently of a religious nature—are thus another important manifestation of the inner-world pattern.

Inner-world contents of the unconscious also manifest themselves in projection, when they appear to the subject in association with conscious contents and are mistaken by him for outer-world experiences, or for attributes of outer-world objects which the latter do not in fact possess when seen from a true outer-world viewpoint. By this means rumours, myths, legends and fabulous images (such as the mermaid) arise: these are therefore another important source of information concerning the inner world. By developing a sense of inner and outer we learn to discriminate between the elements of factual and of psychological truth embodied in them.

Personal consciousness is, however, capable of obtaining access to the inner world by processes of abstraction and reflection, and this technique has been highly developed in the contemporary civilization, but in one sphere only, namely that of thinking. In the sphere of thinking—in the differentiation between theory and practice, abstract and concrete, hypothesis and demonstration—the Two Worlds are familiar to us as equals and counterparts. One of our main difficulties is to perceive and appreciate the nature of all the other contents of the inner world which do not pertain to the realm of thinking:

we must perpetually remind ourselves that the inner world is not confined to thinking alone.

The nucleus of our picture of the outer world is probably our normal, waking sensory experience; it is no less important to remember that sensory experience is not confined to the outer world.

Finally, let it be repeated that inner and outer worlds are equally *within the mind*. Space and time were designated by Kant *Formen der Anschauung*—forms of perception, or, colloquially, 'ways of seeing things'—and the mode in which they predominate is only one of the potentialities of the mind. The mind is not the brain: it is not fixed in space and time but contains them, and with them the 'outer world'. For all ordinary purposes our picture of ourselves as points of awareness 'within' the space-time system is serviceable, but it has the disadvantage of making us averse to recognizing the 'reality', importance and independence of those things which do not fit into that system, and this can only be overcome by concentrating on the viewpoint from which everything—the material no less than the 'invisible' world—is equally a content of universal mind. Both inner and outer are systems or patterns of the impersonal part of the mind, which is independent of our personal volition and therefore seems—and in a sense actually is—external to us. Each is incomplete without the other.

A manner of experience which makes no clear distinction between these two modes is perfectly possible: it is characteristic, as we have seen, of the mental activity of primitives and young children, and it is also a feature of insanity. *But there are only two possibilities*: the subject must either ignore this mode of differentiation or else he must take both inner and outer into account: *it is not possible to confine experience to one while eliminating the other*. The recognition and utilization of either category inescapably entails the activation of the other: this is entailed by the law of equal and opposite reactions. Just as male presupposes female, riches poverty, the seller the buyer or the organic the inorganic, so does outer presuppose inner. If either mode is denied access to consciousness as a result of a one-sided obsession with the other, it will become active in the unconscious part of the mind, hostility and tension will grow up between the two, and trouble will result.

333

Civilization is essentially a matter of mental discrimination in a number of spheres, and the differentiation between inner and outer is one of the most important of them. If we do not wish to revert to savagery we must not only retain this manner of discrimination but even intensify, extend and perfect it yet further: civilization demands it. It therefore follows that we must concentrate on this subject, and that means that we must concentrate particularly on the inner world, or our neglect will certainly have really serious—probably disastrous—consequences.

Persephone is the human soul: we are inescapably bound to two worlds, between which we must share our lives.

334

VII The Two Worlds in Terms
of Life

I HAD hoped to defer the foregoing theoretical exposition of
the theory of the Two Worlds until after some practical
examples of its workings in individual lives had been considered. That would be a far preferable arrangement with
respect to the inner-world pattern, but outer-world exigencies,
in the matter of what can be reasonably expected of the reader,
as well as the requirements of practical publication, have
intervened. It is best here, as nearly always, to seek a working
compromise between the two worlds, and their interaction has
resulted in this volume in its present form.

It consists of the analysis of a story, followed by the exposition
of a thesis in a mainly philosophical context: it is, in fact, almost
entirely confined to inner-world forms. It has not been possible
to offer more than occasional hints at the way in which these
forms work themselves out in that alternative mode of experience which we call the outer world: yet the essence of my thesis
is that the totality of experience which makes up life is a
synthesis of inner- and outer-world experience, and that its
pattern is the product of the interaction, in individual and
collective minds, of factors deriving from both of them.

Such a claim can only be substantiated by the consideration
of examples in which it is possible to set the two categories side
by side, within the framework of an individual life. In this
respect our study of *No Orchids* is set, so to speak, *in vacuo*, since
we know nothing of its author's outer-world life: it will be
necessary to turn to writers of the past, sufficiently celebrated
for details of their outer lives to be easily available for

335

comparison with the records of their inner lives which they have embodied, largely unconsciously, in the symbolism of their writings. This will constitute the matter of later volumes of this study, in which I shall attempt to demonstrate that the inner life of the individual is no mere reflection of the particularities and contingencies of his outer-world circumstances. These play their part, but their significance is determined by the subject's reaction to them, and that, in its turn, is largely the consequence of the universal, non-personal inner-world forces which act on him and through him. It will, I hope, be possible to show that these forces conform to a small number of patterns as universal, intelligible and invariable as those which we call the laws of nature, and of the social sciences such as economics, and with the help of which we succeed in 'making sense' of the complexities of the outer-world mode of experience.

These patterns will be found to embrace not only those universal factors which determine the relationship of the individual element of the mind, as such, with its non-personal elements throughout life, but also a clear, progressive scheme of development within the individual which extends 'from the cradle to the grave'.

One of Freud's most important contributions to psychology lies in his demonstration of the manner in which elements belonging to the mental patterns characteristic of infancy, childhood and adolescence tend to persist unconsciously into adult life, where they come into conflict with the divergent patterns characteristic of that stage, thus producing inner conflicts which manifest themselves in a false and defective attitude towards life. I do not entirely agree with his interpretation of the nature of these patterns: nevertheless the fact that they exist and are incompatible with one another is obvious and incontrovertible. I propose to carry the scheme further, suggesting that universal patterns characteristic of adult youth, of the middle period of life which covers early middle age, and finally of the closing period of mental maturity, may also be discerned, and that the contrasts between them are no less fundamental than those between the periods preceding and following sexual maturity; the persistence of patterns belonging to the youthful adult pattern into the middle period of life, or of those belonging to the latter into the closing period, are in fact no less important than the persistence of childish elements into adult life which Freud has so conclusively demonstrated.

These later changes are not so apparent as the earlier ones because the older person is more individual than the younger. Infancy, childhood and adolescence themselves constitute types, whose typical characteristics predominate over the particular characteristics of the individuals who compose them; in later life, on the other hand, the individual characteristics tend to predominate: the small individual divergencies, which are still insignificant in childhood, give rise later to the development of a wide variety of individual personalities, and of contrasting types whose attitudes are in many respects entirely different, or even diametrically opposed to one another. Thus although, gross abnormalities apart, we know pretty well what we can expect of any boy of ten, the fact that a man is forty means very little in comparison with his individual personality and his type: he may be a retiring poet, a brash politician or a drunken wastrel. Nevertheless these particularities are in the last resort something superimposed on the basic form of human individuality as such, and beneath their bewildering variety it is possible to discern fundamental correspondences within the various age-groups: every human being, irrespective of disposition, sex, psychological type or acquired personality, inevitably passes through the same basic phases of development with striking punctuality, and ignorance of this fact is responsible for many of our troubles.

These changes are apprehended in consciousness with greater or less clarity according to the degree of insight with which the individual is gifted: in many cases—perhaps the majority—they are totally unconscious. Nevertheless they are always revealed in the symbolism of the inner life, and we shall find this confirmed in several examples of those who have recorded that symbolism.

I am particularly anxious to insist that this question of the interaction of the Two Worlds is a matter of life, and not merely of airy theory, for if we continue to ignore it we shall experience the resultant conflict in the form not only of the torments of the mind, but of material disaster as well, and material disaster has the one important consequence that it may bring consciousness to a premature end. The approach, moreover, which the theory suggests in order to escape this tragic outcome, indicates the possibility of a practical working programme which may assist the individual to reorientate his attitude, both to his personal problems and to the collective problems of the times, in such a way that he may be enabled to pay equal and due respect to both these patterns with which, as a psychological or mental being, he is inextricably bound up. Thereby it becomes possible for him to escape the terrible fate of finding himself the helpless and tragic victim of the conflict of two irreconcilable forces, both acting in and through his mind, and each dwarfing the puny resources of the individual personality as the power of the elements dwarfs that of the body.

Man, in both his individual and collective aspects, finds himself in the painful position of the iron between the hammer of his inner and the anvil of his outer nature. By enduring this torment for a time he may, both individually and collectively, suffer the process of being forged into a shape which has significance and value; but the force of the hammer of spirit, and the rigidity of the anvil of space and time, are blind, and the individual or the group which fails to adjust itself to the best posture for sustaining the impact between them is first distorted and eventually annihilated. If it were not for the mysterious identity between the iron and the smith who guides the hammer and sets the iron in the position in which it receives the blows, mankind could never survive the treatment.

The analogy must not be carried too far: we can neither prevent the hammer from striking, nor the anvil from resisting, for hammer and anvil, spirit and matter (the latter being the mental pattern of material objects arranged in space and time) are merely figurative names for the essences of force and resistance. Yet by understanding the nature of this polarity— and that of polarities in general, which consists of their derivation, through the dichotomy produced by consciousness, from the Indeterminate—it is possible for the individual to grasp the identity of the striker with the struck, and his own fundamental identity with both. By this means, and by this means only, he can in a mysterious way control the process of forging as it affects himself, directing the blows which he, as Subject, rains upon himself as Object, in such a way that his personality—

which he must learn to see as something separate from the forces which act on it, and as separate also from the Self—is beaten into a shape which has significance and value, and that it is enabled to survive the strain entailed by the process. If he concentrates exclusively on either hammer or anvil he will fail to make due allowance for the nature of the other, and a distorted form will result; if he sees himself exclusively as either striker or struck—as subject or object—he will fail to appreciate the formative nature of the process, and will either destroy his own particularity or suffer it to be destroyed by forces which he does not understand.

Progress, as Jung says, can come only through the individual, for the impact between the irreconcilables can reach consciousness only in the individual mind. It is useless to attempt to solve our problems by arbitrarily imposing radical changes on the collective system, whether they be political, social or economic. Collective systems cannot be brought into being by dictate: they can only grow up, by trial and error, out of the multitude of individual expedients, originated by the individuals who form the community. Those with insight may discern the overall patterns which govern the slow process of change, and by applying their efforts in the right direction at some critical point they may succeed in liberating dammed-up forces in a beneficial manner, so that great and far-reaching changes, for which they appear to be personally responsible, are associated with their names. The greatness of a man, Bismarck said, is the greatness of the wave which breaks under him.

But two great dangers are associated with such ventures: first, the canalization and regulation of the forces which he unleashes are rarely within the power of the individual, and if no bed is ready to receive them the torrent of the Waters of Life—the released collective libido—is almost invariably transformed into a disastrous flood of the Waters of Death. Free spirit is either creative or destructive, never constructive: construction is the product of bound spirit, requiring restraint, discipline and sustained and often irksome toil. When we come to study the Conquerors we shall see how those who sow the wind must reap the whirlwind.

The second danger is that the reformer should underestimate

the inertia of his material. He expects too much: seeing the shortcomings of the prevailing system, he eliminates them in a tidy theoretical pattern based on the assumption that everybody will behave as he, the reformer, thinks that they ought to behave. But when he comes to put his theory into practice he finds that after the first burst of enthusiasm, if the forces he has released do not wrench themselves from his control and sweep all before them, spreading death and destruction in their path, the collectivity will soon begin to feel uncomfortable under the new, unfamiliar dispensation and will insensibly begin to reconstruct the conditions of the old. Nothing, of course, will ever be quite the same again: some abuses will have been eliminated and new ones will grow up in their places; on balance a certain degree of advance will be discernible, but it will have been purchased at the price of some irreparable losses and of much suffering. G. F. Orwell's bitter little satire *Animal Farm* presents the picture very clearly with respect to the Russian revolution: its only fault is that it inferentially lays the failure to achieve the ideal upon the imputed wickedness of the leaders, instead of in its proper place, which is the incompatibility of the ideal with the mentality of the led. Those who are naïve enough to believe that the ills of humanity may be cured by changes imposed on the social, political or economic system from without (i.e. on the basis of external theory, even with the consent of the populace) are doomed to disappointment, for the systems which it is desired to change are the reflection of the mental world-picture of the community. This picture is deeply ingrained and can only be changed slowly: any attempt to impose radical innovations on it without adequate preparation will be followed by reaction.

Sometimes, of course, outmoded systems are perpetuated by the intolerant obstinacy of a ruling class, in which case an explosion is eventually inevitable; but nobody should be surprised when, after the wreckage has been cleared away, the community sinks back with a sigh of relief into a way of life which is in large measure a reconstruction of the old. The world-picture can only change slowly, for it is deeply rooted in the whole complex system by means of which each individual finds his bearings in life, and which he dare only, and can only, change with infinite precaution.

These considerations have been adduced solely by way of illustration, for we are not concerned with politics or economics, but with a far more fundamental matter, namely contemporary man's basic attitude towards the outer and inner worlds. If a really fundamental change in the collective system is impossible even in such comparatively superficial affairs as politics and economics—of which everybody is at least aware as controversial matters—it is by so much the more out of the question in a sphere which hardly anybody recognizes as controversial at all. It would be otiose to address oneself to the wide public; but every individual who sees the light is not only, so to speak, one soul saved in himself, but he also becomes a source of help and guidance, in however modest a degree, to his fellows.

People are in fact constantly achieving such enlightenment— such a balanced maturity of outlook—of their own accord. It is not necessary to study the psychology of Jung to attain it: Jung himself explicitly asserts that it is a normal and natural process of the Psyche, which takes place spontaneously and automatically in precisely the same way as growth occurs in the body in childhood. The only danger is that the conscious mind may owe allegiance to an artificial, one-sided system which ignores the nature of this natural development and therefore mistrusts and opposes it; the consequence is a state of inner conflict which may not only impair the individual's powers, thus preventing him from fulfilling himself, but may even destroy him and spread a nefarious influence among his fellows. Such a condition, as we shall see when we come to examine individual cases, is like an infectious disease of the Psyche, and may cause terrible harm.

The consideration of individual cases will also demonstrate that it is precisely the most gifted individuals who are liable to get into difficulties of this kind, because to be gifted implies an intensification of the penetrative and differentiating powers of consciousness in one sphere or another. Hence the conflict between the conscious and unconscious parts of the mind is intensified in such individuals, who are compelled to endure the stresses and strains of mental advance at a higher level of consciousness than does the normal man: the conscious mind is therefore, in their case, both more able and more apt to

341

interfere with the process, and thus to bring the subject into conflict with himself.

Jung's system, evolved by a man whose profound insight has clearly compelled him to experience the torments and difficulties of this conflict most intensely in his own mind, is designed to help such people over their difficulties. The mentally sick are not necessarily the mentally inferior: often precisely the opposite is true, for the patients are those who are experiencing the process of forging with exceptional intensity. They are often the potentially creative minds: the only ones who can succeed in presenting new ideas to the world in an intelligible and acceptable form.

Creativeness is not a peculiar property, possessed by some and lacked by others: every individual is potentially creative in his degree, although in the majority, of course, that degree is insignificant from the wider social viewpoint, sufficing only to bring a small inspiration to the individual himself, and to his immediate environment. Even such a small gift is by no means negligible, for the beneficent and vitalizing effect which it may spread in the family circle, the office or the club plays its modest part in helping human beings through the difficult business of living. It is often an almost imperceptible factor, consisting simply in the ability to 'find the right word' which brings comfort in distress, transforms despondency into hope, or resolves hesitation; the capacity to initiate a friendship or an association, or to found a business, or even to transform a waste plot into a garden. If more people brought such small creative gifts to fulfilment the sum of human happiness and the level of human conduct would be notably improved.

People in whom creativeness does not exceed such everyday proportions are in little danger of succumbing to the strain which all creative activity imposes, or from which it derives. But between such modest creators and the great whose names live for ever there is no difference of kind, but of degree only; the interval between them is filled by a gradation of creative potentiality in every degree, and as it rises, the stresses associated with it, and the consequent danger of a disequilibration of the Psyche—of mental sickness or psychopathy in the widest sense —rise with it. The examination of individual cases suggests that an excessive proportion of such exceptionally gifted people succumb to the strain imposed on them by their gifts, and collapse before they have brought them to fruition; not only that: there are grounds for believing that the proportion of such collapses at the present day is greater than it was at various periods in the past. There have been periods in human history, such as the classical epochs of Greece and Rome and the European Renaissance, when genius throve and abounded and the world, although no 'better', nor more secure nor prosperous than it is today, was filled with mental progress. Are we to believe that by some genetic freak the proportion of talented people born at these times exceeded that of our own? It seems to me far more probable that the explanation lies rather in some characteristic of our own times which imposes an excessive strain on the creative mind.

Jung's system appears to me as above all suited to help those in whom the creative gift is developed above the average, and who have got into difficulties as a consequence. By explaining the nature of their problems and showing them that they are no more than an intensification of the problems generic in a species which lives in a self-created artificial mental environment unsuited to the unalterable instinctual characteristics of its mind, it helps them to endure their sufferings, to allay their fears and to reach that dynamic equilibrium of the personality —which is always a possibility—that will enable them to bring forth the best that is in them. The theme of this study is a corollary of Jung's system, and it attempts to explain the nature of one of the most fundamental and pervasive problems with which the contemporary mind is faced.

The essence of Jung's teaching is that we must learn to value and respect the unconscious mind. It is absolutely necessary that we treat it as 'real', i.e. as something which we must take very seriously into account, fearing its antagonism no less than we fear tempest, famine and pestilence, and valuing its benefits, for their own sake, no less than we value the goods and triumphs of the outer world. In this study I have attempted to develop and elaborate some of his ideas of what we are up against and what we may hope to win.

Jung's theme is embodied in the story of Miss Blandish-Persephone: we must make up our minds to adventure outside the light and prosperity, and the apparent security, of This World, into the darkness, the mystery and the perils of the Other Side. We must search there for the root of our troubles in the contention between John Blandish and Ma Grisson and their respective factions; we must expose ourselves for a time to the torment of the strife of the irreconcilables, in which we must participate without taking sides, suffering in ourselves, as Miss Blandish did, the pain of every blow which each directs against the other in the bitterness and hatred which we, in our blindness, have built up between them. And we must learn to overcome our fear and loathing of Slim. Only in this way can we bring about reconciliation—or, rather, can we enable Miss Blandish to do something for us which is beyond our own powers—in the fruitful union of the Opposites in love, and thus win at last the Treasure of wholeness which is the Divine Child, the individuality reborn, the heir to both kingdoms—both worlds—which unites the opposites in itself.

This symbolism is more than an empty form of words: it implies a definite, effectual reorientation towards life. It is a difficult and invidious task to offer practical examples of what I mean, for one man's meat is another's poison, and the circumstances of every individual are different. It has been said that there is no Royal Road to enlightenment: each man must seek and find his own way: it is a matter of hard, patient and persevering work which nobody can do for him. Nevertheless a few suggestions may be useful as indicating the type of thing involved: they are no more than illustrations of what may be profitable in some cases, and there is no guarantee that they will be of the slightest use in others.

Attention to the arts is often useful. I have already suggested that the modern outlook, in its obsession with the interpretation of sensory experience in terms of the logical implications of the pattern of material objects in space and time, tends to overlook the true intrinsic nature and values of that form of experience. The direction of attention towards the arts is calculated to combat this characteristic misuse of the senses by the intellect. Some may find it more profitable to do artistic work themselves, others to study existing works. There was a time when virtually all cultured people thought it incumbent on them to master the technique of at least one of the arts: they painted in water-colours, played the piano, or sang. Their performance, naturally, was pretty low on the average, but that was immaterial: the point was that they attached sufficient value to this mental sphere to take some little trouble with it, and that, even if only to an infinitesimal extent, they were able to experience in its terms. Nowadays this beneficial custom has almost died out—it is characteristic of the times—but Sir Winston Churchill has given a valuable lead by taking up oil-painting, and his explicit statement that this practice afforded him relief from the intolerable strain of affairs, admirably expresses its value in the present context. It is entirely immaterial how good or how bad his paintings may be from the viewpoint of the art critic: we should not admire him so much because he can paint so well, for his ability would derive mainly from the fortuitous possession of a talent; still less because such a busy man could 'find time' to paint in addition to his other activities, because that would imply that he might have been better employed in doing something else. But we should accord him unqualified praise because he discovered how to relieve the tension of a mind overstrained by the conduct of affairs of state by exercising it in another mode; if he had not done so he might well have collapsed under the strain, with the consequence that the fortunes of all of us would have been very different from what they are. It is also worth noting that he tried modelling in clay, brick-laying, novel-writing, and doubtless other activities as well, before he discovered the medium best suited to his bent. There is no particular virtue in painting in oils: the essential is simply to discover what absorbs one and affords relief of tension.

People of a less active and more reflective type may find that they derive greater benefit from studying and contemplating—even from handling—existing objects, or from listening to music. Here again it is entirely immaterial what the object of interest is, provided only that the interest lies solely, or at least mainly, in its aesthetic value. The essential is to go on looking or listening until one discovers something which produces a mental reaction solely by its appearance (or the quality of sound) and to concentrate on that as a starting-point. Alertness should be cultivated for what 'looks right' and what wrong:

whether two pictures at home are too close together or too far apart, whether the teapot and the cream-jug agree or disagree, and so forth. Have this year's cars a harmonious form, or do they merely look modern and shiny? Are the new fashions really pleasanter to look at than the old?

Two pitfalls should be noted: the first is that of persuading oneself that one admires anything because it is regarded as admirable by the best authorities; the second, that of confusing 'knowing about' with the direct sensory relationship with the material. Here again it is completely immaterial, in the present context, what one likes, provided that one likes it for its own sake. In certain company it may be advisable for the novice to keep his judgments to himself, but it is essential to develop the habit of forming aesthetic judgments at every available opportunity, and of formulating them unreservedly to oneself. In the early stages the judgments of others should be ignored, for the purpose of this exercise is not to become a connoisseur, or to be able to talk knowledgeably about artistic matters, but to learn the language of sensory experience.

Nobody should believe that he is congenitally deficient in aesthetic perception, for the aesthetic mode is universal in the human mind, and although, in those who have always ignored it, it may be crude and barely conscious, yet it is always present, and remains capable of development by anybody who is prepared to take the necessary trouble.

That which is commonly called occultism is also worthy of attention: e.g. astrology, or the Chinese system of divination embodied in the *I Ching* or Book of Changes. It is noteworthy that Jung who, as a scientist, automatically adopted an adverse attitude towards astrology, and in several of his earlier works makes the stock deprecatory remarks about it, was compelled in later life to acknowledge that it has value. Space forbids my going into the question here, and it must suffice to point out that astrology must on no account be regarded as a 'science' in the modern meaning of the term. Any suggestion to the effect that the planets exercise a causal influence on human affairs, and, worse still, any attempt to explain it by vague talk of 'vibrations' and the like is, of course, fatuous; but astrologers are unfortunately apt to make fools of themselves by writing in this vein, and by claiming the ability to make reliable forecasts of specific outer-world events. On the other hand, anybody who has studied the matter with an open mind will be compelled to admit that certain more generalized correspondences between planetary movements and human trends are discernible: they cannot invariably be established, yet they do seem to occur more frequently than can be accounted for by the laws of averages and probabilities.

This matter is not susceptible of proof or disproof by scientific methods, since the material cannot be formulated in scientific terms, and so much depends on the interpretation offered by the individual astrologer; on the other hand there is no *a priori* reason for denying that a correspondence might exist. I can, for instance, forecast with considerable confidence that every morning, when the hands of the clock point to 9, the grocer will arrive and open his shop, a train will steam into the station, and the school bell will ring. If I were to point these phenomena out to an intelligent visitor from Mars who had never before seen a clock he might well come to the conclusion that this instrument exercised a mysterious causative or compulsive influence on human beings, or even on inanimate matter. In fact, of course, you and I know that what we are witnessing is the manifestation of a mental pattern which exists in the minds of the grocer, the engine-driver, the schoolmaster, the clockmaker and everybody else in the community, and according to which they voluntarily regulate their activities. Similarly, when the sun reaches a certain degree of elevation the swallows will arrive, and bulbs, even if kept in the dark, will begin to sprout: here we have the manifestation of a pattern which acts without conscious volition. There is no reason why a potentially intelligible pattern should not exist in the universal, non-personal part of the mind, which is not subject to volition and has not yet attained consciousness, in which human tendencies, meteorological phenomena, animal and plant behaviour and the movements of the planets are somehow interrelated, for it must not be forgotten that all these things, as we know them, are themselves patterns of the mind. At present we do not understand how such a pattern could 'work', but that is no adequate reason for categorically denying the possibility of any such thing. The exercise of the function of intuition, which is irrational and anti-logical, suggests that some such pattern may be discerned, and that its 'existence', or presence in universal mind, must be accepted, *although it is irrational, illogical, and completely irreconcilable with the contemporary world-picture*. It is in this that the value of a serious study of such subjects as astrology resides, for it promotes the development of the intuitive faculty and acts as a corrective to the contemporary obsession with the world-picture based on the scientific outlook.

There are many other lessons to be learnt from such a study, *provided that it is interpreted according to the inner-world pattern*; as Jung has pointed out, investigators who have reached the limits of their conscious comprehension tend to project the contents of the unconscious mind, which includes those of the universal, collective mind, into their material, which consequently assumes Archetypal symbolical forms. These symbols, evolved by the ancients as scientific statements (not as deliberate allegories) act directly, through the faculty of intuition, on the unconscious mind of the present-day student. Thus unconscious contents are liberated and the Waters of Life dispensed to a parched consciousness, thereby mysteriously restoring an affirmative attitude to life, and a power of decision, which may have been temporarily lost.[1]

This effect is peculiarly marked if 'the oracle is consulted' by means of the system of divination of the *I Ching*[2] which, for practical purposes, is in many ways preferable to astrology, which has been so extensively vulgarized, and the pursuit of which entails a good deal of 'spadework'. Even the reading of tea-cups, or fortune-telling by cards,[3] are not to be despised: the fact that such practices are associated with uneducated old wives does not detract from the stimulus which they give to

---

[1] The simplest form of this is the effect produced by tossing up a coin when unable to make up one's mind between alternatives. Whichever way the coin falls the fact of having carried out the symbolical act of 'consulting the oracle' often clarifies the situation in a remarkable and inexplicable manner, restoring the power of decision and enabling the questioner to decide according to his true preference. I found this fact, which I had long known, confirmed by Jan Struther in *Mrs. Miniver*.

[2] Published in English by Routledge & Kegan Paul.

[3] This is their proper use, for the Tarot or tarock cards, from which our familiar playing-cards are descended, were originally a system of divination imported into Europe from the East by the gypsies. See A. E. Waite: *The Tarot* (which explains a system of divination and provides the cards.)

the intuitive faculty, and the corrective against obsession with the almightiness of the rational outlook which attention to them produces.

It must be clearly understood that I am not for a moment advocating that anybody should allow his conduct of practical affairs to be directly influenced by practices of this nature. Practical matters are almost exclusively concerned with the subject's relations to an environment which has been shaped by an outer-world system of an entirely opposite nature, and in his dealings with it the subject must be guided by his understanding of that system. One of the main themes of this study is the danger of interpreting inner-world elements in an outer-world sense—of accepting symbolical situations, patterns of behaviour, etc., which have been projected from the unconscious mind, in the capacity of factual elements of the outer-world system. The primary advantage of discriminating clearly between the Two Worlds is that it enables inner-world elements to be taken seriously without doing violence to the outer-world picture. There are, of course, occasions when the two systems correspond and coalesce: these are the creative moments which are the supreme experience of life; but everyday affairs must be conducted on the basis of a strict separation between the Two Worlds.

We must be punctilious in rendering unto Caesar the things that are Caesar's, but in doing so we must beware of forgetting the second half of the precept.

These two suggestions are, as I stated above, no more than examples of the kind of expedient which may be found helpful in the task of reorientation. To many people they may be quite useless: different talents, dispositions and backgrounds demand different manners of expression, and each man must find out for himself what suits him. The essential is that interest and attention should be devoted to matters which are alien to and undervalued by the contemporary conscious attitude, the nature of which I have attempted to indicate in the foregoing chapters. These matters, whatever they are, must be taken seriously enough to justify the devotion of some time and thought to them, although in the clear understanding that they are of no more direct value to the individual's relations with the outer world than Sir Winston Churchill's painting was to his conduct of affairs of state. They will possess indirect value for the subject even in this respect, in that they refresh and revitalize him; but we must attempt a little more than that. Contemporary humanity has reached a stage at which it is no longer enough for people merely to indulge in hobbies and recreations in order to return with renewed energy to the pursuit of their established aims and purposes: these aims, and the system of thought and the values on which they are based, have already been carried too far, so that they threaten to destroy the equilibrium of the collective Psyche. This threat is already calling out compensating reactions of a dangerous nature, and if nothing is done about it they will infallibly bring about the self-destruction of our civilization.

When we come to examine individual cases of such conflicts we shall see how, if the compensating and equilibrating drives produced by the Psyche—which are necessarily opposed in nature to the system whose excesses have evoked them—are opposed and rejected by the conscious part of the mind, they will set up a rebellion in the unconscious part. Their purpose is to thwart the objectionable activities of the conscious mind in every way, and eventually, if driven to desperation, they will set about the complete overthrow of the conscious personality, or the annihilation of the individual. In this enterprise they must inevitably succeed in the end, because they have at their disposal forces of the universal mind before which the individual is powerless. The consequence is that the individual finds himself driven, often against his better judgment, to adopt a perverse course of conduct, the fundamental trend of which is self-destructive. Thus we shall find Oscar Wilde not only gratuitously throwing away the honour and success which he was at last achieving, but also purposefully, although unconsciously, engineering his own utter ruin; we shall see Hitler dragging the whole Third Reich with him into the most colossal suicide recorded in history; we shall find Nietzsche giving up the struggle and seeking a refuge in insanity.

This psychological pattern applies to a collectivity in exactly the same way as to an individual. Our own civilization is revealing an ever-growing tendency towards suicide, for do we not, in recurring bursts of manic destructiveness, periodically tear down so much that we have painstakingly built up, employing for the purpose the very devices which we have evolved for our material enrichment?

One may doubt if it is possible to halt the process at this stage: we are probably going too fast to stop. But any slender chance there is can only come from a reorientation of that conscious attitude which by its arrogant claim to represent the sole truth and the sole criterion of value, its intolerant rejection, as 'superstition', 'escapism', 'mysticism' or 'regression' of everything which is not subservient to its aims and submissive to its scheme of values, is the cause of the trouble. The fact that this attitude is activated by the best intentions and inspired by the conviction of the purest rectitude only makes matters worse.

Such a reorientation can only originate in individuals with sufficient insight to understand the situation; from them it might conceivably spread, through personal example rather than through precept, to the wider circles of what Toynbee has called the creative minority.[1] Such individuals, however, must go further than merely restoring the balance of their own personalities by devoting a minimum of attention to the aesthetic, the intuitive and the irrational modes of the mind: they must go a little out of their way to emphasize the supreme importance of these matters in the present situation.

In doing so they will inevitably incur some derision, even contempt: at best they will be regarded as harmless, if a little queer; at worst as anti-social, for few will have the outer-world prestige of a Churchill to justify their eccentricities. That is a price which they must accept. Having their own position in the world to consider they will have to compromise; they may well disqualify themselves from becoming cabinet ministers, generals or managing directors, but, provided that they confine their eccentricity within reasonable bounds, they will be allowed by a reasonably tolerant community to hold adequate posts of slighter responsibility, and it is in such positions that they can do most good. Prophets in the wilderness are of little use in such a connection: the man who is trusted and believed is the man who can hold his own in this world.[2] And *surtout*,

[1] See Arnold Toynbee, *op. cit.* The creative minority is emphatically not confined to intellectuals, visionaries, artists, etc.

[2] "And I say unto you, *Make to yourselves friends of the mammon of*

pas de zèle. The secret is to understand the difference between the Two Worlds, and that understanding promotes balance and serenity.

Some forty or fifty years ago Albert Einstein devised a harmless-looking equation embodying an abstruse question of mathematical physics: the relation between mass and energy. Seeing it at the time, even a qualified scientist could not have visualized what was to happen at Hiroshima and Nagasaki; hardly, even, could he have imagined lights and machinery fed by the energy of atomic reactors. To the layman it would have been impossible to realize the potential applications of this formula to 'real life', yet it was in these applications, probably not suspected by Einstein himself, that its importance to the mass of humanity lay.

Similarly it is hard, when reading of such things as the conscious attitude and its conflict with Archetypal forces, or the inner and outer modes of experience, to visualize the manifestation of such abstractions in terms of sleepless nights of torment, of the despair and bitterness of Oscar Wilde in prison, the mixture of self-loathing and self-adulation which permeates

unrighteousness; that, when ye fail, they may receive you into everlasting habitations.

He that is faithful in that which is least is faithful also in much: and he that is unjust in the least is unjust also in much.

If therefore ye have not been faithful in the unrighteous mammon, who will commit to your trust the true riches?

And if ye have not been faithful in that which is another man's, who will give you that which is your own?" Luke xvi. 9–12.

This surprising and striking passage, which concludes the extraordinary parable of the unjust steward, with its unexpected insistence on the necessity of conforming to the practices of This World, even when they are not entirely above reproach, is clearly an elaboration of the precept 'Render unto Caesar, etc.' It is the product of a very mature intelligence, which bids us remember that we have to live in This World—even enjoins us 'to make the best of both worlds'. The next verse, 'No servant can serve two masters . . . Ye cannot serve God and mammon', is in direct contradiction to this teaching: in my view it can only be regarded as the interpolation of a puzzled scribe of high principles, who could not bring himself to believe that the Master had really meant what he was reported as having said. It is noteworthy that this emendation of the indisputable purport of the parable, and of the injunction to adopt a 'realistic' attitude which follows it, is far more popular and more widely known than the latter.

Bleak House, the frantic exaltation and hatred of Hitler, and the terror and agony of Auschwitz, Buchenwald and Belsen which resulted from them; yet these things are as truly implicit in the theory as the nuclear fission bomb and the atomic reactor were in Einstein's equation.

It is for this reason that it would have been preferable to defer the theoretical exposition until after a number of examples had been examined: the spectacle of what 'actually happens' when these factors come into play is not unnaturally liable to bring greater conviction to most minds than can be achieved by an abstruse exposition of their nature. The consideration of a number of examples of the inner-world material also may be relied upon to have a cumulative effect, for the contemplation of the various forms assumed by the symbol, which is a living force, acts directly on the unconscious part of the mind. This course, however, has seemed inadvisable, because the material is too extensive: the reader must be informed in advance of the guiding principles which have led to its selection, if he is to be enabled to keep his bearings throughout such a prolonged study, or, indeed, to find the patience to pursue it to the end. Thus I am aware that my thesis is still, at this point, woefully lacking in factual confirmation, and can carry little conviction in the respect in which I intend it, namely as an outlook from which it is possible better to understand life. To those who find it sufficiently interesting, however, further material will be offered in future volumes.

Full conviction, however, can only be based on personal experience: probably it is necessary, in order to believe, to have got into difficulties, to have suffered, to find one's way out— and to blunder back and have to find one's way out again countless times. Sometimes, Gustav Meyrink says, it is terribly hard to understand what is required of one: he gives the instance of a horse which he was training to jump by driving it round, at the end of a rope, on a circular track across which was placed a low hurdle. Every time it refused the jump it received a cut from the whip, and he relates how he sympathized with the animal, in whose eyes he imagined that he could detect the fear of the whip-lash each time it was confronted with the hurdle; but he had a job to do and continued until at last the horse saw the light and jumped: then he shared its triumph and relief. He was, of course, projecting his own feelings into the mind of the horse, for he himself was that horse, driven more cruelly than most men by inner forces which required of him something which he could not understand.

Suffering—even much physical suffering—is evidence that we have failed to adjust ourselves in one or both of the two directions in which, as Jung says, adjustment is necessary: towards the outer world, and towards the demands of our unalterable and ineluctable inner nature. We have to learn to jump, and suffering is generally necessary in order to persuade us to go on trying until we have understood what is required of us. For, to quote Jung yet again, those who undertake what I have called the quest of the Treasure do not do so out of preference, but because they are compelled to. Needs must when the Devil drives—and, as we shall see later, it is literally the Devil who drives us to salvation.[1]

But although suffering is perhaps the price of understanding, suffering alone will not bring understanding. The cases which we shall later consider show numerous examples of men and women who have endured the torments of the soul throughout most of their lives, and have died without ever understanding why they had to suffer. Like Parsifal, we shall obtain no benefit from witnessing the ceremony of the Graal until we ask what it means. The question which we have to ask today concerns the relationship between the Two Worlds, and, in particular, the nature of the inner, for of the outer we already know far more than is good for us.

---

[1] Mephistopheles' introduction of himself in Goethe's *Faust* reveals this situation: *Ich bin ein Teil von jener Kraft Die stets das Böse will, und stets das Gute schafft*—I am a part of that force which always works for evil, and always achieves good.

VIII Conclusion

THE supreme symbol of the inner world is the dream: it is
the normal, commonplace, ever-present reminder of that
alternative manner of experience in which the Subject in us
manifests Its sovereign independence of that cherished, petty,
circumscribed continuity which is our personal life. It is above
all with respect to our dreams, and to those spontaneous waking
fantasies which are so close to them in character, that we can
assert the reality of the inner world. When we have dreamed,
or when some image has presented itself to us in fantasy, we
must purposefully insist, in face of the contempt and derision
of that voice of outer-world prejudice which speaks from within
us no less than from without: 'This was real: it happened; just
as surely and just as really as it happened that I undressed and
went to bed.' It happened, to be sure, in another world, and
is not to be interpreted according to the principles of This
World, in which I must now get up and dress again, nor must
it be considered in any but an indirect relationship to the latter;
nevertheless it happened. It had significance and importance
and must not be ignored.

It may take some time to discover what it meant, and it
may not, in the event, be of any great importance. Dreams, like
outer-world events, vary in importance and significance, and
we must not be disappointed if, all too frequently, nothing very
sensational results from our efforts. Nevertheless, if it is written
down, thought about seriously and 'carried about with one',
almost any dream will prove to have a meaning. It is not the
single interpretation but the general attitude that counts, and
with it the cumulative understanding of the unconscious mind,
and of the inner world, which results from a sustained attention

to dreams and fantasies over a period of years. If this attitude i
perseveringly cultivated it will bear fruit in a better balanced
more harmonious and richer relationship to life in general
and the individual who cultivates it may progress some little
way towards transcending that small vortex of experience
in universal mind which he regards as himself. If it were
universally practised there might even be peace on earth.

Having started with Chuang Tzu we may close with him:

Those who dream of the banquet wake to lamentation and sor
row. Those who dream of lamentation and sorrow wake to join th
hunt. While they dream they do not know that they dream. Som
will even interpret the very dream they are dreaming; and onl
when they awake do they know it was a dream. By and by come
the Great Awakening, and then we find out that this life is really a
great dream. Fools think that they are awake now, and flatter them
selves that they know if they are really princes or peasants. Con
fucius and you are both dreams; and I who say you are dreams—
I am but a dream myself.[1]

To which we may add what is perhaps the sublimest of al
statements of the relativity of what we call existence:

> Our revels now are ended. These our actors,
> As I foretold you, were all spirits and
> Are melted into air, into thin air:
> And like the baseless fabric of this vision,
> The cloud-capp'd towers, the gorgeous palaces,
> The solemn temples, the great globe itself,
> Yea, all which it inherit, shall dissolve
> And, like this insubstantial pageant faded,
> Leave not a rack behind. We are such stuff
> As dreams are made on, and our little life
> Is rounded with a sleep.

[1] Giles' translation. Wilhelm's corresponds exactly, except for the las
sentence, which he renders, 'And my saying that you are a dreamer, tha
also is a dream.'

Index

I. GENERAL

357

INDEX

II. TITLES OF WORKS MENTIONED